OBJECTIVE	CHAPTER

Operating System Fundamentals

Identify the operating system's functions, structure, and major system files to navigate the operating system and how to get to needed technical information. — **2, 4**

Content may include the following: Major Operating System functions (Create folders; Checking OS Version); Major Operating System components (Explorer; My Computer; Control Panel); Contrasts between Windows 9x and Windows 2000

Major system files: what they are, where they are located, how they are used and what they contain:

System, Configuration, and User Interface files: IO.SYS; BOOT.INI; WIN.COM; MSDOS.SYS; AUTOEXEC.BAT; CONFIG.SYS; COMMAND LINE PROMPT

Memory management: Conventional; Extended/upper memory; High memory; Virtual memory; HIMEM.SYS; EMM386.exe

Windows 9x: IO.SYS; WIN.INI; USER.DAT; SYSEDIT; SYSTEM.INI; MSCONFIG (98); COMMAND.COM; REGEDIT.EXE; SYSTEM.DAT; RUN COMMAND; COMMAND LINE PROMPT

Windows 2000: Computer Management; BOOT.INI; REGEDT32; REGEDIT; RUN CMD; NTLDR; NTDETECT.COM; NTBOOTDD.SYS

Command Prompt Procedures (Command syntax): DIR; ATTRIB; VER; MEM; SCANDISK; DEFRAG; EDIT; XCOPY; COPY; SETVER; SCANREG

Identify basic concepts and procedures for creating, viewing and managing files, directories and disks. This includes procedures for changing file attributes and the ramifications of those changes (for example, security issues). — **4, 9**

Content may include the following: File attributes—Read Only, Hidden, System, and Archive attributes; File naming conventions (Most common extensions); Windows 2000 COMPRESS, ENCRYPT; IDE/SCSI; Internal/External; Backup/Restore; Partitioning/Formatting/File System (FAT; FAT16; FAT32; NTFS4; NTFS5; HPFS)

Windows-based utilities: ScanDisk; Device manager; System Manager; Computer Manager; MSCONFIG.EXE; REGEDIT.EXE (View information/Backup registry); REGEDT32.EXE; ATTRIB.EXE; EXTRACT.EXE; DEFRAG.EXE; EDIT.COM; FDISK.EXE; SYSEDIT.EXE; SCANREG; WSCRIPT.EXE; HWINFO.EXE; ASD.EXE (Automatic Skip Driver); Cvt1.EXE (Drive Converter FAT16 to FAT32)

Installation, Configuration, and Upgrading

Identify the procedures for installing Windows 9x, and Windows 2000 for bringing the software to a basic operational level. — **3, 4**

Content may include the following: Start Up; Partition; Format drive; Loading drivers; Run appropriate set up utility

Identify steps to perform an operating system upgrade. — **3, 4**

Content may include the following: Upgrading Windows 95 to Windows 98; Upgrading to Windows NT Workstation 4.0 to Windows 2000; Replacing Windows 9x with Windows 2000; Dual boot Windows9x/Windows NT 4.0/2000

Identify the basic system boot sequences and boot methods, including the steps to create an emergency boot disk with utilities installed for Windows 9x, Windows NT, and Windows 2000. — **3, 4, 7**

Content may include the following: Startup disk; Safe Mode; MS-DOS mode; NTLDR (NT Loader), BOOT.INI; Files required to boot; Creating emergency repair disk (ERD)

Identify procedures for loading/adding and configuring application device drivers, and the necessary software for certain devices. — **3, 4, 5, 6**

Content may include the following: Windows 9x Plug and Play and Windows 2000; Identify the procedures for installing and launching typical Windows and non-Windows applications. (Note: there is no content related to Windows 3.1); Procedures for set up and configuring Windows printing subsystem (Setting Default printer; Installing/Spool setting; Network printing (with help of LAN admin))

W9-BKA-526

OBJECTIVE	CHAPTER

SYBEX

A+®: Operating System Technologies
Technologies
Study Guide
Third Edition

David Groth and Dan Newland

with

Lisa Donald, Joseph Dreissen, Dan Haglund

San Francisco • Paris • Düsseldorf • Soest • London

Associate Publisher: Neil Edde
Contracts and Licensing Manager: Kristine O'Callaghan
Acquisitions and Developmental Editor: Elizabeth Hurley
Editors: Brianne Hope Agatep, Sally Engelfried, Judy Flynn
Production Editor: Shannon Murphy
Technical Editors: Mark Kovach, Michelle A. Roudebush
Book Designer: Bill Gibson
Graphic Illustrators: Duane Bibby, Tony Jonick
Electronic Publishing Specialists: Judy Fung, Jill Niles
Proofreaders: Nanette Duffy, Dennis Fitzgerald, Laurie O'Connell, Yariv Rabinovitch, Nancy Riddiough
Indexer: Rebecca R. Plunkett
CD Coordinator: Kara Eve Schwartz
CD Technician: Keith McNeil
Cover Designer: Archer Design
Cover Photographer: Tony Stone Images

Library of Congress Card Number: 00-112012

ISBN: 0-7821-2807-6

SYBEX

To Our Valued Readers:

In recent years, CompTIA's A+ program has established itself as one of the most resepcted entry-level IT certifications. Sybex is proud to have helped thousands of A+ candidates prepare for their exam, and we are excited about the opportunity to continue to provide people with the skills they'll need to succeed in the highly competitive IT industry.

CompTIA recently revised the exams required for the A+ certification, updating the material to reflect new developments in hardware and operating systems technologies. They have also expanded the question pool in order to make the exams more challenging and prevent the dreaded paper-certification syndrome, in which individuals obtain a certification without a thorough understanding of the technology. Sybex supports this philosophy, as we have always advocated a comprehensive instructional approach to certification courseware. It has always been Sybex's mission to teach exam candidates how new technologies work in the real world, not to simply feed them answers to test questions. Sybex was founded on the premise of providing technical skills to IT professionals, and we have continued to build on that foundation, making significant improvements to this edition based on feedback from readers, suggestions from instructors, and comments from industry leaders.

Our authors and editors have worked hard to ensure that this new edition of the A+ Study Guide is comprehensive, in-depth, and pedagogically sound. We're confident that this book will meet and exceed the demanding standards of the certification marketplace and help you, the A+ exam candidate, succeed in your endeavors.

Good luck in pursuit of your A+ certification!

Neil Edde
Associate Publisher—Certification
Sybex, Inc.

SYBEX Inc. 1151 Marina Village Parkway, Alameda, CA 94501
Tel: 510/523-8233   Fax: 510/523-2373   HTTP://www.sybex.com

To those who thought I couldn't do it, and for those who thought I could.

—David Groth

For Steph, who makes everything in my life better.

—Dan Newland

Acknowledgments

Thanks first of all to you, the reader, for buying this book. You could've spent your money on any A+ book, but you chose mine. Thank you.

Thanks very much to all those who supported me while I was writing and developing this book. Thanks first to my coauthors. You can be proud of your work here. These people are at the top of the field in their areas. I couldn't ask for better people to work with.

A very special thanks to my wife, family, and friends for understanding when I was under deadlines and didn't have as much time as they wanted to spend with them.

Also much thanks to the all the people at Sybex who published this book under incredible time constraints: Elizabeth Hurley, Shannon Murphy, Brianne Agatep, Judy Flynn, Sally Engelfried, Mark Kovach, Michelle A. Roudebush, Jill Niles, Judy Fung, Jennifer Campbell, Nanette Duffy, Dennis Fitzgerald, Leslie Higbee Light, Laurie O'Connell, Yariv Rabinovitch, Nancy Riddiough, Kara Eve Schwartz, Keith McNeil, Duane Bibby, Tony Jonick, and Rebecca R. Plunkett.

I hope all of you enjoy this book and it is useful to you. If you have questions or comments, positive or negative, please e-mail me at `dgroth@chief-geek.com`. I'm always striving to make my books better.

—David Groth

I would like to thank David for including me on this project, and the staff at Sybex for all their help and encouragement. Writing is often referred to as a lonely art, and while that is true to an extent, it is also very much a collaborative effort. Specifically, Elizabeth and Shannon did a great job of keeping the project (and me) on track, and Brianne, Judy, and Sally were spectacular at the difficult task of turning my initial drafts into a finished product.

—Dan Newland

Contents at a Glance

Contents

Introduction

The A+ certification tests are sponsored by the Computing Technology Industry Association (CompTIA) and supported by several of the computer industry's biggest vendors (for example, Compaq, IBM, and Microsoft). This book was written to provide you with the knowledge you need to pass the Operating System Technologies Exam (formerly known as the A+ DOS/Windows Exam) for A+ certification. A+ certification gives employers a benchmark for evaluating their employees' knowledge. When an applicant for a job says, "I'm A+ certified," the employer can be assured that the applicant knows the fundamental computer service concepts. For example, an A+ certified technician should know the difference between the various types of hard disk subsystems and how to configure them.

This book was written at an intermediate technical level; we assume that you already know how to *use* a personal computer and its basic peripherals, such as modems and printers, but recognize that you may be learning how to *service* some of that computer equipment for the first time. The exam itself covers basic computer service topics as well as some more advanced issues, and it covers some topics that anyone already working as a technician, whether with computers or not, should be familiar with. The exam is designed to test you on these topics in order to certify that you have enough knowledge to fix and upgrade some of the most widely used types of personal desktop computers.

We've included review questions at the end of each chapter to give you a taste of what it's like to take the exam. If you're already working as a technical service or support person, we recommend you check out these questions first to gauge your level of knowledge. You can use the book mainly to fill in the gaps in your current computer service knowledge. You may find, as many service technicians have, that being well versed in all the technical aspects of the equipment is not enough to provide a satisfactory level of support—you must also have customer relations skills. We include helpful hints to get the customer to help you help them.

If you can answer 80 percent or more of the review questions correctly for a given chapter, you can probably feel safe moving on to the next chapter. If you're unable to answer that many correctly, reread the chapter and try the questions again. Your score should improve.

WARNING DON'T just study the questions and answers—the questions on the actual exam will be different from the practice ones included in this book and on the CD. The exam is designed to test your knowledge of a concept or objective, so use this book to learn the objective *behind* the question.

What Is A+ Certification?

The A+ certification program was developed by the Computer Technology Industry Association (CompTIA) to provide an industry-wide means of certifying the competency of computer service technicians. The A+ certification, which is granted to those who have attained the level of knowledge and troubleshooting skills that are needed to provide capable support in the field of personal computers, is similar to other certifications in the computer industry. For example, Novell offers the Certified Novell Engineer (CNE) program to provide the same recognition for network professionals who deal with its NetWare products, and Microsoft has its Microsoft Certified Service Engineer (MCSE) program. The theory behind these certifications is that if you need to have service performed on any of their products, you would sooner call a technician who has been certified in one of the appropriate certification programs than you would just call the first so-called expert in the phone book.

The A+ certification program was created to offer a wide-ranging certification, in the sense that it is intended to certify competence with personal computers from many different makers/vendors. There are two tests required to become A+ certified! You must pass the A+ Operating System Technologies exam, which covers the DOS and Windows operating environments. You must also pass the A+ Core Hardware Service Technician exam, which covers basic computer concepts, hardware troubleshooting, customer service, and hardware upgrading. You don't have to take the Core Hardware and the Operating System Technologies exams at the same time; you have 90 days from the time you pass one test to pass the second test. The A+ certified "diploma" is not awarded until you've passed both tests.

Why Become A+ Certified?

There are several good reasons to get your A+ certification. The CompTIA Candidate's Information packet lists five major benefits:

- It demonstrates proof of professional achievement.
- It increases your marketability.
- It provides greater opportunity for advancement in your field.
- It is increasingly found as a requirement for some types of advanced training.
- It raises customer confidence in you and your company's services.

Provides Proof of Professional Achievement

The A+ certification is quickly becoming a status symbol in the computer service industry. Organizations that contain members of the computer service industry are recognizing the benefits of A+ certification and are pushing for their members to become certified. And more people every day are putting the "A+ Certified Technician" emblem on their business cards.

Increases Your Marketability

A+ certification makes individuals more marketable to potential employers. Also, A+ certified employees may receive a higher base salary, because employers won't have to spend as much money on vendor-specific training.

What Is an AASC?

More service companies are becoming A+ Authorized Service Centers (AASCs). This means that over 50 percent of the technicians employed by that service center are A+ certified. At the time of the writing of this book, there are over 1,400 A+ Authorized Service Centers in the world. Customers and vendors alike recognize that AASCs employ the most qualified service technicians. Because of this, an AASC will get more business than a non-authorized service center. Also, because more service centers want to reach the AASC level, they will give preference in hiring to a candidate who is A+ certified over one who is not.

Provides Opportunity for Advancement

Most raises and advancements are based on performance. A+ certified employees work faster and more efficiently, thus making them more productive. The more productive employees are, the more money they will make for their company. And, of course, the more money they make for the company, the more valuable they will be to the company. So if an employee is A+ certified, their chances of getting promoted will be greater.

Fulfills Training Requirements

A+ certification is recognized by most major computer hardware vendors, including (but not limited to) IBM, Hewlett-Packard, Apple, and Compaq. Some of these vendors will apply A+ certification toward prerequisites in their own respective certification programs. For example, an A+ certified technician is automatically given credit towards HP laser printer certification without having to take prerequisite classes and tests. This has the side benefit of reducing training costs for employers.

Raises Customer Confidence

As the A+ certified technician moniker becomes more well known among computer owners, more of them will realize that the A+ technician is more qualified to work on their computer equipment than a non-certified technician is.

How to Become A+ Certified

A+ certification is available to anyone who passes the tests. You don't have to work for any particular company. It's not a secret society. It is, however, an elite group. In order to become A+ certified, you must do two things:

- Pass the A+ Core Hardware Service Technician exam
- Pass the A+ Operating System Technologies exam

As mentioned earlier, you don't have to take both exams at the same time; you have 90 days from the time you pass one test to pass the second test.

The exams are administered by Prometric and can be taken at any Prometric Testing Center. If you pass both exams, you will get a certificate in the mail from CompTIA saying that you have passed, and you will also receive a lapel pin and business card. To find the Prometric training center nearest you, call (800) 755-EXAM (755-3926).

To register for the tests, call Prometric at (800) 77-MICRO (776-4276) or register online at www.2test.com. You'll be asked for your name, Social Security number (an optional number may be assigned if you don't wish to provide your Social Security number), mailing address, phone number, employer, when and where (i.e., which Prometric testing center) you want to take the test, and your credit card number (arrangement for payment must be made at the time of registration).

Although you can save money by arranging to take more than one test at the same seating, there are no other discounts. If you have to take a test more than once in order to get a passing grade, you have to pay both times.

It is possible to pass these tests without any reference materials, but only if you already have the knowledge and experience that come from reading about and working with personal computers. But even experienced service people tend to have what you might call a 20/80 situation with their computer knowledge—they may use 20 percent of their knowledge and skills 80 percent of the time, and they have to rely on manuals, guesswork, the Internet, or phone calls for the rest. By covering all the topics that are tested by the exams, this book can help you to refresh your memory concerning topics that, until now, you might have only seldom used. (It can also serve to fill in gaps that, let's admit, you may have tried to cover up for quite some time.) Further, by treating all the issues that the exam covers (i.e., problems you may run into in the arenas of PC service and support), this book can serve as a general field guide, one that you may want to keep with you as you go about your work.

In addition to reading the book, you might consider practicing these objectives through an internship program. (After all, all theory and no practice make for a poor technician.)

Who Should Buy This Book?

If you are one of the many people who want to pass the A+ exam, and pass it confidently, then you should buy this book and use it to study for the exam. The Operating System Technologies exam is intended to certify that the exam candidate has the necessary skills to work on microcomputer hardware and typically will have at least 6 months of on-the-job experience. This book was written with two goals in mind: to prepare you for the challenges of the real IT world and to pass the A+ exams. This study guide will do that by describing in detail the concepts on which you'll be tested.

How to Use This Book Kit and CD

This book includes several features that will make studying for the A+ exam easier. At the beginning of the book (right after this introduction, in fact) is an assessment test that you can use to check your readiness for the actual exam. Take this exam before you start reading the book. It will help you determine the areas you may need to brush up on. You can then focus on these areas while reading the book. The answers to the assessment test appear on a separate page after the last question of the test. Each answer also includes an explanation and a note telling you in which chapter this material appears.

To test your knowledge as you progress through the book, there are review questions at the end of each chapter. As you finish each chapter, answer the review questions and then check to see if your answers are right—the correct answers appear on the page following the last review question. You can go back to reread the section that deals with each question you got wrong to ensure that you get the answer correctly the next time you are tested on the material.

On the CD-ROM you'll find four sample exams. Because the CD-ROM covers all the material written in both books in this boxed set, our four sample exams will cover both of the A+ exams. You should test your knowledge by taking both the Core Hardware and Operating System Technologies practice exams when you have completed the books and feel you are ready for the A+ exams. Take these practice exams just as if you were actually taking the A+ exams (i.e., without any reference material). When you have finished the practice exams, move onto the two bonus exams to solidify your test-taking skills. If you get more than 90 percent of the answers correct, you're ready to go ahead and take the real exam.

On the CD-ROM that is included with this book, there are several "extras" you can use to bolster your exam readiness:

Electronic flashcards   You can use these 150 flashcard-style questions to review your knowledge of A+ concepts. They are available for PCs and hand-held devices. You can download the questions right into your Palm device for quick and convenient reviewing anytime, anywhere—without your PC!

Test engines   The CD-ROM includes all of the questions that appear in this book: the assessment questions at the end of this introduction and all of the chapter review questions. Additionally, it includes two practice exams and two bonus exams for each A+ module. The book questions appear much like they did in the book, but they will be randomized. The randomized test will allow you to pick a certain number of questions to be tested on, and it will simulate the actual exam. Combined, these test engine elements will allow you to test your readiness for the real A+ exam.

Full text of the book in PDF   If you are going to travel but still need to study for the A+ exam and you have a laptop with a CD-ROM drive, you can take this entire book with you just by taking the CD-ROM. This book is in PDF (Adobe Acrobat) format so it can be easily read on any computer.

The Exam Objectives

Behind every computer industry exam you can be sure to find exam objectives— the broad topics in which the exam developers want to ensure your competency. The official CompTIA exam objectives are listed here.

Exam objectives are subject to change at any time without prior notice and at CompTIA's sole discretion. Please visit the A+ Certification page of CompTIA's Web site (www.comptia.org/certification/aplus/index.htm) for the most current listing of exam objectives.

The A+ Core Hardware Service Technician Exam Objectives

As mentioned previously, there are two tests required to become A+ certified: the Core Hardware Service Technician exam and the Operating System Technologies exam. The following are the areas (or "domains" according to CompTIA) in which you must be proficient in order to pass the A+ Core Module exam.

Domain 1.0: Installation, Configuration, and Upgrading

This content area deals with the installation, configuration, and upgrading of common computer Field Replaceable Units (FRUs). Most technicians spend a lot of time performing these operations. To that end, CompTIA has made sure that questions from this content area will make up 30 percent of the exam.

1.1   Identify basic terms, concepts, and functions of system modules, including how each module should work during normal operation and during the boot process.

1.2   Identify basic procedures for adding and removing field replaceable modules for both desktop and portable systems.

1.3   Identify available IRQs, DMAs, and I/O addresses and procedures for configuring them for device installation and configuration.

1.4   Identify common peripheral ports, associated cabling, and their connectors.

1.5   Identify proper procedures for installing and configuring IDE/EIDE devices.

1.6   Identify proper procedures for installing and configuring SCSI devices.

1.7   Identify proper procedures for installing and configuring peripheral devices.

1.8   Identify hardware methods of upgrading system performance, procedures for replacing basic subsystem components, unique components and when to use them.

Domain 2.0: Diagnosing and Troubleshooting

Before a technician can install or upgrade a component, he or she must determine which component needs to be replaced. A technician will normally use the skills addressed by the diagnosing and troubleshooting content areas to make that determination. Questions about these two topics together make up 30 percent of the exam.

2.1   Identify common symptoms and problems associated with each module and how to troubleshoot and isolate the problems.

2.2   Identify basic troubleshooting procedures and how to elicit problem symptoms from customers.

Domain 3.0: Preventive Maintenance

Most people don't think of computer service as a dangerous job. Most often, safety precautions are taken to prevent damage to the components. In actuality, there are a few components that can cause severe injury. This topic also covers maintenance and cleaning of computer components. Questions about these topics constitute 5 percent of the exam.

3.1   Identify the purpose of various types of preventive maintenance products and procedures and when to use and perform them.

3.2   Identify issues, procedures, and devices for protection within the computing environment, including people, hardware, and the surrounding workspace.

Domain 4.0: Motherboards, Processors, and Memory

Several of the items in these content areas give people the most problems (for example, learning the differences between all the various types of processors). This content area makes up 15 percent of the exam.

4.1 Distinguish between the popular CPU chips in terms of their basic characteristics.

4.2 Identify the categories of RAM (Random Access Memory) terminology, their locations, and physical characteristics.

4.3 Identify the most popular type of motherboards, their components, and their architecture (bus structures and power supplies).

4.4 Identify the purpose of CMOS (Complementary Metal-Oxide Semiconductor), what it contains, and how to change its basic parameters.

Domain 5.0: Printers

As we were writing this book, we asked A+ certified technicians what they thought was the hardest part of the Core Hardware exam. With a single, resounding voice they all said, "Printers!" For this reason, we have tried to make the printer section as comprehensive as possible. Although there are only two objectives here and the questions on printers make up 10 percent of the test, we have dedicated an entire chapter to printer components and operation to make sure that this area won't give you any problems.

5.1 Identify basic concepts, printer operations, and printer components.

5.2 Identify care and service techniques and common problems with primary printer types.

Domain 6.0: Basic Networking

With the explosion of the Internet into the service world, the line between a service technician and networking technician has blurred. Frequently, computers that come in for service have problems that are related to their networking hardware. An A+ certified technician should know how both the hardware and software components of networking can affect the operation of the computer. CompTIA has put basic networking concepts on the A+ Core Hardware exam, and they make up 10 percent of the total exam questions.

6.1 Identify basic networking concepts, including how a network works and the ramifications of repairs on the network.

Operating System Technologies Exam Objectives

The following are the areas in which you must be proficient in order to pass the A+ Operating System Technologies exam.

Domain 1.0: Operating System Fundamentals

This domain requires knowledge of DOS, Windows 3.*x*, Windows 95/98, Windows NT, and Windows 2000 operating systems. You will need to know the way they work, as well as the components that compose them. You will also need to know topics relating to navigating the operating systems and, in general, how to use them. Operating system fundamentals make up 30 percent of the exam.

1.1 Identify the operating system's functions, structure, and major system files to navigate the operating system and how to get to needed technical information.

1.2 Identify basic concepts and procedures for creating, viewing, and managing files, directories, and disks. This includes procedures for changing file attributes and the ramifications of those changes (for example, security issues).

Domain 2.0: Installation, Configuration, and Upgrading

This domain basically tests your knowledge of the day-to-day servicing of operating systems. This includes topics such as installing, configuring, and upgrading the various operating systems (DOS, Windows 9*x*, NT, and 2000). You will also be expected to know system boot sequences. These topics make up 15 percent of the exam.

2.1 Identify the procedures for installing Windows 9*x* and Windows 2000 for bringing the software to a basic operational level.

2.2 Identify steps to perform an operating system upgrade.

2.3 Identify the basic system boot sequences and boot methods, including the steps to create an emergency boot disk with utilities installed for Windows 9*x*, Windows NT, and Windows 2000.

2.4 Identify procedures for loading/adding and configuring device drivers and the necessary software for certain devices.

Domain 3.0: Diagnosing and Troubleshooting

Questions in this domain will test your ability to diagnose and troubleshoot Windows 9*x*, NT, and 2000 systems and will make up a whopping 40 percent of the test.

3.1 Recognize and interpret the meaning of common error codes and startup messages from the boot sequence, and identify steps to correct the problems.

3.2 Recognize common problems and determine how to resolve them.

Domain 4.0: Networks

This domain requires knowledge of network capabilities of DOS and Windows and how to connect to networks. It includes what the Internet is, its capabilities, basic concepts relating to Internet access, and generic procedures for system setup. Network questions make up 15 percent of the exam.

4.1 Identify the networking capabilities of Windows including procedures for connecting to the network.

4.2 Identify concepts and capabilities relating to the Internet and basic procedures for setting up a system for Internet access.

Tips for Taking the A+ Exams

Here are some general tips for taking your exam successfully:

- Bring two forms of ID with you. One must be a photo ID, such as a driver's license. The other can be a major credit card or a passport. Both forms must have a signature.

- Arrive early at the exam center so you can relax and review your study materials, particularly tables and lists of exam-related information.

- Read the questions carefully. Don't be tempted to jump to an early conclusion. Make sure you know exactly what the question is asking.

- Don't leave any unanswered questions. Unanswered questions are scored against you.

- There will be questions with multiple correct responses. When there is more than one correct answer, a message at the bottom of the screen will prompt you to "Choose all that apply." Be sure to read the messages displayed.

- When answering multiple-choice questions you're not sure about, use a process of elimination to get rid of the obviously incorrect questions first. This will improve your odds if you need to make an educated guess.

- On form-based tests, because the hard questions will eat up the most time, save them for last. You can move forward and backward through the exam. (When the exam becomes adaptive, this tip will not work.)

- For the latest pricing on the exams and updates to the registration procedures, call Prometric at (800) 755-EXAM (755-3926) or (800) 77-MICRO (776-4276). If you have further questions about the scope of the exams or related CompTIA programs, refer to the CompTIA site at www.comptia.org/.

Assessment Test

1. Which Windows 98 command-line utility is used to delete files and directories, even if the subdirectories contain additional files?

   A. DEL

   B. REMOVE

   C. DELTREE

   D. REMTREE

2. Which key would you use in Windows 98 to select non-contiguous files for a file action such as a copy?

   A. CTRL

   B. SHIFT

   C. ALT

   D. F5

3. Which Windows 98 utility would you use to check a disk drive for disk-related errors?

   A. Disk Cleanup

   B. Disk Manager

   C. Disk Defragmenter

   D. SCANDISK

4. What is the minimum amount of RAM a computer must have to run Windows 98?

   A. 8MB

   B. 12MB

   C. 16MB

   D. 32MB

5. Which of the following commands would you use to partition your disk drives prior to a Windows 98 installation?

   A. PARTDISK

   B. FDISK

   C. MAKEPART

   D. FORMAT

6. What is the purpose of the MSCDEX.EXE file on the Windows 98 startup disk?

A. Memory manager

B. Video manager

C. Provides hard drive support

D. Provides CD-ROM support

7. Which Windows 95 option would you use if you did not want your system checked for Plug-and-Play devices?

A. SETUP /pi

B. SETUP /np

C. SETUP /-np

D. SETUP /-npnp

8. Which of the following options best describes what happens when you install Windows 95 with the portable configuration?

A. No networking is installed.

B. PCMCIA support and APM support is installed.

C. The minimum Windows 95 files are installed.

D. The GNP components are installed.

9. Which of the following options is not an upgrade enhancement when upgrading from Windows 95 (original version, not OSR2) to Windows 98?

A. Better Internet support through the integration of Internet Explorer

B. Support for newer hardware such as USB, AGP, and DVD

C. Support for the FAT32 file system

D. DOS 6 replaced by DOS 7

10. Which Windows 98 startup file allows the rest of the operating system and its programs to interact directly with the system hardware and the system BIOS?

A. MSDOS.SYS

B. BIOS.SYS

C. IO.SYS

D. OSIO.SYS

11. Which Windows 98 utility is used to easily edit configuration files such as CONFIG.SYS and WIN.INI?

   A. MSCONFIG

   B. WINCONFIG

   C. W98CONFIG

   D. REGEDIT

12. Which Windows 98 utility would you use if you wanted to upgrade a FAT16 partition to a FAT32 partition?

   A. Disk Converter

   B. FDISK

   C. Disk Manager

   D. Disk Administrator

13. How much free disk space is required on a computer that will have Windows 2000 Professional installed?

   A. 650MB

   B. 1.2GB

   C. 1.6GB

   D. 2GB

14. You want to install Windows 2000 on a computer that has just had its hard drive formatted. What command would you use on a Windows 98 computer that had the Windows 2000 Professional CD to make Windows 2000 Startup Disks?

   A. BOOTDISK

   B. MAKEBOOT

   C. MAKEBT16

   D. MAKEBT32

15. What command would you use to install Windows 2000 Professional on a computer that needs to have the accessibility options installed?

   A. SETUP /A

   B. SETUP /H

   C. WINNT /A

   D. WINNT /H

16. Which of the following operating systems can be upgraded directly to Windows 2000 Professional? (Select all that apply.)

   A. Windows 3.1

   B. Windows 95

   C. Windows 98

   D. Windows NT Workstation 4.0

17. Which Windows 2000 boot file is used in a dual-boot configuration to keep a copy of the DOS or Windows 9x boot sector?

   A. NTBOOT.SYS

   B. NTBOOT.DOS

   C. BOOTSECT.SYS

   D. BOOTSECT.DOS

18. What file extension is associated with Microsoft Installer files?

   A. .APP

   B. .MSI

   C. .INS

   D. .DAT

19. Which of the following options provides the most reliable way to uninstall a Windows 98 application?

   A. Control Panel ➤ Windows Configuration

   B. Control Panel ➤ System Configuration

   C. Control Panel ➤ Add/Remove Programs

   D. Delete the application files with Windows Explorer and remove any Registry entries

20. Which printer option is used to bypass printer spooling?

   A. Print Directly to Printer.

   B. Bypass Print Spooling.

   C. Disable Spooling.

   D. This option can only be set by directly editing the Registry.

21. Which of the following backup options backs up the files on a disk that have changed since the last Full backup and does not mark the files that are backed up during the session as archived?

A. Full

B. Differential

C. Incremental

D. Partial

22. Which of the following commands is not located on a Windows 98 startup disk?

A. FDISK

B. FORMAT

C. SYS

D. DELTREE

23. What command-line utility would you use to create a Windows NT Emergency Repair Disk?

A. ERD

B. MAKEERD

C. RDISK

D. MAKEDISK

24. Which of the following network protocols is not a default protocol that can be loaded with Windows 98?

A. NetBEUI

B. DLP

C. NWLink

D. TCP/IP

25. What software must be loaded on a Windows 98 client so that the computer can access other Microsoft network clients?

A. Microsoft Client for Microsoft Networks

B. Client Connect

C. TCP Connect

D. File and Print Sharing Manager

26. What UNC path would you use to connect to a folder called DATA and a share called ACCT on a computer called WS1 on a domain called ACME?

   A. \\ACME\WS1\ACCT\DATA

   B. \\ACME\WS1\ACCT

   C. \\WS1\ACCT\DATA

   D. \\DATA\ACCT\WS1\ACME

27. Which service is responsible for managing Internet host names and domain names as well as resolving the names to IP addresses?

   A. DHCP

   B. WINS

   C. DNS

   D. SMS

28. What key do you press to access Safe Mode when Windows 98 is booting?

   A. F1

   B. F2

   C. F6

   D. F8

29. Which utility would you use to troubleshoot hardware problems on a Windows 98 computer?

   A. Task Manager

   B. Device Manager

   C. SCANDISK

   D. System Services Manager

30. What command is used on Windows 98 computers to check the consistency of the Registry and to back up the Registry?

   A. REGEDIT

   B. REGEDT32

   C. SYSREG

   D. SCANREG

Answers to Assessment Test

1. C. The DEL command is used to delete files. RD is used to remove empty directories or subdirectories. DELTREE is used to delete files and directories, even if they contain files. See Chapter 2 for more information.

2. A. The CTRL key is used to select non-contiguous files, while the SHIFT key is used to select contiguous files. See Chapter 2 for more information.

3. D. SCANDISK is used to check a disk drive for errors or problems. Disk Cleanup is used to delete unneeded files. Disk Defragmenter is used to arrange data so that it is more easily accessed. See Chapter 2 for more information.

4. B. While 12MB is the bare minimum to load the operating system, Microsoft actually recommends at least 16–32MB of memory. See Chapter 3 for more information.

5. B. The FDISK utility is used to manage disk partitions. With FDISK you can create, delete, and mark the active partition. See Chapter 3 for more information.

6. D. The MSCDEX.EXE file is used to provide CD-ROM drive support prior to Windows 98 being loaded. You also need to load the proper CD-ROM driver. See Chapter 3 for more information.

7. A. The SETUP /pi switch skips the check for any Plug-and-Play devices. See Chapter 3 for more information.

8. B. When you install a portable or laptop computer and use the portable configuration, the PCMCIA support is added as well as Advanced Power Management for when the laptop is running from battery power. See Chapter 3 for more information.

9. D. When you upgrade from Windows 95 to Windows 98, DOS 7 (16-bit) is replaced by DOS32 (32-bit). See Chapter 3 for more information.

10. C. The IO.SYS file allows the rest of the operating system and its programs to interact directly with the system hardware and the system BIOS. A part of this file's code is hardware drivers for common devices (such as serial and communication ports and disk drives). See Chapter 3 for more information.

11. A. The MSCONFIG utility is used to edit configuration files easily and graphically. See Chapter 3 for more information.

12. A. The FAT32 file system offers several enhancements to the FAT16 file system. You can convert existing FAT16 partitions to FAT32 partitions through System Tools ➤ Disk Converter utility. See Chapter 3 for more information.

13. D. Windows 2000 installations require a minimum of 2GB of free disk space for the installation process. See Chapter 4 for more information.

14. B. The MAKEBOOT command is used from Windows *9x* computers while the MAKEBT32 command is used from Windows NT or Windows 2000 computers. See Chapter 4 for more information.

15. D. Windows 2000 uses the WINNT command to start the installation process. The /H switch specifies that the accessibility options should be installed. See Chapter 4 for more information.

16. B, C, D. If the hardware requirements for a Windows 3.1 computer meet the Windows 2000 requirements you can install Windows 2000, but there is no supported upgrade path for this operating system. See Chapter 4 for more information.

17. D. If your computer has an operating system installed and you install Windows 2000 (as opposed to an upgrade), your computer will be capable of dual-booting. The previous operating system's boot information will be stored in a file called BOOTSECT.DOS. See Chapter 4 for more information.

18. B. Files used to install applications are .MSI files. Microsoft Installer files have many advantages over traditional installation processes. See Chapter 5 for more information.

19. C. The best and safest way to remove Windows applications is through the Add/Remove Programs applet within the Control Panel. See Chapter 5 for more information.

20. A. When you access a printer's properties, you can bypass printer spooling by selecting the Print Directly to Printer option. See Chapter 6 for more information.

21. B. A Differential backup does not mark the files that are backed up as archived. An Incremental backup would mark the files that are backed up as archived. See Chapter 7 for more information.

22. D. The Windows 98 startup disk is a bootable disk that contains most of the commands needed to set up the computer prior to the Windows 98 installation. However, this disk does not contain the DELTREE command by default. See Chapter 7 for more information.

23. C. The RDISK command is used in Windows NT computers to create the ERD. This disk is not bootable and is specific to the computer that it was created on. See Chapter 7 for more information.

24. B. Windows 98 does not support a protocol called DLP. See Chapter 8 for more information.

25. A. The Microsoft Client for Microsoft Networks software is used to allow the computer to access network resources located on other Microsoft computers. See Chapter 8 for more information.

26. C. Universal Naming Convention (UNC) paths specify the computer name, followed by the share name, followed by the path. See Chapter 8 for more information.

27. C. The Domain Name System (DNS) is used to resolve Internet host names or domain names to IP addresses. See Chapter 8 for more information.

28. D. When prompted during the Windows 98 boot process, press the F8 key to access Windows Safe Mode. This is useful for troubleshooting purposes. See Chapter 9 for more information.

29. B. The Device Manager utility can be used to see all of the devices and their status that are recognized by the Windows 98 operating system. See Chapter 9 for more information.

30. D. The SCANREG command is used to check and back up the Registry. It will also attempt to fix any problems it diagnoses with the Registry structure. See Chapter 9 for more information.

A+: Operating System Technologies Exam

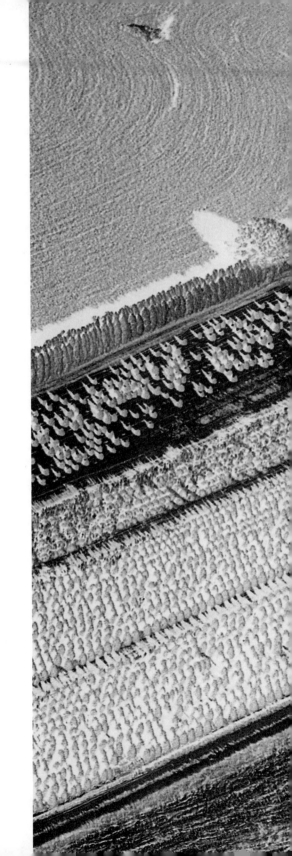

Chapter 1

Introduction to Computer Operating Systems

"I think there is a world market for maybe five computers."

Thomas Watson
Chairman of IBM, 1943

When poor Mr. Watson made his prediction 60 years ago, he was looking at a very different machine from the ones we have today. At that time computers were bulky—as in room-sized—slow and difficult to use. As recently as the 1970s most machines were still using punch cards as a primary data input tool, and anyone wanting to use a computer had to navigate a complex, uninviting interface with only a keyboard to help them. In such an environment, Watson probably was correct to believe that few people would go through the time, effort, and expense to use computers.

> After years of training people to pass A+ certification exam, we realize how important this material is to passing the test. Even though it doesn't directly cover any objectives, this chapter provides crucial context for working in the field.

As computer technology has evolved towards smaller, more powerful machines, the personal computer has made significant strides towards Microsoft's grandiose stated goal of "a computer in every home." The incredible global computer revolution is not due just to hardware, though. In many ways the acceleration of computer usage over the last decade has more to do with the ever-improving operating systems that humans use to interact with these machines. Computers require programmed code (called software) to run, and they require an input-output mechanism to allow users to give the machine instructions and view the results of those commands. The operating system is the primary software used to achieve these ends, and the evolution of more powerful and user-friendly operating systems has made computers less difficult to use and more enjoyable.

In order to understand the emergence of modern personal computer operating systems, you should know about the technologies that led to our present systems and about the critical relationship between hardware and software over the course of the PC's development. Graphics, speed, GUI interfaces, and multiple programs running concurrently are all made possible by software designers taking full advantage of the hardware for which they are designing their software. Because of this, we will see that as computer hardware has improved, software has improved with it. Because the operating system is the platform on which all other software builds, it is generally the development of a new operating system that drives the development of other software. This chapter is therefore the story of that very special, and crucial, type of software—the personal computer operating system. This chapter is spent looking at where operating systems have been, and we will focus the rest of the book looking at where they are currently by focusing on Microsoft's Windows 95/98 and Windows 2000 operating systems.

Types of Software

There are a number of different types of personal computer software, and each has a specific role in the operation of the machine. Among these are the following major distinctions:

Operating System (OS)   Provides a consistent environment for other software to execute commands. The OS gives users an interface with the computer so they can send commands to (input) and receive feedback or results back (output). To do this the operating system must communicate with the computer hardware to perform the following tasks:

- Disk and file management
- Device access
- Memory management
- Output format

Once the operating system has organized these basic resources, users can give the computer instructions through input devices (such as a keyboard or a mouse). Some of these commands are built into the operating system, while others are issued through the use of applications. The OS becomes the center through which the system hardware, other software, and the user communicate, and all the rest of the components of the system work together through the OS, which coordinates their communication.

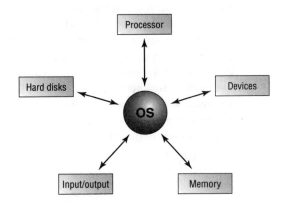

Network Operating System (NOS)　Similar to a standard operating system, except that the NOS is optimized to provide services to other machines on the network. NOS software is examined briefly in Chapter 8, "Configuring Network Software," but is discussed in-depth in Sybex's *Network+ Study Guide.*

Application　Used to accomplish a particular task, an application is software that is written to supplement the commands available to a particular operating system. Each application is specifically compiled (configured) for the operating system it is going to run on. For this reason, the application relies on the OS to do many of its basic tasks. Examples of an application might include complex programs, such as Microsoft Word or Netscape Navigator, or simple programs, such as a command line FTP program. Either way, when accessing devices and memory the programs can simply request that the OS do it for them. This arrangement saves substantially on programming overhead, as much of the executable code is "shared," meaning that it is written into the operating system and can therefore be used by multiple applications running on that OS.

Driver　Extremely specific software written for the purpose of instructing a particular OS on how to access a piece of hardware. Each modem or printer has unique features and configuration settings, and the driver allows the OS to properly understand how the hardware works and what it is able to do.

Types of PC Operating Systems

$\mathbf{T}$his chapter will introduce a few of the major operating systems of the past 20 years and will briefly describe how they work. These are not the only operating systems out there but are simply the ones that were accepted by a large enough segment of the PC market to become *de facto* standards. As you read about these different software products, try to think about the ways they differ from one another and the reasons they were designed in the fashion they were. The A+ exam focuses only on OS options available on Intel, and it will be those systems that are given the most time in this chapter. Although Macintosh, for instance, has a strong following in certain niche markets, it is little used in corporate settings. Intel/Windows machines dominate the corporate market almost completely. By knowing some of the OS options available to you, it will be easier to decide which operating system will work best in a particular situation and you can be better prepared to recommend a particular OS to your customers. The following OSs will be will be discussed over the course of the chapter:

- CP/M
- DOS

- Windows (1–3.*x*)
- OS/2
- Windows 95
- Windows NT Workstation
- Linux
- Macintosh OS 9

To understand the emergence of modern graphical operating systems, you should know about the technologies that led to our present systems and about the critical relationship between hardware and software. Graphics, speed, GUI interfaces, and multiple programs running concurrently are all made possible by software designers taking full advantage of the hardware for which they are designing their software.

Operating System Terms and Concepts

Before we actually get too far into our discussion of PC operating systems, it may be useful to define a few key terms. Below are some terms you will come across as you study this chapter, and visit with people in the computer industry.

Version   A version is a particular revision of a piece of software, normally described by a number, which tells you how new the product is in relation to other versions of the product. MS-DOS, for instance, is currently in its sixth major version. Major revisions are distinguished from minor ones in this manner: DOS 5.0 to 6.0 was a major revision, while 6.0 to 6.2 was a minor revision. This way of marking changes is now relatively standard in marking changes in other OS and application software. Additionally, very minor revisions are indicated with an additional decimal point. Upgrading from DOS version 6.21 to 6.22 involved only a few new files, but it was still an upgrade.

Source   The actual code that defines how a piece of software works. Computer operating systems can be "open source," meaning that the OS can be examined and modified by users, or it can be "closed source," meaning users cannot modify or examine the code.

Shell   A shell is a program that runs "on top of" the operating system and allows the user to issue commands through a set of menus or some other graphical interface. Shells make using an operating system easier to use by changing the user interface. The two shells we will be looking at most closely are Microsoft's DOS Shell (a menuing system) and Windows (a fully graphical user interface).

Graphical user interface (GUI)   The user interface is the method by which a person communicates with a computer. GUIs use a mouse, touch pad, or another mechanism (in addition to the keyboard) to interact with the computer to issue commands.

Network   A network is any group of computers that have a physical communication link between them. Networks allow computers to share information and resources quickly and securely.

Cooperative multitasking   A multitasking method that depends on the application itself to be responsible for using and then freeing access to the processor. This is the way that Windows 3.1 managed multiple applications. If any application locked up while using the processor, the application was unable to properly free the processor to do other tasks, and the entire system locked, usually forcing a reboot.

Preemptive multitasking   A multitasking method in which the operating system allots each application a certain amount of processor time and then forcibly takes back control and gives another application or task access to the processor. This means that if an application crashes, the operating system takes control of the processor away from the locked application and passes it on to the next application, which should be unaffected. Although unstable programs still lock, only the locked application will stall, not the entire system.

Multithreading   The ability of a single application to have multiple requests in to the processor at one time. This results in faster application performance, because it allows a program to do many things at once. Only 32-bit or higher operating systems support multithreading.

"Classic" Operating Systems

The word "classic" sounds so much better than "obsolete", doesn't it? Still, this isn't exactly the type of heading that makes you want to take notes, is it? That's the point, in a lot of ways, as the material in this chapter is not going to be on the A+ exam. Then why, you may ask, is it in the *A+ Complete Study Guide* at all? Two reasons, really. The first is that it is easier to understand the modern OS versions you will be tested on if you understand where they come from. The second is that being a technician isn't just about passing a test, and these systems will come up in discussions all through your career, as someone reminisces about the "good old days" of DOS or OS/2. It is important that we know where we have been and how we have gotten to where we are. Knowing this background is an essential part of being an informed and effective computer-support person or service technician and certainly is in accordance with the overall goals of certification. Customers and clients will be more confident of your abilities when you can show that you have a solid understanding of your industry. That said, those of you obsessed with certification can skip ahead a few pages to the "Current Operating Systems" section while the rest of us take a stroll down memory lane on the 16-bit bus.

CP/M

The *Control Program for Microcomputer (CP/M)* is an operating system you may never have heard of because it is not in use on modern PCs. Gary Kildall wrote this OS in 1973, using his PL/M programming language. It initially ran on the Intel 8008. It was later ported to the 8080 chip and was, in many ways, very similar in function to DOS. As a matter of fact, it looks quite similar to DOS, as you can see in Figure 1.1.

FIGURE 1.1   Control Program for Microcomputer (CP/M)

```
Z80 C>SUBMIT AUTOEXEC.Z80
Z80 C>set_bdos min
Z80 C>set_cpmecho off
Z80 C>set_cpmlist lpt1
Z80 C>set_cpmpun com1
Z80 C>set_cpmrdr com1
Z80 C>set_cpu z80
Z80 C>set_fake off
Z80 C>set_illop fault
Z80 C>set_iobase 400
Z80 C>set_mask on
Z80 C>set_source z80
Z80 C>set_term h19
Z80 C>set_vars on
Z80 C>coldboot
Z80 C>
Z80 C>
```

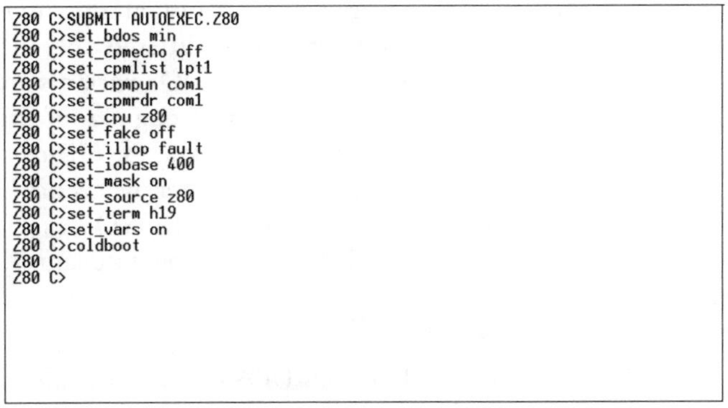

The following bit of computer folklore, which, despite questionable authenticity, has become well known in the industry, underscores the relationship between CP/M and DOS: In 1981, IBM decided to begin marketing machines to home users and small offices. They decided that, for reasons of time and efficiency, they would simply license an operating system rather than develop and support one of their own. To that end, they scheduled a meeting with Gary Kildall. The IBM representative arrived for the meeting at Kildall's house, but Gary wasn't there; he was out flying his plane. After an unsuccessful meeting with Kildall's wife and lawyer, the IBM representative left without an OS. Not long after, IBM found a different system, entering into a contract with Bill Gates by which Gates' fledgling company Microsoft (you may have heard of them) agreed to license their DOS operating system to IBM. Kildall says that this story is not accurate and, in fact, claims that Bill Gates was the first to tell the apocryphal story. One way or the other, the fact remains that Kildall's OS lost a huge opportunity. At the time that IBM allegedly came calling, CP/M was in fact the industry standard for low-cost computers on the Intel platform. Within a few years of losing the IBM contract, it was nothing but a memory.

A copy of CP/M itself is as hard to find these days as a baby sauropod, but the good folks at ZDNet have a great emulator called 22Nice available for download if you are interested in digging into computer history. Go out to zdnet.com.au/swlib/ Utilities/System_Utilities/0000CB.html to read more about it. Warning: Downloading and using command line operating systems will quickly earn you the "geek" label.

MS-DOS and PC-DOS

In the 1980s or early 1990s, the operating system that shipped with most PCs was a version of the *Disk Operating System (DOS)* created by Microsoft: *MS-DOS*. (There were a number of manufacturers of DOS, but most of them produced similar versions—they differed only in syntax and a few utilities. The important differences among DOS variants are to be found from one chronological version to the next, not among manufacturers.)

In next section, you will look at the origins of DOS and the way it has evolved, version by version, over time. After the history lesson, we will also examine some of the commands and syntax of the DOS OS, as you will need some knowledge of command line syntax before taking the A+ exam.

The Origins of DOS

The story behind MS-DOS is one of the most often told of all computer fables. But the intrigue goes further than the mystery of why Gary Kildall missed his meeting with IBM. As noted, Microsoft contracted with IBM to write the operating system for their new Intel-based microcomputer project. Although Bill Gates and his partner, Paul Allen, were both experienced programmers, they had gained their success through the creation of programming languages, not operating systems.

Gates and Allen had created the BASIC language in 1976 and had also released versions of COBOL and FORTRAN for Intel-based machines. However, they had never created an operating system from scratch, which is exactly what they promised to do for IBM. In an interesting twist, just as Seattle-based Microsoft was finishing up a very secretive deal with IBM, Tim Patterson of Seattle Computer Products began writing an operating system specifically for use with the 8086-based computer. Patterson was dissatisfied with how long it was taking for an x86 version of CP/M to be released, so he named his operating system *Quick-and-Dirty Disk Operating System (QDOS)*, and showed it to Microsoft, even as they were in the middle of talks with IBM. Paul Allen soon contracted with Seattle Computer Products to purchase QDOS to then sell to an unnamed client (IBM, of course). The purchase price of around $100,000 bought Microsoft an operating system, and a few months later, Patterson followed his operating system—he quit SCP and took a job with Gates and Allen. Microsoft soon acquired all rights to QDOS and renamed it MS-DOS.

From there, MS-DOS was modified for use with the new IBM minicomputer, and in the fall of 1981, IBM announced the IBM 5150 PC Personal Computer. The 5150 had a 4.77MHz Intel 8088 CPU, 64KB RAM, 40KB ROM, one 5.25-inch floppy drive, color graphics capability, and an OS called *PC-DOS 1.0*. PC-DOS, of course, was simply IBM's moniker for the MS-DOS they were licensing from Microsoft.

Before the PC, most computers were sold as kits. This meant that the customer had to assemble the machine, install the OS, etc. IBM debuted their IBM PC as a machine that anyone could use, because it was "ready to go" right out of the box.

Gates and Allen had contracted to allow IBM to *use* their operating system, rather than allowing IBM to *buy* it outright. Moreover, IBM had not been granted any type of exclusivity over DOS, hence Microsoft was also able to license versions of DOS to other companies, allowing the creation of what were originally called "IBM clone" machines. These machines ran on the same Intel chip as the IBM PC and used a similar version of the operating system. From 1981 on, the future of the personal computer was to be largely determined by the increasingly powerful processors created by Intel and the increasingly sophisticated operating systems Microsoft wrote to take advantage of Intel's enhancements.

MS-DOS Versions

Next we will look at the evolution of the MS-DOS operating system and will examine the major changes in microcomputer architecture and standards that are reflected in each revision. Smaller revisions—1.0 to 1.1, 6.0 to 6.1—are not enumerated, but their changes are included in the overall enhancements made to the overall version.

You will notice as you read about and use DOS that most of the versions of this operating system are very similar, as the OS proved to be very stable in its original design. Although various enhancements or features may or may not be available to you, depending on the version you are using, in a general sense you can trust that if you learn one version, you can probably use any of them.

MS-DOS 1

The original version of MS-DOS was, to put it mildly, a "no-frills" operating system. It had no provisions for networking, did not include any sort of graphical shell program, and had limited ability to manage system resources. Approximately a year after the release of DOS 1.0, a revision—DOS 1.1—added support for double-sided 320KB floppy drives. Double-sided disks were important, as they effectively doubled the machine's storage and retrieval capacity. It is difficult to grasp this concept today, when a 10- or 20-gigabyte hard drive is standard on most new desktop machines, but in 1981 internal hard drives were neither easily available nor supported by DOS. Users generally had only a single 5.25" drive, so the OS, any programs the users wanted to run, and any data they wanted to retrieve all had to be accessed through the 5.25" floppies!

MS-DOS 2

In early 1983, IBM introduced the IBM PC XT. The XT featured a 10MB hard drive, a serial interface, and three additional expansion slots. It also had 128KB of RAM and a 360KB floppy drive (40KB more capacity than that of single-sided floppies on the previous PC) and could support a 10MB internal hard drive. Users of this new PC needed an operating system that would allow them to take advantage of this new hardware, and Microsoft did not disappoint them.

MS-DOS 3

With DOS 3.0, released in summer 1984, Microsoft continued to include additional DOS features and to support more powerful hardware. DOS 3.0 supported hard drives larger than 10MB, as well as enhanced graphics formats. Three revisions—3.1, 3.2, and 3.3—provided additional innovations. The IBM PC AT was the first machine shipped with DOS 3. It had 256KB of RAM, an Intel 80286 processor (6 MHz!), and a 1.2MB 5.25" floppy drive. A 20MB hard drive and color video card were also available. Later upgrades to version 3 of MS-DOS included support for networking and 32MB partition sizes, as well as 1.44MB floppy drives.

Version 3.1 was notable because it featured the first DOS support for networking. The IBM PC Network was a simple local area network structure that was similar to today's workgroup networks.

DOS 3.2 introduced the XCOPY command, enabling the user to identify more than one file at a time to be copied, and it made important modifications to other DOS commands. It was also the first version to support IBM's Token Ring network topology and the first to allow for 720KB 3.5" floppies. Version 3.3, introduced in 1987, offered additional enhancements to numerous existing commands and introduced support for 1.44MB floppy disks. Logical partition sizes could be up to 32MB, and a single machine could support both a primary and a secondary partition on each disk. It is important to note that DOS 3 was released in 1984, the same year as Apple's infamous "1984" ad aired during the Super Bowl, marking the release of the Apple Macintosh. IBM had a great thing going with the PC, but they had gotten lazy and just made occasional improvements to DOS as needed, rather than really trying to make significant changes to it. As the challenge came in from Apple, whose graphical Macintosh OS was clearly superior to DOS, Microsoft and IBM announced the creation of a second PC operating system, OS/2. Unfortunately, "announcing" and "delivering" are very different things, and the story of OS/2's production problems is a long one. We will look at both Apple and OS/2 later in the chapter.

MS-DOS 4

By 1988 it was apparent that the wave of the future was the graphical interface, and DOS 4 provided users with the DOS Shell, a utility much like the Windows File Manager. Actually, DOS Shell was simply a scaled-down version of Windows (which we will look at in a minute) that allowed users to manage files, run programs, and do routine maintenance, all from a single screen. The DOS Shell even supported a mouse. (That's right, there was no ability to use a mouse within DOS before this version. Oh, how Mac lovers must have mocked Microsofties back in the dark days of '88!)

MS-DOS 5

There were several important features introduced in the 1991 release of DOS 5.0. First of all, the ability to load drivers into reserved (upper) memory was a relief to those people who were constantly running out of conventional memory. This feature allowed more complex DOS programs (that took up more conventional memory) to be developed.

In addition to this feature, several software utilities made their debut. The most commonly used utility introduced at this time was EDIT.COM. This ASCII text editor has since become one of the most popular text editors for simple text files (and a welcomed relief from the single-line view of EDLIN.COM—previously the only choice for a text editor). Also added in DOS 5 were QBASIC.EXE, DOSKEY, UNFORMAT, and UNDELETE.

MS-DOS 6

Released in 1993 to excellent sales (and a lawsuit for patent infringement), DOS 6.0 offered a number of new commands and configurable options. Another enhancement in DOS 6.0 was EMM386.EXE, which allowed the system to pool extended and expanded memory. DOS 6.0 has subsequently been revised a number of times—once (DOS 6.2 to 6.21) because of a court order. Microsoft was found to have violated Stac Electronics' patent rights in the creation of the DoubleSpace utility for 6.0 and 6.1, and the only real difference between 6.2 and 6.21 is that DoubleSpace is removed. Never to be denied, Microsoft soon released DOS 6.22 with a disk compression program called DriveSpace.

As of this writing, DOS 6.22 is the most current MS-DOS version available as a stand-alone operating system. Microsoft has included certain DOS-style command line utilities for use within Windows 95, Windows NT and Windows 2000, but these are actually Windows programs that simply mimic the familiar, old command-prompt environment of DOS.

Microsoft Windows

Any real understanding of the success of DOS after 1987 requires knowledge of Windows. In the early years of its existence, Microsoft's DOS gained great acceptance and became a standard as a PC operating system. Even so, as computers became more powerful and programs more complex, the limitations of the DOS command-line interface were becoming apparent (as well as the aforementioned conventional memory limitation).

The solution to the problem was to make the operating system easier to navigate, more uniform, and generally more "friendly" to the user. IBM had understood that the average user did not want to receive their computer in pieces but preferred to have it ready-to-go out of the box. Oddly, they did not understand that the same user who wanted their *hardware* to be ready-to-go also wanted their *software* to be the same way. They did not want to edit batch files or hunt through directories using CD or DIR commands either. Because of this, when Microsoft came to IBM with a graphical user interface (GUI) based on groundbreaking work done by Xerox labs, IBM was not interested, preferring to go onward with the development of OS/2, a project it had already started with Microsoft.

The Xerox Corporation maintained a think-tank of computer designers in Palo Alto, California called the Palo Alto Research Center (PARC). One of the results of their work was the Alto workstation, which is generally thought to be the forerunner of all modern graphical operating systems. The Alto had a mouse and a GUI interface, and it communicated with other stations via Ethernet. Oh, and it was finished in 1974! Although it was never promoted commercially, both Microsoft and Apple viewed the Alto and incorporated its technology into their own systems. The accomplishments of the PARC lab in laying the groundwork for modern graphical computing systems simply cannot be overstated. Check out www.parc.xerox.com for more information on PARC past and present.

Regardless of IBM's interest, Microsoft continued on its own with its development of the GUI—which it named *Windows* after its rectangular work areas—and released the first version to the market in 1985. Apple filed a lawsuit soon after, claiming that the Microsoft GUI had been built using Apple technology, but the suit was dismissed. Apple's Macintosh and Microsoft's DOS-with-Windows combo have both continued to evolve, but until a recent deal between Apple and Microsoft, tensions have always been high. Mac and PC *users*, of course, still remain adamantly chauvinistic about their respective platforms.

Oh, the stories that have been told around the glow of a monitor about Gates vs. Jobs. Even so, one of the easiest ways to get a bit of the flavor of the struggle is through a recent movie called "Pirates of the Silicon Valley," in which Anthony Michael Hall of "The Breakfast Club" plays Gates and Noah Wyle of "ER" fame plays Jobs. More info at tnt.turner.com/movies/tntoriginals/pirates.

The Windows interface to MS-DOS is really just a shell program that allows users to issue DOS commands through a graphical interface—a prettier extension of Microsoft's earlier DOS Shell work. The integration of a mouse for nearly all tasks—a legacy of the Xerox Alto computer on which both the Macintosh and Windows GUIs are based—further freed users from DOS by allowing them to issue common commands without using the keyboard. Word processors, spreadsheets, and especially games were revolutionized as software manufacturers happily took advantage of the ease of use and flexibility that Windows added to DOS.

Windows Versions

After the development of Windows, many of the enhancements made to subsequent versions of DOS were designed to help free up and reallocate resources to better run Windows and Windows-based applications. Similarly, PC hardware continued to evolve far past the limits of DOS's ability to effectively use the power available to it, and later versions of Windows would be designed to hide and overcome the limitations of the operating system. The combination of MS-DOS and its Windows shell would make Microsoft the industry leader, and spurred the PC movement to new heights in the early 1990s. Following is a brief examination of the development of the Windows shell and a look at its different versions.

Windows 1

Version 1 of Windows featured the tiling windows, mouse support, and menu systems that still drive next-generation operating systems such as Windows 98, Windows CE, and Windows 2000. It also offered "cooperative multitasking," meaning that more than one Windows application could run concurrently. This was something that MS-DOS, up to this point, could not do.

Windows 1 was far from a finished product. For one thing, it didn't use icons, and it had few of the programs we have come to expect as Windows standards. Windows 1 was basically just an updated, more graphical version of the DOS SHELL.EXE program.

Windows 2

Version 2, released in 1987, added icons and allowed application windows to overlap each other, as well as tile. Support was also added for PIFs (program information files), which allowed the user to configure Windows to run their DOS applications more efficiently.

Windows 3.*x*

Windows 3.0 featured a far more flexible memory model, allowing it to access more memory than the 640KB limit normally imposed by DOS. It also featured the addition of the File Manager and Program Manager, allowed for network support, and could operate in "386 Enhanced mode." 386 Enhanced mode used parts of the hard drive as "virtual memory" and was therefore able to use disk memory to supplement the RAM in the machine. Windows today, in fact, is still quite similar to the Windows of version 3.0.

In 1992, a revision of Windows 3, known as Windows 3.1, provided for better graphical display capability and multimedia support. It also improved the Windows error-protection system and let applications work together more easily through the use of object linking and embedding (OLE).

Windows after the introduction of version 3.1 took a marked turn for the better, because Microsoft started making a serious effort to change to a full 32-bit application environment. With version 3.11, also known as Windows for Workgroups, Windows could offer support for both 16-bit and 32-bit applications. (Windows 3.1 could only support 16-bit applications.) Significant progress on the 32-bit front was not to be made, however, until very late in 1995, when Microsoft introduced Windows 95. Since that time the venerable DOS/Windows team has been largely replaced by newer, more advanced systems. You may occasionally still run into a Windows 3.1 machine, but it is not a common occurrence.

With the introduction of Windows for Workgroups, people speaking generically about the two "flavors" of Windows—3.1 and 3.11—started referring to them collectively as *Windows 3.x*, as in the heading of this section.

OS/2

Even as Windows 3.1 was in development, Microsoft was participating in a joint effort with IBM to create a next-generation operating system for use with 286 and higher processors. This operating system was to be IBM/Microsoft's second generation OS, or OS/2, intended to replace DOS. Differing goals for the design of the new system caused a number of disagreements, though, and the partnership soon broke up. IBM continued the development of OS/2 on their own, while Microsoft took their part of the technology and began to develop LAN Manager, which would eventually lead to the development of Windows NT.

With the second version, IBM made OS/2 a 32-bit system that required at least a 386 processor to run. Although this made it vastly more stable and powerful than Windows 3.1, both it and Microsoft's NT product had a problem finding a market. The main reason for this was probably that most users simply did not have powerful enough computers to properly use the system, and few pieces of software were available that leveraged the new architecture and OS properly.

With version 3 (OS/2 Warp), IBM created a multitasking, 32-bit OS that required a 386 but preferred a 486. Warp also required a ridiculous 4MB of RAM just to load. With a graphical interface and the ability to do a great deal of self-configuration, the Warp OS was a peculiar cross between DOS and a Macintosh. Warp featured true preemptive multitasking, did not suffer from the memory limitations of DOS, and had a desktop similar to the Macintosh.

For all of its tremendous features, OS/2 Warp had a funny name and was badly marketed. It never really established a wide user base. Nonetheless, until Windows NT 3.51 was released in 1995, OS/2 was the operating system of choice for high-end workstations, and up until recently the OS retained a small but faithful following. The last year or so has been harsh on OS/2 fans, though, as IBM has essentially abandoned the high-end desktop market to Windows NT, Windows 2000, and Linux. OS/2 has been largely forgotten, and IBM now ships Windows 2000 Professional with its own desktops. When even the company that makes an OS stops pushing it, it drops into the "obsolete" section real quick. For more info on OS/2, including current support options, go out to IBM's OS/2 information page at www-4.ibm.com/software/os/warp.

Windows 95

Although it dominated the market with its DOS operating system and its add-on Windows interface, Microsoft found that the constraints of DOS were rapidly making it difficult to take full advantage of rapidly improving hardware and software developments. The future of computing was clearly a 32-bit, preemptively multitasked system such as IBM's OS/2, but many current users had DOS-based software or older hardware that was specifically designed for DOS and would not operate outside of its Windows 3.1, cooperatively multitasked environment.

Because of this problem, in the fall of 1995 Microsoft released a major upgrade to the DOS/Windows environment. Called Windows 95, the new product integrated the operating system and the shell. Where previous versions of Windows simply provide a graphic interface to the existing DOS OS, the Windows 95 graphical interface *is* part of the OS. Moreover, Windows 95 was designed to be a hybrid of the features of previous DOS versions and newer 32-bit systems. To this end, it is a preemptively multitasked system that is able to emulate and support cooperative multitasking for programs that require it. It also supports both 32-bit and 16-bit drivers as well as DOS drivers, although the 32-bit drivers are strongly recommended over the DOS ones, as they are far more stable and faster.

Among the most important of the other enhancements debuted by Microsoft with Windows 95 was support for the Plug-and-Play standard (PnP). This meant that if a device was designed to be plug-and-play, a technician could install the device into the computer, start the machine, and have the device automatically recognized and configured by Windows 95. This was a major advance, but unfortunately for Plug and Play to work properly, three things had to be true:

1. The OS had to be PnP compatible.
2. The computer motherboard had to support PnP.
3. All devices in the machine had to be PnP compatible.

Unfortunately, at the time Windows 95 came out many manufacturers were creating their hardware for use in DOS/Windows machines, and DOS did not support PnP, so most pre-1995 computer components were not PnP compliant. Because of this, these components—generally referred to as "legacy" devices— often interfered with the Plug-and-Play environment. Legacy devices are sound cards, modems, etc. that do not support the Plug-and-Play standard. Such devices are not able to dynamically interact with newer systems. They therefore require manual configuration or must be replaced by newer devices, which don't usually need manual configuration. Due to problems managing legacy hardware under Windows 95, many people soured on PnP technology. Worse, they blamed Windows 95 for their problems, not the old hardware. "It worked fine in DOS" was the standard logic! Now, half a decade later, nearly all PC components are PnP compliant, and configuring computer systems is far easier than it was under DOS.

The foibles of PnP aside, to say that the new system was a success would be a major understatement. Within just a few years of its release, the Windows 95–style GUI had won over nearly all Windows users, and the more resilient architecture of 95 had won over network administrators and computer technicians. While it was far from perfect, Windows 95 was a tremendous advance out of the DOS age. Perhaps the only ones not thrilled were the folks at Apple, who continued to make a cottage industry out of starting lawsuits against Microsoft. This time Apple was contending that the Windows 95 interface itself was stolen from the Macintosh. While it is undeniable that the 95 interface is an evil twin of the Mac interface, it turned out that Apple themselves had gotten their GUI from somewhere else...the PARC Alto! Unbelievably, Xerox had evidently not only designed the first computer GUI, but they had created an interface that could not be significantly improved upon in over 20 years of OS development, and which both Apple and Microsoft settled on as the basis for their GUIs! All subsequent versions of Windows (98, NT, and 2000) use an interface essentially identical to the Windows 95 GUI.

Chapter 2, "Introduction to the Windows Interface," goes into depth on the nature of the Windows 95/98/NT/2000 interface, and overall Windows 95 OS is only marginally different from its Windows 98 upgrade, which is one of the operating systems you will be tested on during the A+ exam. As such, Windows 95 will be grouped with 98 for the rest of the book, and we will be more concerned with the differences between Windows 9x and Windows 2000 than we will be by differences between Windows 95 and Windows 98.

Other Current Operating Systems

And then there were only five. As this book is written, the desktop operating system market is dominated by one operating system, while four others are viable options...or pretenders to the throne. Clearly, Windows 95/98 is the primary desktop OS in the world, with a stranglehold on the desktops of the corporate environment and a strong lead in the home market. It is not, though, the only OS you may run across, and many high-end workstations are running one of the other options listed below. Without further ado, the five current OS options are

- Windows 98
- Windows NT Workstation
- Windows 2000 Professional
- Linux (all distributions)
- Mac OS 9

We will be talking about Windows 98 and Windows 2000 in depth throughout the rest of the study guide, as they are the two operating systems that you will be tested on. As such, the remainder of this chapter will focus on the other OS options available to the daring PC owner.

On the horizon: Microsoft released Windows Me just as the A+ test objectives were being finalized. Because of the timing of its debut, Me will not be part of the exam. Me is an upgrade to Windows 98 and is expected to be the last version of the Windows 95/98/Me architecture. Plans are for future releases of Microsoft's home/low-end desktop product to be based on the more stable Windows 2000 architecture instead of on the Windows 95 architecture.

Windows NT Workstation

As previously noted, Windows 98 is currently the most common PC operating system on the market. Still, for users who need more power, other options are available. One of these is the Windows NT operating system. NT (which unofficially stands for New Technology) is an OS that was designed to be far more powerful than any previous Windows version. It uses an architecture based entirely on 32-bit code and is capable of accessing up to four gigabytes (4,000 megabytes) of RAM.

Windows NT can support huge drive sizes and more than one processor, and has numerous advantages over Windows 95 and DOS. NT comes in two varieties—Workstation and Server, each intended for a particular role. NT Server is designed as the centerpiece of a network and is able to carry out numerous tasks for organizing and managing networked computers. Windows NT Workstation, on the other hand, is intended for users who work with large files or complex programs. CAD (computer-aided design) programs are a good example of the sort of applications that run better under NT than under other versions of Windows.

Windows NT also allows for better security than previous versions of Windows and is more stable. Naturally, each version of NT that has come out has been more expensive than the current version of Windows 3.*x* or 95 and needed a significantly more powerful machine to run well. A quick rundown of the evolution of NT follows.

Windows NT Workstation 3.*x*

Windows NT was first released in 1993, under the title of *Windows NT 3.1*. Where, you may ask, were Windows NT 1.0 and 2.0? Perhaps in the same closet at Microsoft where all of the copies of Word 5.0 are hidden....NT was essentially a reworking of the LAN Manager software which had come out of Microsoft's aborted OS/2 partnership with IBM, but part of the "New Technology" (hence NT) offering was a workstation option that had not been available on LAN Manager. Windows NT 3.1 debuted at the familiar 3.1 version number to stay in line with the rest of the 3.*x* Windows family. It was subsequently upgraded to 3.5 and then to 3.51.

In 1993 Windows NT 3.1 was definitely a step up from DOS/Windows and was adopted in many CAD and number-crunching environments. When Windows NT 3.51 arrived in the fall of 1995, it featured a number of improvements, such as a fully 32-bit OS, file-level security, support for more RAM, and support for multiple processors.

Windows NT Workstation 4.0

With the release in 1996 of Windows NT 4.0, the NT platform was given a facelift and now sported the popular Windows 95 GUI. (NT 3.*x* had used the Windows 3.*x* Program Manager GUI.) This and the increasing availability of NT-compatible application software allowed NT 4.0 Workstation to solidify its place in the market as a high-end desktop. NT was positioned directly against its cousin, OS/2 Warp. With the 95 GUI and the power of Microsoft marketing, NT quickly took over most of the "power user" market. NT workstations are excellent for any of the following tasks:

- Database client
- Graphics station
- CAD station

Probably the only real problem that the Windows NT system had when compared to Windows 95 was that both NT 3.*x* and NT 4.0 lacked plug-and-play capabilities, a fact that would irritate many a technician over the next few years.

LINUX

Over the past couple of years the "open-source" movement has been rallying around Linus Torvalds and his Linux OS. Linux is a Unix-type operating system that has been released into the public domain and is being developed as an operating system standard, much as TCP/IP is a protocol standard. There are a number of computer users who are uncomfortable with Microsoft's dominance of the crucial OS market, and, as a result, Linux has been positioned as an excellent alternative to the Microsoft juggernaut. There were suspicions that CompTIA would be adding Linux questions into the A+ exam, but in the end it was decided that Linux' time had not yet come.

This was probably the right decision, for two reasons. The first of these is that while it is making inroads with knowledgeable home users and is even being used as a server in many corporate environments, Linux has simply not been able to break into the mass home or corporate desktop markets that the A+ objectives prepare you to serve. The second reason follows from this. Because most Linux users are computer junkies themselves, few of them will be taking their computers in for professional (i.e., paid) configuration or support. As an A+ certified tech, you will be working for the people who will pay you, and most of them are still running Windows.

That said, Linux is a nifty idea. The theory behind it is to make core operating system code available to anyone who wants it, so that the code can then be explored and enhanced by users. Those who choose to can even create a full Unix-type OS from the Linux source code, modify it as they see fit, and release it to the world as a Linux "distribution." Distributions are similar to versions, but where versions are chronological enhancements to a single company's OS, distributions are variations on a single OS theme. For a list of Linux distributions, refer to `www.linux.org/dist/english.html`.

The architecture of Linux is based on Unix, the OS used in mainframes and other high-end computers, and it is extremely powerful and stable. Linux also is commonly used as a Web server or e-mail server on the Internet, and can function as either a network operating system or a desktop operating system, just as Windows NT can.

There are few creatures more rabid in defense of their cause than Linux fans, and for good reason. The basic philosophy of Linux is that the people who use an operating system are the ones who know best what needs to be improved on it and that user feedback should be respected and acted upon. Linux has not always been an OS for the masses, as early distributions were complex to install and had little application support, but through a small army of users sending suggestions it has improved markedly.

The Linux vs. Microsoft debate is an interesting one in the computer world, as it is a face-off between idealism and corporate power, open-source and proprietary code. It is a battleground where we will eventually see whether users prefer a system which gives them power (but requires a bit more work) or one that makes everything easy (but gives them fewer choices). Should be fun to watch, if nothing else.

For detailed information of the world of Linux, two Web sites are obvious starting points: `www.linux.org` and `www.linux.com`. Linux.org is probably the better of the two for those interested in simply learning about what Linux is, and it has a great online course called "Getting Started with Linux."

Macintosh OS 9

Finally, we come to the venerable old man of the graphical operating system world, the Apple Macintosh. Apple was founded by Steve Jobs and Steve Wozniak. Wozniak built the first Apple, and was the technical wizard. Jobs was the sales and marketing guy, and together they built and marketed the Apple II, which Jobs dubbed "the computer for the rest of us." The Apple II was an immediate success, as it had color graphics, and useful applications such as Visicalc were available for it. For 1977, it was quite a spiffy machine.

The Apple was a relatively simple computer, though, and was operated via an OS like CP/M or BASIC. In 1984 all that changed, as Apple unveiled the Macintosh, a new machine with a revolutionary graphic user interface. Or at least an interface revolutionary to everyone outside the PARC labs. The original Mac had its faults—it was too expensive, it didn't have a hard drive, etc.—but nonetheless it laid the groundwork for many Macs (and Windows enhancements) to come. The Mac II came out in 1987, and included color support (the original Mac was b/w), but overall the Macintosh was undermined by problems within Apple (that caused Steve Jobs to be forced out) and limited Macintosh software development. The Apple philosophy was always one of producing both the hardware and the software for their machines and not licensing anyone else to do either. Eventually this backfired, as consumers chose cheaper and better-supported Intel/Microsoft options instead.

Fast forward to 2000, and the Macintosh is relatively popular again after nearly a decade of decline. A good part of this renaissance is due to the extremely successful iMac line, and the continuing success of the PowerBook (a Macintosh notebook). Mac computers are often found in artsy places—design houses, marketing departments, etc.—and are still the choice of people who want their computer to be simple to use and pretty to look at. Mind you, there's nothing wrong with that, but thank heavens we aren't tested on these things.

Choosing an Operating System

Now that we have sampled the variety of PC operating systems, it is time to take a more in-depth look at the two systems that dominate the current environment: Windows 95/98 and Windows 2000.

If you have users who have older hardware, Windows 95 may be the best bet, simply because of its low resource usage. Most other home users will be happiest with Windows 98 (or now Windows Me), and corporate users are generally divided between Windows 98/Me and Windows NT Workstation/Windows 2000 Professional. As we will see, users who need higher performance or strong security should be nudged toward NT or 2000 Professional. Really, the choices that you will probably be dealing with come down to the two OS options dealt with in-depth in the following chapters: Windows 98 for home/casual users and Windows NT for high-end systems.

Now that we have discussed the various types of PC operating systems, it is time to take a quick look at which ones you may want to recommend for users who are looking to upgrade. First off, Macintosh and Linux are sort of off on their own. The Mac OS runs on a different processor than Intel PCs, so if you own an Apple machine, you will be running the Mac OS on it. Linux is a great system, but is only for the adventurous at this time and is generally not something you want to recommend to the casual user. Linux will certainly work for anyone, but experienced computer users will be happier with it than novices will. That leaves us with the Microsoft family of products. If you have users who have older hardware, Windows 95 may be the best bet, simply because of its low resource usage. Most other home users will be happiest with Windows 98 or Windows Me, and corporate users are generally divided between Windows 98/Me and Windows NT Workstation/Windows 2000 Professional. Users who need higher performance or strong security should be nudged toward NT or 2000 Pro.

Summary

In this chapter we have looked at the evolution of the personal computer and how it has changed over the past two decades. The PC and especially its ever-improving operating systems have revolutionized the way that computing is done. From the Xerox Alto GUI to DOS to Macs and Windows, a number of different solutions have been found to the problem of allowing humans to communicate with machines. Over the rest of this book, we will leave behind most of the operating systems, just as CompTIA has done, and focus on just two platforms—Windows 98 and Windows 2000. The choices that you will probably face come down to the two OS options dealt with in-depth in the following chapters, where we will explore Windows 98 for home/casual users and Windows NT for high-end systems.

Key Terms

Before you take the exam, be certain you are familiar with the following terms:

Control Program for Microcomputer (CP/M)

PC-DOS 1.0

co-operative multitasking

preemptive multitasking

Disk Operating System (DOS)

Quick-and-Dirty Disk Operating System (QDOS)

graphical user interface (GUI)

shell

MS-DOS

source

multithreading

version

network

Review Questions

1. All of the following are important developments in Intel platform PC operating systems except _____.
   A. CP/M
   B. MS-DOS and PC-DOS
   C. Windows Interfaces to DOS
   D. OS/1

2. CP/M stands for _____.
   A. Control Processing Management
   B. Control Program for Microcomputer
   C. Control Power for Microcomputer
   D. Control Processing Microcomputer

3. What was the original version of MS-DOS?
   A. MS-DOS 2
   B. MS-DOS 3
   C. MS-DOS -1
   D. MS-DOS -5

4. What was the major innovation that came after MS-DOS -1?
   A. The 5.25" disk drive
   B. The 3.5" disk drive
   C. Double-sided 3.35" disks were created
   D. Double-sided 320K floppy drives were created

5. In early 1983 IBM introduced the IBM PC-XT. The PC-XT featured all of the following except _____.
   A. DOS 1.25 was the operating system
   B. 10MB hard drive
   C. Serial interface
   D. Three additional expansion slots
   E. 128K of RAM

6. The XT shipped with which version of DOS?
   A. MS-DOS 3
   B. MS-DOS 2
   C. MS-DOS 4
   D. MS-DOS 1

7. All of the following were features of MS-DOS 3 except _____.
   A. Supported hard drives larger than 10MB
   B. Enhanced graphics formats
   C. Support for networking
   D. Could not support 1.44MB floppy drives

8. The IBM PC-AT introduced in 1984 featured all but which the following?
   A. 128KB RAM
   B. An Intel processor 80286
   C. 1.25MB floppy drive
   D. 20MB hard drive

9. What was the first graphical interface that was introduced with MS-DOS 4?
   A. GUI
   B. DOSwin
   C. DOS Shell
   D. DOSini

10. The XCOPY command was introduced with which DOS version?
    A. DOS version 3.2
    B. DOS Version 3.1
    C. DOS Version 3.0
    D. DOS Version 4

11. All of the following were features introduced by MSDOS-5 except _____.
    A. The ability to load drivers into reserved or upper memory
    B. EDIT.COM utility
    C. EDLIN.COM
    D. QBASIC.EXE

12. What version of MS-DOS was DOSKEY.COM and UNDELETE.EXE introduced?
    A. MS-DOS version 6
    B. MS-DOS version 5
    C. MS-DOS version 4
    D. MS-DOS version 3

13. The ability to pool EMS and XMS memory using EMM386.EXE was introduced in which version of DOS?

  A. MS-DOS 5

  B. MS-DOS 4

  C. MS-DOS 6

  D. MS-DOS 3

14. Windows featured tiling windows, mouse support, and menu systems in which versions?

  A. Windows 1

  B. Windows 2

  C. Windows 3

  D. Windows 95

  E. All of the Above

15. What was the first Windows version that allowed more memory than the 640KB limit normally imposed by DOS?

  A. Windows 1

  B. Windows 2

  C. Windows 3

  D. Windows 95

16. What was the first 32-bit preemptive multitasking system?

  A. Windows 2

  B. Windows 3

  C. Windows 1

  D. Windows 95

17. _____ is the best of these Microsoft operating system for users needing to deal with large files or complex programs.

  A. Windows NT

  B. Windows 95

  C. Windows 3.11

  D. Windows 2

18. What was the minimum processor that version 2 of OS/2, a 32-bit system, required?

  A. 486

  B. 586

  C. 686

  D. 386

19. Which Windows operating system would provide high performance and file security?

   A. Windows 95

   B. Windows 98

   C. Windows NT

   D. Windows Me

20. Which of these "classic" operating systems can be looked at as the model on which modern graphical systems such as Windows 2000 and the Apple Macintosh are based?

   A. Windows 1.0

   B. OS/2

   C. CP/M

   D. Alto

Answers to Review Questions

1. D. CP/M, MS-DOS and PC-DOS, and Windows Interfaces are all are important developments in Intel platform PC operating systems.

2. B. This OS was written in 1973 by Gary Kildall, using Kildall's PL/M programming language, and it initially ran on the Intel 8008. It was later ported to the 8080 chip and was in many ways very similar in function to DOS.

3. C. This DOS version had a "no-frills" operating system. It had no provisions for networking, did not include any sort of graphical shell program, and had limited ability to manage system resources.

4. D. Double-sided 320K floppy drives were created was the major innovation that came after MS-DOS -1. At the time, hard drives were not easily available; therefore, all information was stored on 5.25" floppy disk.

5. A. The XT featured a 10MB hard drive, a serial interface, and three additional expansion slots. It also had 128KB of RAM and a 360KB floppy drive.

6. B. The XT shipped with MS-DOS 2.0, a revision of the DOS operating system that had to be redone almost from the ground up. It closely fit the machine it was built for, and it supported 10MB hard drives and the new 360KB floppy disks.

7. D. MS-DOS 3 could not support 1.44MB floppy drives. MS-DOS used 5.25" floppy drives.

8. A. The IBM PC-AT introduced in 1984 did not feature 128KB RAM. The IBM PC-AT was the first machine shipped with DOS 3. It had 256KB of RAM, an Intel 80286 processor (6 MHz!), and a 1.2MB, 5.25" floppy drive. A 20MB hard drive and color video card were also available.

9. C. MS-DOS 4 introduced the first graphical interface, which was called DOS Shell. The DOS Shell was simply a scaled-down version of Windows that allowed users to manage files, run programs, and do routine maintenance all from a single screen. The DOS Shell even supported a mouse.

10. A. The XCOPY command was introduced with DOS version 3.2. The XCOPY command enables the user to identify more than one file at a time to be copied. It also copies file attributes.

11. C. MS-DOS introduced all of the features listed except EDLIN.COM which was introduced in MS-DOS 3.0 and is a line editor.

12. B. DOSKEY.COM and UNDELETE.EXE were introduced in MS-DOS version 5. The DOSKEY.COM command loads the DOSKEY program into memory. DOSKEY is a program that runs in the background of other programs. The UNDELETE.EXE command makes it possible to recover a deleted file if the space on the disk has not been written over by a new file.

13. C. The ability to pool EMS and XMS memory using EMM386.EXE was introduced in MS-DOS 6. EMS stands for Expanded Memory Specification and provides access for the microprocessor to the upper memory area. XMS is Extended Memory Specification and is loaded by HIMEM.SYS.

14. E. Windows featured tiling windows, mouse support, and menu systems in all Windows versions from Windows 1 through Windows 95.

15. C. Windows 3 substantially increased the size and complexity of programs that could be executed under DOS/Windows and was a crucial step in making Windows a viable product.

16. D. The first 32-bit preemptive multitasking system was Windows 95. Windows 95 is a preemptively multitasked system that is able to emulate and support cooperative multitasking for programs that require it. It also supports both 32-bit and 16-bit drivers as well as DOS drivers, although the 32-bit drivers are strongly recommended over the DOS ones, as they are far more stable and are faster.

17. A. Support for large files or complex programs was the specialty of Windows NT, and its mantle has now been passed to Windows 2000. These operating systems are designed to support more and faster hardware and to provide greater stability and security.

18. D. IBM made version 2 of OS/2 a 32-bit system that required at least a 386 processor to run. This made it immensely more stable and powerful.

19. C. Windows NT is a 32-bit OS that offers file-level security and support for multiple processors.

20. D. Although all of these systems have had some effect on the composition of modern GUIs, it was the Xerox Alto that was first with many of the innovations that we now look at as the basis of a GUI system, including the mouse and windowing capability.

Using the Microsoft Operating System GUI

THE FOLLOWING OBJECTIVES ARE COVERED IN THIS CHAPTER:

✓ **1.1 Identify the operating system's functions, structure, and major system files to navigate the operating system and how to get to needed technical information.**

Content may include the following:

- Major operating system functions
  - Create folders
  - Checking OS version
- Major operating system components
  - Explorer
  - My Computer
  - Control Panel
- Contrasts between Windows 9x and Windows 2000
- Major system files: what they are, where they are located, how they are used, and what they contain:

  System, configuration, and user interface files
  - IO.SYS
  - BOOT.INI
  - WIN.COM
  - MSDOS.SYS
  - AUTOEXEC.BAT
  - CONFIG.SYS
  - Command line prompt

  Memory management
  - Conventional
  - Extended/upper memory
  - High memory
  - Virtual memory

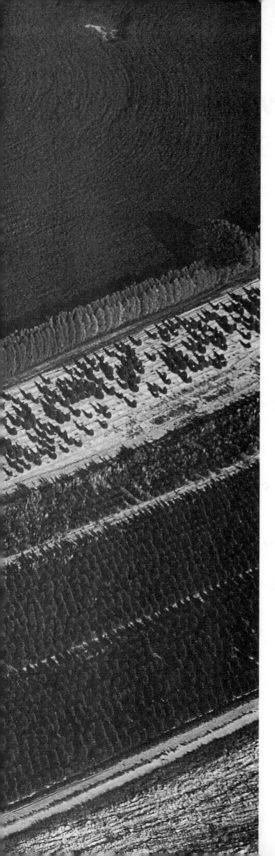

- HIMEM.SYS
- EMM386.EXE

Windows 9x

- IO.SYS
- WIN.INI
- USER.DAT
- SYSEDIT
- SYSTEM.INI
- MSCONFIG (98)
- COMMAND.COM
- REGEDIT.EXE
- SYSTEM.DAT
- Run command
- Command line prompt

Windows 2000

- Computer management
- BOOT.INI
- REGEDT32
- REGEDIT
- RUN CMD
- NTLDR
- NTDETECT.COM
- NTBOOTDD.SYS

Command prompt procedures (command syntax)

- DIR
- Attrib
- VER
- MEM
- SCANDISK
- DEFRAG
- EDIT
- XCOPY
- COPY
- SETVER
- SCANREG

As mentioned in the previous chapter, the Windows 95 graphical user interface (GUI) has been incredibly successful since its debut. Because of this, all Microsoft operating system GUIs since then have drawn heavily from Windows 95. Among these are both Windows 98 and Windows 2000, the two key operating systems you will need to know for the A+ operating systems exam.

For complete coverage of objective 1.1, please also see Chapter 4. For coverage of the Memory management subobjectives of objective 1.1, refer to Chapter 3 of *A+: Core Module Study Guide*, the other book in this boxed set.

The development of the graphical user interface from the Alto to Windows 2000 was discussed in Chapter 1, "An Introduction to Computer Operating Systems," and made out to be a major reason the personal computer industry has taken off in the last decade or two. What exactly is it all about, though? In this chapter, we will look at the post-Windows 95 Microsoft GUI from the ground up, beginning with a detailed look at its key components and ending with an exploration of basic tasks common to both Windows 98 and Windows 2000. The following general topics will be covered:

- Windows GUI components
- Using Windows Explorer and Internet Explorer
- Using Control Panel
- The command prompt

The Windows 9x/2000 Interface

When you look at the monitor of a machine running Windows 98 and then look at the monitor of a machine running Windows 2000, it is difficult to tell the two apart. If you look closely, you will notice that the names of some icons have changed, but for the most part the two are identical and look very much like the screen in Figure 2.1.

FIGURE 2.1 The Windows interface

As a technician, you will quickly realize that this is very good for you! Because of Microsoft's standardization of a single graphical interface for all of its operating systems, most basic tasks are accomplished in identical fashion on everything from a Windows 95 workstation computer to a Windows 2000 Advanced Server computer. Also, while the tools that are used often vary between Windows 98 and 2000, the way you use those tools remains remarkably consistent across *platforms*.

We will begin by taking an overview look at the common elements of the Windows GUI. We will then look at some tasks that are similar across Windows 98 and 2000. If you have a copy of Windows 9*x* or Windows NT4/2000 available, you may want to follow along by exploring each of the elements as they are discussed. If you are able to follow along, you may also notice that there are numerous additional icons and options we are not mentioning. Some of these will be covered in later chapters, so for now simply ignore them, or browse through them on your own and then return to the text.

The Desktop

The Desktop, simply put, is the virtual desk upon which all of your other programs and utilities run. By default it contains the *Start menu*, the *Taskbar*, and a number of *icons*. The Desktop can also contain additional elements, such as Web page content, through the use of the Active Desktop option. Because it is the base on which everything else sits, how the Desktop is configured can have a major effect on how the GUI looks and how convenient it is for users.

You can change the Desktop's background patterns, screen saver, color scheme, and size by right-clicking any area of the Desktop that doesn't contain an icon. The menu that appears allows you to do several things, such as creating new Desktop items, changing how your icons are arranged, or selecting a special command called Properties, as shown in Figure 2.2.

FIGURE 2.2   The Desktop right-click

The Three Clicks in Windows

- Primary mouse click. A single click used to select an object or place a cursor.

- Double-click. Two primary mouse clicks in quick succession. Used to open a program through an icon or for other specific application functions.

- Secondary mouse click. Most mice have two buttons. Clicking once on the secondary button (usually the one on the right side, although that can be modified) is interpreted differently from a left mouse click. Generally in Windows this displays a context-sensitive menu from which you are given the ability to perform tasks or view object properties.

When you right-click the Desktop and choose Properties, you will see the Display Properties screen shown in Figure 2.3. From this screen you can click the various tabs at the top to move to the different screens of information about the way Windows looks. Tabs are similar to index cards, in that they are staggered across the top so you can see and access large amounts of data within a single small window. Each Properties window has a different set of tabs. Among the tabs in the Display Properties are the following:

Background   Used to select an HTML document or a picture to display on the desktop.

Screen Saver   Sets up an automatic screen saver to cover your screen if you have not been active for a certain period of time. Originally used to prevent "burned" monitors, they are now generally used for entertainment or to password-protect user's desktops. The Screen Saver tab also contains other power settings.

Appearance   Used to select a color scheme for the Desktop or to change the color or size of other Desktop elements.

Effects   Contains numerous options best described as "assorted visual options."

Web   Allows for configuration of Active Desktop settings.

Settings   Used to set color depth or screen size. Also contains the Advanced button, which leads to graphics driver and monitor configuration settings.

FIGURE 2.3   The Display Properties screen

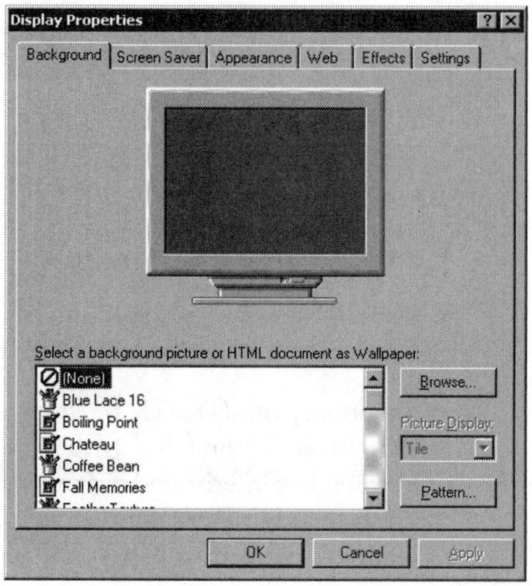

, You can also access the Display Properties settings by using the Display Control Panel under Start ➢ Settings ➢ Control Panel.

EXERCISE 2.1

Changing a Screen Saver

To change the Windows screen saver on Windows 98 or Windows 2000, perform the following steps:

1. Right-click the Desktop.

2. Choose Properties from the context menu.

3. Click the Screen Saver tab.

4. Choose Starfield Simulation. Click Preview to see the new screen saver. Move the mouse to cancel the screen saver and return to your Desktop.

5. Click the OK or the Apply button. (OK performs two tasks: Apply and Exit window, while Apply leaves the window open.)

The Taskbar

The Taskbar (see Figure 2.4) is another standard component of the Windows interface. It contains two major items: the Start menu and the System Tray. The Start menu is on the left side of the Taskbar and is easily identifiable by the fact that it is a button that has the word "Start" on it. The System Tray is located on the right side of the Taskbar and contains only a clock by default, but other Windows utilities (for example, screen savers or virus-protection utilities) may put their icons here when running to indicate that they are running and to provide the user with a quick way to get access to their features.

FIGURE 2.4   The Taskbar

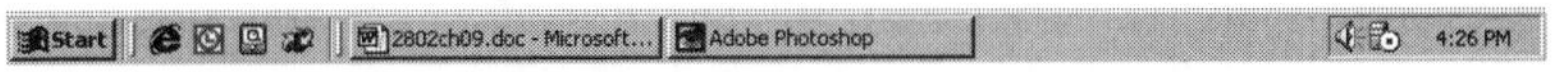

Besides the Start button and the System Tray, the middle area of the Taskbar is also used by Windows. Whenever you open a new window or program, it gets a button on the Taskbar with an icon that represents the window or program. To bring that window or program to the front (or to maximize it if it was minimized), click its button on the Taskbar. As the middle area of the Taskbar fills up with buttons, the buttons become smaller in order to display all of them.

You can increase the size of the Taskbar by moving the mouse pointer to the top of the Taskbar and pausing until the pointer turns into a double-headed arrow. Once this happens, you can click the mouse and move it up to make the Taskbar bigger. Or, you can move it down to make the Taskbar smaller. You can also move the Taskbar to the top or sides of the screen by clicking the Taskbar and dragging it to the new location.

EXERCISE 2.2

Hiding the Taskbar

You can make the Taskbar automatically hide itself when not being used (thus freeing up that space for use by the Desktop or other Windows):

1. Right-click the Taskbar.

2. Choose Properties, which will bring up the Taskbar Properties screen.

3. Check the Auto Hide option on the General tab.

4. Click OK.

5. Move your mouse to the top of the Desktop. The Taskbar will retract off the screen.

6. Move the mouse pointer back to the bottom of the screen, and the Taskbar will pop up and can be used as normal.

The Start Menu

When Microsoft officially introduced Windows 95 to the world, it bought the rights to use the Rolling Stones' song "Start Me Up" in its advertisements and at the introduction party. They chose that particular song because the Start menu was the central point of focus in the new Windows interface, and it has been in all subsequent versions.

To display the Start menu, click the Start button in the Taskbar, as shown in Figure 2.5. From the Start menu, you can select any of the various options the menu presents. An arrow pointing to the right means that there is a submenu. To select a submenu, move the mouse pointer over the submenu title and pause. The submenu will then appear; you don't even have to click. (You have to click to choose an option *on* the submenu, though.) We'll discuss each of the default Start menu's submenu options and how to use them momentarily.

FIGURE 2.5   The Start menu

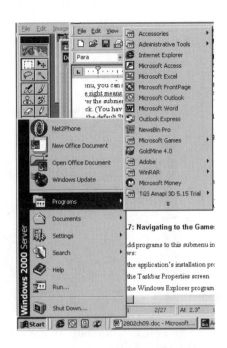

One handy feature of the Start menu is that it usually displays the name of the operating system type along its side when you activate it. This provides an excellent way to quickly see whether you are on Windows 95, 98, NT, or 2000. You can also check which operating system you are using by right-clicking the My Computer icon on the Desktop and selecting Properties. The operating type and version will be displayed on the first tab.

Programs Submenu

The Programs submenu holds the program groups and program icons that you can use. When you select this submenu, you will be shown yet another submenu, with a submenu for each program group (see Figure 2.6). You can navigate through this menu and its submenus and click the program you wish to start.

FIGURE 2.6   Navigating to the Games program group

You can add programs to this submenu in many ways. The three most popular ways are as follows:

- Using the application's installation program
- Using the Taskbar Properties screen
- Using the Windows Explorer program

The first (and simplest) way is to use the application's installation program. The installation program will not only copy the files for the program, but it will also automatically make a program group and shortcuts for the programs under the Programs submenu.

You can add shortcuts to the top of the Start menu (above the Programs submenu) by clicking a program or shortcut and dragging it onto the Start menu. A shortcut for that item will then appear in the Start menu above a divider between Programs and the new shortcut.

Another way to add programs to the Programs submenu is to use the Taskbar Properties screen. To get to this screen, right-click the Taskbar and choose Properties. When the Taskbar Properties screen appears, click the Start Menu Programs tab to bring it to the front. You will then see the screen shown in Figure 2.7. From here, you can click Add to add a new program or Remove to remove one. A *Wizard* (a special sequence of screens designed to walk you through the necessary steps to accomplish certain tasks) will help you create or delete the shortcut(s).

FIGURE 2.7 Use the Taskbar Properties screen to add and remove programs from the Programs submenu.

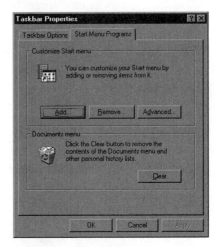

Finally, you can add programs to the Programs submenu on Windows 98 or Windows 2000 by using another new component introduced in Windows 95: Windows Explorer (EXPLORER.EXE). We will talk more about using Explorer later in the chapter.

Documents Submenu

The Documents submenu has one and only one function: to keep track of the last 15 data files you opened. Whenever you open a file, a shortcut to it is automatically made in this menu. To open the document again, just click the document in the Documents menu to open it in its associated application.

If you want to clear the list of documents shown in the Documents submenu, go to the Taskbar Properties screen. Then click the Clear button within the Documents Menu section.

Settings Submenu

The Settings submenu provides easy access to the configuration of Windows. There are numerous submenus to the Settings submenu including Control Panel, Printers, and Taskbar & Start Menu. Additional menus are available depending on which version of Windows you are using. These submenus give you access to the Control Panel, printer driver, and Taskbar configuration areas, respectively. You can also access the first two areas from the My Computer icon; they are placed here together to provide a common area to access Windows settings.

Search (Find) Submenu

The name of this menu changes between Windows 98 and Windows 2000, but the purpose doesn't. The Windows 98 Find submenu is used to locate information on your computer or on a network. The Search menu of Windows 2000 has the same functionality.

To find a file or directory, select the Find or Search submenu and then select Files or Folders (see Figure 2.8). In the Named field in this dialog box, simply type in the name of the file or directory you are looking for and click Find Now. Windows will search whatever is specified in the Look In parameter for the file or directory. Matches will be listed in a window underneath the Find window. You can use wildcards (* and ?) to look for multiple files and directories. You can also click the Advanced tab to further refine your search. This will be discussed in more detail later in the chapter in the "File Management" section.

FIGURE 2.8 Options in the Find submenu

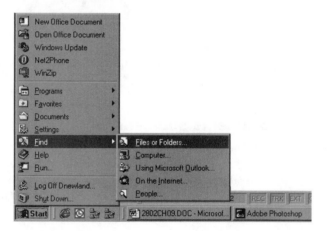

Help Command

Windows includes a *very* good help system. Not only is it arranged by topic, but it is fully indexed and searchable. Because of its usefulness and power, it was placed into the Start menu for easy access. When you select this command, it will bring up the Windows Help screen (see Figure 2.9). From this screen, you can double-click a manual to show a list of subtopics and then click a subtopic to view the text of that topic.

FIGURE 2.9   Windows 98 Help screen

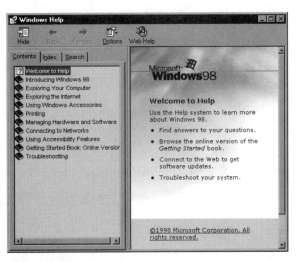

Or, you can click the Index tab to show an alphabetic listing of topics (see Figure 2.10). To select a topic, type the first few letters of the topic (for example, type **print** to move to the section that talks about printing), then click Display to display the text on the topic.

FIGURE 2.10   The Index tab on the Help screen

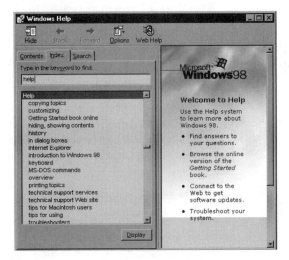

You can also click the Search tab to find any text you want in the help files. Simply type the text. As you type, Help will display a list of topics that contain the characters you are typing. You will see the list of topics get shorter as you type, because the more you type the more you are narrowing down your search.

When the topic you want appears in the list, click the one(s) you want to read about, then click Display.

Run Command

The Run command can be used to start programs if they don't have a shortcut on the Desktop or in the Programs submenu. When you choose Run from the Start menu, the screen in Figure 2.11 appears. To execute a particular program, just type its name and path in the Open field. If you don't know the exact path, you can browse to find the file by clicking the Browse button. Once you have typed in the executable name and path, click OK to run the program.

FIGURE 2.11 The Start menu's Run command

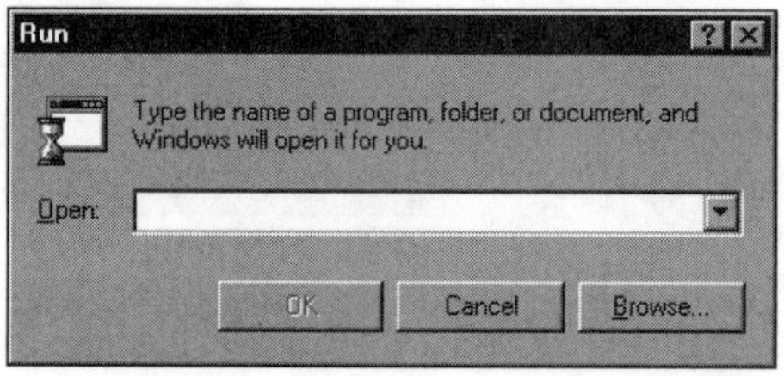

EXERCISE 2.3

Starting a Program from the Run Window

1. Click Start ➢ Run.

2. In the Open window, type **notepad**.

3. Click OK. Notepad will open up in a new window.

If the program you want to run has been run from the Run window before, you can find it on the Open field's drop-down list. Click the down arrow to display the list, then select the program you want by clicking its name and then clicking OK. More about starting and using applications later.

Shut Down Command

Windows 9*x* and 2000 are very complex operating systems. At any one time, there are several files open in memory. If you accidentally hit the power switch and turn the computer off while these files are open, there is a good chance these files will be corrupted. For this reason, Microsoft has added the Shut Down command under the Start menu. When you select this option, Windows presents you with three choices, as shown in Figure 2.12.

FIGURE 2.12   Shut Down command options

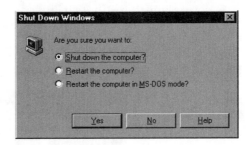

The three Shut Down choices are as follows:

Shut Down the Computer   This option will write any unsaved data to disk, close any open applications, and get the computer ready to be powered off. When you see a black screen with the message It's now safe to turn off your computer in orange text, it is, in fact, safe to power off the computer. You can also hit Ctrl+Alt+Del to reboot the computer at this point.

Restart the Computer   This option works the same as the first option but instead of shutting down completely, it will automatically reboot the computer with a warm reboot.

Restart the Computer in MS-DOS Mode (Windows 9*x* only)   This option is special. It does the same tasks as the previous options, except upon reboot, Windows 9*x* will execute the command prompt only and will not start the graphic portion of Windows 9*x*. You can then run DOS programs as though the machine were a DOS machine. When you are finished running these programs, type **exit** to reboot the machine back into the "full" Windows 9*x* with the GUI.

Icons

Icons are not nearly as complex as windows can be, but they are very important nonetheless. Icons are shortcuts that allow a user to open a program or a utility without knowing where that program is or how it needs to be configured. Icons consist of four elements:

- Icon label
- Icon graphic
- Program location
- Working directory location

The label and graphic simply tell the user the name of the program and give a visual hint as to what that program does. Solitaire, for instance, is labeled Solitaire, and its icon graphic is a deck of cards. By right-clicking an icon once, you make that icon the active icon, and a drop-down menu appears. One of the selections is Properties. Clicking Properties will bring up the attributes of an icon (see Figure 2.13) and is the only way to see exactly which program an icon is configured to start.

FIGURE 2.13   The Properties window with its icon to the left

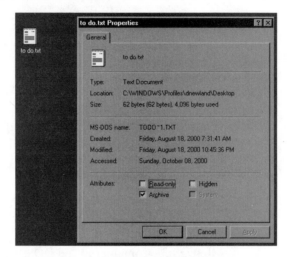

The *working directory* simply tells Windows where to save documents created through this icon. This is default and can be over-ridden.

Standard Desktop Icons

In addition to the options in your Start menu, there are a number of icons that are placed directly on the Desktop. Two of the most important icons are My Computer and the Recycle Bin.

The My Computer Icon

If you double-click the My Computer icon, it will display all the disk drives installed in your computer as well as the Control Panel and Printers folders (see Figure 2.14), which can be used to configure the system. If you double-click a disk drive, you will see the contents of that disk drive.

FIGURE 2.14   Using My Computer to open folders

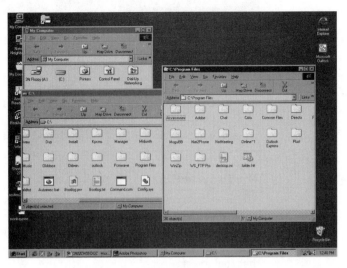

You can delve deeper into each disk drive and open a window for each sub-directory by double-clicking it. You can also copy and move files between drives and between directories using these windows.

In addition to allowing you access to your computer's files, the My Computer icon allows you a view of your machine's configuration and hardware, also called the System Properties, as shown in Figure 2.15. The following exercise shows you how to view these properties.

FIGURE 2.15   System Properties screen

EXERCISE 2.4

Viewing System Properties

1. Right-click the My Computer icon.

2. Choose Properties.

3. On the System Properties screen, look to see what type of processor your computer uses and how much RAM is installed. It also will tell you what version of Windows is being used.

The Recycle Bin

All files, directories, and programs in Windows are represented by icons and are generally referred to as objects. When you want to remove an object from Windows, you do so by deleting it. Deleting doesn't only remove the object, though. It also removes the ability of the system to access the information or application that the object represents. Because of this, Windows includes a special directory where all deleted files are placed: the Recycle Bin. This Recycle Bin holds the files until it is emptied and allows users the opportunity to recover files that they deleted accidentally.

You can retrieve a file that you have deleted by opening the Recycle Bin icon, then dragging the file from the Recycle Bin back to the disk it came from. To permanently erase the file, you need to empty the Recycle Bin, thereby permanently deleting any items in it and freeing up the hard drive space they took up. If the Recycle Bin has files in it, its icon will look like the full trash can shown on the left of Figure 2.16; after it is emptied, its icon will reflect this, as shown on the right.

Deleting a file from the Recycle Bin frees up space on the drive by simply deleting the file's record from the drive's File Allocation Table (FAT). The information in the file will actually remain on the drive until it has been overwritten by new information.

FIGURE 2.16 A full (left) and empty (right) Recycle Bin

EXERCISE 2.5

Emptying the Recycle Bin

1. Right-click the Recycle Bin.

2. Choose Empty Recycle Bin.

3. A window appears asking if you are certain you want to permanently delete the objects. Click Yes.

What's in a Window?

We have now looked at the nature of the Desktop, the Start menu, and the Taskbar. Each of these was created for the primary purpose of making access to user applications easier, and these applications are in turn used and managed through the use of windows, the rectangular application environments for which the Windows family of operating systems is named. We will now examine how windows work and what they are made of.

Program Windows

A program *window* is a rectangular area created on the screen when an application is opened within Windows. This window can have a number of different forms, but most windows include at least a few basic elements. Figure 2.17 shows the Control box, Title bar, Minimize button, Restore button, Close button, and resizable border in a text editor called Notepad (NOTEPAD.EXE) that has all of the basic window elements and little else!

FIGURE 2.17   The basic elements of a window

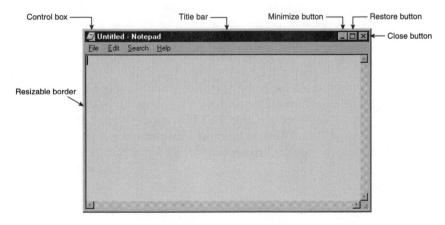

Elements of a Window

Control box   In the upper-left corner of the window. Used to control the state of the application. It can be used to maximize, minimize, and close the application. Clicking it once brings into view a selection menu. Double-clicking it closes the window and shuts down the application.

Minimize and Restore buttons   Used to change the state of the window on the Desktop. They will be discussed in the "States of a Window" section later in this chapter.

Close button   Used to easily end a program and return any resources it was using to the system. It essentially does the same thing as double-clicking the control box, but with one less click.

Title bar   The area between the Control box and the Minimize button. It simply states the name of the program and in some cases gives information as to the particular document being accessed by that program. The color of the Title bar indicates whether or not a particular window is the active window.

Menu bar   Used to present useful commands in an easily accessible format. Clicking one of the menu choices will display a list of related options you may choose from.

Active window   The window that is currently being used. It has two attributes: first, any keystrokes that are entered are directed there by default. Second, any other windows that overlap the active window will be pushed behind it.

Border   A thin line that surrounds the window in its restored state that allows it to be widened and shortened.

These elements are not all found on every window, as programmers can choose to eliminate or modify them. Still, in most cases these will be constant, with the rest of the window filled in with menus, toolbars, a workspace or other application-specific elements. For instance, Microsoft Word, the program with which this book was written, adds an additional control box and minimize and maximize buttons for each document. It also has a menu bar, a number of optional toolbars, scroll bars at the right and bottom of the window, and a status bar at the very bottom. Application windows can become very cluttered.

Notepad is a very simple Windows program. It has only a single menu bar and the basic elements seen previously in Figure 2.17. Figure 2.18 shows a Microsoft Word window. Both Word and Notepad are used to create and edit documents, but Word is far more configurable and powerful and therefore has many more optional components available within its window.

FIGURE 2.18   A window with more components

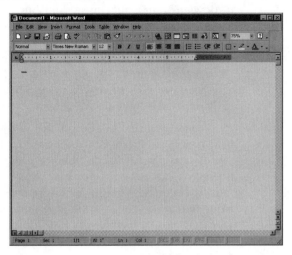

States of a Window

There is more to the Windows interface than the physical parts of a window itself, though. Windows also are movable, stackable, and resizable, and they can be hidden behind other windows (often unintentionally!).

When an application window has been launched, it will exist in one of three states:

Maximized   A maximized window is one that takes up all available space on the screen. When it is in front of the other programs, it is the only thing visible—even the Desktop is hidden. In Figure 2.19, note that Microsoft Word is maximized; it takes up the entire space of the Desktop, and the middle button in the upper-right corner displays two rectangles rather than one. The sides of the window no longer have borders. The window is flush with the edges of the screen. Maximizing a window provides the maximum workspace possible for that window's application, and the window can be accessed actively by the user. In general, maximized mode is the preferred window size for most word processing, graphics creation, and other user applications.

Restored   A restored window is one that can be used interactively and is identical in function to a maximized window, with the simple difference that it does not necessarily take up the entire screen. Restored windows can be very small, or they can take up almost as much space as maximized windows. Generally, how large the restored window becomes is the user's choice. Restored windows display a restore box (the middle button in the upper-right corner) with a single rectangle in it; this is used to maximize the window. Restored windows have a border. Figure 2.19 shows an example of Notepad in a restored state.

Minimized   The last window state is minimized. Minimized program windows are represented by nothing but an icon on the Taskbar, and they are not usable until they have been either maximized or restored. The only difference between a minimized program and a closed program is that a minimized program is out of the way but is still taking up resources and is therefore ready to use if you need it. It will also leave the content of the window in the same place when you return to it as when you minimized it. In Figure 2.19, Adobe Photoshop is minimized.

When a program is open and you need to open another program (or maybe need to stop playing a game because your boss has entered the room), you have two choices. First, you can close the program and reopen it later. If you do this, however, your current game will be lost and you will have to start over. Minimizing the game window, on the other hand, will remove the open window from the screen and leave the program open but display nothing more than an icon in the lower-left corner of the Taskbar, as with my Photoshop icon in Figure 2.19. Later, you can restore the window to its previous size and finish the game in progress.

FIGURE 2.19   Windows in different states

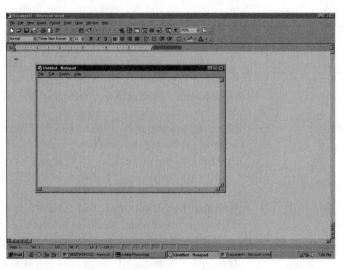

Using the Command Prompt

The Microsoft Disk Operating System, or MS-DOS, was never meant to be extremely friendly. It had its roots in CP/M, which, in turn, had its roots in UNIX. Both of these older operating systems were command line–based, and so was MS-DOS. In other words, they all used long strings of commands typed in at the computer keyboard to perform operations. This type of interaction with the computer is preferred by some people, most often folks with technical backgrounds (including yours truly). Although Windows has now left the full command-line interface behind, there is still a bit of DOS in Windows, and the way to get to it is through the command prompt.

We will look at a number of graphical utilities in the next few chapters and, believe it or not, the command prompt is one of them. Although you can't tell from looking at it (see Figure 2.20), the crazy thing about the Windows command prompt is that it is actually a 32-bit Windows program that is intentionally *designed* to have the look and feel of a DOS command line!

Because it is, despite its appearance, a Windows program, the command prompt provides all of the stability and configurability that you would expect from Windows.

FIGURE 2.20   The Windows command prompt

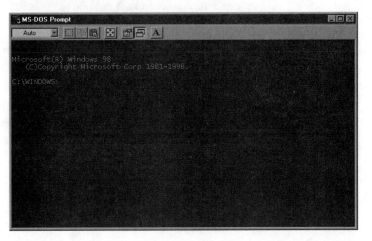

Running a Utility or Program from the Command Prompt

Windows includes a number of command-line utilities. Among these is the IPCONFIG utility of Windows 2000. If you are running Windows 2000, this is the utility that allows you to check on the TCP/IP settings of the machine. (TCP/IP is the protocol which allows networked computers to use the Internet, and as such is something you will probably see a lot of. It will be discussed further in Chapter 8, "Configuring Network Software.")

Other than that, there are very few actual text-based applications in newer versions of Windows. For a bit of a taste of the old days, though, check out the EDIT program (See Figure 2.21), still provided free of charge with both Windows 98 and Windows 2000. EDIT is still often used to modify batch files and text configuration files.

FIGURE 2.21 The EDIT program

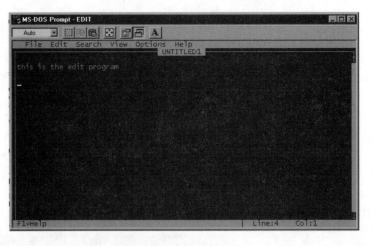

EXERCISE 2.6

Using the EDIT Program

1. Open a command prompt. To do this in Windows 98, click Start ➢ Programs ➢ MS-DOS Prompt. In Windows 2000, click Start ➢ Programs ➢ Accessories ➢ Command Prompt.

2. Type **EDIT**.

3. The **EDIT** utility will open. In the text area, type **hello**.

4. To save the file, press Alt+F. This brings up the File menu. From this, press A.

5. In the Save As window, type **hello.txt** and click OK.

6. To exit from **EDIT**, press ALT+F and press X for Exit.

Issuing Text Commands

In general, Windows 98 uses more text-based commands than Windows 2000, and a number of standard commands are stored in the Windows 98 command directory. This can be found in whichever directory (usually Windows) that Windows 98 is installed into. See Table 2.1 for a list of Windows text commands, some of which are available only in Windows 98, while others are available in Windows 2000 as well.

TABLE 2.1 Windows Text Commands

Command	Purpose
ATTRIB	Allows the user to set or remove file attributes.
CD	Changes your current folder to another folder.
CHECKDSK	Examines the hard drives of the machine.
COPY	Copies a file into another directory.
DEFRAG	Used to defragment (reorganize) the files on your machine's hard drives, which can result in better performance.
DEL	Deletes a file from the folder.
DELTREE	Deletes files and subdirectories. A more powerful extension of the DEL command.
DIR	Displays the contents of the current folder.
DISKCOPY	Duplicates floppy disks.
DOSKEY	Lists recently issued commands with a prompt session.
FDISK	Creates, deletes, and manages hard disk partitions.
FORMAT	Prepares a drive for use.
MD	Creates a new folder.
MEM	Provides information on how much memory is available to the system.
MOVE	Moves files from one folder to another.
MSCDEX	Accesses CD-ROMs.
REN	Renames a file.
SCANDISK	Similar to CHECKDSK.
SCANREG	Scans the Registry by starting a Windows application that checks for errors and allows you to back up the Registry files.

TABLE 2.1 Windows Text Commands *(continued)*

Command	Purpose
SETVER	Sets the version and reports version numbers of DOS utilities.
SYS	Prepares a drive to be used to start a computer.
VER	Checks the current version of the operating system.
XCOPY	Duplicates files and subdirectories. An extension of the COPY command.

To issue a command from the command prompt, you need to know the structure that the command uses, generally referred to as its *syntax*. The following exercise shows how to learn about a command and then run that command. The command in the exercise is ATTRIB, which is used to allow a user to set one of four attributes on a file: Read Only, Archive Needed, System, or Hidden.

If you don't know the options for a DOS command, you can usually find them out using the online help for that command. Simply type the command followed by a forward slash (/) and a question mark (?). This will display all the options for that command and how to use them properly, as in Figure 2.22.

FIGURE 2.22 Options available for ATTRIB.EXE

EXERCISE 2.7

Changing a File Attribute on Windows 98

1. Open a command prompt. To do this, click Start ➤ Programs ➤ MS-DOS Prompt.

2. Type `CD C:\` and press Enter.

3. Type `DIR` and press Enter. A list of all the files in the root of C: will be shown.

4. Type `ATTRIB /?` and press Enter.

5. Type `ATTRIB autoexec.bat`. The current attributes of the file will be displayed.

6. Type `ATTRIB autoexec.bat +R`.

7. Repeat step 5 to view the changed attribute, and then repeat step 6 with a `-R` to return the file to its original attributes.

Windows Configuration

Simply navigating the Start menu and running `EDIT` does not an A+ certified tech make! Most of the tasks that you will be called on to deal with are more complex than minimizing a window. The Windows OS provides numerous utilities to aid you in changing system configuration elements or identifying and diagnosing problems. Many of these are specific to the particular operating system, but nonetheless their location and general usage is similar on both Windows 98 and Windows 2000. Because of this, system management in Windows can be loosely grouped into the following areas:

- File management
- System tools
- Control Panel programs
- The Registry Editor

File Management

File management is the process by which a computer stores data and retrieves it from storage. The process of actually preparing drives for storage, called *disk management*, is significantly different on Windows 98 and Windows 2000 and will be dealt with in later chapters. The process of managing files, though, is similar across both platforms.

Files and Folders

For a program to run, it must be able to read information off of the disk and write information back to it. In order to be able to organize and access information—especially in larger new systems that may have thousands of files—it is necessary to have a structure and an ordering process.

Windows provides this process by allowing you to create *directories*, also known as folders, in which to organize files. Windows also regulates the way that files are named and what the properties of the file are. Each file created in Windows has to follow certain rules, and any program that accesses files through Windows must comply with these rules. Files created on a Windows system will follow these rules:

- It will have a filename of up to 256 characters.
- Certain characters such as a period (.) and a slash (\ or /) are prohibited in the filename.
- An optional extension (generally three or four characters) can be added to identify the file's type.

The Windows file system is arranged like a filing cabinet. In a filing cabinet, paper is placed into folders, which are inside dividers, which are in a drawer of the filing cabinet. In the DOS file system, individual files are placed in subdirectories that are inside directories, which are stored on different disks. Windows also protects against duplicate filenames, as no two files on the system can have exactly the same name and *path*. A path indicates the location of the file on the disk; it is composed of the logical drive letter the file is on, and if the file is located in a directory or subdirectory, the names of those directories. For instance, a file named AUTOEXEC.BAT is located in the root of the C: drive—meaning it is not within a directory—so the path to the file is simply C:\AUTOEXEC.BAT. Another important file, FDISK.EXE, is located in the Command directory under Windows under the root of C:, so the path to FDISK is therefore C:\WINDOWS\COMMAND\FDISK.EXE.

The *root directory* of any drive is simply the place where the hierarchy of that drive begins. On a C: drive, for instance, C:\ is the root directory of the drive.

Capabilities of the Windows Explorer

Although it is technically possible to simply use the command-line utilities provided within the command prompt to manage your files, this generally is not the most efficient way to accomplish most tasks. The ability to use drag-and-drop techniques and other graphical tools to manage the file system makes the process far simpler, and the Windows Explorer is a utility that allows the user to accomplish a number of important file-related tasks from a single graphical interface, as shown in Figure 2.23.

FIGURE 2.23   The Windows Explorer program

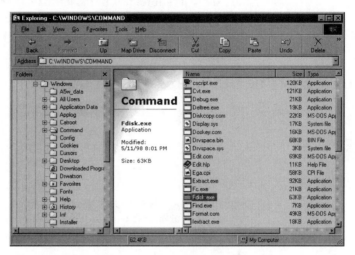

Some of the tasks you can accomplish using the Explorer include:

- Viewing files and directories
- Opening programs or data files
- Creating directories and files
- Copying objects (files or directories) to other locations
- Moving objects (files or directories) to other locations
- Deleting or renaming objects (files or directories)
- Searching for a particular file or type of file
- Changing file attributes
- Formatting new disks (such as floppy disks)

Navigating and Using the Explorer

Using the Windows Explorer is actually pretty simple. Just a few basic instructions will be all you will need to start working with it. First off, the Explorer interface itself has a number of parts, each of which serves a specific purpose. The top area of the Explorer is dominated by a set of menus and toolbars that allow easy access to common commands. The main section of the window is divided into two panes. The left pane displays the drives and folders available to the user, while the right pane displays the contents of the currently selected folder. Along the bottom of the window, the Status Bar displays information about the used and free space on the current directory. Some common actions in Explorer include:

Expanding a folder   You can double-click a folder to expand the folder (i.e., show its subfolders in the left panel) and display the contents of the folder in the right pane. Simply clicking the "+" sign to the left of a folder will expand the folder without changing it (see Figure 2.24).

Collapsing a folder   Clicking the "−" sign next to a folder will unexpand it.

FIGURE 2.24   The Expand and Collapse symbols

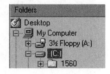

Selecting a file   If you click the file in the right pane , Windows will highlight the file by marking it with a darker color.

Selecting multiple files   The Ctrl and Shift keys allow you to select multiple files at once. Holding down Ctrl while clicking individual files will select each new file while leaving the currently selected file or files selected as well. Holding down Shift while selecting two files will select both of them and all files in between.

Opening a file   Double-clicking a file in the right pane will open the program if it is an application; if it is a file, it will open it using whichever file extension is configured for it.

Changing the view type   There are four different primary view types: Large Icons, Small Icons, List, and Details. You can move between these views by clicking the View menu and selecting the view you prefer.

Finding specific files   This is accessed under View ➢ Find in Windows 98 or by using the Search button in Windows 2000. Either way, you can search for files based on their name, file size, file type, and other attributes, as shown in Figure 2.25.

FIGURE 2.25 Searching for a file in Windows

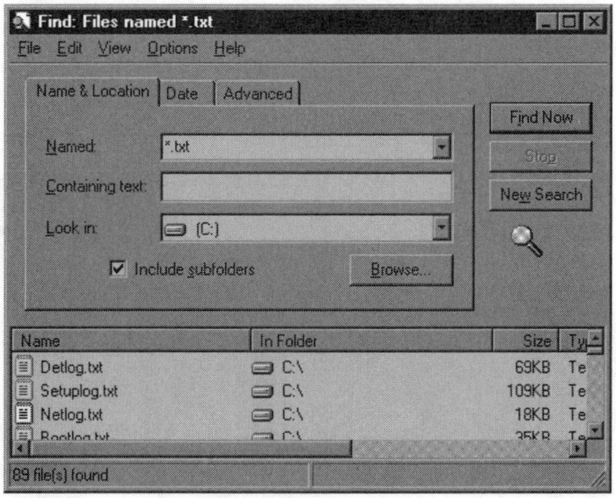

![Find: Files named *.txt dialog box showing the Name & Location tab with Named field set to *.txt, Look in field set to (C:), Include subfolders checked, and search results listing Detlog.txt, Setuplog.txt, Netlog.txt, Bootlog.txt with 89 file(s) found]

EXERCISE 2.8

Searching for a Type of File

1. In Windows 98, click Tools ➤ Find ➤ Files or Folders. In Windows 2000, simply click the Search button on the toolbar.

2. Either the Search window (Windows 98) or Search pane (Windows 2000) will appear. You will be prompted for the Search information.

3. Type ***.TXT** in the Named field.

4. In the Look In field, enter **C:**, and click Find Now.

5. Make sure the Include Subfolders check box is checked, and click OK.

6. Windows will now search the C: drive and will eventually display a Search Results window with all of the files it has found.

When searching, wildcards can also be used. Wildcards are characters which act as placeholders for a character or set of characters, allowing, for instance, a search for all files with text (TXT) extensions. To perform such a search, you'd type an asterisk (*) as a stand-in for the filename: ***.TXT**. Asterisks are used to take the place of any number of characters in a search, while question marks (?) are used to take the place of a single number or letter, for example, AUTOEX??.BAT would return the file AUTOEXEC.BAT as part of its results.

Creating new objects To create a new file, folder, or other object, navigate to the location where you want to create the object, and then right-click in the right pane. In the menu that appears, select New and then choose the object you want to create, as shown in Figure 2.26.

FIGURE 2.26 Creating a new folder

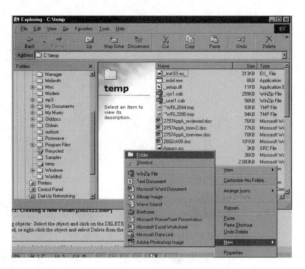

Deleting objects Select the object and press the Del key on the keyboard, or right-click the object and select Delete from the menu that appears.

 The simplicity of deleting in Windows makes it very likely that you or one of the people you support will delete or misplace a file or a number of files that are still needed. In such a case the Recycle Bin (mentioned earlier) is a lifesaver!

EXERCISE 2.9

Using Windows Explorer

1. Open the Windows Explorer. In Windows 98, click Start ➢ Programs ➢ Windows Explorer. In Windows 2000, click Start ➢ Programs ➢ Accessories ➢ Windows Explorer.

EXERCISE 2.9 *(continued)*

2. To see what applications are installed in the Program Files directory, navigate the hierarchy from My Computer to C: to Program Files. You may need to click the "+" sign next to one or more of the folders to expand them and see their contents.

3. Navigate back to the root of C: and right-click in the right pane. Select New ➢ Folder and type **TEST** as the name of the folder.

4. Double-click the new **TEST** folder, and examine the right pane after its contents are displayed. As the folder was just created, it is empty. Right-click in the right pane and select New ➢ Text Document. Give the file the name **NEW.TXT**.

5. To delete the file you just created, select it by clicking it once and then right-click it. Choose Delete. You are asked whether you are sure you want to send the file to the Recycle Bin. Click Yes.

Besides simplifying most file management commands as shown above, the Explorer also allows you to easily complete a number of disk management tasks. Floppy disks can be formatted and labeled and the Windows system files can be copied to a floppy so that a disk may be used to boot a machine.

 Disk management will be covered more fully in Chapters 3 and 4, "Windows 95/98" and "Windows 2000," respectively.

System Tools

Windows 98 and Windows 2000 also include a number of applications that a user can run to check on the health and performance of their computer. Windows 98 undoubtedly has more of these gadgets, but Windows 2000 has a good number of them as well. In both cases, these utilities, if installed, can be found in the same folder on the Start menu: Start ➢ Programs ➢ Accessories ➢ System Tools, as shown in Figure 2.27. The programs in this folder can be very useful to a technician. Some common Windows 98 utilities found there, along with their purpose, are listed in Table 2.2. Some, but not all, of these tools are also available on Windows 2000.

FIGURE 2.27 The System Tools program group

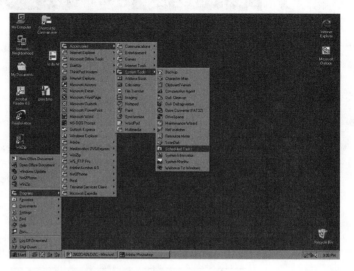

TABLE 2.2 System Tools

System Tool	Function
Backup	Makes archival copies of important files.
Character Map	Determines which type of letters, numbers, and nonalphanumeric characters the machine will use.
Clipboard Viewer	Allows you to see what has been copied onto the system clipboard.
Drive Space 3	Allows you to compress the files on a drive to get more information onto it (although compressing files makes them slower to access).
Compression Agent	Used with Drive Space 3. Allows you to set up parameters for automatically determining which files to compress.
Disk Cleanup	A utility which goes through the system and deletes unneeded files to free up drive space.
Disk Defragmenter	Arranges data on the computer's disk drives so that it will be more easily available.

TABLE 2.2   System Tools *(continued)*

System Tool	Function
Maintenance Wizard	Sets up a system maintenance plan.
Net Watcher	Checks the performance of the network.
Resource Meter	Gives a quick, graphical display of how heavily basic system resources are being used.
Scandisk	Checks a disk drive for errors or problems
Scheduled Tasks	Enables the running of recurring tasks automatically.
System Information	Finds information on the hardware and software installed on a PC.
System Monitor	A more complex version of Resource Meter. Monitors specific resources and watches how they are used in real time.

Windows 2000 also has a folder called Administrative Tools where many of its system configuration utilities are kept. Many of these tools are available in both Windows 98 and Windows 2000 but by different names or in different locations. For instance, Windows 98's System Monitor is expanded into a more powerful tool in Windows 2000 called Performance, which you can access by clicking Start ➢ Control Panel ➢ Administrative Tools folder.

EXERCISE 2.10

Scheduling a Disk Cleanup Task

1. Click Start ➢ Programs ➢ Applications ➢ System Tools ➢ Scheduled Tasks.

2. In the Scheduled Tasks window that appears, double-click the Add a Scheduled Task icon.

3. Read the introduction screen, then click Next. (After filling out any screen in a Wizard, you must click Next to continue. At the end of a Wizard, you will need to click Finish.) In the next screen, choose Disk Cleanup as the application to run, as shown in the graphic.

4. Choose to run it monthly.

5. Click the Day radio button and accept the default times.

6. Choose to view advanced properties and click Finish.

7. Under the Settings tab, check the Wake the Computer to Run This Task option and click OK. Your task will now run on the first day of each month with the options you have selected.

8. If you do not want to keep this task, simply delete it.

The Control Panel

Although for the most part the Windows system is functional from the time it is first installed, Microsoft realized that if someone were going to be using computers regularly, they would probably want to be able to customize their environment so that it would be better suited to their needs—or at least more fun to use. Because of this, the Windows environment has a large number of utilities that are intended to give the user control over the look and feel of the Desktop.

This is, of course, an excellent idea. It is also a bit more freedom than some less-than-cautious users seem to be capable of handling, and you will undoubtedly serve a number of customers who call you in to restore their configuration after botched attempts at changing one setting or another.

More than likely, you will also have to reinstall Windows yourself a few times because of accidents that occur while you are studying or testing the system's limits. This is actually a good thing since no competent computer technician can say that they have never had to reinstall because of an error. You can't really know how to fix Windows until you are experienced at breaking it. Because of this, it is extremely important to experiment and find out what can be changed in the Windows environment, what results from those changes, and how to undo any unwanted results. To this purpose, we will be examining the most common configuration utility in Windows: the Control Panel.

The Control Panel is the graphical entryway to the heart of Windows' configurable settings. One of the few applications in Windows that contains icons of its own, the Control Panel utility houses a number of separate configuration options. Some standard Control Panel icons are shown in Figure 2.28, but various applications and add-on products can add others. We will be taking only a brief look at the uses of these panels, but many of them are worth exploring closely on your own. Table 2.3 lists a number of common Control Panel options and what they are used for.

FIGURE 2.28   The Control Panel interface

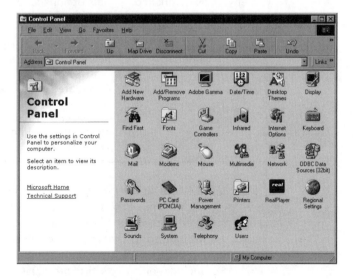

TABLE 2.3   Selected Windows Control Panel Programs (Windows 2000 Names)

Program Name	Function
Add/Remove Hardware	Adds and configures new hardware.
Add/Remove Programs	Changes, adds, or deletes software.

TABLE 2.3 Selected Windows Control Panel Programs (Windows 2000 Names) *(continued)*

Program Name	Function
Date/Time	Sets the system time and configures options such as time zone.
Display	Configures screen savers, colors, display options, and monitor drivers.
Fonts	Adds and removes fonts.
Internet Options	Sets a number of options which are discussed in more detail in Chapter 18, "Configuring Network Software."
Multimedia	Configures audio and video options. Discussed in more detail in Chapter 16, "Using and Configuring Additional Peripherals."
Network (Network and Dial-up Connections)	Sets options for connecting to other computers. Discussed further in Chapter 18.
Modems (Phone and Modem Options)	Sets options for using phone lines to dial out to a network or the Internet. Again, see Chapter 18.
Printers	Configures printer settings and print defaults.
System	Allows you to view and configure various system elements. Very different in Windows 98 and Windows 2000.

For a quick look at how the Control Panel programs work, the following exercise looks at some of the settings in the Date/Time program. The Date/Time program is used to configure the system time, date, and time zone settings, which can be important for files that require accurate timestamps or to users who don't have a watch. Because it is a very simple program, it's a perfect example to use. Date/Time includes only two sets of tabs: Date & Time and Time Zone, and only includes one option, to use Daylight Savings or not.

EXERCISE 2.11

Changing the Time Zone

1. Click Start ➢ Settings ➢ Control Panel.

2. From Control Panel, double-click the Date/Time icon (by default, the programs are listed alphabetically).

3. Click the Time Zone tab and use the drop-down menu to select (GMT –03:30) Newfoundland, as shown in the graphic.

4. Hop a plane to Newfoundland, secure in the knowledge that you will know what time it is once you get there.

5. If you skipped step 4, change the time zone back to where it should be before closing the window.

The Registry Editor

Configuration information is also stored in a special configuration database known as the *Registry*. This centralized database contains environmental settings for various Windows programs. It also contains what is known as *registration* information, which details which types of file extensions are associated with which applications. So, when you double-click a file in Windows Explorer, the associated application runs and opens the file you double-clicked.

The Registry was introduced with Windows 95 and is a database of configuration information. Most operating systems up until Windows 95 were based on text files, which can be edited with almost any text editor. However, the Registry database is contained in special binary file which can be edited only with the special Registry Editor provided with Windows. The Registry Editor program is called **REGEDIT.EXE**, and its icon is not typically created during Windows installation—you must create the icon manually. You can also run the program manually by selecting Start ➢ Run, typing **REGEDIT**, and clicking OK.

Windows 2000 has two applications which can be used to edit the Registry, REGEDIT and REGEDT32 (with no /). Both work similarly, but each has slightly different options for navigation and browsing.

The Registry is broken down into a series of separate areas called hives (see Figure 2.29). These keys are divided into two basic sections—user settings and computer settings. In Windows 9*x,* Registry information is stored in the user .dat and system.dat files, while in Windows 2000 a number of files are created corresponding to each of the different hives. The basic hives of the Registry include:

HKEY_CLASSES_ROOT   This hive includes information about which file extensions map to particular applications.

HKEY_CURRENT_USER   This hive holds all configuration information specific to a particular user, such as their desktop settings and history information.

HKEY_LOCAL_MACHINE   This hive includes nearly all configuration information concerning the actual computer hardware and software.

HKEY_USERS   This hive includes information on all users who have logged on to the system. The HKEY_CURRENT_USER hive is actually a subkey of this hive.

HKEY_CURRENT_CONFIG   This hive provides quick access to a number of commonly needed keys that are otherwise buried deep in the HKEY_LOCAL_MACHINE structure.

Modifying a Registry Entry

If you find it is necessary to modify the Registry, you can modify the values in the database, or can even create new entries or keys. You will find the options for adding a new element to the Registry under the Edit menu. To edit an existing value, simply double-click the entry and modify it as needed. On Windows 2000 systems, you will need administrative-level access to modify the Registry.

Windows extensively uses the Registry to store all kinds of information. Indeed, it holds most, if not all, of the configuration information for Windows 98 and 2000. It is a potentially dangerous task to modify the Registry in Windows. The reason that the Control Panel and other configuration tools are provided for you is so that you will have graphical tools for modifying system settings. Directly modifying the Registry can have unforeseen—and unpleasant—results. You should only modify the Registry when told to do so by an extremely trustworthy source.

FIGURE 2.29 The Registry Editor

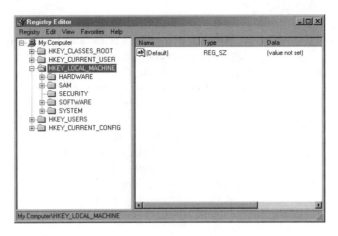

Restoring the Registry in Windows 9*x*

As you may have noticed, the Registry is extremely important to the functioning of Windows. Because of this, any problems with the Registry can cause system-wide trouble. If your Windows 9*x* Registry files (`system.dat` or `user.dat`) become corrupted, there are two primary ways for them to be repaired:

Automatically Windows keeps backups of each of your Registry files and checks the current Registry for errors each time you boot the system. If errors are found, the backup copy of the Registry will be located and will be used to replace the corrupt Registry. As long as you have not purposely deleted the Windows backup files, this works fine.

Manually If the Registry backups are damaged or lost, you will then need to use a different plan. In Windows 95, you can manually restore the Registry by simply replacing the `system.dat` or `user.dat` file with the `system.da0` or `user.da0` files that hold Windows 95's Registry backup. Windows 98 stores the Registry backups differently, and manual restores require that files be backed up previously using a backup program.

Restoring the Registry in Windows 2000

Windows 2000 also stores Registry information in files on the hard drive. These can be restored through the use of the Last Known Good Configuration, which restores the Registry to a backup of its last functional state. To use this option, simply click F8 during startup, and then select Last Known Good Configuration from the menu that appears. The Registry files can also be backed up to the systemroot\repair directory by using the Windows 2000 Backup program, or can be saved to tape during a normal backup. To repair the Registry from a backup simply overwrite the Registry files in `systemroot\system32\config`.

Summary

Because Windows is a graphical system, the key to success in learning to use it is to click every option and examine every window. By exploring the system to find out what it can do, you will be better prepared to later decipher what a user has done. Moreover, remember that when you are first learning Windows, the solution to a support issue is most often found through your eyes, not your memory. If you have a problem to troubleshoot, begin by looking in all of the windows you can find that may have settings relating to the problem. Often, the answer actually is staring you in the face!

With the basic knowledge gained in this chapter, we are now ready to look at installing and configuring each of the specific applications you will be tested on during the A+ Operating System exam: the Windows 95/98 and Windows 2000 chapters are next!

Key Terms

Before you take the exam, be certain you are familiar with the following terms:

directories	syntax
icons	tabs
path	Taskbar
platforms	window
Registry	Wizard
root directory	working directory
Start menu	

Review Questions

1. What is the Desktop?

   A. The top of the desk where the computer sits

   B. The virtual desk upon which all of your other programs and utilities run

   C. It keeps track of all the data on disk

   D. Where all of a computer's memory is stored

2. When you right-click with the mouse, a menu appears. This menu allows you to do all of the following except:

   A. Create new icons

   B. Create new directories

   C. Change the TCP/IP address

   D. Arrange icons

3. The screen saver can be changed in the _____ dialog box.

   A. Properties

   B. Taskbar

   C. Menu Bar

   D. Shortcut Menu

4. There are three types of mouse clicks in Windows. What are they?

   A. Primary click, triple-click, and right-left click

   B. Double-click, right-left click, and primary click

   C. Primary click, left-right click, and triple-click

   D. Secondary click, primary click, and double-click

5. The Taskbar can be increased in size by:

   A. Right-clicking the mouse and dragging the Taskbar to make it bigger

   B. Left-clicking the mouse and double-clicking the Taskbar

   C. Moving the mouse pointer to the top of the Taskbar and pausing until the pointer turns into a double-headed arrow

   D. Highlighting the Taskbar and double-clicking in the center

6. Which submenu holds the program groups and program icons that you can use?

   A. Programs

   B. Document

   C. Settings

   D. Find

7. Which of the following will not let you add programs to the Programs submenu?

    A. The application program

    B. File Manager

    C. The Taskbar

    D. Windows Explorer

8. The Windows Explorer Program can be accessed by: (Select all that apply.)

    A. Selecting Start ➤ Run ➤ Programs

    B. Selecting Start ➤ CMD ➤ Programs

    C. Selecting Start ➤ Programs ➤ Explorer

    D. Right-clicking My Computer with the mouse and selecting Explore

9. How many functions does the Documents submenu have?

    A. Three

    B. Two

    C. One

    D. Four

10. Which submenu keeps track of the last 15 data files that you opened?

    A. Programs

    B. Taskbar

    C. Settings

    D. Documents

11. Which submenu provides you with easy access to the configuration of Windows $9x$?

    A. Settings

    B. Programs

    C. Documents

    D. Find

12. What are three submenus of the Settings submenu?

    A. Control Panel, Printers, Start

    B. Control Panel, Printers, Taskbar

    C. Control Panel, Taskbar, Help

    D. Find, Printers, Taskbar

13. You can start programs if they don't have a shortcut on the Desktop or in the Programs submenu by:

   A. Using the Shut Down command

   B. Typing **cmd** in the Start Run box

   C. Using the Run command and typing in the name of the program

   D. Typing **cmd** in the Start box and then the program name

14. The My Computer icon will display all of the following except:

   A. All the disk drives installed in your computer

   B. Control Panel

   C. Dial-up Networking

   D. Printers

   E. Modems

15. Icons consist of which elements?

   A. Icon label, icon graphic, program location, working directory location

   B. Working directory location and program assistance

   C. Programming, working directory, and program location

   D. Programming, program assistance, and program location

16. In Windows 9*x*, a deleted file can be retrieved using the:

   A. My Computer icon

   B. Recycle Bin

   C. Control Panel

   D. Settings panel

17. To turn off a Windows 9*x* machine you should:

   A. Run Shut Down

   B. Turn off the switch and unplug the machine

   C. Press Ctrl+Alt+Del

   D. Select Start ➢ Shut Down, choose Shut Down and turn the computer off

18. The Control Panel in Windows 9*x* is accessed by: (Select all that apply.)

   A. Selecting ➢ Start ➢ Settings ➢ Control Panel

   B. Selecting Start ➢ Control Panel

   C. Selecting Start ➢ Programs ➢ Control Panel

   D. Double-clicking My Computer and double-clicking the Control Panel icon

19. How can you find files in Windows *9x*?

    A. Through the Program Manager

    B. By selecting Start ➢ Find

    C. By using `FINDFILE.EXE`

    D. You cannot search for files in Windows *9x*.

20. What file is needed to enable CD-ROM support under MS-DOS?

    E. `CDLDR`

    F. `MSCDEX.EXE`

    G. `CDLRD.EXE`

    H. `CDEX.EXE`

Answers to Review Questions

1. B. By default, the Desktop contains the Start menu, the Taskbar, and a number of icons. Because it is the base on which everything else sits, how the Desktop is configured can have a major effect on how the GUI looks and how convenient it is for users.

2. C. The menu that appears when you right-click a mouse allows you to: create new icons, create new directories, and arrange icons.

3. A. The screen saver can be changed in the Properties dialog box. To access the Properties dialog box, you can either right-click anywhere on the Desktop and choose Properties from the menu that appears or go to the Control Panel and click Display.

4. D. There are three mouse clicks in Windows. A primary click is used to select an object or place a cursor. A double-click is used to open a program through an icon or for other specific application functions. A secondary click (usually a click on the right mouse button, although that can be modified) is interpreted differently than a left mouse click. In Windows, it generally displays a context-sensitive menu from which you are given the ability to perform tasks or view object properties.

5. C. The Taskbar can be increased in size by moving the mouse pointer to the top of the Taskbar and pausing until the pointer turns into a double-headed arrow.

6. A. When you select the Programs submenu, you will be shown yet another submenu, with a submenu for each program group. You can navigate through this menu and its submenus and click the program you wish to start.

7. B. You can add programs to the Programs submenu in many ways. The three most popular ways are through the application's installation program, the Taskbar Properties screen, and the Windows Explorer program. If you use the application's installation program, it will automatically make a program group and shortcuts for the programs under the Programs submenu.

8. C, D. The Windows Explorer program can be accessed by clicking Start ➢ Programs ➢ Explorer or right-clicking My Computer and selecting Explore.

9. C. The Documents submenu has one function: to keep track of the last 15 data files you opened.

10. D. Whenever you open a file, a shortcut is automatically made to the file in the Documents menu. To open the same document again, just click on its name in the Documents menu.

11. A. The Settings submenu provides you with easy access to the configuration of Windows $9x$. To open it, select Start ➢ Settings.

12. B. In Windows 2000, Network and Dial-Up Connections is also a submenu of Settings.

13. C. To run any program, select Start ➤ Run and type in the name of the program in the Open field. If you don't know the exact path to the program, you can find the file by clicking the Browse button. Once you have typed in the executable name and path, click OK to run the program.

14. E. To locate your modems, you must go into Control Panel and click the Modems icon.

15. A. The label and graphic tell the user the name of the program and give a visual hint as to what that program does. By right-clicking an icon once, you make that icon the active icon, and a drop-down menu appears. One of the selections is Properties. Clicking Properties will bring up the attributes of an icon and is the only way to see exactly which program an icon is configured to start.

16. B. The Recycle Bin is where all deleted files are placed. Deleted files are held here until the Recycle Bin is emptied. Users can easily recover accidentally deleted files from the Recycle Bin.

17. D. To turn off a Windows 9x machine, select Start ➤ Shut Down, choose Shut Down and turn the computer off.

18. A, D. Control Panel in Windows 9x can be accessed by either selecting Start ➤ Settings ➤ Control Panel or by double-clicking My Computer and double-clicking the Control Panel icon.

19. B. Files can be found in Windows 9x by selecting Start ➤ Find and selecting the appropriate drive.

20. B. MSCDEX.EXE, along with the drivers for the particular device, is used to access a CD-ROM drive from DOS.

Chapter 3

Installing and Using Windows 95/98

THE FOLLOWING OBJECTIVES ARE COVERED IN THIS CHAPTER:

✓ **2.1 Identify the procedures for installing Windows 9x, and Windows 2000 for bringing the software to a basic operational level.**

  Content may include the following:

  - Start Up
  - Partition
  - Format drive
  - Loading drivers
  - Run appropriate set up utility

✓ **2.2 Identify steps to perform an operating system upgrade.**

  Content may include the following:

  - Upgrading Windows 95 to Windows 98
  - Upgrading Windows NT Workstation 4.0 to Windows 2000
  - Replacing Windows $9x$ with Windows 2000
  - Dual boot Windows $9x$/Windows NT 4.0/2000

✓ **2.3 Identify the basic system boot sequences and boot methods, including the steps to create an emergency boot disk with utilities installed for Windows 9x, Windows NT, and Windows 2000.**

  Content may include the following:

  - Startup disk
  - Safe Mode
  - MS-DOS mode
  - NTLDR (NT Loader), BOOT.INI
  - Files required to boot
  - Creating emergency repair disk (ERD)

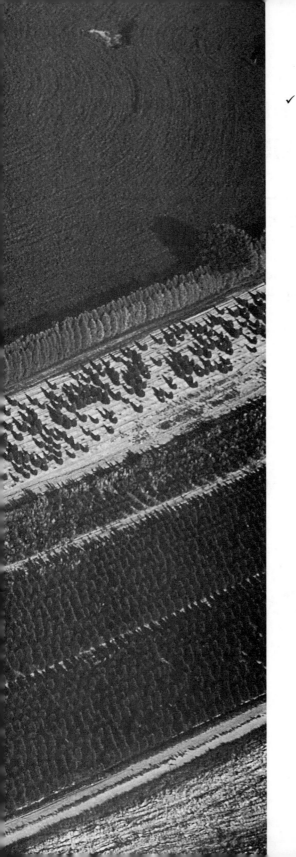

✓ **2.4 Identify procedures for loading/adding and configuring application device drivers, and the necessary software for certain devices.**

> **Content may include the following:**
>
> - Windows 9x Plug and Play and Windows 2000
> - Identify the procedures for installing and launching typical Windows and non-Windows applications (Note: there is no content related to Windows 3.1.)
> - Procedures for set up and configuring Windows printing subsystem.
>   - Setting Default printer
>   - Installing/Spool setting
>   - Network printing (with help of LAN admin)

ver the past two years, Windows 98 has become the operating system of choice for thousands of users. Most people who have computers today have upgraded to Windows 98 so that they can take advantage of its many features. There is still a significant user base for Windows 95 as well, though, and as such this section details the steps needed to install Windows 95 on a computer, as well as the steps needed to upgrade to Windows 98 from an existing Windows 95 system.

In this chapter, we will therefore take a look at what sort of hardware is required to install Windows 95 and Windows 98 (referred to generically as Windows 9*x* hereafter), what you need to know to get each installed and running, and what some of the major files and boot processes are for each.

For additional coverage of objective 2.1, please see Chapter 4. Additional coverage of objective 2.2 can be found in Chapter 4. Objective 2.3 is also covered in Chapters 4 and 7, and there is additional coverage of objective 2.4 in Chapters 4, 5, and 6.

Installation Prerequisites

Although they are very similar operating systems, Windows 95 and Windows 98 do have some significant differences. For instance, whereas Windows 95 can be installed from either floppy disks or from CD-ROM, Windows 98 is an extremely large operating system and is generally installed either from CD-ROM or over a network connection. (It is also technically possible to install Windows 98 using floppy disks, but at over 70 disks, you simply don't want to go there.)

Hardware Requirements

In an earlier edition of this book, published in 1997, we referred to Windows 95 by saying, "Let there be no doubt about it, Windows 95 is a resource hog." Ah, how times change. Although it's true that Windows 95 requires substantially more RAM, hard disk space, and processor speed than any of its predecessors, compared to the requirements of Windows 98 and Windows 2000, it seems extremely compact. As a reference, Table 3.1 lists the hardware requirements for installing each of the Windows 9*x* platforms.

TABLE 3.1 Windows Hardware Prerequisites

Hardware	95 Requirement	98 Requirement
Processor	386DX or higher processor (486 recommended).	386DX or higher processor (Pentium recommended).
Memory	4MB (8MB recommended).	8MB (16–32MB recommended).
Free hard disk space	50–55MB for typical install (40MB if upgrading from a previous version of Windows). Could go as high as 85MB for a custom install with all options.	120MB for typical install. Could go as high as 250MB for a custom install with all options.
Floppy disk	One 3½-inch disk drive (if doing installation from floppy disks).	One 3½-inch disk drive (if doing installation from floppy disks).
CD-ROM	Required if installing from CD (preferred method).	Required if installing from CD (preferred method).
Video	VGA or better.	VGA or better.
Mouse	Required.	Required.
Keyboard	Required.	Required.

The installation needs of Windows 2000 will be examined in Chapter 4.

If there is one thing to be learned from Table 3.1, by the way, it is that Microsoft is nothing if not optimistic. For your own sanity, though, we *strongly* suggest that you do not try to run Windows 98 on a 386DX machine with 8MB of RAM. Windows 95 seems to perform acceptably—in our opinion—if the machine has a Pentium-class processor and at least 16MB of RAM, but Windows 98 has a few more built-in gizmos and normally should be run on a 200+ megahertz machine with at least 32MB of RAM. As this book is being written, machines of that description can be purchased on eBay for about $75 (with shipping), or less than the price of a copy of the Windows 98 upgrade. If someone comes to you with a 486/33 and 8MB of RAM wanting to upgrade to Windows 98, do them—and yourself—a favor and direct them to a hardware upgrade first! Also, anyone who does have better hardware but is still running Windows 95 should seriously consider upgrading. Windows 98 is better supported by software vendors, and its ability to support more powerful memory and storage make it preferable on new machines.

Other hardware—sound cards, network cards, modems, video cards, and so on—may or may not work with Windows 95 or Windows 98. If the device is fairly recent, you can be relatively certain that it was built to work with Windows 9*x*, but if it is older, you may need to find out who made the hardware and check their Web site to see if they have Windows 9*x* drivers. If they don't, you can also use DOS 16-bit "real-mode" drivers, but this should be done only as a last resort because they are more difficult to configure and are less effective than Windows 9*x* 32-bit drivers. We will talk more about this distinction in the discussion of the hardware detection phase of setup later in this chapter, and in the chapters on multimedia (Chapter 5) and networking (Chapter 8) later on.

Briefly, a real-mode driver is one that directly accesses hardware, as was the standard in DOS; 32-bit Windows drivers work through the Windows system, allowing Windows to optimize and control hardware access. Although they are slow, real-mode drivers will usually work with Windows 9*x* if you cannot obtain updated drivers for your hardware. Before using an old driver, always search vendor Web sites for updated versions.

Preparing the Computer for Installation

Once you have verified that the machine on which you are planning to install Windows 9*x* is capable of running it properly and that all hardware is supported, you will need to make certain that the system is ready for the install. The primary question here is whether you are planning to perform a fresh install of Windows or whether you are going to be upgrading an existing system. Upgrading will be dealt with later in the chapter; for now, we'll focus on new installations.

The Windows Startup Disk

If you are installing Windows 9*x* onto a system that does not already have a functioning operating system, you have a bit of work to do before you get to the installation itself. New disk drives need to have two critical functions performed on them before they are able to be used—partitioning and formatting:

Partitioning   The process of assigning part or all of the drive for use by the computer

Formatting   The process of preparing the partition to store data in a particular fashion

These two procedures are dealt with in Windows 9*x* by using the FDISK.EXE and FORMAT.EXE commands. Running any sort of command on a machine that has no operating system is, well, impossible, though, so in order to do this, you need to boot the computer using a floppy disk that is bootable to MS-DOS or the Windows 9*x* command line. Windows 9*x* solves this problem through the use of a startup disk that allows you to boot a computer and run these and other basic commands. It should be included in the Windows 95/98 package you are installing from, but if it is not, you will need to make one.

 Neither the Windows 95 nor the Windows 98 CD-ROM is bootable, which is why the startup disk is so crucial.

In a paradox every bit as difficult to resolve as the chicken-or-egg debate, you are only able to make the startup disk (a) during setup or (b) once 95/98 is installed. If you have lost your startup disk and need to prepare a new drive, your best bet is to find a machine with an existing installation of Windows 95 or 98 and an create a startup disk off of it. To do this, go to Start ➢ Settings ➢ Control Panel and double-click the Add/Remove Programs icon. Within Add/Remove Programs is a tab called Startup Disk (Figure 3.1).

FIGURE 3.1   The Windows 98 Startup Disk tab

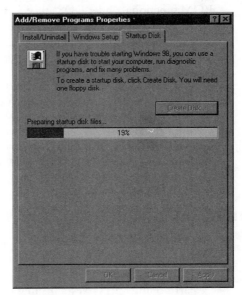

Click the Startup Disk tab to bring it to the front. Click the Create Disk button to start the startup disk creation process. You will need a single floppy disk for this, and all information on it will be deleted and replaced. If you can't find a floppy disk and even a single machine already running Windows 9x, well, you may be in the wrong business....

If you are performing the installation via CD, you must also make certain that the startup disk is capable of accessing the CD-ROM drive on your machine. In Windows 98, the startup disk automatically loads standard CD-ROM drivers and presents you with an option to load CD-ROM support on startup. Some Windows 95 startup disks also have this, but if not, you can modify the AUTOEXEC.BAT and CONFIG.SYS to load a CD-ROM driver. The exact modifications you will need to make depend on the type and manufacturer of your CD-ROM drive, but a sample CONFIG.SYS and AUTOEXEC.BAT follow:

```
CONFIG.SYS:
        Files=25
        Buffers=9,256
        DEVICE=C:\PANCD.SYS /B:25 /N:PANCD001

AUTOEXEC.BAT
        PATH=C:\;C:\DOS
        MSCDEX.EXE /D:PANCD001 /L:D /M:100
```

Notice that these aren't big changes, but they are crucial to make the CD-ROM functional under DOS; once Windows 95 or 98 is loaded, these files won't be needed because Windows has its own drivers for accessing the CD drive, and they will be loaded during the install. These lines can be added to and later removed from AUTOEXEC.BAT and CONFIG.SYS using any text editor.

Once you have a basic Windows startup disk, you will want to continue to make other small improvements upon it as well by adding tools to allow you to perform common tasks more easily. SMARTDRV.EXE and XCOPY.EXE are two we recommend adding. Smart drive (SMARTDRV.EXE) increases file copy speed, and XCOPY.EXE allows you to copy multiple files and directories easily.

Partitioning Using a Windows 95 Boot Disk

Once you have a DOS or Windows startup disk, it is time to boot the computer and prepare it for the Windows installation. When the computer first boots up, the Windows 95 boot disk will simply bring you to an A:\> prompt.

Partitioning refers to establishing large allocations of hard drive space. A partition is a continuous section of sectors that are next to each other. In DOS and Windows, a partition is referred to by a drive letter, such as C: or D:. Partitioning a drive into two or more parts gives it the appearance of being two or more physical hard drives.

When a drive is partitioned in DOS, the first partition you create will be a *primary partition*, which is marked *active*. The active partition is the location of the boot-up files for DOS or Windows. If there is more than one partition, the second and remaining DOS partitions are found inside of another partition type called an *extended partition*. An extended partition contains one or more *logical partitions*; it is the logical partitions that have drive letters associated with them. Only one primary and one extended partition can be created per disk using the Windows 95 disk utility, which is called FDISK. This two-partition limit is a characteristic of Windows 95, not a limitation of the hard drive.

When FDISK is executed, a screen appears that gives four or five options (Figure 3.2 shows the screen with four options). The fifth option, which allows you to select a hard drive, appears only when there is more than one physical hard drive. FDISK will only partition one hard drive at a time.

FIGURE 3.2   The introductory screen in FDISK.EXE

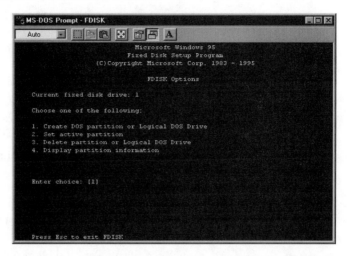

With FDISK, you can create partitions, delete partitions, mark a partition as active, or display available partitioning information. You must create a primary partition before you can create any other partitions. If space is still available on the drive, then a second, extended partition may be created. No drive letter is assigned to the extended partition. One or more logical partitions must be defined within the extended partition, and they can then have drive letters attached to them so users can access them.

It is possible for no partitions to be marked active on a particular drive. In this case, the machine will not be able to boot to the drive. If this is the case, you must use FDISK to set an active partition before you will be able to properly install Windows 9x. One and only one partition can be marked active.

FDISK creates a start and an end to a section of hard drive space. At the beginning of that space, it creates a special file called the Master Boot Record, or MBR. The MBR contains the partition information about the beginning and end of the primary and extended partitions. At the beginning of the partitions, this record is called the DOS Volume Boot Sector.

The size of a partition will determine certain aspects of a file pointer table called the *file allocation table*, or *FAT* for short. The larger the drive partition, the more space will be wasted on the drive.

Formatting

The next step in management of a hard drive is formatting, initiated by the FOR-MAT command. Technically the sort of formatting that we are talking about is high-level formatting. This should not be confused with low-level formatting, although it can be just as destructive to information on the hard drive. High-level formatting is, these days, normally the only formatting a technician will do. When high-level formatting is performed, the following actions take place:

- The surface of the hard drive platter is briefly scanned to find any possible bad spots, and the areas surrounding a bad spot are marked as bad sectors.

- Magnetic tracks are laid down in concentric circles. These tracks are where information is eventually encoded. These tracks, in turn, are split into pieces of 512 bytes called sectors. Some space is reserved in between the sectors for error correction information, referred to as CRC, or Cyclic Redundancy Check, information. The operating system may use CRC information to re-create data that has been partially lost from a sector.

- Additionally, a file allocation table (FAT) is created. This table will contain information about the location of files as they are placed onto the hard drive. The FAT has a limited number of entries. Therefore, the space allocated for the partition may need to be divided into clusters of sectors, where a sector is the smallest part of a hard drive.

Low-level formatting is the first step in preparing to install an operating system into a computer. It is the process of getting the surface material of the hard drive platters prepared to accept information. Low-level formatting creates the tracks and sectors that higher-level processes look for. This formatting process destroys any information that is already present on the hard drive. For this reason, low-level formatting is rarely used on IDE hard drives, which contain some special information written at the factory. SCSI hard drives will occasionally be low-level formatted; on very rare occasions, an IDE drive will also be low-level formatted. Fortunately, these days hard drives are usually low-level formatted at the factory and never need to have this done to them again. For most technicians, this is just a historical fact of past times.

Optimization

Each FAT has a set number of entries; the number depends on the size of the hard drive. On a very small hard drive, the FAT could theoretically be large enough to track all the sectors, but in practice this never occurs. Only high-density floppy disks have FATs that track individual sectors. Sectors on hard drives will be clumped together in what is called a *cluster* or *allocation unit*. In general, as the drive or drive partition increases in size, the number of sectors per cluster increases.

A drive between 16MB and 128MB will have four sectors per cluster. A larger drive of up to 256MB will have eight sectors per cluster. In fact, every time you double the hard drive size, you double the number of sectors per cluster. Thus, drives of up to 512MB will have 16 sectors per cluster, drives of up to 1024MB will have 32 sectors per cluster, and so on. Clusters of 32 sectors are 16KB in size.

Allocation units may not be used by two different files, thus any empty space in an allocation unit (any space not filled by the file assigned to that allocation unit) is wasted. Many files almost fill the last cluster allocated to them, but many files barely use this last allocated cluster. On the average, files use half of the last cluster allocated to them.

Imagine large clusters with one cluster per file being only half filled. If these clusters are 16KB and there are 5,000 files, then roughly 40MB of hard drive space is designated but unused. For example, if a hard drive has almost 25,000 files on one partition, that translates to 200MB of wasted space.

One solution to optimizing hard drive space is to set up multiple partitions that are smaller in size and therefore use smaller clusters. It is not unusual for a 1GB drive to regain 200MB or more when split into two partitions. You should also avoid partition sizes that are just over the limit for cluster sizes. A 528MB partition has less available space on it than a 512MB partition does, simply because the clusters are large enough to waste more than the extra space on the larger partition. As new drives get larger, though, the difference between 528MB and 512MB becomes largely irrelevant. Because of this, a new file system—FAT32—solves many of these problems (and will be discussed later).

EXERCISE 3.1

Preparing a New Disk for Windows 95

1. Insert the Windows 95 boot disk and start the computer.

2. At the prompt, type **FDISK**.

3. In the main FDISK screen, select option 4, Display partition information.

4. If the drive is already partitioned properly, the partitions and their sizes will be listed.

5. Return to the main screen by clicking the ESC key on your keyboard. If the partitions were properly created already, click ESC again to leave FDISK.

6. If the disk is not yet partitioned, select 1, Create DOS partition or logical DOS drive.

EXERCISE 3.1 *(continued)*

7. Click 1, Create a primary DOS partition. You will be asked if you want to use the maximum space available and make the partition startable. In most cases, this is best, but if you wish to make the partition a particular size, you can do so. *IMPORTANT: If there are partitions on the disk already, you must delete them to create new ones. If you do this, all information currently on those partitions will be lost!*

8. After you have created the new C: partition, click ESC until you are asked to reboot.

9. Reboot, and again use the startup disk to start the system. At the A: prompt, type **FORMAT C:** to format the drive with the standard FAT file system.

10. You will be warned that all information on the drive will be deleted. Type **Y** to confirm, and the format will begin. This can take some time. When the format is completed, you may begin the installation of Windows. You do not need to reboot after a format.

Using the Windows 98 Boot Disk

If you are using a Windows 98 boot disk to prepare a drive, you will notice that a few things are different. First, when the machine first starts up, you will be presented with two options: boot with CD-ROM support or boot without it. The default is to boot with CD support. If you are planning to install from CD-ROM, this makes life easy because most supported CD drives are simply loaded automatically.

Second, as you start the Windows 98 FDISK program, you will be presented with the message about working with large hard drives. Standard FAT (FAT16) has problems dealing with large drives, both due to its maximum partition size of 4GB and because it uses extremely large cluster sizes for large partitions. As the size of computer hard drives increased, this became a serious problem, so Microsoft added support for a second format type—FAT32. Earlier versions of the file allocation tables are known as FAT12 and FAT16 (because the size of the FAT entries are 12 bits and 16 bits respectively). First implemented in Windows 95 "Revision B," FAT32 support became standard in later versions of Windows—98 and 2000. As a comparison of how the new system saves you space, a 2GB drive with FAT16 has clusters of 32KB; with FAT32, the cluster sizes are 4KB. Because of this, if you save a 15KB file, FAT will need to allocate an entire 32KB cluster. FAT32 would use four 4KB clusters, for a total of 16KB. FAT32 wastes an unused 1KB, while FAT wastes 15 times as much!

The disadvantage of FAT32 is that it is not compatible with older DOS, Windows 3.*x*, and Windows 95 operating systems. This means that when you boot a Windows 95 Rev B. or Windows 98 FAT32–formatted partition with a DOS boot floppy, you can't read the partition.

FAT32 supports drives of up to 2 terabytes. If you have a disk that is over 2,000GB in size, you will have to create multiple partitions on it.

Starting a Windows 9x Installation

Once you have the drive prepared, you are ready to start the Windows install process. To do this, boot to the startup disk and put either the CD-ROM or the first setup disk into the machine.

The program that performs the installation is called SETUP.EXE, and it's located either in the root directory of Disk 1 of the set of installation floppies or in the WIN95/WIN98 directory of the installation CD-ROM. It examines your hard disk and makes sure there is enough room to install Windows 95, then copies a few temporary files to your hard disk. These temporary files are the components of the Installation Wizard that will guide you through the installation of Windows 9x.

There are a few options that you can use with the Setup program. To use them, you place them after the SETUP at the command line, separated by a single space. Table 3.2 details these Setup startup switches.

TABLE 3.2 Windows 95 SETUP Command-Line Options

Option	Function
/d	Tells Setup to ignore your existing copy of Windows. It only applies during an upgrade.
<filename>	Used without the < and >, specifies the preconfigured setup file that Setup should use (e.g., SETUP MYFILE.INI causes Setup to run with the settings contained in MYFILE.INI).
/id	Tells Setup to skip the disk space check.
/iq	Tells Setup to skip the test for cross-linked files.
/is	Tells Setup to skip the routine system check.
/it	Tells Setup to skip the check for Terminate and Stay Resident programs (TSRs) that are known to cause problems with Windows 95 Setup.

TABLE 3.2   Windows 95 SETUP Command-Line Options *(continued)*

Option	Function
/1	Enables a Logitech mouse during setup.
/n	Causes Setup to run without a mouse.
/p	Tells Setup to skip the check for any Plug-and-Play devices.
/T:C:\tmp	Specifies which directory (C:\tmp in this case) Setup will copy its temporary files to. If this directory doesn't exist, Setup will create it.

In this portion of the chapter, we will look at the Windows 95 setup specifics. To start the installation, you simply change to the drive letter where the installation files are and type **SETUP** (with the appropriate startup switches), like so:

```
C:>D:
D:>SETUP
```

Setup will tell you that it's going to check your system and that you must press Enter to continue. If you want to cancel the installation without continuing, you can press Esc. When you press Enter, Setup copies a very basic Windows system to your computer from the CD and starts it. Setup then executes in a Windows environment and welcomes you to the installation (Figure 3.3).

FIGURE 3.3   Windows 95 Setup Welcome screen

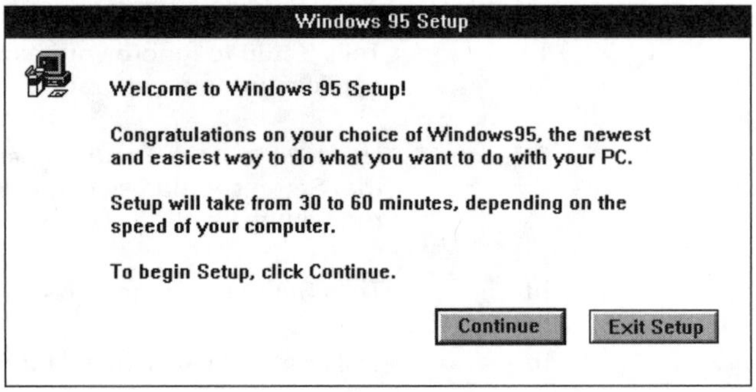

Because Windows may need these files later, it is often a good idea to simply copy all of the needed files (the Win95 directory on the CD or all of the files on each setup disk) to a directory on the local drive of the machine. Some folks use a directory called C:\disks for this purpose.

To begin the installation, click Continue. Setup will then copy some more files your to computer while it builds the Setup Wizard. The Windows 95 Setup Wizard guides you through the installation step by step. At each step, you will be asked questions about how you would like Windows 95 configured. Then you simply click the Next or Continue button.

The Setup Wizard will ask you questions about three main categories:

- Gathering information
- Copying files to your computer
- Finishing the installation

These three general steps will be presented to you when you begin the installation and at various times during the installation.

After the Welcome screen, Setup will present you with the text of the license agreement. The Windows 95 license agreement basically says that you are being sold a copy of this software for use on one computer and that you won't give it away or sell it to anyone else for a profit. There's a bunch more to it, so you should read the entire agreement. When you've read it, click Yes to accept the agreement and move on. If you click No, you are telling Setup (and Microsoft) that you don't agree to the terms of the contract. This will cancel the installation.

Step 1: Collecting Information about Your Computer

Next you'll be presented with the screen in Figure 3.4. This screen gives you the basic outline of the Windows 95 Installation process. In the first step, Setup asks you questions about how your computer is currently configured and which options you would like to install.

FIGURE 3.4 Windows Setup start screen

From this point in the setup process on, the Setup screens will have a Back button and a Cancel button. You click the Back button to go back to the preceding screen, and click the Cancel button to completely exit the installation. If you exit the installation before it's completely finished, Setup will restore your system to its former state.

To begin the gathering of information, click the Next button (or press Enter).

Choosing the Windows Installation Directory

Setup will allow you to choose where you would like to install Windows 95. Setup chooses C:\WINDOWS by default. However, if you want to have both Windows 3.*x* and Windows 95 on the same system, you should install Windows 95 to a directory other than C:\WINDOWS. To do so, click the Other Directory radio button and then click Next. Setup will then ask you which directory you want to put Windows 95 in.

For most installations, you will want to install Windows 95 to the C:\WINDOWS directory. If this is the case, leave C:\WINDOWS checked and click the Next button to continue. Setup will check to see if you have enough disk space and memory to install Windows 95. If either of these two requirements are below the recommendations, Setup will issue an error and quit. If they pass, Setup will continue to the next step, choosing the type of setup you want to perform.

Choosing the Setup Options

The screen shown in Figure 3.5 allows you to select which type of installation you want. There are four options, outlined in Table 3.3.

FIGURE 3.5   Selecting the type of setup you want to perform

TABLE 3.3   Windows 95 Setup Types

Setup Option	Description
Typical	Allows Setup to choose the most popular features during the rest of the setup process.
Portable	Sets up the most common applications and utilities for portable computers. This option will install PCMCIA support and Advanced Power Management (APM).
Compact	Installs the minimum components Windows 95 needs to function.
Custom	Allows you to choose which components to install. If you select this option, Setup will present you with a list of utilities and programs to install. This option allows you to make the most choices about how Windows 95 gets installed. This is the method most commonly used by technicians to install Windows 95.

Because it's the most popular option for technicians, select the Custom radio button. Then click Next to continue the installation.

Entering User Information

In the next screen, you enter information about yourself and your company (if applicable). This information will be used when you install most other Microsoft applications. Simply start typing your name in the Name field. Then press the Tab key to move to the next field, Company. Type in your company name (or the name of the company that owns the computer) and click Next to continue.

Entering the Product Identification Number

The product identification number helps to ensure that you aren't illegally installing Windows 95 from a pirated copy. The number you must enter is usually found on the back cover of the CD case (look for a yellow sticker with the words *CD KEY*). It might also be found on the warranty registration card. You should send this card in so that you can receive technical support if you ever need it. From this screen (Figure 3.6), simply type in the number *exactly* as it appears on the back of the CD case.

FIGURE 3.6   Entering the product identification number

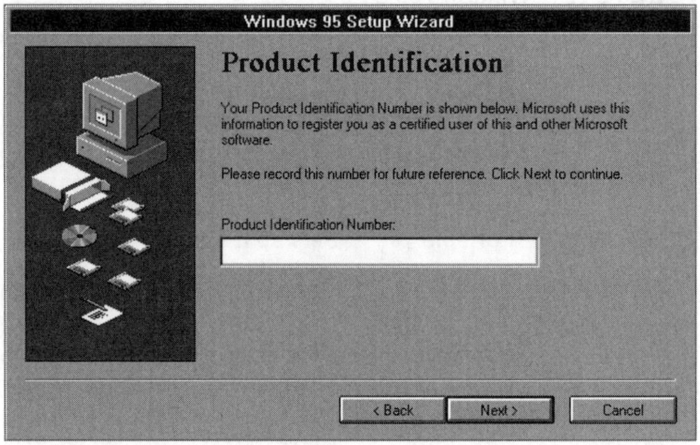

After you finished typing the number, you can click Next. If you type the wrong number, Setup will tell you and ask you to enter it again.

Analyzing Your Computer and Setting Up Hardware

Setup is now ready to start looking for the hardware devices it needs to install drivers for. To let Setup search for the devices, select the Yes (Recommended) option in the screen that appears. To specify all the hardware that your computer has manually, select the No, I Want to Modify the Hardware List option. Windows 95 does a pretty good job of detecting hardware in the computer and installing device drivers for those devices. For most computers, you'll want to select the Yes option and click Next.

After you click Next, Setup will present you with a screen like the one shown in Figure 3.7. If you have a network adapter, sound card, or CD-ROM drive, mark the appropriate check box(es). A check box will appear to tell Setup to install drivers and software for those items. When you have finished selecting hardware drivers from this screen, click Next to continue the installation and begin the hardware detection process.

FIGURE   3.7   Choosing special setup options

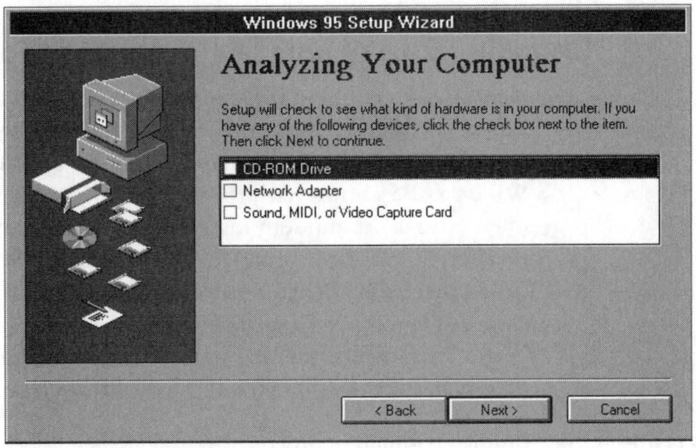

The hardware detection process may take several minutes. During this time, you will see a screen like the one in Figure 3.8 and you will hear the hard drive searching for files (or at least you'll see the hard drive light flash madly). When Setup finds a piece of hardware, it will make a note of which driver to install; if it finds something it doesn't have a driver for, it will ask you whether you want to provide one or not install the device at all.

FIGURE   3.8   Analyzing the computer's hardware to determine which drivers to install

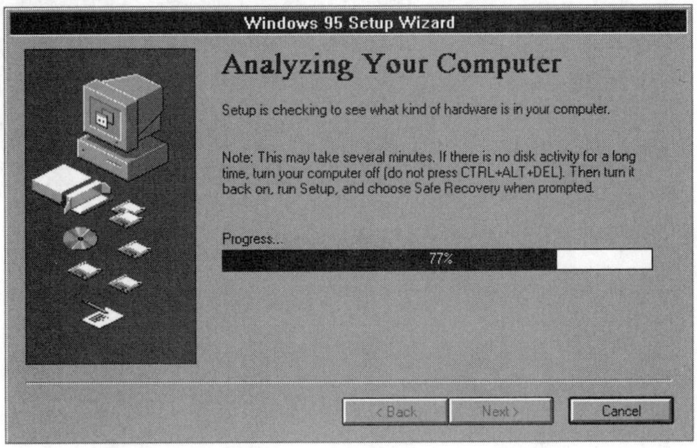

If the progress bar stops moving for more than 10 minutes and there is no hard disk activity, more than likely the machine is locked up. Reboot the computer and rerun Setup. Setup will detect that a previous installation wasn't completed and it will try to resume where it left off. Neat, huh?

After the hardware detection is finished, Setup will automatically move on to the next step.

Choosing E-Mail and Fax Software to Install

Windows 95 comes with several pieces of software to get you connected to the rest of the world. From the screen shown in Figure 3.9, you can choose to install Microsoft's online service, the Microsoft Network (MSN). In addition, Windows 95 comes with the software to send and receive faxes (although you must have a fax modem installed in your computer to use it). This software is called Microsoft Fax and it's integrated into Windows 95's Universal Mailbox called the Exchange Client (meaning you must have the Exchange Client installed to use MS Fax). The Exchange Client is actually called Microsoft Mail in the Setup window. This name, although confusing, stems from the fact that this mail client has its roots in the old MS Mail software.

FIGURE 3.9 Choosing which online tools to install

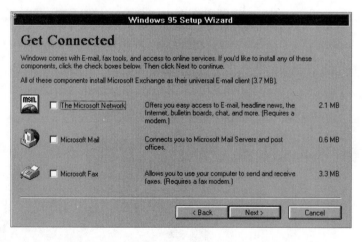

If you want to install any of these components, check the appropriate box. When you're finished selecting items, click Next to continue.

These check boxes just tell Setup whether you want the e-mail and fax software installed. Setup doesn't let you configure these components until after Windows 95 is installed.

Choosing Which Windows 95 Components You Want Installed

If you choose a Standard installation type, Setup will ask you whether you want it to choose all the components automatically or see a list of components. If you choose the latter, the screen in Figure 3.10 appears. If you chose a Custom installation type, Setup will automatically present you with the screen in Figure 3.10.

FIGURE 3.10 Custom setup component selection

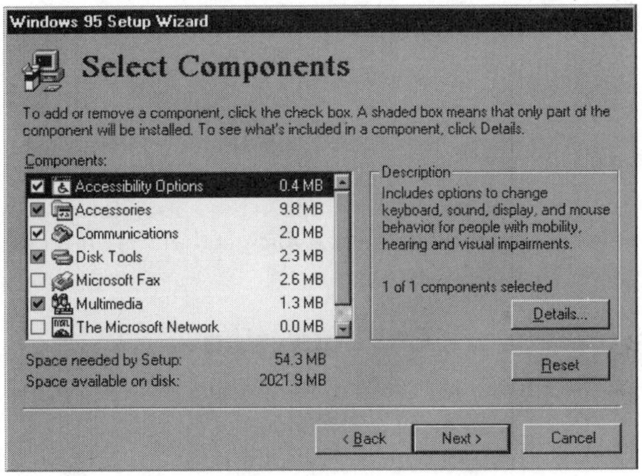

Windows 95 Setup Wizard

Select Components

To add or remove a component, click the check box. A shaded box means that only part of the component will be installed. To see what's included in a component, click Details.

Components:

☑	Accessibility Options	0.4 MB
☑	Accessories	9.8 MB
☑	Communications	2.0 MB
☑	Disk Tools	2.3 MB
☐	Microsoft Fax	2.6 MB
☑	Multimedia	1.3 MB
☐	The Microsoft Network	0.0 MB

Description
Includes options to change keyboard, sound, display, and mouse behavior for people with mobility, hearing and visual impairments.

1 of 1 components selected

Details...

Space needed by Setup: 54.3 MB
Space available on disk: 2021.9 MB

Reset

< Back   Next >   Cancel

If a check box is gray with a check mark in it, that means that not all the components of that category are going to be installed. If you highlight the category that has the gray check box and click the Details button, a screen will appear that will allow you to select or deselect additional components. Figure 3.11 shows the screen that appears when you highlight Accessories and click Details. Notice that Games is not checked by default. If you want Solitaire installed (and most people do), click the check box next to Games and click OK.

FIGURE 3.11 Adding or removing components from an installation group

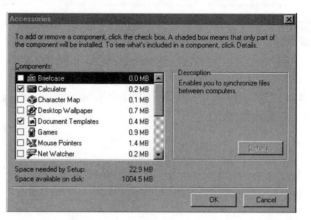

Once you have selected all the components you want installed, accept all selections by clicking OK until you get back to the screen shown in Figure 3.10. Then, click the Next button to continue the installation.

If you make a mistake selecting items, you can click the Reset button (see Figure 3.10) to reset the selections to the Setup defaults. However, be aware that the selections made in the e-mail/fax section of the installation will also be reset to their defaults, which is that they are not installed.

Network Configuration

The next step in the installation of Windows 95 shows up only if there is a network card installed in the machine. From this screen (Figure 3.12), you can customize which networking components are installed and how they are configured. Click Next to continue this installation.

FIGURE 3.12   The Network Configuration screen

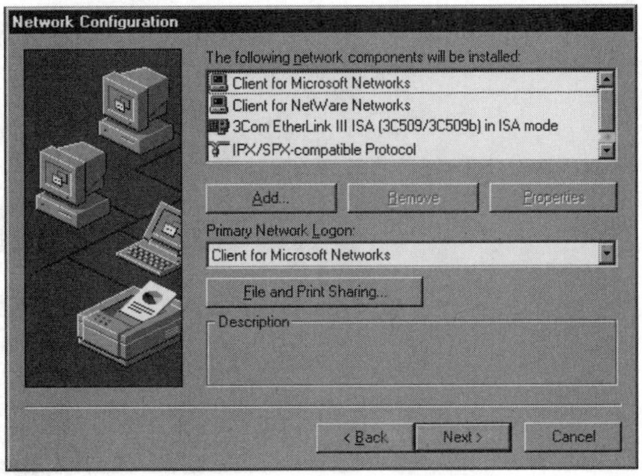

Because Windows 95 Networking configuration is covered in Chapter 8, we won't cover it again here. Refer to Chapter 8 for information about the details of configuring the Network Configuration screen.

If you have networking installed, the next screen you will see will be the computer identification screen. This only applies if you have the Client for Microsoft Networks installed because, on Microsoft networks, each computer has to have a name and should belong to a workgroup (these concepts will also be discussed in Chapter 8). After entering the information for Computer Name and Workgroup parameters, click Next to continue to the next step in the installation.

Verifying Computer Settings

Now that Setup has detected all the hardware in your machine in a Custom setup, the Setup Wizard will present you with a list of the hardware (Figure 3.13) that it found and allow you to modify which driver Windows 95 will use. If any of the drivers in the list are incorrect or have the word *Unknown* next to them, click the driver description, then click the Change button. Setup will present you with a list of alternatives. If none of the alternatives fit, leave the driver unchanged and install a new one after the installation.

FIGURE 3.13 Verifying computer settings

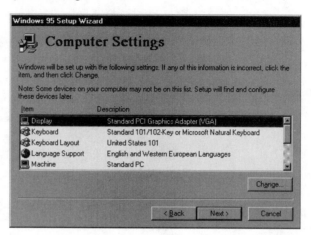

Once you have verified that all hardware drivers are correct, click Next to continue.

Installing and updating drivers for peripheral hardware is covered in Chapter 6, and updating current drivers is covered later in this chapter.

Creating a Startup Disk

The next step in the Windows 95 installation is to decide whether you want a startup disk (see Figure 3.14). This is the same disk we discussed earlier. You can choose to make one at this time (the Yes option) or to make one at a later time (the No option). Most technicians make their own Windows 95 startup disk, copy all their diagnostic utilities to it, and never use this option again. Because you booted using the one you created earlier, select No and click Next to continue the installation.

FIGURE 3.14   Choosing not to create a startup disk

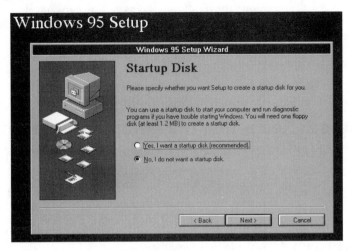

Step 2: Copying Files to Your Computer

At this point, you have given the Setup Wizard all the information it needs to begin installing Windows 95. It will present you with a screen (Figure 3.15) telling you this and giving you one last chance to cancel before copying files to your computer. If you think you made any mistakes, you can click the Back button. You can also click Cancel to abort the entire installation. If you believe you have entered all information correctly, click Next to start the file copy.

FIGURE 3.15   Starting the file copy

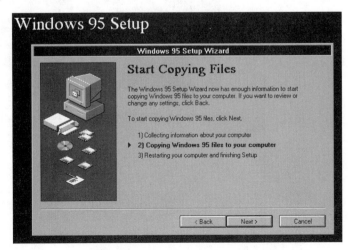

The bottom of the next screen displays a progress bar to indicate how far along the file copy process is. You can cancel the file copy at any time by clicking the Exit button in the lower-right corner of the screen or by pressing the F3 key on your keyboard. The file copy may take several minutes, depending on the speed of your computer. The nice part is, you don't have to watch a boring, blue bar go across the screen. Instead, you get to read several screens that give you information about the features of Windows 95.

Step 3: Restarting the Computer and Finishing Setup

When the file copy is finished, you will see a screen like the one in Figure 3.16. This screen is telling you that the majority of the installation is finished. You just need to reboot the computer and customize the way Windows 95 operates. To restart the computer and run Windows 95, remove any disks from their respective disk drives and click Finish. This will cause the computer to reboot.

FIGURE 3.16   Finishing the installation

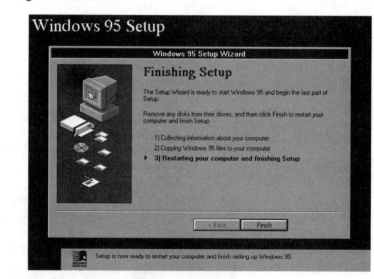

Upon rebooting, you'll see a blue screen with the message Getting ready to run Windows 95 for the first time... in red at the bottom of the screen.

If you have a network client installed, you may see a network login screen. The first time you run Windows 95, you won't be able to use your network connection anyway, so click Cancel for any screens you see that deal with network logins.

Setting Up Hardware and Software After Installation

The next screen you will see will tell you that Windows 95 is setting up hardware and any Plug-and-Play devices you might have (Figure 3.17). If there are any devices for which Windows 95 can't determine the settings (or find drivers), it will pop up a screen asking you to specify them. It will then pop up another screen telling you what settings it is configuring. It will automatically continue to the next screen.

FIGURE 3.17   Setting up hardware

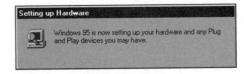

Briefly, a *driver* is a small program or piece of program code that runs in the background and translates the information going to and from an application and a piece of hardware. For example, a program such as WordPerfect doesn't keep track of all the different types of printers that are available; instead, it uses a printer driver. (Windows 95 and DOS applications use their own specific printer drivers.) WordPerfect is loaded into memory along with a printer driver that is specific to the user's printer. If a different printer is attached to that system, then a different printer driver may be required.

Setting the Date/Time Properties

After you set the hardware and software parameters, Windows 95 will present you with a screen that will allow you to set the date, time, and time zone (Figure 3.18) of the computer.

FIGURE 3.18 The Time Zone tab of the Date/Time property box

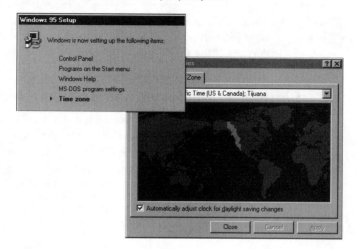

There are two tabs at the top of the window:

- In the Time Zone tab, you can click a map to set your time zone (click your current location on the map and it will set the time zone to the correct zone automatically, or if you know it, you can select your time zone from a drop-down list). You can click the check box next to Automatically Adjust Clock for Daylight Saving Changes and Windows 95 will set the clock automatically forward or backward on the appropriate day.

- The other tab is the Date & Time tab. From here you can set the current date and time by clicking the appropriate date in the calendar. You move to different months by selecting them from the drop-down list. If you need to move forward or backward a year, click the up or down arrows that are to the right of the year. To change the time, click the area that indicates the time and use the arrows to the right to move the hours, minutes, and seconds forward or backward.

When you've finished setting the date, time, and time zone, you can click OK to continue the installation.

Setting Up Your Universal Inbox

If you chose to install either Microsoft Mail or Microsoft Fax, Windows 95 will ask you to install Microsoft Exchange using the Inbox Setup Wizard. This wizard will guide you through the setup of the e-mail and fax services. If you have a modem installed in your computer, the wizard will help you configure it to work with these services. Because this material isn't covered on the exam, we'll refer you to the Windows 95 Help file that comes on the installation CD.

Setting Up a Printer

The final step to configuring Windows 95 is setting up a printer. To do this, Windows 95 starts up the Add Printer Wizard. This wizard is designed to guide you through the installation of a printer. We will cover this in more detail in Chapter 8, so we won't devote a great deal of time to discussing it here. If you don't want to install a printer now (or don't have one connected to your computer), click Cancel.

Final Installation Steps

After you configure a printer, Windows 95 is finally fully configured and will present you with a screen instructing you that it will reboot one final time. To reboot your computer and bring up Windows 95, click OK. Windows 95 is installed!

Once Windows 95 opens for the first time (without any wizards), you can start using it. You can also further customize the interface using the techniques discussed in Chapter 2 or those covered in "Configuring Windows 9*x* Software" later in this chapter.

Upgrading to Windows 98 from Windows 95

If you are currently running Windows 95 and want to upgrade to Windows 98, you're not alone. Most corporate and many home users have upgraded to Windows 98 at the time this book is being written in late 2000. This is due, in part, to some of the features that Windows 98 added to enhance Windows 95. It can also be attributed to the fact that the upgrade process is very easy (almost painless, in fact) and to the fact that the Microsoft marketing machine did a great job of selling it as a significant upgrade. Some of the major enhancements with Windows 98 include the following:

- Better Internet support through the integration of Internet Explorer
- Year 2000 fixes
- Support for newer hardware, such as USB, AGP, and DVD
- FAT32
- DOS 7 (16-bit) is replaced by DOS32 (32-bit)
- Enhancements for MMX processors, better use of RAM and disk resources

In truth, Windows 98 is a relatively basic upgrade. Besides the fact that most of the changes were relatively modest, most of them were generally also available to interested Windows 95 users through free Internet updates. As you will see, for most configuration and troubleshooting tasks, Windows 95 and 98 are identical.

Still, time marches on, and if you are asked to upgrade a machine from Windows 95 to Windows 98, the procedure is relatively straightforward. Let's run through a typical upgrade.

Starting the Upgrade

For the most part, the major steps that you need to follow when upgrading from an earlier version of Windows to Windows 98 are the same steps used to install Windows 98 on a machine without an operating system. These are divided by Setup into the following areas:

1. Preparing to run Windows 98 setup
2. Collecting information about your computer
3. Copying Windows 98 files to your computer
4. Restarting your computer
5. Setting up hardware and finalizing settings

The Windows 98 installation program, SETUP.EXE, performs these steps. In order to start the upgrade, you need to start the SETUP.EXE program. If you are upgrading to Windows 98 using a CD-ROM with a working installation of Windows 95, things couldn't be much simpler. Insert the disk into the CD drive and a window similar to the one in Figure 3.19 appears. In addition to this window, a box will appear noting that you are using an earlier version of Windows and offering to upgrade you to Windows 98.

FIGURE 3.19 The Windows 98 Autorun window

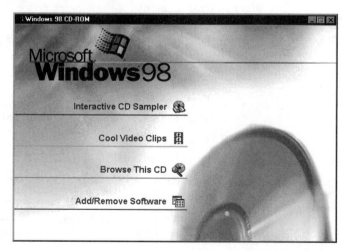

Simply click Yes, and the SETUP.EXE program will load. You will be able to see the progress of the setup process along the left side of the window as the Setup program shows you which part of the install you are in and approximately how much time is remaining.

Preparing to Run Windows 98 Setup

The first part of the setup routine is pretty basic. All that happens during the initial preparation is that the drives are given a quick examination and the files needed to run the setup are loaded. There are a couple of things that Windows checks for at this time, such as whether you have enough free drive space for the install and whether you have any programs running that may interfere with the upgrade.

During a system upgrade, you will generally want to shut down all nonessential programs, including those that are sitting in your system tray. This will help avoid conflicts and make it more likely that the install will go smoothly.

Collecting Information about Your Computer

Once the Setup program is convinced that you are ready to install, it will begin to gather the details needed for this install. A wizard appears and goes through the following screens:

License agreement This is where you give Bill your firstborn. Few people bother to read these, and fewer still understand them. The most important thing that you need to remember is that if you don't accept the license agreement, you can't complete the install. That simple.

Product Key These just keep getting longer, and more annoying. Microsoft keys have gone from 10 keys in Windows 95 to 25 in Windows 98. Remember that if a user has purchased the software, you need to put in their actual key, not just any one you have handy.

Install Directory Here you enter the directory in which the Windows 98 files will be stored. By default, this is the same directory that the current version of Windows is in—generally C:\WINDOWS. You can change this directory, but if you do, the upgrade will no longer migrate existing programs and you will have to install all programs and drivers over again (as in a new install).

At this point, Setup does some system checks and again checks for drive space. It also looks at the install directory you have specified. If you are upgrading over an existing Windows install, you're given the option to save your existing system files so that you can revert back if you have problems with Windows 98. If you decide to save these files, they will be saved at this point.

To save the files needed to revert back to Windows 95, you must have about 50MB of extra disk space. In most cases, you will not need these files and will choose not to save them. If you have any doubt about the compatibility of the hardware or software on the machine, though, this is a reassuring option.

Next you are presented with choices as to which Windows components you wish to install. There are four basic installation types, each of which gives you a different set of components:

Typical   If you are installing a system for someone else, and are not sure which options to install, this is a good base install of most elements.

Portable   This type installs fewer components, but it includes a number of communication tools left out of the typical install, including Dial-Up Networking.

Compact   The no-frills install. It installs a minimal set of options.

Custom   The technician's special. It allows you to go in and choose exactly which components you want and which you don't from the component groups. Each group generally has a number of options included with it, and you can choose to install all, some, or none of any component group. The component groups are Accessibility (used to install options for those with mobility, hearing, or visual impairments), Accessories, Communications, Desktop Themes, Internet Tools, Microsoft Outlook Express, Multilanguage Support, Multimedia, Online Services, System Tools, and Web TV for Windows.

If a box is checked, all components for that group will be installed. If it is clear, none will be. If the box is gray, only some of the components will be installed. To see exactly which components are selected, use the Details button (see Figure 3.20).

FIGURE 3.20   The component check boxes

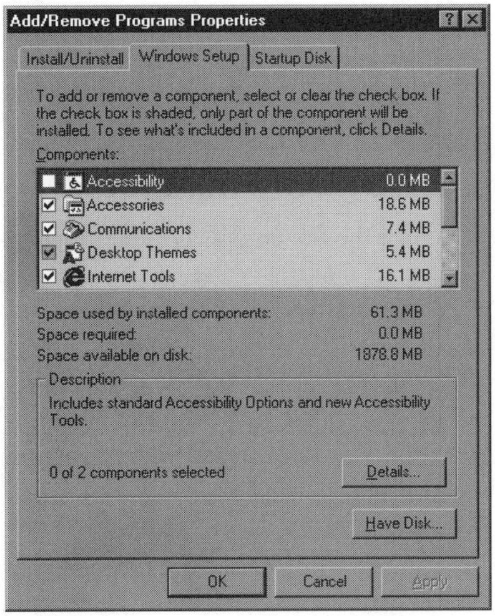

Once you have selected your components, you will be asked for a computer name, a workgroup, and a description of the machine. The computer name can be up to 15 characters with no spaces, as can the workgroup name. The Description field can be longer and can include spaces. Their functions are as follows:

Computer Name   Used to uniquely identify the machine on a Microsoft network. This name cannot be the same as any other machine's computer name.

Workgroup   Used to organize computers, a workgroup is a group of machines that participate in a loose grouping on the network. If your workgroup name is different than everyone else's, you will be the only person in that workgroup.

Description   Simply a text field in which you can describe what the machine is, where the machine is, or why the machine is. It can also be left blank.

Once these fields have been filled in, Setup confirms keyboard layout and regional settings, as well as country or regional information. You are then given the opportunity to make a Windows 98 startup disk. As this is an upgrade, you may not have a Windows 98 startup disk, and this is an excellent time to create one. Click Next past the first screen, and then either OK or Cancel, depending on whether you need a 98 startup disk or not. If you choose to create one, place a floppy into the A: drive. Any data already on this disk will be completely erased.

After you have completed the startup disk screens, the "collecting information about your computer" phase of the installation is over. The next phase of the install begins immediately.

Copying Windows 98 Files to Your Computer

Not a lot happens during this phase, at least as far as user interaction. Files will copy from the CD to the hard drive, and during this time, Microsoft marketing information about various Windows 98 features will be displayed to keep you occupied. This is an excellent time to wander off and make coffee.

Restarting Your Computer

Once the file copy is complete, you will be asked to reboot the machine. If you are off making coffee, as recommended, the Setup program will simply reboot for you after a 15-second delay.

Setting Up Hardware and Finalizing Settings

During the reboot, Windows collects information about the hardware installed in the machine, exactly as it did during an installation under Windows 95. Plug-and-Play devices are listed and activated if possible. Setup will load and test drivers to detect other hardware.

Once your hardware has been detected, you will be given the chance to specify driver locations for any devices that are not supported out of the box by Windows 98.

If you are upgrading, Windows 98 will generally find and use the device drivers that were in use under Windows 95. This is good, in that it makes for an easy install, but you should check vendor Web sites to see if they have updated Windows 98 drivers. If so, you will need to upgrade to the new driver.

Once Windows has detected and installed drivers for all of the hardware it can find, it will reboot a second time in order to initialize the new configuration and present your Desktop.

Windows 98 Setup

After the reboot, you're almost there. You can be pretty sure that you are nearing the end of the setup when you see in the Windows 98 Setup window that the basic settings for each of the following are being configured:

    Control Panel

    Programs on the Start Menu

    Windows Help

    MS-DOS Program Settings

    Tuning up Application Start

    System Configuration

These are user-based settings that are configured for each user the first time they use Windows 98. Windows 98 sets up the Desktop and other user-specific system elements according to the system defaults, after which point you are presented with a Windows 98 Desktop.

That didn't hurt at all, now, did it? Of course, the setup was completed without any problems, too, which always helps. For more information about what to do when the setup doesn't go so well, check out Chapter 9.

If the computer seems to start up fine but Windows 9x doesn't function properly, try rebooting in *Safe mode*. This mode of operation loads Windows 98 with a minimal set of drivers and can help you determine if the problem is hardware or software related. To boot the computer, turn it on and press the F8 key when you see the words *Starting Windows 98*. Doing so will present you with a list of boot-up choices, the third of which is Boot Computer in Safe Mode. Select this option (number 3) and press Enter. When Windows 98 comes up, it will be running in Safe mode, indicated by the words *Safe Mode* in all four corners of the screen. You can then check on drivers, conflicts, and so on and make changes to the configuration as needed. To exit Safe mode, restart the computer. If you have fixed the problem, upon reboot, the computer will be operating normally. For more on Safe mode, see Chapter 9 on troubleshooting.

Configuring Windows 9x Software

Once you have the system up and running, you may want to know just what you have installed. Windows 95 and Windows 98 are pretty much identical under the hood, so we will simply look at this as a 9x discussion.

Because Windows 9x is a very different operating system than Windows 3.x (which it replaced), most of its configuration is done using different tools than were used in Windows 3.x. Even so, Windows 9x shares a few configuration similarities with its ancestors (Windows 3.x and DOS) for compatibility's sake. The AUTOEXEC.BAT and CONFIG.SYS are used to a limited extent, but they're not needed and remain only for older hardware and software compatibility. Additionally, INI files are still used for some Windows programs (generally, older 32-bit apps) to hold configuration settings.

The Registry was completely overhauled between Windows 3.1 and Windows 95 and has taken the place of most INI files. In addition to software extension information, it also contains software configuration information and hardware configuration information. Generally speaking, most of the Windows 9x settings that were previously stored in INI files are now stored in the Registry.

Let's discuss some Windows 9*x* configuration files and the tools used to edit them.

Important System Files

There are a number of files stored in the root of C:, as well as in the WINDOWS directory, which can be used to modify your system's configuration and affect how your computer works. Some of the files listed in the following subsections are critical to the functioning of a Windows 9*x* computer, whereas others are simply holdovers from earlier operating systems.

Due to the fact that the Registry actually handles most of the startup tasks in Windows 9*x*, many system files are there mostly for compatibility with older programs. Because of that, you may never use them. Regardless, many of these obsolete files are listed in CompTIA's test objectives, so you need to know about them!

Examining the Windows 9*x* Boot Process

First, let's look at the process you use when you boot the system. When Windows 9*x* first starts up, it goes through a number of steps before presenting you with a Desktop. The basic elements of a Windows 9*x* startup are as follows:

- *System self-checks and enumerates hardware resources.* Each machine has a different startup routine, called the POST (power on self-test), which is executed by the commands written to the motherboard of the computer. Newer Plug-and-Play boards not only check memory and processors, they also poll the systems for other devices and peripherals.

- *MBR loads and finds the boot sector.* Once the system has finished with its housekeeping, the master boot record is located on the first hard drive and loaded into memory. The MBR finds the bootable partition and searches it for the boot sector of that partition. Information in the boot sector allows the system to locate the root directory of C: and to find and load into memory the IO.SYS file located there.

- *IO.SYS loads into memory and starts the processor in real mode.* The IO.SYS file performs a number of tasks, each of which is done in real mode. Real mode is simply a method of accessing the processor in 16-bit mode. Drivers loaded through the CONFIG.SYS file therefore can continue to function in real mode even after the next step, unless they are replaced by 32-bit Windows drivers. The IO.SYS file performs the following tasks:

  - Provides basic file system access to allow the rest of the boot files to be found

  - Accesses the MSDOS.SYS file to obtain boot configuration parameters

- ▪ Loads `LOGO.SYS` (Windows bitmap display) and `DRVSPACE.BIN` (compressed drive access) if they are present and needed
- ▪ Loads the Registry file `SYSTEM.DAT` into memory, but does not access it
- ▪ Selects a hardware profile (or allows the user to)
- ▪ Processes the commands in the `CONFIG.SYS` and `AUTOEXEC.BAT` files if they are present

- ▪ *WIN.COM loads and transfers the processor to protected mode.* Once the `AUTOEXEC.BAT` file is parsed and processed, the `WIN.COM` file is automatically executed. This file then loads various drivers as instructed by the Registry. It also examines the `SYSTEM.INI` and `WIN.INI` files to obtain additional configuration information. Once the Registry files have been loaded, the processor is transferred into 32-bit protected mode.

- ▪ *Virtual device drivers, the Windows kernel, and the GDI load.* Once the system is in 32-bit mode, various 32-bit virtual device drivers load to manage hardware resources, often replacing 16-bit real-mode drivers. The Windows kernel, which controls access to the processor from Windows 9x, is loaded into memory, and once the graphical display interface (GDI) loads to manage screen I/O, the system is ready to accept customers.

- ▪ *The Explorer shell loads and the user is presented with a Desktop.* The last part of the boot process is the loading of the "shell" program: `EXPLORER.EXE`. The Explorer is the program that manages the graphical interface—the toolbar, the Desktop, and the Start menu. Once this loads, network connections are restored and programs in the `STARTUP` folder are run, all of which is determined by settings read out of the `USER.DAT` Registry settings for that user.

Listing the Important Files

Among the things you will have to be familiar with in preparation for the A+ exam are the startup and system files used by Windows 9x. We will now look at each of these individually, but Windows makes nosing around in the startup environment difficult, and as such there is a change you'll need to make first.

To protect them from accidental deletion, and to simply get them out of the way of the average user, Windows 9x system files are hidden from the user by default. Because of this, many of the files we are about to talk about will not be visible to you. To change this, you will need to change the display properties of the Windows Explorer. To do so, follow these steps:

1. Open the Windows Explorer.
2. Browse to the root of the C: drive. Look for the `IO.SYS` system file. It should be hidden and will not appear in the file list.
3. Choose View ➢ Folder Options. The Folder Options window opens.

4. Select the View tab, and scroll until you find the Hidden Files option (see Figure 3.21).

FIGURE 3.21 The Explorer View options

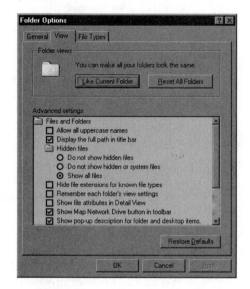

5. Select Show All Files.

6. Also uncheck the Hide File Extensions for Known File Types box.

7. Click OK. You will now be able to see the IO.SYS file and the others discussed in the following sections. For security, you should set these attributes back after you've read this chapter.

Startup Files

We discussed a number of files in the section "Examining the Windows 9*x* Boot Process." Now we will take a minute to explain each one further (there is an asterisk next to the names of the files that are required to boot Windows 9*x*):

MSDOS.SYS* Functions primarily to handle disk I/O, hence the name *disk operating system (DOS)*. Just like IO.SYS, MSDOS.SYS is loaded into memory at bootup and remains in memory at all times.

EMM386.EXE Provides the operating system with a mechanism to see additional memory. The memory space that EMM386.EXE controls has come to be known as *upper memory*, and the spaces occupied by programs in that region are known as *upper memory blocks (UMBs)*.

HIMEM.SYS Used to access upper memory.

IO.SYS* Allows the rest of the operating system and its programs to interact directly with the system hardware and the system BIOS. IO.SYS includes hardware drivers for common hardware devices. It has built-in drivers for such things as printer ports, serial or communication ports, floppy drives, hard drives, auxiliary ports, console I/O (input and output), and so on.

WIN.INI Sets particular values corresponding to the Windows environment. It's used extensively by 16-bit Windows 3.*x* applications; it's almost entirely replaced by the Registry for Windows 9*x* 32-bit apps.

WIN.COM* Initiates the Windows 9*x* protected load phase.

SYSTEM.INI Used in DOS and Windows 3.1 to store information specific to running the operating system. This and other INI files were used to configure 16-bit DOS and Windows apps.

COMMAND.COM Called the *DOS shell* or the *command interpreter*. It provides the command-line interface that the DOS user sees. This is usually, but not always, the C:\> prompt.

CONFIG.SYS Loads device drivers and uses the information from the AUTOEXEC.BAT to configure the system environment. Memory management tools and DOS peripheral drivers can be added here.

AUTOEXEC.BAT Used to run particular programs during startup. Also declares variables (such as search paths).

A batch file, named with a .bat extension, is simply a set of commands that Windows can execute or run. These commands may run utilities, or they may point toward full-blown applications. The AUTOEXEC.BAT is a batch file that is automatically executed when the system starts up.

Startup Files Configuration Tools

There are a number of ways to modify the INI files on a Windows 9*x* machine. First, you can open up a copy of Notepad, or the text editor of your choice, and go to town. This is still probably the most common method of modifying INI configuration files. If you prefer to have things a bit easier, though, there are a couple of tools provided with Windows 9*x* for dealing with these files. Both Windows 95 and Windows 98 allow you to use a tool called SYSEDIT.EXE to modify certain files, and Windows 98 has added MSCONFIG.EXE as well.

SYSEDIT

To run SYSEDIT, choose Start ➢ Run and type **SYSEDIT** at the prompt. You will see a window with a number of key configuration files open, as shown in Figure 3.22.

FIGURE 3.22 Main SYSEDIT window

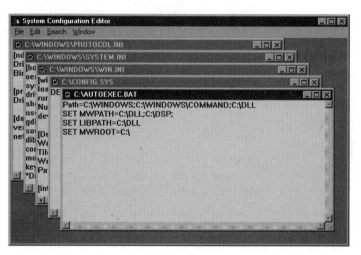

From here, you can examine, compare, and if needed, modify any of these files. All that the SYSEDIT program really does is open multiple text editors, each of which has one of the key text files in it.

SYSEDIT can be used to view and edit the PROTOCOL.INI, SYSTEM.INI, WIN.INI, CONFIG.SYS, and AUTOEXEC.BAT files.

MSCONFIG

Provided as a new addition to Windows 98, the System Configuration Utility is accessed by opening a Run window and typing **MSCONFIG**. The System Configuration Utility has a number of tabs, each of which has specific options you can manage (see Figure 3.23).

FIGURE 3.23   The System Configuration Utility

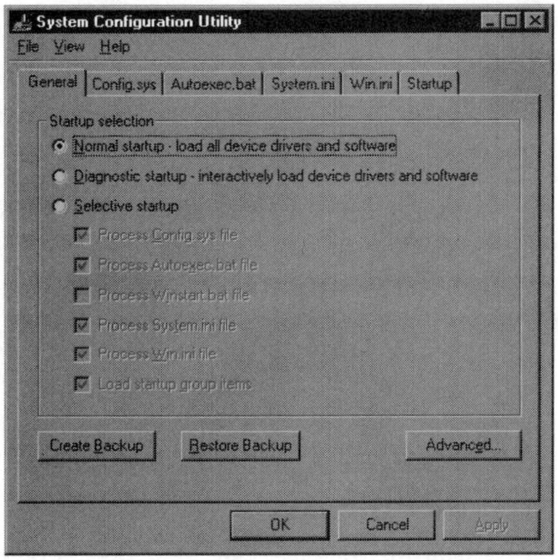

The thing that makes the System Configuration Utility different is that it lets you use your mouse to browse and modify settings that previously were accessible only through manual text configuration. You can also enable or disable Windows 98–specific elements, such as those shown in Figure 3.24. The MSCONFIG utility therefore merges Windows 98 configuration info with a way for non–DOS savvy users to work with DOS-era configuration files. Table 3.4 lists the tabs on the System Configuration Utility window.

FIGURE 3.24   The Advanced window from the SCU's General tab

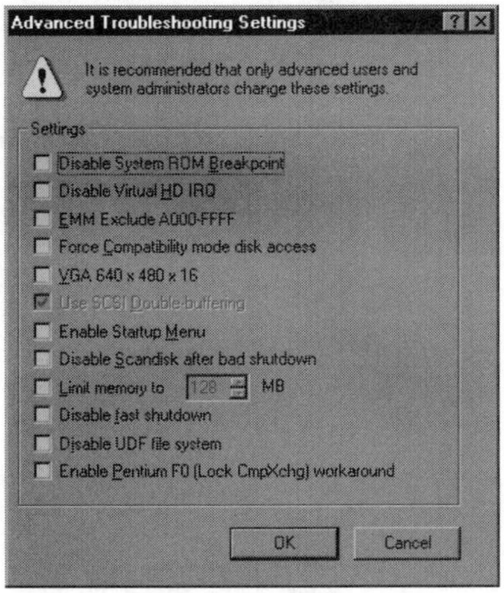

TABLE 3.4   System Configuration Utility Tabs

Tab	Function
General	Used to set startup options, as well as to determine which files to load during startup
Config.sys	Used to graphically view and edit the CONFIG.SYS file
Autoexec.bat	Used to graphically view and edit the AUTOEXEC.BAT file
System.ini	Allows you to modify the SYSTEM.INI file using a Registry-type interface
Win.ini	Allows you to modify the WIN.INI file using a Registry-type interface
Startup	Can be used to enable or disable particular startup options

Note that in the copy of Notepad in Figure 3.25, the contents of the AUTOEXEC.BAT file are displayed. The Autoexec.bat tab of the System Configuration Utility shows the same information. If you uncheck the last item and then reopen the AUTOEXEC.BAT file, the REM statement is added to block the execution of a line without actually deleting the command, in case you need it again later (Figure 3.26). This is very useful for troubleshooting.

FIGURE 3.25   The AUTOEXEC.BAT file before modification

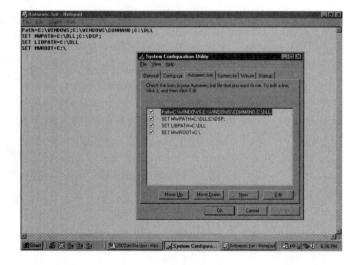

FIGURE 3.26   The AUTOEXEC.BAT file after modification

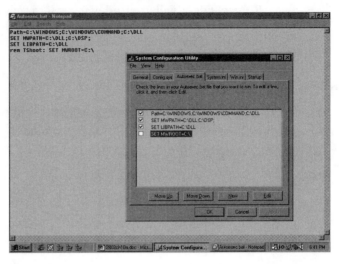

The Windows 9x Registry

The two major types of configuration files are the INI files and the Registry. The INI files are still used in Windows 9x, but as previously mentioned, they have less responsibility. The Registry, on the other hand, is used almost exclusively for holding configuration settings. It holds them not only for applications, but also for the system itself. Additionally, it contains different settings for different users.

The Windows 9x Registry is a database that is made up of two files: USER.DAT and SYSTEM.DAT. USER.DAT contains environmental settings for each user who logs in to Windows 9x. SYSTEM.DAT contains information about the hardware configuration of the computer that Windows is running on.

You can also create a third file—CONFIG.POL—which you can configure to specify particular security settings for a particular user or group of users. This file is used to "lock down" the Windows 9x interface so a user can't change it (useful if you have a user who is constantly changing their settings and messing up their computer). The CONFIG.POL file is created and edited with a utility called the Policy Editor, which is available on the Windows 95 and 98 installation CD-ROM. Normally you do not need to modify the system using the Policy Editor unless you are managing a network environment.

USER.DAT and SYSTEM.DAT cannot be edited with a text editor because they aren't ASCII text files (like AUTOEXEC.BAT, CONFIG.SYS, or the INI files). To edit the Windows 95 Registry, you need to use a tool specifically designed for that purpose: the aptly named Registry Editor (REGEDIT.EXE).

To start the editor, choose Start ≻ Run and type **REGEDIT**. Click OK and the Registry Editor will open, allowing you to view the Registry. The screen shown in Figure 3.27 shows a typical Registry. On the left side of this screen you will see the areas of the Registry. Each area (called a *key*) contains different types of settings. Table 3.5 explains these six keys and their functions.

FIGURE 3.27 A typical REGEDIT screen

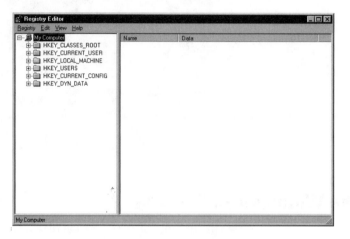

 If you make changes to the Registry, you will have to reboot your computer to have them take effect. The Registry is loaded into memory at start up.

TABLE 3.5 Registry Keys and Their Functions

Key	Description
HKEY_CLASSES_ROOT	Contains file extension associations. This tells Windows when a file with a particular extension should be opened in a particular application. Much of the data in this key is duplicated in the HKEY_LOCAL_ MACHINE key.

TABLE 3.5   Registry Keys and Their Functions *(continued)*

Key	Description
HKEY_CURRENT_USER	Contains user profile information for the person currently logged in to Windows. It contains the preferences for color settings and Desktop configuration. It is a subset of the HKEY_USERS key (described below).
HKEY_LOCAL_MACHINE	Contains settings and information for the hardware that is installed in the computer. When troubleshooting hardware issues, you might make changes to this section.
HKEY_USERS	Contains the default user profile and the profile for the current user (HKEY_CURRENT_USER, described above).
HKEY_CURRENT_CONFIG	Contains the current hardware configuration. This key is a subset of the HKEY_LOCAL_MACHINE (described above).
HKEY_DYN_DATA	Contains the dynamic settings for any Plug-and-Play devices in your computer. This setting is kept in RAM and doesn't require a reboot when changes are made to it.

Whenever you need to make changes to the Registry, open REGEDIT. The next step is to locate the subkey (the folders underneath the keys shown) that contains the setting you want to change. You can find it two ways. You can browse to it by clicking the plus sign (+) next to a folder to display the subkeys inside. Keep clicking until you find the subkey you're looking for. This can take a while because there may be several hundred folders to browse through. The other method is much more logical. In REGEDIT, select Edit ➢ Find (Figure 3.28). Then type in the string of characters you are looking for and click Find Next. REGEDIT will search the database until it comes across a string that matches what you typed in. If it isn't the entry you are looking for, press F3 to find the next entry that contains the string.

FIGURE 3.28 Performing a Find in REGEDIT

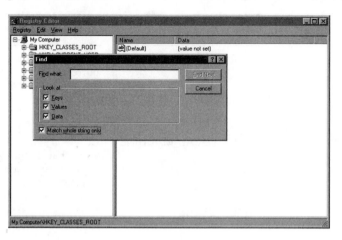

Thankfully, there aren't many times you need to go into the Registry to make changes. Most often, when you use the Windows 9*x* configuration utilities to make changes, changes will be made to the Registry as well. Let's discuss three of the tools that allow you to make these changes: the Properties menu option, the Control Panels, and the Device Manager.

And Now for the Real World...

If it's not apparent by now, the Registry is very important for correct Windows 9*x* operation. That's why every time Windows 9*x* successfully loads the Registry, it makes a backup of the two Registry files: USER.DAT and SYSTEM.DAT. These backup files are called USER.DA0 and SYSTEM.DA0, respectively, and can be used to restore a good Registry over one that's broken. In case of a Registry corruption, boot in Safe Mode Command Line by pressing F8 at system start up and choosing Safe Mode Command Line. Or boot to a Windows 9*x* startup disk. Then change the extension of the Registry files from .dao to .dat and reboot the computer. The Registry will be current as of the last successful boot.

Managing Hardware in Windows 9*x*

Configuring your software is just half of the work you have to deal with when working on Windows 9*x*. The system's hardware can also be configured, and there are a number of tools and options for letting you install, update, and configure your system. We will first look at how you can examine the hardware that is installed on your machine, and then we'll examine how to install a new device.

Device Manager

The *Device Manager* is a graphical view of all the hardware installed in your computer that Windows 9*x* has detected. You can open it by right-clicking My Computer, choosing Properties, then clicking the Device Manager tab. Or you can open the System Control Panel program (from Start ➢ Settings ➢ Control Panel) and choose Device Manager. In either case, you will see a screen similar to the one in Figure 3.29.

FIGURE 3.29   An example of a Device Manager screen

As you can see, one of the devices (COM 2) is marked with a red *X*. That is because the COM 2 port needed to be disabled so that the modem (which is installed to use COM 2) can use it.

The Device Manager is used to display all the hardware that Windows 9*x* "knows about" and to configure the hardware settings of those devices. If you click the plus sign (+) next to a category of devices, it will "tree out" that category and allow you to see the devices in the category. If you then click a device and click Properties, you can view the information about that device. Figure 3.30 shows the result of selecting a network card and clicking Properties. Notice that there are three tabs: General, Driver, and Resources. Most devices will have these tabs (although some devices may have only one or two). The General tab (shown in Figure 3.30) shows general information about the device and status information. It also allows you disable the device in the current hardware profile.

FIGURE 3.30 Displaying the properties of a device in the Device Manager

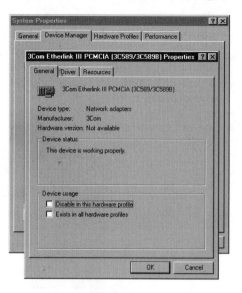

 For more information about hardware profiles, refer to either the Windows 95 or 98 Help file or the Windows 95 (or 98) Resource Kit by Microsoft. Don't worry, hardware profiles aren't covered on the exam.

Updating a Device's Properties or Driver

The next tab is usually the Driver tab (Figure 3.31). This tab allows you to see the driver name for the device as well as the driver version, if available. You can see in the figure that no drivers have been loaded for this device, or the drivers specified for the device are not compatible. If you need to load a driver (or update a driver), click the Update Driver button. Windows 9*x* will present you with a list of drivers to select from or allow you to install your own from floppy disk or CD-ROM. If you have upgraded to Windows 98 from Windows 95, you may find that a number of updated Windows 98 drivers are available on vendor Web sites.

FIGURE 3.31   The Driver tab of a device in the Device Manager

    To add drivers available on the Web, you usually must download the compressed driver files and then expand them onto a floppy disk or into a hard drive folder. At that point, you can run the update, and point to the location you extracted the files to. My personal favorite is www.windrivers.com.

The rightmost tab is usually Resources. From this tab, you can view and configure the system resources that the device is using (Figure 3.32). Most often, the check box next to Use Automatic Settings is checked, meaning that Windows 9*x* Plug-and-Play has determined the settings for the device and is managing it. However, if the device is not a Plug-and-Play device and needs to be configured manually, simply uncheck the Use Automatic Settings check box. You can then select the setting (for example, the Interrupt Request) and click the Change Setting button to pick the correct setting from a list. When you configure settings manually, Windows 9*x* will let you know if the setting you have chosen conflicts with another device. However, if you are in Safe mode, this feature can't be used and Windows 9*x* will not tell you.

FIGURE 3.32 The Resources tab of a device in the Device Manager

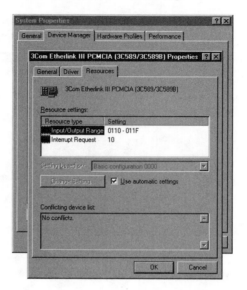

 Occasionally, Windows will not automatically detect a device that you have installed. In such a case, you will have to install the device manually. To learn about more complex peripheral device installs, refer to Chapter 6.

Windows 9x Management

Once you have the system configured and running, you may also want to go in and optimize certain settings. We will be focusing on three areas in which you can view and modify the Windows system to (potentially!) improve performance:

- Disk management
- Resource monitoring
- DOS application management

Disk Management

Several configuration settings that previously had to be manually adjusted are now automatic with Windows 9x. Among the most notable of these settings are the swap file and disk drive caching. There are essentially just three resources that a computer operating system needs to manage: processor, memory, and disk drives. Two of these three are managed completely automatically in Windows 9x. The third, disk drives, affects how both of the others perform, though, and can be configured in a number of ways.

Virtual Memory

The swap file is used to provide "virtual memory" to the Windows 9x system. What this means is that the swap file is hard drive space that idle pieces of programs are placed in, while other active parts of programs are kept in or swapped into main memory. The programs running within Windows believe that their information is still in RAM, but Windows has simply moved it into "near-line" storage on the hard drive. When the application needs the information again, it is "swapped" back into RAM so that it can be used by the processor. When you are working in your office and need a document, you may have to walk over to a file cabinet to get it. You then return to your seat and read the document. When you have finished and need to go on with another task, you need to put down the current document. If you don't need it again in the near future, you should get up and put it back in the file cabinet. If you will be needing it again, though, you may just set it on your desk for easier access. As with a document, though, when you need it again you do still have to pick it back up (unless you can remember what it said without looking again). Generally, you can think of a computer's disk drive as the file cabinet and virtual memory as the desk. Real memory (RAM) is the computer's memory. The more RAM you put into the machine, the more things it is able to remember without looking anything up. The larger the swap file, the fewer times it has to do intensive drive searches.

The moral of the story: As with most things virtual, a swap file is not nearly as good as actual RAM, but it is better than nothing!

As shown Figure 3.33, the default behavior for virtual memory is that Windows 9x simply handles it for you. This is a good thing, and unless you have a particular need to modify the file, you are best served by letting the computer handle it. If a particular application does require extensive virtual memory, you can modify it easily, though. To find the Virtual Memory button, choose Start ➤ Settings ➤ Control Panel. Double-click the System icon and select the Performance tab. The Virtual Memory button is along the bottom of the window.

FIGURE 3.33 The Windows 98 Virtual Memory window

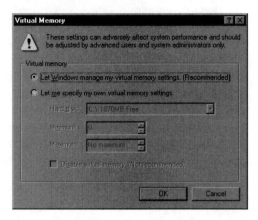

 Locate the swap file on a drive with plenty of empty space. As a general rule, try to keep 20 percent of your drive space free for the overhead of various elements of the operating system, like the swap file.

 Do not set the swap file to an extremely low size. Another general rule would be that the swap file should be at least as big as the amount of RAM in the machine. If you make the swap file too small, the system can become unbootable, or at least unstable.

Disk Caching

Disk caching in Windows 9x is no longer handled by SMARTDRIVE, as it was in earlier versions of Windows. Instead, Windows 9x uses a 32-bit caching program called VCACHE, originally introduced with Windows 3.11. This protected-mode driver runs more efficiently than its real-mode predecessor, SMARTDRIVE. It uses a more efficient set of rules for predicting the needed hard drive data. Further, it caches data from the network and from the CD-ROM; thus it is able to speed up the access to data from these devices.

Disk Conversion

Because many users upgraded their systems to Windows 98 from Windows 3.1 or Windows 95 Rev. A, they did not have the opportunity to choose between FAT16 and FAT32 because those earlier systems only supported FAT16. Because of this, you may want to convert their existing drives to the newer, faster file system using the Drive Converter utility. This utility is located in the Start ➢ Programs ➢ Accessories ➢ System Tools folder and will convert a partition from FAT16 to FAT32 without destroying the information that is on it.

Although conversion generally works without a hitch, a power outage or accidental shutdown during the conversion could be *very* bad. Make sure to back up all crucial files before the conversion!

Disk Compression

The disk compression utility that comes with Windows 9x is still called DriveSpace, but unlike the earlier DriveSpace, it is now a protected-mode driver with faster performance. Older drives that have been doubled in space by using DriveSpace or DoubleSpace should be switched to the new protected-mode version. DriveSpace is automatically loaded, but not activated, when Windows 9x is installed.

Microsoft has been improving compression over time. Windows 95 used an awful system with a .CSV file and a host drive (usually H:) to compress information. Windows 98 does much the same, but uses an advanced utility called DriveSpace3 which allows you to set compression levels and to compress just parts of a drive. Both the Windows 95 and Windows 98 compression utilities work well enough, but they are difficult to understand and use and have limits. Only FAT16 drives can be compressed, and as FAT partitions under 9x can only be 2GB, that means any partition over 2GB cannot be compressed. Moreover, the FAT system itself is relatively inefficient because of its larger cluster sizes on bigger drives. Often a user can free up a lot of space on a FAT drive simply by converting it to FAT32. Refer to the next chapter for more advanced compression options in Windows 2000.

Resource Monitoring

Sometimes you just need to know a bit about what a machine is running, and what its current configuration settings are, before you start to reconfigure it. To do this, there are a couple of key utilities that you can gather information through.

Microsoft System Information

This is a great tool! It gives you a ton of information—everything from the username and swap file information to detailed displays of the exact resource usage of a particular device. You can't modify anything using this tool, so there isn't much else to say, but it is a great troubleshooting/configuration snooping utility (see Figure 3.34). The following categories are available for browsing:

- Hardware Resources
- Components
- Software Environment
- Applications

FIGURE 3.34 MS System Information Display info

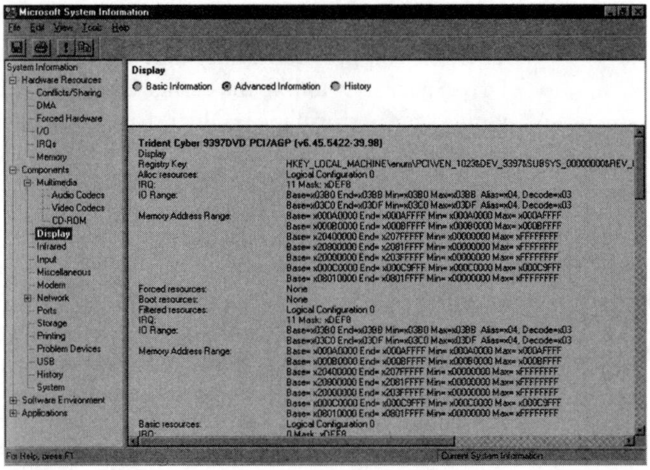

System Monitor

If you are interested in finding out what effect a particular application has on a Windows 9x system, you can use the System Monitor to plot key system resources in real time. Each resource you choose to monitor will be given a separate line that you can watch. In Figure 3.35, for instance, you can see that the Reads/second (in blue) spiked when a Word document was opened from the hard drive.

FIGURE 3.35 Watching resource usage with System Monitor

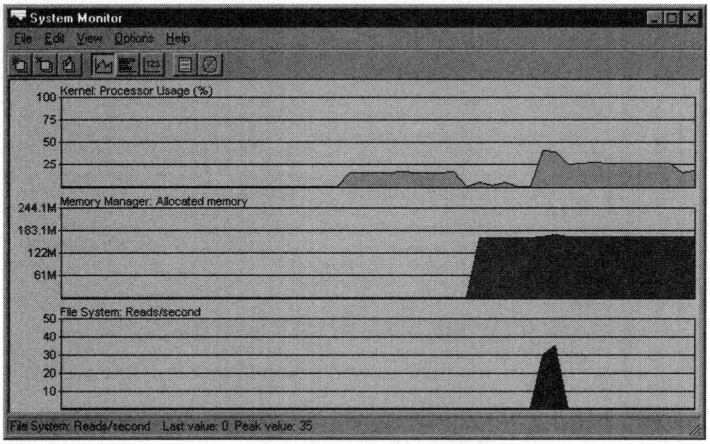

The general categories you can monitor include the following:

- Disk Cache
- File System
- Kernel
- Memory Manager
- Microsoft Network Client

Each of these categories then has specific counters beneath them that allow you to monitor particular elements. You can even change the polling interval from the default 5 seconds if you would like more specific results.

For a quick look at system resources, you can also just open up the Resource Meter (also in the SYSTEM TOOLS folder). It has just three counters—System resources, User resources, and GDI resources. Also, it shows you what is *free*, whereas the System Monitor shows you what is *used*. The Resource Meter is shown in Figure 3.36.

FIGURE 3.36 The Resource Meter

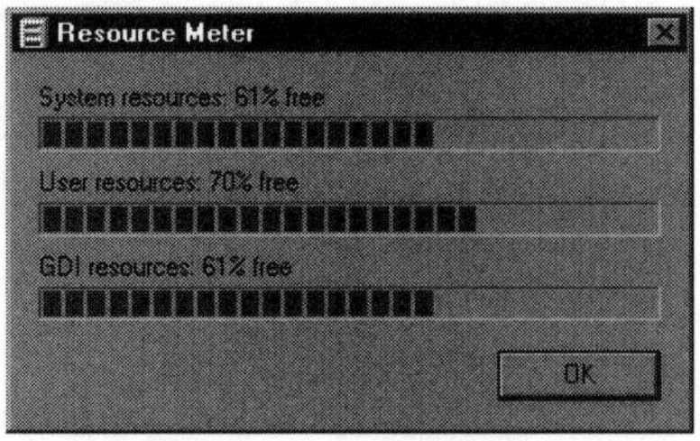

The Joy That Is Shareware

If, for some reason, you decide that the tools provided with Windows 9x simply aren't right for the exact problem you are having, it's no one's fault but your own if you don't find a better utility. The unending river of free or inexpensive utilities available is actually enough to dwarf all but the most active imaginations. If you need it, head out to www.download.com or www.tucows.com, and it's probably there. Rarely are any of us blessed with a truly unique problem, and there are lots of folks out there producing nifty solutions to your problems.

DOS Optimization

Compatibility with older programs is important because people have a significant investment in the money spent on their programs and in their time learning how to use them. Microsoft built a number of features into Windows 9x that allow previous users of DOS and Windows 3.x to capitalize on their investment and that allow technicians access to DOS-based troubleshooting.

According to Microsoft (see, for example, the Microsoft Windows 95 Resource Kit), memory management for conventional memory while running the Windows 9x operating system is the same as for MS-DOS 6.x. This applies to the management of conventional memory only because all other memory management in Windows 9x is essentially automatic. If 16-bit DOS and 16-bit Windows 3.x programs are not even going to be used, then these techniques are not necessary.

If you do need to use DOS/Windows 3.1 "real-mode" programs, you have three options:

- The user can initiate a DOS shell from inside of Windows 9x. This Virtual DOS Machine (VDM) is actually a 32-bit Windows application that emulates a DOS environment.

- The user can exit from Windows 9x into DOS mode. To do this, simply choose Start ➢ Shut Down ➢ Restart in MS-DOS Mode. Any programs you are currently running will be shut down and a DOS session will be opened. The advantage of this is that some DOS applications require actual control of the computer, and will not work through a VDM.

- In some cases, the user can boot the computer straight into DOS. This requires having a copy of MS-DOS installed on the machine and using a dual-boot scenario, with Windows 9*x* installed and DOS coexisting as a totally different, stand-alone system.

In any of these cases, special configuration tasks can potentially make DOS/3.1 programs function more efficiently. To maximize available memory for real-mode programs, load the extended memory manager, HIMEM.SYS, and the expanded memory manager, EMM386, in the CONFIG.SYS file. If possible, remove the real-mode drivers from the AUTOEXEC.BAT file and utilize the protected-mode drivers that are built into Windows 9*x*. You should not load SMARTDRIVE because the VCACHE disk caching that comes with Windows 9*x* is superior and does not detract from conventional memory.

MEMMAKER, which came with DOS 6.2*x*, is found on the Windows 9*x* CD in the directory OTHER\OLDDOS. MEMMAKER may be used to optimize the CONFIG.SYS and AUTOEXEC.BAT files for conventional memory.

 If you want to dual-boot to DOS, you must use the FAT file system and keep your C: partition below 2GB; FAT32 and partition sizes over 2GB are not supported by DOS. Don't worry about this too much, though, because finding a machine that is still running DOS 6.*x* or lower is extremely rare. Because Windows 95 (DOS 7) and 98 (DOS32) support DOS applications well enough in most cases and have far more functionality, "real" 6.*x* and earlier DOS has largely gone the way of the Atari 2600 and laserdiscs.

Summary

So that was Windows 9*x* in a nutshell. We have looked at the hardware requirements of Windows 95 and 98, how they are installed, and what is involved in an upgrade. We have also examined the Windows 9*x* boot process, and the files needed to start the system. Past that, we looked at the tools provided by Microsoft to view and configure Windows 9*x* and the hardware of the computer it is running on.

Installing Windows 9*x* starts with creating a startup disk and preparing the drive using the FDISK and FORMAT commands. At that point, you boot to the CD (or the network) and run the SETUP.EXE program that starts the Windows 9*x* install routine. You then work through the interactive Setup Wizard and provide information as needed.

Upgrading to Windows 98 from Windows 95 is pretty straightforward and usually involves little more than putting the CD into a CD-ROM drive and running Setup. You will be presented with a wizard that allows you to keep your current configuration even as you upgrade to the newer OS and update your file system to FAT32.

Understanding the boot process is crucial to knowing what is going on if errors occur during start up, and as such, we looked at the files needed for a Windows 9x machine to start and how system start up occurs, including what some of those files are and what they do.

Once the machine is up and running, getting it to run better, or to support certain applications, may require additional configuration. Tools such as the Registry Editor and Device Manager facilitate this, as do configuration options such as the Virtual Memory settings.

Last, some older DOS/Windows 3.1 programs require additional support, such as DOS mode. These applications often use configurations that must be specifically customized for them.

With this chapter, we have looked at one of the big two Microsoft operating systems. Next up is Windows 9x's younger—and stronger—brother, Windows 2000.

Key Terms

Before you take the exam, be certain you are familiar with the following terms:

Active Directory	extended partition
allocation unit	File Allocation Table (FAT)
cluster	key
Device Manager	logical partitions
disk operating system (DOS)	primary partition
DOS shell	Safe mode
driver	upper memory blocks (UMBs)

Review Questions

1. Which of the following is not a requirement of installing Windows 95?

   A. 386DX or higher processor

   B. 2MB of memory

   C. 50–55MB free hard disk space

   D. One 3½-inch disk drive

   E. CD-ROM

   F. VGA video card or better

   G. Mouse and keyboard

2. Which of the following is not a requirement to install Windows 98?

   A. 386 or higher processor; Pentium recommended

   B. 8MB of memory; 16 to 32MB recommended

   C. 120MB free hard disk space

   D. One 3½-inch disk drive

   E. CD-ROM

   F. VGA or better video card

   G. Mouse and keyboard is required

3. A real-mode driver is one that _____ .

   A. Directly accesses hardware

   B. Indirectly accesses hardware

   C. Is software configurable

   D. Is a 32-bit Windows driver

4. What is the first step when installing Windows 9*x* onto a system that doesn't already have a functioning operating system?

   A. Formatting

   B. Partitioning

   C. Redirecting

   D. Installing the operating system

5. The DOS command that partitions the hard drive is called what?

   A. `FORMAT.EXE`

   B. `XCOPY.EXE`

   C. `FDISK.EXE`

   D. `FDISK.COM`

6. When a drive is partitioned, what is the first partition that is created called?

   A. Secondary partition

   B. Extended partition

   C. Expanded partition

   D. Primary partition

7. How many primary and extended partitions can be created using the Windows 95 FDISK utility?

   A. Two

   B. Three

   C. One

   D. Four

8. Which option on the FDISK utility allows you to select the hard drive and appears only when there is more than one physical hard drive?

   A. First option

   B. Second option

   C. Third option

   D. Fifth option

9. Which of the following is not performed by formatting the hard drive?

   A. Formatting scans the surface of the hard drive platter to find bad spots and marks the areas surrounding a bad spot as bad sectors.

   B. High-level formatting lays down magnetic tracks in concentric circles.

   C. The tracks are split into pieces of 512 bytes called sectors.

   D. Low-level formatting creates a file allocation table that contains information about the location of files.

10. A drive between 16MB and 128MB will have how many sectors per cluster?

    A. One

    B. Four

    C. Three

    D. Five

11. Drives up to 1,024MB will have how many sectors per cluster?

    A. 24

    B. 36

    C. 32

    D. 45

12. When you use a Windows 98 boot disk when the machine first starts up, what is the first option?

    A. Boot with CD-ROM support or without it.

    B. Boot from a floppy disk.

    C. Boot from the hard drive.

    D. Format the hard drive.

13. What is the disadvantage of FAT32?

    A. It supports drives up to 2 terabytes.

    B. It's not compatible with older versions of DOS or with Windows 3.*x* and Windows 95 operating systems.

    C. It is compatible with all versions of DOS and other operating systems.

    D. You don't have to create multiple partitions.

14. The program that performs the Windows 9*x* installation is called _____ .

    A. INSTALL.BAT

    B. SETUP.DAT

    C. SETUP.EXE

    D. INSTALL.DAT

15. Which switch tells Windows 95's Setup program to ignore settings from your current copy of Windows?

    A. /is

    B. /it

    C. /id

    D. /d

16. Which switch causes Setup to run without a mouse?

    A. /n

    B. /l

    C. /p

    D. iq

17. The Setup Wizard will ask questions about how many main categories?

    A. One

    B. Two

    C. Three

    D. Four

18. Which of the following is not a category Setup asks questions about?
    A. Gathering information
    B. Networking information
    C. Copying files to your computer
    D. Finishing the installation

19. How many different types of setups are there?
    A. One
    B. Two
    C. Three
    D. Four

20. Which setup type allows Setup to choose the most popular options?
    A. Typical
    B. Portable
    C. Compact
    D. Custom

Answers to Review Questions

1. B. Windows 95 requires 4MB memory (and recommends 8MB).

2. A. To install Windows 98, you must have a 386DX or higher processor; Pentium is recommended.

3. A. A real-mode driver is one that directly accesses hardware, as was the standard in DOS. 32-bit Windows drivers work through the Windows system to access hardware, allowing Windows to optimize and control hardware access.

4. B. New disk drives or PCs with no operating system need to have two critical functions performed on them before they are able to be used: partitioning and formatting. These two functions are performed by using two commands, `FDISK.EXE` and `FORMAT.EXE`, which can be copied to a bootable floppy.

5. C. FDISK is usually performed on a computer that has no operating system or has a new hard drive. FDISK creates a start and an end to a section of hard drive space. At the beginning of that space, it creates a special file called the Master Boot Record, or MBR. The MBR contains the partition information about the beginning and end of the primary and extended partitions.

6. D. When a drive is partitioned, the first partition that is created is called the primary partition. The primary partition must be named drive C:, must contain the system files, and must be marked active for the system to boot up.

7. C. Only one primary and one extended partition can be created in Windows 95 using FDISK. You can have one of each; however, the extended partition can be subdivided so you can have 23 logical drives.

8. D. The fifth option on the FDISK utility allows you to select the hard drive and appears only when there is more than one physical hard drive. The fifth option is Select Hard Drive.

9. D. The file allocation table is created by high-level formatting, not low-level formatting.

10. B. A drive between 16MB and 128MB will have four sectors per cluster. Sectors on a hard drive clumped together are called clusters or allocation units. As the drive or drive partition increases in size, the number of sectors per cluster increases.

11. C. Drives up to 1,024MB will have 32 sectors per cluster. As the drive or drive partition increases in size, the number of sectors per cluster increases: 16MB to 128MB have 4 clusters, 129MB to 256MB have 8 clusters, 256MB to 512MB have 16 clusters, 512MB to 1,024MB have 32 clusters.

12. A. When you use a Windows 98 boot disk when the machine first starts up, the first option is whether to boot with CD-ROM support or without it. The default is to boot with CD-ROM support.

13. B. The disadvantage of FAT32 is that it's not compatible with older versions of DOS or with Windows 3.*x* and early Windows 95 operating systems.

14. C. The program that performs the Windows 9*x* installation is called SETUP.EXE. You cannot boot from the CD-ROM to install Windows 9*x*.

15. D. The /d switch in Windows 95 ignores the setup of your existing copy of Windows. The /id switch tells Setup to skip the disk space check, /it tells it to skip the check for Terminate and Stay Resident programs (TSR) that are known to cause problems with Windows 95 Setup, and /is skips the routine system check.

16. A. The /n switch causes Setup to run without a mouse. Use /l if you have a Logitech mouse and want it enabled during setup. The /p switch tells Setup to skip the check for any Plug-and-Play devices, and /iq tells Setup to skip the test for cross-linked devices.

17. C. The Setup Wizard will ask questions about three main categories. The three main categories are gathering information, copying files to your computer, and finishing the installation.

18. B. Setup does not ask questions about networking.

19. D . Windows 95 has four different types of setups: Typical, Portable, Compact, and Custom.

20. A. The Typical option allows Setup to choose the most popular options.

Chapter 4

Installing and Using Windows 2000 Professional

THE FOLLOWING OBJECTIVES ARE COVERED IN THIS CHAPTER:

✓ **1.1 Identify the operating system's functions, structure, and major system files to navigate the operating system and how to get to needed technical information.**

    Content may include the following:

- Major operating system functions
  - Create folders
  - Checking OS version
- Major operating system components
  - Explorer
  - My Computer
  - Control Panel
- Contrasts between Windows 9x and Windows 2000
- Major system files: what they are, where they are located, how they are used, and what they contain:

    System, configuration, and user interface files

- IO.SYS
- BOOT.INI
- WIN.COM
- MSDOS.SYS
- AUTOEXEC.BAT
- CONFIG.SYS
- COMMAND LINE PROMPT

    Memory management

- Conventional
- Extended/upper memory
- High memory

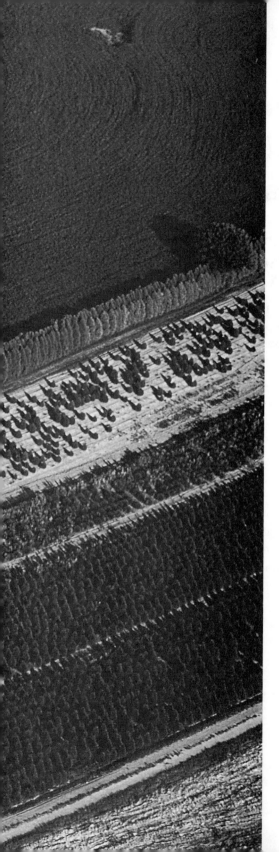

- Virtual memory
- HIMEM.SYS
- EMM386.exe

Windows 9x

- IO.SYS
- WIN.INI
- USER.DAT
- SYSEDIT
- SYSTEM.INI
- MSCONFIG (98)
- COMMAND.COM
- REGEDIT.EXE
- SYSTEM.DAT
- RUN COMMAND
- COMMAND LINE PROMPT

Windows 2000

- Computer Management
- BOOT.INI
- REGEDT32
- REGEDIT
- RUN CMD
- NTLDR
- NTDETECT.COM
- NTBOOTDD.SYS

Command Prompt Procedures (Command syntax)

- DIR
- ATTRIB
- VER
- MEM
- SCANDISK
- DEFRAG
- EDIT
- XCOPY
- COPY
- SETVER
- SCANREG

✓ **1.2 Identify basic concepts and procedures for creating, viewing, and managing files, directories, and disks. This includes procedures for changing file attributes and the ramifications of those changes (for example, security issues).**

Content may include the following:

- File attributes—Read Only, Hidden, System, and Archive attributes
- File naming conventions (most common extensions)
- Windows 2000 COMPRESS, ENCRYPT
- IDE/SCSI
- Internal/External
- Backup/Restore
- Partitioning/Formatting/File System
  - FAT
  - FAT16
  - FAT32
  - NTFS4
  - NTFS5
  - HPFS

Windows-based utilities

- ScanDisk
- Device Manager
- System Manager
- Computer Manager
- MSCONFIG.EXE
- REGEDIT.EXE (View information/backup Registry)
- REGEDT32.EXE
- ATTRIB.EXE
- EXTRACT.EXE
- DEFRAG.EXE
- EDIT.COM
- FDISK.EXE
- SYSEDIT.EXE
- SCANREG
- WSCRIPT.EXE
- HWINFO.EXE
- ASD.EXE (Automatic Skip Driver)
- Cvt1.EXE (Drive Converter FAT16 to FAT32)

✓ **2.1 Identify the procedures for installing Windows 9x and Windows 2000 for bringing the software to a basic operational level.**

Content may include the following:

- Start Up
- Partition
- Format drive
- Loading drivers
- Run appropriate set up utility

✓ **2.2 Identify steps to perform an operating system upgrade**

Content may include the following:

- Upgrading Windows 95 to Windows 98
- Upgrading Windows NT Workstation 4.0 to Windows 2000
- Upgrading Windows 9x with Windows 2000
- Dual boot Windows 9x/Windows NT 4.0/2000

✓ **2.3 Identify the basic system boot sequences and boot methods, including the steps to create an emergency boot disk with utilities installed for Windows 9x, Windows NT, and Windows 2000.**

Content may include the following:

- Startup disk
- Safe Mode
- MS-DOS mode
- NTLDR (NT Loader), BOOT.INI
- Files required to boot
- Creating emergency repair disk (ERD)

✓ **2.4 Identify procedures for loading/adding and configuring application device drivers and the necessary software for certain devices.**

Content may include the following:

- Windows 9x Plug and Play and Windows 2000
- Identify the procedures for installing and launching typical Windows and non-Windows applications (Note: there is no content related to Windows 3.1)
- Procedures for set up and configuring Windows printing subsystem.
  - Setting Default printer
  - Installing/Spool setting
  - Network printing (with help of LAN admin)

While most users will find that Windows 98 is sufficient for their needs, Microsoft does have a more powerful desktop operating system option, which we will look at over the course of this chapter. This advanced OS is called Windows 2000 Professional, and it is designed as the preferred OS for corporate users or home *power users*. The rationalization for the extra expense of Windows 2000 Pro is that it provides the following enhancements to the Windows platform:

- Advanced security
- Support for more hardware
- Greater application stability

For complete coverage of objective 1.1, please also see Chapter 2. For complete coverage of objective 2.1, please also see Chapters 3 and 6. For complete coverage of objective 2.2, please also see Chapter 3. For complete coverage of objective 2.3, please also see Chapters 3 and 7. For complete coverage of objective 2.4, please also see Chapters 3, 5 and 6.

For coverage of the Memory management subobjectives of objective 1.1, please refer to Chapter 3 of *A+: Core Module Study Guide*, the other book in this boxed set.

Over the course of this chapter we will look at these enhancements, along with examining the basic steps needed to install and configure Windows 2000 Professional. In the process, we will also look at a number of the critical files used to start and run Windows 2000.

Although the A+ objectives talk almost exclusively about Windows 9*x* and Windows 2000, you may see exam questions on Windows NT as well. Because NT and 2000 are very similar in their architecture and key files, you should be able to answer most NT questions by simply providing the answer that would be appropriate in Windows 2000. This is not always the case, however. To cover all your bases (for the exam and in the real world), you may want to read up on Windows NT a bit more before the test.

Installing Windows 2000

Windows 9*x* and Windows 2000 may look a lot alike when they are running, but one of the most important concepts you will have to deal with in becoming a computer technician is that no two operating systems are completely alike. As such, the installation process we used for Windows 9*x* is completely different than the installation process for Windows 2000. We will begin this chapter by looking into the 2000 installation process and, in doing so, cover the following topics:

- Installation requirements
- Accessing the Setup files
- Running the Setup program
- Partitioning
- Formatting
- Customizing Setup

Installation Prerequisites

As with last chapter, we will start off by looking at what you will need to consider before installing or upgrading to Windows 2000. Because of the fact that it is a "power workstation," the hardware requirements for Windows 2000 are higher than that of Windows 9*x*, and it also is less forgiving of older, less efficient software.

Hardware Requirements

The hardware requirements to install Windows 2000 Professional are actually rather low—a Pentium 133 and 32MB of RAM. Almost any machine that is still being used in a corporate environment will meet these basic requirements. More than any other OS we have looked at, though, more is better for Windows 2K, and as such your clients will be far happier with their system performance if you ensure that they have PII-class machines with 64MB–128MB of RAM.

The "recommended" levels are simply a guideline from Microsoft. Remember the hardware levels in the first column of Table 4.1 are the ones you need for the test!

TABLE 4.1   Windows 2000 Hardware Prerequisites

Hardware	Required	Recommended
Processor	Pentium 133	Pentium II or higher
Memory	64MB	128MB or higher
Free hard disk space	2GB	2GB plus what is needed for your applications and storage
Floppy disk	Required only if installing from the boot disks	Yes
CD-ROM	Required only if installing from CD	Yes
Video	VGA	SVGA
Mouse	Yes	Yes
Keyboard	Yes	Yes

Once you have found hardware that you feel is going to run Professional acceptably, your next step is to determine whether this hardware is compatible with the OS. There are a number of ways to do this, but probably the most dependable is to go to www.microsoft.com/windows2000 to download a copy of the most recent *Hardware Compatibility List (HCL)*. This list will tell you which hardware has been tested with Windows 2000 and should run properly. If your hardware is not on the HCL, contact your vendor for compatibility information and updated Windows 2000 drivers. Many Windows NT drivers will work with 2000, while Windows 95 or 98 drivers will NOT work!

Most hardware on the HCL also has drivers that ship with Windows 2000, so the hardware should be installed and configured automatically with the new drivers by plug-and-play during setup. If your hardware is extremely new or if your vendor did not submit the hardware to Microsoft for testing, you may find that you need to supply your own drivers.

Accessing the Setup Files

Unlike Windows 9x Setup, which must run from a functioning operating system (an earlier version of DOS or Windows or a boot disk), Windows 2000 will generally be a breeze to install on a machine. To start the install process, simply place the Windows 2000 Professional CD into the CD-ROM drive and restart the computer. After the POST routine for the computer has completed, a message will appear that says, "Press any key to boot from CD..." Hit a key, any key, and the Windows 2000 Setup program will start.

That is a "perfect world" situation, and sometimes reality intrudes. If the message discussed above does not appear, that generally means that your PC is not configured to boot from CD-ROM or does not have that capability. In such a case, you will need to do one of two things:

1. Go into the BIOS to set the machine to boot to its CD drive. Consult your computer's user guide for more information on examining and making changes to the BIOS.

2. Create and use Windows 2000 boot disks to start the setup.

The Windows 2000 Boot Disks

Although most modern machines support booting from CD-ROM, you may occasionally need to use a boot disk to start Setup. This disk can either be a Windows Boot Disk with CD-ROM support or the startup disk set that can be made from the Windows 2000 CD. To create the 2000 boot disks, you will need access to the Windows 2000 CD and a computer with a CD-ROM drive. There is a directory on the CD called BOOTDISK. In this directory is an executable file called MAKEBOOT, which is used to make Windows 2000 startup disks from any version of DOS or Windows.

The above information should be only informational, as starting Setup from boot disks is slow and requires changing disks. If you need to use a boot disk, use a Windows 98 startup disk with the CD-ROM support option, and then run SETUP from the root of the CD or WINNT from the i386 directory.

Starting a Windows 2000 Installation

The startup options listed above all eventually lead you to the same point: executing the setup routine for Windows 2000 Professional. Professional has two different executables used to start Setup, depending on the OS you are using to start the install. These executables are WINNT (used from DOS or Windows 9*x*) and WINNT32 (used from Windows NT or 2000). These commands have various options associated with them, as shown in Tables 4.2 and 4.3.

TABLE 4.2   Common WINNT.EXE Options

Option	Function
/s:*sourcepath*	Allows you to specify the location of the Windows 2000 source files.
/t:*tempdrive*	Allows you to specify the drive the setup uses to store temporary installation files.
/u:*answer file*	Used in an unattended installation to provide responses to questions the user would normally be prompted for.
/udf:*id* [,UDB_*file*]	If you are installing numerous machines, each must have a unique computer name. This setting lets you specify a file with unique values for these settings.
/e:*command*	Allows you to add a command (such as a batch script) to execute at the end of Setup.
/a	Tells Setup to enable accessibility options.

TABLE 4.3   Common WINNT32.EXE Options

Option	Function
/s:*sourcepath*	Allows you to specify the location of the Windows 2000 source files.
/tempdrive: *drive_letter*	Allows you to specify the drive Setup uses to store temporary installation files.
/unattend	Used to run install without user intervention.
/unattend[*num*]: [*answer_file*]	Allows you to specify custom settings for machines during an unattended installation.

TABLE 4.3 Common WINNT32.EXE Options *(continued)*

Option	Function
/cmd: *command_line*	Executes a command (such as a batch file at the end of Setup).
/debug[*level*]: [*filename*]	Used to troubleshoot problems during an upgrade.
/udf:*id* [,*UDB_file*]	Allows certain values that need to be unique to be set separately for each machine installed.
/checkupgradeonly	Performs all the steps of an upgrade, but only as a test. The results are saved to an upgrade.txt file that can be examined for potential problems.
/makelocalsource	Specifies that the i386 installation directory from the CD should be copied to the hard drive, allowing for easier updates later.

If you simply start the install from CD-ROM or create the Windows 2000 boot disks, WINNT.EXE will start the install by loading a number of files, and then present you with a screen that says, "Welcome to Setup."

If you use a Windows 98 boot disk, change to the i386 directory and run WINNT from that directory.

Partitioning the Drive

To start Setup, click Enter at the welcome screen, and you will be shown a list of the partitions currently configured on the machine. If one of these is acceptable, simply select that partition, then click Enter. If you wish to create a new partition, you can do so using the Setup program itself, which replaces FDISK as a way to set up the system's hard drive(s).

To delete an existing partition, highlight the partition and press D. You will be asked to confirm your choice and will be reminded that all information on the partition will be lost. If the disk is new or if the old information is no longer needed, this is fine.

If you are not sure what is on the drive, find out before you repartition it!

To create a new partition, highlight some free space, and click C. You will be asked how big you want the partition to be. Remember that Windows 2000 Professional wants you to have about 2GB as a minimum, but can be as large as the entire drive.

Formatting

Once you have created or decided on a partition to use, you will be asked to format that partition. In doing so, you will need to choose between the NTFS file system and the FAT file system. FAT is the file system of DOS, and its advantages include the following:

- Compatible with DOS and Windows 9*x* dual-boot configurations
- Excellent speed on small drives
- Accessible and modifiable with many standard DOS disk utilities

The *NTFS* file system, as one might expect, comes from Windows NT and is a more sophisticated file system that has a number of enhancements that set it apart from FAT:

- Supports larger partition sizes than FAT
- Allows for file-level security to protect system resources
- Supports compression, encryption, disk quotas, and file ownership

In most cases, you will find that it will be better to go with the newer and more advanced NTFS system.

When you choose one of the format options, the machine will go out and format the installation partition. This generally takes a few minutes, even on a fast PC.

Advanced Attributes

NTFS gives you a number of options that are not available on FAT or FAT32 drives. A number of these are implemented through the use of the Advanced Attributes window, shown in Figure 4.1. To reach these options, simply right-click the folder or file you wish to modify and select Properties from the menu. On the main properties page of the folder or file, click the Advanced button in the lower right corner.

FIGURE 4.1 The Advanced Options window

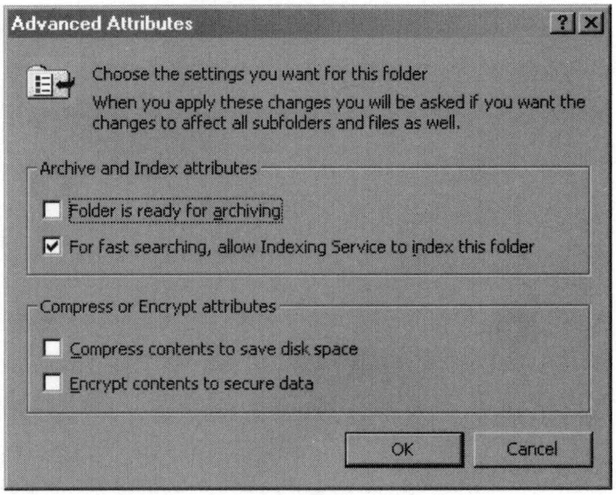

On the Advanced Attributes screen you will have access to the following settings:

Archiving Identical to the Archive attribute on a FAT or FAT32 drive. This tells the system whether the file has changed since the last time it was backed up. Technically it is known as the "Archive Needed" attribute; if this box is selected, the file should be backed up. If it is not selected, a current version of the file is already backed up.

Indexing Windows 2000 implements an Index Service to catalog and improve the search capabilities of your drive. Once files are indexed you can search them more quickly by name, date, or other attributes. Setting the index option on a folder will cause a prompt to appear, asking whether you want the existing files in the folder to be indexed as well. If you choose to do this, Windows 2000 will automatically reset this attribute on subfolders and files. If not, only new files created in the directory will be indexed.

Compression Windows 2000 supports advanced compression options first introduced in Windows NT. NTFS files and folders can be dynamically compressed and uncompressed, often saving a great deal of space on the drive. As with Indexing, turning on Compression for a folder will result in your being prompted as to whether you want the existing files in the folder to be compressed. If you choose to do this, Windows 2000 will automatically compress the subfolders and files. If not, only new files created in the directory will be compressed.

Compression works best on files such as word processing documents and uncompressed images. Word files or MS Paint bitmaps can be compressed to up to 80 percent using compression. Files that are already packed well do not compress as effectively; EXE and Zip files generally compress only about 2 percent. Similarly GIF and JPG images are already compressed (which is why they are used in Internet Web pages), so they compress little or not at all.

Encryption   This last advanced attribute is totally new to Windows 2000. Encryption allows a user to secure their files against anyone else being able to view them by actually encoding the files with a key that only the user has access to. This can be useful for those who are worried about extremely sensitive information, but in general, encryption is not necessary on the network. NTFS local file security is usually enough to provide users access to what they need and prevent others from getting to what they shouldn't. If users do want to encrypt a file, they simply go through the same process as they would in indexing or compressing.

If a user forgets their password or is unable to access the network to authenticate their account, they will not be able to open encrypted files. If the user's account is lost or deleted, the only other user who is able to decrypt the file is the Administrator account.

Yet another file type—HPFS—is mentioned in the exam objectives. HPFS is the advanced file system for OS/2, and, due to Microsoft's desire to replace OS/2 in the market, they added support for HPFS into Windows NT. Windows 2000 no longer supports HPFS, though.

Installing Windows 2000

After the installation partition is formatted, the system checks the new partition for errors, and then begins to copy files.

While the files are being copied, a progress indicator will display on the screen showing you how far along the process is. Windows will install files into temporary installation folders on the drive and will ask you to reboot once the copy is complete. If you do not reboot within 15 seconds of the end of the file copy, the system will automatically reboot for you.

If Setup detects any problems during the partition check, it will attempt to fix the problem and will immediately ask you to reboot. At that point the install will need to start over. If problems are found, this can often be an indicator that there are problems with the hard drive, and you may want to run a full scandisk before returning to the install.

The Graphical Phase of Setup

When Windows 2000 Professional reboots, it will automatically bring you into a graphical setup, which resembles a massive Windows wizard (as shown in Figure 4.2). This is generally referred to as the "graphical phase" of Windows 2000 Setup. This is due to the contrast between this phase and the earlier blue-background and text "non-graphical" phase where we configured partitions and copied temporary files.

FIGURE 4.2 The Windows 2000 Setup Wizard

During this phase Windows will attempt to identify and configure the hardware in the computer, which may take a few minutes. One of the more unsettling parts of Setup occurs during this time, as the screen flickers—and often goes completely black—while monitor detection occurs.

Windows 2000 comes packaged with an impressive array of drivers and is able to identify and load most modern hardware. Still, not all devices have compatible drivers on the Windows 2K CD-ROM, so if your hardware is not detected during startup, you can install additional device drivers after Setup completes, as shown later in the chapter.

After hardware detection is completed, the ever-polite Windows 2000 Setup Wizard welcomes you once again. To move through the wizard, simply click on the Next and Back buttons along the bottom of the window. The screens of the setup process are as follows:

Regional Settings   The first screen rarely needs to be modified if you are configuring the machine for use in the U.S., but users in other countries will find that this is where they can change keyboard and language settings.

Personalize Your Software   This is used to enter the name (required) and organization (optional) of the person to whom the software is registered. Both fields are just text boxes. Enter any values that apply.

Computer Name and Administrator Password   The *computer name* is the name by which a machine will be known if it participates on a network. This name is generally 15 characters or less. The administrator password is used to protect access to the powerful Administrator account. Unlike Windows 9*x*, where usernames and password security is optional, all users must log on with a username and password to use a Windows 2000 Professional desktop.

Modem Dialing Information   If a modem has been detected, you will be asked for country, area code, and dialing preference information. If you do not have a modem, this screen will be skipped.

Date and Time Settings   The Date and Time dialog box also has time zone and daylight savings time information. Any data on this screen can easily be changed later as well.

Networking Settings/Installing Components   After the date and time, you will be waiting for a minute or two as Windows 2K installs any networking components that it has found and prepares to walk you through the configuration of the network. As you are waiting, you will see which components are being installed in the Status area.

Performing Final Tasks   Once you have made it through the component install, the setup process is in the home stretch. The Final Tasks page reports on the setup's progress while it does the following:

Installs Start menu items   This is where shortcuts are created to the applications and options installed during the setup.

Registers components   The Registry is updated with setup information.

Saves settings   Configuration information is saved to disk, and other defaults and user selections are applied (such as area code, time zone, etc.).

Removes any temporary files used   The temporary files saved to the hard drive at the start of Setup and used to install Windows are removed to free drive space.

This last screen can take quite a long time to complete, and in general the install of Windows 2000 takes about twice as long as an install of Windows 9x.

Eventually, the wizard will complete, and you will be asked to reboot by clicking the Finish button. When the system restarts, Windows 2000 Professional Setup will be complete, and the standard 2000 boot process will initiate.

Upgrading to Windows 2000

If the machine that you want to install Windows 2000 on already has Windows 9x or Windows NT up and running, you may want to upgrade to the advanced security and performance of Windows 2000 without losing your installed programs or system configuration. Windows 2000 allows for this by providing a very sophisticated upgrade mechanism that can check your hardware and software, and then update an existing Windows 9x install while preserving the look, feel, and functionality of your current environment.

Windows 2000 can not upgrade Windows 3.1 or DOS systems to 2000 Professional. Most machines running 3.1 or DOS probably will be running older hardware, but if you do want to upgrade such a system, you will need to perform a new full install rather than an upgrade. All programs or drivers that were installed on DOS or Windows 3.x will then need to be reinstalled under 2000.

Starting Setup

Compared to the work involved in setting up a new Windows 2000 install, running the 2000 upgrade is almost completely effortless. The basic requirements are the same for an upgrade as they are for a new install, and again you will have the option of either doing a CD-based install or a network-based install.

Generally, the simplest option is to place the Windows 2000 Professional disk into the CD-ROM drive of the machine to be upgraded. A window (see Figure 4.3) should automatically appear asking if you want to upgrade to Windows 2000.

FIGURE 4.3   The Windows 2000 Upgrade Autorun screen

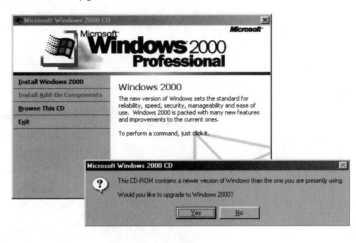

When a compact disc is inserted into a drive, it often automatically starts a program, such as an install routine. This is done through the *Autorun* option.

Upgrading to Windows 2000 Professional from Windows 9*x* and Windows NT
Workstation is essentially the same process. Just pop the disk in and go. One of
the big advantages of the Windows NT upgrade is that because it is a very similar
OS to Windows 2000, you should have fewer compatibility issues. Also, Windows
NT drivers can be used in Windows 2000, where Windows 9*x* drivers cannot,
meaning more hardware may be automatically detected and installed.

If you click Yes to accept the offered upgrade, the Windows 2000 Setup Wizard will begin. This wizard will perform a number of pre-upgrade tasks and will
then start the upgrade itself. The screens you may see during the Upgrade Wizard
include the following:

Welcome to the Windows 2000 Setup Wizard   The first choice of the wizard is also probably the most important. The screen (shown in Figure 4.4) is
where you decide whether to perform an upgrade to your existing system or
to simply install a fresh copy of Windows 2000 onto the drive. Both of these
have their advantages.

Upgrade to Windows 2000 (Recommended)   The upgrade allows you
to keep your existing programs, but it also retains any existing *problems*.
Because of this, any system configuration glitches or files that are no
longer used will continue to plague you in the new install, just like they
had in Windows 9*x*.

Install a new copy of Windows 2000 (Clean Install)   A clean install has two major advantages. First, it allows you to start fresh without the baggage of your Windows 9x Setup. Second, it allows you to "dual boot" back to your original Windows 9x OS. The disadvantage, of course, is that you will have to re-install all of your programs in this scenario.

FIGURE 4.4   The Upgrade or Install Option

 Windows 2000 and Windows 9x can't exist on the same partition in a dual-boot scenario, since certain drive locations (such as the location of Internet Explorer) are hard-wired to the same directory for both. To install a new copy of Windows 2000 and dual-boot to Windows 9x, you need to have a second partition on your disk or a second disk. Windows 9x should be installed on the C partition first, and then Windows 2000 can be installed afterwards on the D partition. The installation of Windows 9x *after* Windows 2000 is not supported as a dual-boot scenario.

If you choose to upgrade, you will continue through the wizard. If you choose to install a new copy of the OS, you will be immediately funneled into the process described in the "Installing Windows 2000" section.

 In most cases, I use upgrades as an opportunity to clean up a system. In order to do this I generally back up any needed data and then simply reformat the machine's drives and start over from ground zero. It takes a bit more time, but it is often worth it. Before doing this, though, make sure you still have installation disks for all of the applications and other software you will need to reinstall.

License Agreement and Product Key   Assuming you have continued the upgrade, you're required to complete the next two screens, License Agreement and Product Key. They allow you to accept the Microsoft licensing terms and ask you for a Windows 2000 *product key*. As with the regular install, this key is an obscene 25 characters in length and can usually be found on the case of the CD.

Preparing to Upgrade to Windows 2000   With the bookkeeping out of the way, you can now get down to the business of the upgrade itself. Before you start copying files, the Upgrade Wizard will examine your existing configuration to see whether there are any problems that will make upgrading difficult. Figure 4.5 illustrates this. The Upgrade Wizard provides a link to Microsoft's Windows Compatibility Web site for product updates and compatibility information.

FIGURE 4.5   Preparing to Upgrade to Windows 2000

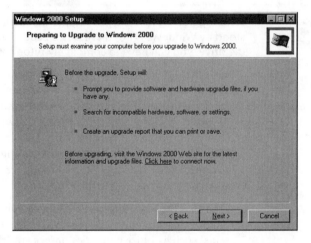

During the upgrade, Setup will try to contact Microsoft's site for information and updates, including the upgrade packs it's looking for on the next page of the wizard. If you do not have a connection to the Web as you are upgrading, you will be asked to connect, but you can choose to continue to work offline. If you do work offline, any updates must be applied manually later. If you have an Internet connection, it is recommended to go out to the Web site and look for updates.

Provide Upgrade Packs   If you do work offline, one of the things you may need to provide are application upgrade packs. Most 32-bit applications will continue to function without any problems. If you have any 16-bit DOS or Windows 3.*x* applications, though, they may not work. Also, any new or odd hardware may not be upgraded properly, as we will see in the next section. If you have been out to the Microsoft upgrade site of a vendor site and have obtained updated files for 2000, you may add them now by choosing the Yes, I Have Upgrade Packs option. If not, simply select the No, I Don't Have Any Upgrade Packs option. In such a case you can still apply upgrades later if applications do not function after the upgrade.

Upgrading to the Windows 2000 NTFS File System   Another upgrade option you will be given is to upgrade your drive's file system to Windows 2000's advanced NTFS. The upgrade to NTFS enables increased file security, disk quotas, and disk compression. NTFS also makes better use of large drives by using a more advanced method of saving and retrieving data.

To enable NTFS and sever all ties to Windows 9x, select the Yes, Upgrade My Drive option. To retain your links to the past and allow for dual-boot scenarios, select the No, Do Not Upgrade My Drive option.

While upgrading to NTFS has a number of advantages, the file system is only understood by Windows NT and Windows 2000. If you want to reinstall Windows 9x on the drive, you will have to completely reformat.

Preparing an Upgrade Report   Once you have made your choices, Setup will finally go through and examine your system for compatibility issues. This involves checking all hardware and software that is currently installed can be found, and it also involves creating a detailed upgrade report. Once it is finished you will be allowed to do two things: provide updated files for any incompatible hardware and view a report of what the compatibility check has found.

Provide Updated Plug-and-Play Files   In upgrading any system there is a chance that incompatible hardware may be found. In upgrading certain systems, such as older machines or laptops, the chances are even greater. IBM's ThinkPad series, for example, has hardware support for DVD playback available through an MPEG-2 Decoder Card. This is an optional piece of hardware which is specifically built by IBM for IBM, and as such it is not common enough to be recognized by the setup process. In order for this device to work, updated files must be obtained from IBM.

If you don't have updated files at present for any unsupported hardware, you can still continue with the install but will have to update the files before the hardware will function under Windows 2000. If the functioning of the hardware is essential to the operation of the system (network card, video card, etc.) you may want to stop the install and get the new drivers before continuing. For non-essential hardware such as a DVD decoder, you can continue and simply fix the problem later, but it is a good idea to at least verify that the hardware is compatible with Windows 2000, just so you won't be surprised later.

As noted earlier, you cannot use the same Windows 9x or Windows NT drivers that are currently installed.

Upgrade Report   Once you have added any plug-and-play drivers, the Setup Wizard will provide you with a detailed report (see Figure 4.6) of what it thinks may cause you "issues" as you upgrade. The following topics are included:

Hardware   Any devices that cannot be confirmed as compatible with Windows 2K will be listed here.

FIGURE 4.6   The completed upgrade report

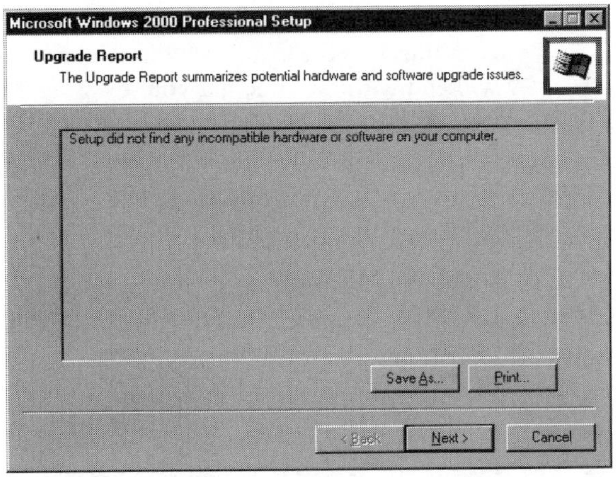

Software   Programs that do not work with Windows 2K are listed here. The ThinkPad upgrade, for instance, found that not only was the DVD decoder not supported, but the installed DVD player also will not work. In these cases you are directed to uninstall the program before the upgrade, because it will not function and may not uninstall properly after the upgrade.

This particular IBM DVD player should be expected to fail, as it was designed to link directly to the IBM DVD decoder card. Such direct access of hardware is explicitly restricted in Windows NT and 2000, and as such this software will be prevented from executing without an acceptable Windows 2000 driver.

Program Notes   Besides incompatibilities, some programs simply need to be reconfigured to work with Windows 2000. The Program Notes area details some of these known issues, such as how Microsoft Outlook 2000 works with Windows 2000 but must be reinstalled after the upgrade.

General Information   This section details information best described as "other." Some of the upgrade issues that came up during a recent upgrade included notes on issues concerning hardware profiles, backup files, and the recycle bin.

If you wish to save the upgrade report information for later use, you have two options: print it or save it to a file. If you feel that the machine has major compatibility issues, you should probably save or print the report, and visit the www.microsoft.com/windows2000/compatible and www.hardwareupdate.com for information or updates.

Once you have checked out the upgrade report, you have to choose whether to proceed with the upgrade immediately or to exit from the upgrade in order to regroup and obtain needed updates. If you are ready to proceed, click Next to continue with the install. If you would rather wait, click Cancel, and the upgrade will end without affecting your existing Windows 9x or NT install.

Ready to Install Windows 2000   If you have made it this far, the tough part is now over. As the wizard states, "This process is completely automatic, and you will not have to answer any additional questions."

All you need to do is click the Next button and head off to get some coffee, or preferably some lunch. About one hour and three restarts later you should find that the process has completed, and a Windows 2000 logon screen should be waiting for you when you return.

After the first reboot the existing Windows install will be deleted, and Windows 2000 files will be copied to the drive. After that a second graphical setup will start, and your settings from Windows 9x or NT will be automatically reapplied.

Logging On to Windows 2000

As shown in Figure 4.7, users are presented with a number of options when they start Windows 2000. The user logon system comes up immediately at the end of the Windows 2000 startup process, and the system requires, at the very least, a username and password, but it allows for other choices. This is due to the fact that its security structure requires that every user on a Windows 2000 Professional system have a unique name and password to identify them and their configuration.

FIGURE 4.7 The Windows 2000 Logon screen

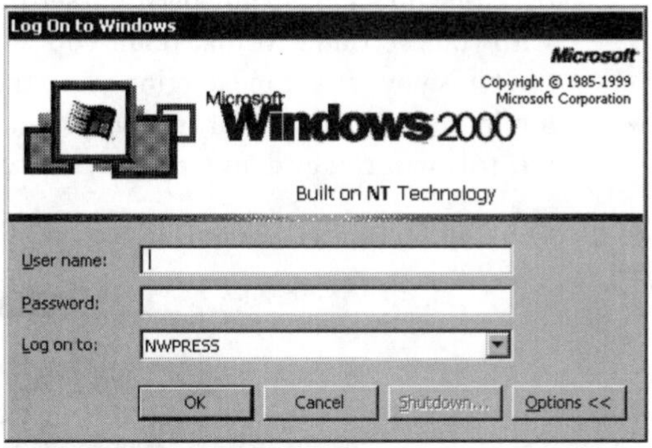

The options available on this screen include the following:

Username The *username* is the name that defines a particular individual on the computer. Each user has their own desktop and personal settings and can be given or restricted from particular files or tasks. This field displays your letters as you type them and is not case sensitive.

Password A *password* is a personal identifier that is used to verify that the user is who they say they are. Without a verified username and password set, a user cannot log onto a Windows 2000 Professional workstation. The password field displays only asterisk (*) characters as you type, and the field is case sensitive.

From This allows the user to set the security context from which they will be authenticated. Windows 2000 Professional workstations have their own user database, but they can also authenticate using a shared database, such as the Windows 2000 Server Active Directory. You cannot type new information into the From field, but if you have multiple authentication options configured, you will be able to select from among them using the down arrow.

Logon using Dial-Up Networking Allows a user to establish a dial-up connection to a remote network, and then authenticate against a database over that connection. This option is rarely used, but it may be needed in high-security environments.

> **NOTE** For now we will only discuss logging on to the local computer. In Chapter 8, "Configuring Network Software," we will look into other logon options during an examination of Windows 2000 Professional networking options.

In order to log on you will need to enter valid credentials. You may have created an administrator account and password during the setup, or you may need to get this information from a network administrator.

Once you have entered your credentials, Windows 2000 will configure your desktop and will load any personal settings and any user policy settings associated with your account. At that point you will be able to begin using Windows 2000.

If it is your first time logging on to the system as a particular user, it may take a minute or two for your initial system environment to be set up. A number of wizards will run and an introduction screen will be displayed, as in Figure 4.8.

FIGURE 4.8 The Getting Started screen

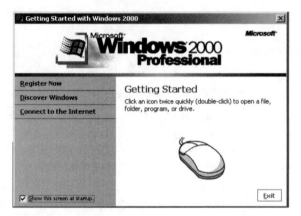

Windows 2000 System Information

Once you have completed the upgrade, you will immediately notice that Windows 2000 has some differences from Windows 9x. Windows 2K uses different startup procedures and different startup files. In this section we will discuss how Windows 2000 boots and what files are needed to keep it healthy and happy.

Key Boot Files

Almost all of the files needed to boot Windows 3.1 or 9x are unnecessary for Windows 2000. Windows 2K requires, in fact, only a very few files, each of which performs specific tasks:

NTLDR   This file "bootstraps" the system. In other words, it is the file that starts the loading of an operating system on the computer.

BOOT.INI   Holds information about what operating systems are installed on the computer.

BOOTSECT.DOS   In a dual-boot configuration this keeps a copy of the DOS or Windows 9x boot sector so that the Windows 9x environment can be restored and loaded as needed.

NTDETECT.COM   Parses the system for hardware information each time Windows 2000 is loaded. This information is then used to create dynamic hardware information in the Windows 2000 Registry.

NTBOOTDD.SYS   On a system with a SCSI boot device, this file is used to recognize and load the SCSI interface. On EIDE systems this file is not needed and is not even installed.

System files   Besides the previously listed files, all of which are located in the root of the C partition on the computer, Windows 2000 also needs a number of files from its system directories, including the hardware abstraction layer (HAL.DLL) and the Windows 2000 command file (WIN.COM).

Numerous other DLL (dynamic link library) files are also required, but usually the lack or corruption of one of these will simply produce a non-critical error, while the absence of WIN.COM or HAL.DLL will cause the system to be nonfunctional.

The Boot Process

When Windows 2000 starts, the computer's BIOS performs a number of system checks, and then it looks for an operating system to load. What it finds is Windows 2000's NTLDR (NT loader) file, which is then read into memory. The NTLDR prepares the system for the boot process and invokes a rudimentary file system access that allows it to read the BOOT.INI file in the root of C. This file is then used to construct a menu from which a user may select an operating system. If Windows 2000 is the only OS installed on the machine, the choice is moot, but if the system dual-boots, you may choose your OS at this point and boot directly into your selected OS. You may also make additional selections by pressing the F8 key.

The system waits a predetermined amount of time for a user choice, and then simply loads the default OS. Both the default option and the time can be configured in Windows 2K's System properties.

Using the F8 Options

In most cases you will be able to just boot into Windows 2000 without worrying about the advanced options. Occasionally, though, problems may arise. If you have a problem which makes it difficult to get 2000 up and running, the advanced options offer a number of useful tools.

Safe Mode   Starts Windows 2000 using only basic files and drivers (mouse, except serial mice; monitor; keyboard; mass storage; base video; default system services; and no network connections). Once in Safe Mode, you can restore files that are missing or fix a configuration error.

Safe Mode with Networking   Same as Safe Mode, but tries to load networking components as well.

Safe Mode with Command Prompt   Similar to Safe Mode, but doesn't load the Windows GUI. Presents the user with a Windows 2000 command prompt interface.

Enable Boot Logging   Logs all boot information to a file called `ntbtlog.txt`. This file can be found in the `\WINNT` directory. You can then check the log for assistance in diagnosing system startup problems.

Enable VGA Mode   Starts Windows 2000 using the basic VGA driver, but loads the rest of the system as normal. If you happen to install an incorrect video driver or a video driver corrupts, this allows you to get into the system to fix the problem.

Last Known Good Configuration   This option is useful if you have changed a configuration setting in the Registry, which then causes the system to have serious problems. LKGC will not save you from a corrupt file or a deleted file error.

Debugging Mode   A sort of advanced boot logging, Debugging Mode requires that another machine be hooked up to the computer through a serial port. The debug information is then passed to that machine during the boot process. This is rarely used and should not be bothered with in most cases. If it comes to this, reinstalling is far faster!

For more on Safe Mode and Windows troubleshooting, refer to Chapter 9, "Software Troubleshooting."

Starting Windows 2000

Once you have chosen to start Windows 2000 Professional, NTLDR will invoke NTDETECT.COM to check the system's hardware, and will load NTBOOTDD.SYS if the system uses a SCSI boot device. Once this is complete, NTLDR will then pass control of the system to WIN.COM, and the graphical phase of startup will begin.

During this time you will be presented with a series of screens that show the system's progress during startup; the interface is initiated and network connections and computer policies (if present) are loaded. Once this has completed, Windows 2000 presents you with a Logon screen as discussed earlier, (see Figure 4.7), and you can now start to use the system.

If you choose to boot back to a previous OS, NTLDR will immediately pass control to BOOTSECT.DOS, and the other files mentioned will not be used.

Modifying Windows 2000 Settings

Once Windows 2000 Professional is up and running, you probably will have relatively few additional configuration options that need to be set, but there are a few things that may need to be done. With Windows 2000 Professional, Microsoft has provided a one-stop shopping environment for finding system information in the Computer Management tool, while most system-wide configuration changes are made using the System icon in the Control Panel. In this section we will look at each of these.

The 2000 Professional Administrative Tools

Windows 2000 includes a number of tools for administration and management of the system. These can be found in the *Administrative Tools* icon in the Control Panel, which has a number of utilities. Component Services, Data Sources, and Telnet Server Administration are beyond the scope of this book, as is the local security policy. The rest of these tools are available through Computer Management, and that is where we will examine them.

Computer Management

The Computer Management tool (see Figure 4.9) is new to Windows 2000, and combines many Windows-based administrative tools into a single interface. There are three basic classes of tasks available from this console:

- System Tools
- Storage
- Services and Applications

FIGURE 4.9   The Computer Management interface

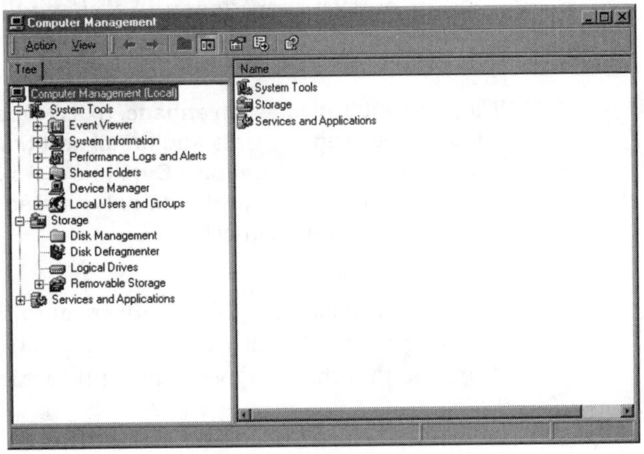

System Tools

The System Tools area provides access to a number of different utilities, many of which are also available elsewhere on the system. Even so, this provides a central interface for the following information:

Event Viewer Logs data about the computer. It is also accessible through Computer Management.

System Information Allows you to poll the system to find out information on installed hardware and software.

Performance Logs and Alerts Used to monitor system resource usage in real time or to log performance.

Shared Folders A place to get a quick look of what is being shared on your computer. Sharing will be discussed more fully in Chapter 8, "Configuring Network Software."

Device Manager Used to view and modify information about system hardware. We will look at this more in the "Hardware" section.

Local Users and Groups As the Windows 2000 Professional station maintains its own list of security accounts, this is where those accounts are stored and modified. For a user to log onto a Windows 2000 station, they must have a user account defined in the Local Users and Groups utility or they must use a *network security provider*, such as a Windows 2000 Active Directory or Novell's NetWare Directory Services.

Storage

The storage tools are used to manage and maintain the hard drives and other storage devices on your machine.

Disk Management Known as Disk Administrator in Windows NT 4, Disk Management is Windows 2000's replacement for FDISK. You can use it to create or delete partitions and even modify drive types.

Windows 2000 includes an enhanced disk type called a "dynamic disk." Dynamic disks can be used to create additional partitions and can also allow you to create advanced disk configurations. Dynamic disks can only be used by Windows 2000 machines, so this change should only be made if Windows 2K is the only OS that will be running on the machine.

Disk Defragmenter Nearly identical to the Disk Defragmenter program in Windows 9x, this checks the drive for errors, and rearranges (defragments) files so that they are more efficiently arranged on the drive.

Removable Storage   This option allows you to manage a backup tape drive or a ZIP-type removable disk drive with your system. It also is the place where you can go to check up on your CD-ROM or DVD drive, as they are also considered to be removable storage.

Services and Applications

The last of the options, the Services and Applications tree, contains only one option that most of you will use, that being the Services option. WMI Control and Indexing Service almost never need to be modified.

WMI Control   Used to configure and control the Windows Management Instrumentation service.

Services   Used to start and stop services that are on the machine. A *service* is simply an application or a function that the computer runs in the background. Services are also accessible through Computer Management. If a service is unable to start, any of a number of things could be the problem. For more on this refer to Chapter 9, "Software Troubleshooting."

Indexing Service   In order to speed searches of your drives or information, the Indexing Service keeps an index of your drive. From this location, you can configure how the Indexing Service is carried out.

We simply don't have the time to go into each of these in great depth, but if you have access to a Windows 2000 Professional machine, I highly recommend that you go through and examine each of these tools.

The System Properties Icon

While many of the tools in Computer Management are informational, the System Properties control panel (see Figure 4.10) is nearly all business. From within this one relatively innocuous panel you can make 90+ percent of all configuration changes that need to be done to a Windows 2000 Professional machine. The System Properties panel is divided into five tabs: General, Network Identification, Hardware, User Profiles, and Advanced. The General tab simply gives you an overview of the system, such as OS version, registration information, and basic hardware levels (Processor and RAM). For the rest of the tabs, we will look a bit more closely at their functionality.

FIGURE 4.10 The System Properties window

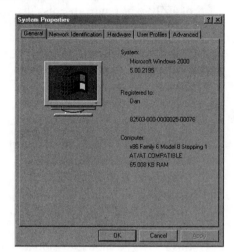

Network Identification

This tab is used to define whether the machine is in a workgroup or a domain environment. We will talk more about networking in Chapter 8, "Configuring Network Software," but in general terms, the difference between a workgroup and a domain is this:

Workgroup Loosely associated computers, each of which is their own security authority.

Domain A group of computers that is tightly connected, due to the fact that they have a single authority (called a domain controller) which manages security for all of them.

As a trainer, I am always looking for analogies to help explain things, and it seems that the best way to think of this is in relation to the difference between the United States and Europe. In the U.S. a single authority (the Federal Government) controls our military and has a strong degree of control over the individual states of the Union. In Europe, the European Union is a far weaker bond, and each country in the EU still maintains their own armies and more independent governments. The EU, essentially, is a workgroup model; the US Federal system is a domain model, at least it has been since the Civil War. But that is a completely different argument...

Hardware

This tab includes a number of tools, all of which allow you to change how the hardware on your machine is used. Because Windows 2000 is a plug-and-play system, it does many hardware-related functions similarly to Windows 9x. As it is a more advanced system, though, certain things are different.

Hardware Wizard

The Hardware Wizard is used, as it says, to "install, uninstall, repair, unplug, eject, and configure" hardware in the system. What this essentially means is that if you want to add a new device into the system or to uninstall drivers that are already there, this is the place to go. You can also use this to temporarily eject *PC Card* devices or other removable components.

Even in a plug-and-play system, it is important to properly unplug a device if you wish to remove it while the system is running. If you don't do this, nothing may go wrong at all, but you can sometimes damage the device or cause the system to become unstable.

Driver Signing

This is an option new to Windows 2000. In order to minimize the risks involved with adding third-party software to your Windows 2000 Professional machine, Microsoft has come up with a technique called *driver signing* (see Figure 4.11). Installing new hardware drivers onto the system is a situation in which both viruses and badly written software can threaten your system's health. To minimize the risks of this, you can choose to only use drivers which have been "signed." The signing process is meant to ensure that you are getting drivers that have been checked with Windows 2000 and that those drivers have not been modified maliciously.

FIGURE 4.11   Driver signing options

Driver Signing Options

To ensure their integrity, all files on the Windows 2000 CD are digitally signed by Microsoft and are automatically verified during Setup.

When you install new software, the following verification settings will be used.

File signature verification

○ Ignore - Install all files, regardless of file signature

● Warn - Display a message before installing an unsigned file

○ Block - Prevent installation of unsigned files

Administrator option

☑ Apply setting as system default

OK   Cancel

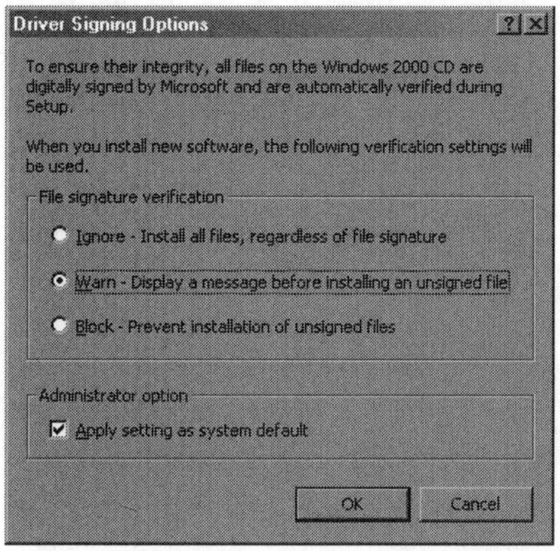

Device Manager

Although many hardware changes can be made through the Hardware Wizard, it is often easier to use the Device Manager, which provides a very simple and well-organized method to manage hardware in the system. In Figure 4.12, for instance, a modem can be disabled or uninstalled simply through a right-click.

FIGURE 4.12 Device Manager

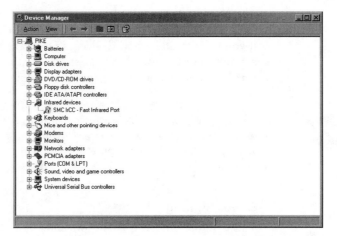

You can also go into a device's properties and modify other information, including the device's software drivers. If a new driver is made available for a device, you will want to update your existing driver to the newer (and purportedly better) software.

UPDATING DRIVERS

If you have upgraded to Windows 2000 from Windows NT this can be especially important, as 2000 can use Windows NT drivers, but prefers drivers specifically written for it. If you are upgrading, you should collect as many Windows 2000–specific drivers as possible and upgrade them either during or soon after the upgrade. To upgrade an existing driver, simply open the Device Manager and find the hardware you want to update drivers for. Right-click the device and select Properties from the menu. On the Properties window that appears, select the Drivers tab, and you should see an Update Drivers button. Clicking it will start the Update Device Driver Wizard, which will then require that you provide the location of the new Windows 2000 drivers for the device.

Hardware Profiles

A hardware profile is used to allow you to start the computer with different hardware configurations. This is most useful on laptops, which often have docking stations, or at the very least are moved from place to place often. These are very similar (i.e., exactly the same) as the hardware profiles discussed for Windows 9x.

User Profiles

Unlike Windows 9x, where *user profiles* are an optional setting, in Windows 2000 every user will automatically be given a user profile when they log on to the workstation. This profile is stored in the Documents and Settings folder on the drive that 2000 is installed on, and it contains information about the user's settings and preferences. Although this does not happen often, occasionally a user profile will become corrupt or will need to be destroyed. Alternatively, if a particular profile is set up exceptionally well, you can copy it so that it is available for other users as well. To do either of these, use the User Profiles tab (as shown in Figure 4.13) to select the user profile that you want to work with. At that point you will be given three options:

Delete   Use this to remove the user's profile entirely. When that user logs on again they will be given a fresh profile taken from the system default. Any settings that they have added will be lost, as will any profile-related problems that they have caused themselves.

FIGURE 4.13   The User Profiles tab

Change Type   This is used to configure a profile as local (the default) or roaming. In a standard Windows 2000 Professional Setup, if a user works at two machines, each of them will use a different profile. Updates to one machine will not be reflected on the other. If you have a network, though, roaming profiles can be configured to allow a user to have a single profile anywhere on the network. Getting into this any further is beyond the scope of this book.

Copy To Used to copy a profile from one user to another. Often the source profile is a template set up to provide a standard configuration.

Advanced

Finally we arrive at the Advanced tab, which has three subheadings, each of which can be configured separately. This could also be called the "Etc." tab rather than the Advanced tab. Among its options are the following:

- Performance
- Environment Variables
- Startup and Recovery

Performance

Although it is hidden away in the backwaters of Windows 2000's system configuration settings, the Performance button holds some of the most important settings you may need to configure on a 2000 Professional system. Among the settings in the Performance window are the size of your virtual memory and the maximum size of the Registry.

The initial Performance window has two options: application response and virtual memory. Application response is normally not something you will need to modify. It is set by default to optimize the system for foreground applications, making the system most responsive to the user who is running programs. This is generally best, but it does mean that any applications (databases, network services, etc.) that are run by the system are given less time by the system.

If the Windows 2000 Professional machine is going to be primarily working as a network server, you may want to change this to background services. Otherwise leave it as is.

VIRTUAL MEMORY

The virtual memory settings (see Figure 4.14) tell you how much hard drive space is allocated to the system as a swap file. For a review of what *virtual memory* is, return to Chapter 3, "Windows 95/98." Windows 2000 recommends a particular virtual memory level, but you can add to or subtract from this as you need. Often, certain applications (SQL Server for instance) will need to have Windows 2000 Professional's virtual memory limit raised in order to work properly. Graphics and CAD applications also require raising the virtual memory level, but if this is the case, the setup instructions for the application will generally tell you what modifications need to be made.

Adding to the pagefile size is not always helpful and can sometimes actually slow down the system. Only modify this setting if you have been instructed to or if you are testing to see whether the change speeds up or slows down the computer. Reducing the pagefile size is generally not recommended and can have serious consequences on performance.

FIGURE 4.14 The Virtual Memory window

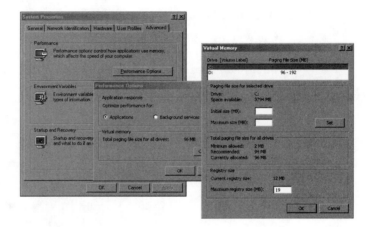

REGISTRY SIZE

Another option that is available in the Virtual Memory window is the ability to change the maximum Registry size. In most cases the default size is fine, but if a number of users are on a machine each of their settings must be stored separately, and the Registry can fill up. To prevent this, you can allow the Registry to continue to grow using this setting.

Letting the Registry fill up is a serious problem. If you think this may happen, you should change this option. An extra 10MB today could save a lot of pain tomorrow....

Environment Variables

There are two types of *environment variables*, and each can be added through the Environmental Variables button.

User Variables   These specify settings that are specific to an individual user, and do not affect others who log on to the machine.

System Variables   These are set for all users on the machine. System variables are used to provide information needed by the system when running applications or performing system tasks.

System and user variables were extremely important in DOS and Windows 3.1. If you are going to try to run DOS/Win3.1 applications on Windows 2000, you will likely have to add additional variables in this window to support those applications.

Startup and Recovery

The Windows 2000 Startup and Recovery options are relatively straightforward (Figure 4.15). They involve two areas: what to do during system startup and what to do in case of unexpected system shutdown.

FIGURE 4.15   The Startup and Recovery window

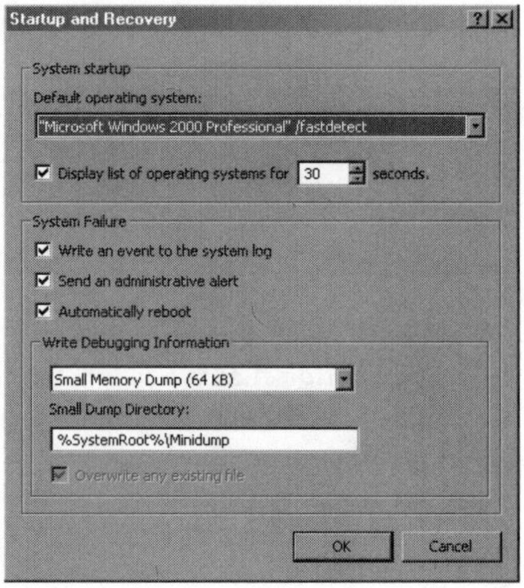

Startup and Recovery

System startup
Default operating system:
"Microsoft Windows 2000 Professional" /fastdetect
☑ Display list of operating systems for 30 seconds.

System Failure
☑ Write an event to the system log
☑ Send an administrative alert
☑ Automatically reboot
Write Debugging Information
Small Memory Dump (64 KB)
Small Dump Directory:
%SystemRoot%\Minidump
☑ Overwrite any existing file

OK   Cancel

System Startup

The System Startup option defaults to Windows 2000 Professional when you install Windows 2000 Professional, but you can change this default behavior if you would like. Unless you are *dual-booting*, there is only one option available, but if you have another OS installed, you can change the Windows 2000 boot manager to load that as the default. You can also reduce the time that the menu is displayed or remove the menu entirely.

If you choose to completely disable the menu on a dual-boot system, you will find that this may cause you annoyance in the future when you want to boot into a different OS but no longer have a choice to do so. Even if you almost always boot into Professional, you will still want to let the boot menu appear for at least 2–5 seconds if you are dual booting.

System Failure

A number of options are available in the Startup and Recovery screen for use in the case of problems as well. These include writing an event about the problem, sending out an alert of the network, and saving information about the problem to disk. These options only come into play in case of a major system problem, though.

Your options for handling system failures will be covered along with the trouble-shooting information in Chapter 9, "Software Troubleshooting."

Summary

Although similar in many ways to Windows 9*x*, Windows 2000 is also very different in significant ways. The installation process for Windows 2000 is far more straightforward, as it allows booting to set up directly from the CD and integrates disk preparation tools into the setup process.

Upgrading from Windows 9*x* to Windows 2000 is, similarly, a relatively simple task, although you will have to take into account that not all applications that run on Windows 9*x* will also run on 2000, and hardware may need to be pumped up a bit for the newer OS.

In this chapter, we looked at how you will soon find that, once you have installed Windows 2000 Professional, the startup process, the logon process, and the process of changing settings are different in 2000 than in 9*x*. Also, we looked at additional features that are available in 2000, such as the Administrative Tools.

Key Terms

Before you take the exam, be certain you are familiar with the following terms:

Administrative Tools	password
Autorun	PC card
computer name	power users
driver signing	product key
dual-booting	service
environment variables	user profiles
Hardware Compatibility List (HCL)	username
network security provider	virtual memory
NTFS	

Review Questions

1. What three basic classes of tasks are available in the Computer Management tool in Windows 2000? (Select all that apply.)

   A. Storage

   B. Network

   C. System Tools

   D. Services and Applications

2. When installing Windows 2000, you realize that you need to create a new partition. What would your next step be?

   A. Exit Setup, reboot the computer with a system disk, and use the DOS program FDISK to create your partition.

   B. Exit Setup, open the control panel of your current operating system, click the device applet, and choose the Disk Partition option.

   C. Create new partitions from within the Setup program itself.

   D. There is nothing that can be done. Once Setup has begun, there is no stopping it.

3. You want to change the size of your virtual memory and the maximum size of the Registry. Within Windows 2000, how can you accomplish your goal?

   A. You can change the size of virtual memory and the maximum size of the Registry by accessing the Control Panel, clicking System Panel, selecting the Advanced tab, clicking the Performance button, and making your changes.

   B. You can change the size of virtual memory and the maximum size of the Registry by accessing the Control Panel and clicking the Virtual Memory icon. Registry size may also be changed within that option.

   C. Virtual memory and Registry size are changed during the setup process. From that point on, they automatically change based upon the user profile.

   D. Virtual memory and Registry size should not be modified.

4. Which of the following is NOT required hardware for Windows 2000?

   A. Pentium 133

   B. 64MB of RAM

   C. 2GB hard drive

   D. SVGA video

5. You have successfully completed the installation of Windows 2000 Professional on a machine with minimum hardware requirements. Upon accessing one of your older graphics programs and opening a large BMP file, your computer seems sluggish and it takes many seconds for the image to be displayed. What can you do to improve performance?

   A. Nothing, short of adding more RAM.

   B. Open the Control Panel, click the System Panel button, select the Advanced tab, click the Performance button, and then increase the size of your virtual memory.

   C. Open the Control Panel, select the Hardware tab, and then change the size of your virtual memory.

   D. Reinstall the graphics program.

6. You successfully install Windows 2000 Professional and want to check your drives for errors. What is one way this can be accomplished?

   A. Open the Control Panel, click Administrative Tools, click Computer Management, and within the Storage tab, click Disk Defragmenter.

   B. Open the Control Panel, click Administrative Tools, click Computer Management, and within the Storage tab, click Disk Management.

   C. Open the Control Panel, select the Systems tab, and click Device Manager.

   D. Type **C:\defragment** at the DOS prompt.

7. The Hardware Compatibility List (HCL) lists hardware that has been tested with Windows 2000. If your hardware is NOT on the HCL, what should you do?

   A. Reload your Windows 95 or 98 drivers.

   B. Reinstall the device. The correct driver will load automatically.

   C. Contact the vendor and get updated Windows 2000 drivers.

   D. Download an updated HCL from Microsoft, which will then include the drivers for any device on your PC.

8. You want to set up a dual-boot scenario between Windows 98 and Windows 2000. Which option would work?

   A. Install Windows 2000 in the same partition as Windows 98 for efficient use of disk space.

   B. Partition your hard drive. Install Windows 2000 first. Once it is working, install Windows 98 in a second partition.

   C. Partition your hard drive. Install Windows 98 first. Then install Windows 2000 in a second partition.

   D. It is not possible to set up a dual-boot between Windows 98 and Windows 2000.

   E. Answer: C.

9. During Setup, all system hardware and software is tested. When the test is complete, a detailed upgrade report is generated. Which of the following topics are included as part of the upgrade report? (Select all that apply.)

   A. Hardware

   B. Software

   C. Program Notes

   D. General Information

10. Windows 2000 was installed and running on a PC. After making a change in the Registry, the system failed to reboot properly. Which troubleshooting option would work best?

   A. Reboot the computer using the F8 option, choose Safe Mode, reopen the Registry, and try to undo your change.

   B. Reboot the computer using the F8 option, choose the Last Known Good Configuration option, and complete the boot sequence.

   C. Reboot the computer using the F8 option, choose the Debugging Mode option, and complete the boot sequence. The system will debug itself.

   D. Reinstall your operating system. Any change made to the Registry is irreversible.

11. Logging onto a Windows 2000 system requires, at the very least, which of the following? (Select all that apply.)

   A. A username

   B. The Windows 2000 product key

   C. A password

   D. A remote access account

12. During the Windows 2000 Setup, you are asked to choose between the NTFS file system and the FAT file system. Which of the following is NOT an advantage of NTFS?

   A. NTFS supports compression, encryption, disk quotas, and file ownership.

   B. NTFS can be accessed and modified with standard DOS disk utilities.

   C. NTFS supports larger partitions than FAT.

   D. NTFS allows for file-level security.

13. What does the command `/checkupgradeonly` do?

   A. It instructs the Setup program that the procedure is an upgrade, not a full installation.

   B. It checks the computer for upgrade compatibility with Windows 2000 and generates a report.

   C. There is no such a command.

   D. It instructs the Setup program to thoroughly scan the hard drive only during the upgrade process.

14. During a routine installation of Windows 2000, Setup detected a problem during the partition check. After rebooting and reattempting setup, the problem continues. What should you do?

    A. Nothing, Windows 2000 Setup is designed to fix any problem encountered.

    B. Reboot the computer, access the system BIOS, change the boot sequence to boot from the CD-ROM, and reboot. The problem will go away.

    C. Install Windows 2000 to an alternate partition.

    D. Terminate Setup and run a full scandisk.

15. After a successful upgrade to Windows 2000, what should you do with the temporary files generated during the setup process?

    A. Nothing, all temporary files saved to your hard drive and used during setup are automatically removed.

    B. Nothing, these temporary files are actually needed, as they contain all user settings from the previous operating system.

    C. Emptying your Recycle Bin will remove these temporary files from your hard drive.

    D. If you install Windows 2000 from a CD-ROM, no temporary files are created, so there is nothing to delete.

16. You are preparing a computer for a dual-booting between Windows 98 and Windows 2000. Your drive is partitioned, and Windows 98 is already installed. Which of the following must you also consider?

    A. You must choose NTFS for the Windows 2000 partition for file-level security.

    B. You must choose FAT for the Windows 2000 partition. NTFS is not compatible with Windows 98 dual-boot configurations.

    C. Choose either FAT or NTFS, as long as you install Windows 2000 into a different partition than Windows 98.

    D. You cannot create a dual-boot configuration between Windows 98 and Windows 2000.

17. Which of the following is NOT a part of the graphical phase of Windows 2000 Setup?

    A. Date and Time settings

    B. Partitioning the hard drive

    C. Networking Setting/Installing Components

    D. Regional Setting

18. Driver Signing is an option new to Windows 2000. What exactly does driver signing do?

    A. It controls access to the Internet.

    B. It minimizes the risk involved with installing new hardware drivers.

    C. It has to do with the pre-determined times certain system tasks are performed, such as disk defragmenting, virus checking, and so on.

    D. It has to do with which folder drivers are stored.

19. What is the key difference between a workgroup and a domain, as defined in this chapter?

    A. A workgroup consists of several computers sharing a single security authority. A domain allows each computer to handle its own security.

    B. A workgroup and a domain handle security in much the same way. There is no difference.

    C. In a workgroup, each computer is responsible for security. In a domain, there is a single authority for managing security.

    D. A workgroup can only include Windows 9x machines, while a domain can include Windows 2000 workstations.

20. Which of the following is not a Windows 2000 Key Boot file?

    A. AUTOEXEC.BAT

    B. NTLDR

    C. BOOTSECT.DOS

    D. BOOT.INI

Answers to Review Questions

1. A, C, D. Windows 2000 includes the Computer Management tool, which combines many Windows-based administrative tools into a single interface. The three basic classes of tasks available from the Computer Management console are System Tools, Storage, and Services and Applications.

2. C. During the Windows 2000 Setup, you are shown a list of current partitions. If you wish to create a new partition, you can do so from within the Setup program. There is no need to exit Setup.

3. A. There are three subheadings under the Advanced tab: Performance, Environment Variables, and Startup and Recovery. The Performance button allows you to change the size of your virtual memory and Registry.

4. D. A Pentium 133, 64MB of RAM, and a 2GB hard drive are minimum hardware requirements for the installation of Windows 2000. However, VGA is the minimum for video. While SVGA will enhance the performance of Windows 2000, it is only recommended.

5. B. The virtual memory settings tell the user how much hard drive space is allocated to the system as a swap file. With minimum RAM on the system illustrated in this question, this setting may need to be modified.

6. A. The Disk Defragmenter is located within the Storage tab. This program checks for drive errors, as well as defragmenting the hard drive.

7. C. The Hardware Compatibility List (HCL), while comprehensive, does not include every legacy driver ever made. It may thus be necessary to contact the vendor for compatibility information.

8. C. Windows 2000 cannot exist in the same partition as Windows 98. It is thus necessary to partition the hard drive, install Windows 98 first, and then Windows 2000. Installing Windows 98 after Windows 2000 is not supported as a dual-boot option.

9. A, B, C, D. Setup performs a thorough check, or test of all hardware and software. The upgrade report details those issues that may require upgrading. Hardware, Software, Program Notes, and General Information are the four topics listed.

10. B. There are several advanced boot options available when pressing F8 during the boot process. Last Known Good Configuration works when a configuration setting in the Registry is changed, causing a problem. This option will not restore a corrupt or deleted file, however.

11. A, C. While there are other login options available for logging into a Windows 2000 system, at the very least, a user needs a username and a password.

12. B. NTFS is a more sophisticated file system. However, it is not compatible with DOS.

13. B. There are many Setup commands with various options associated with them. `/checkupgradeonly` does exactly what it says it does. It checks a computer for upgrade compatibility with Windows 2000 and generates either a `.log` or a `.txt` report.

14. D. Although Setup will detect and attempt to fix any problem encountered during installation, persistent drive problems need to be fixed before installation can be continued.

15. A. One of the final tasks performed by the Setup program is the removal of any temporary file saved to the hard drive at the start of the setup.

16. B. During a Windows 2000 Setup, you must choose which file system to use. Only a FAT file system is compatible with a Windows 98, Windows 2000 dual-boot configuration.

17. B. The graphical phase of Windows 2000 Setup begins after the hard drive is formatted and/or partitioned. Thus, partitioning the hard drive occurs before the graphical phase begins.

18. B. Installing new hardware drivers can cause system problems. To minimize this, Windows 2000 has pre-tested most drivers. Thus, you can install only those drivers that have "signed" or screened for reliability.

19. C. A domain is a group of tightly connected computers managed by a domain controller that handles security for the entire group. In a workgroup, however, each computer is responsible for its own security.

20. A. Almost all of the files needed to boot Windows 3.1 or 9*x* are unnecessary for Windows 2000. Thus, AUTOEXEC.BAT is not a key Windows 2000 boot file.

Application Installation and Configuration

THE FOLLOWING OBJECTIVES ARE COVERED IN THIS CHAPTER:

✓ **2.4 Identify procedures for loading/adding and configuring application device drivers and the necessary software for certain devices.**

Content may include the following:

- Windows 9x Plug and Play and Windows 2000

- Identify the procedures for installing and launching typical Windows and non-Windows applications. (Note: there is no content related to Windows 3.1.)

- Procedures for setup and configuring Windows printing subsystem.

  - Setting default printer

  - Installing/spool setting

  - Network printing (with help of LAN admin)

Buying a computer back in the 1980s was sort of like buying a DVD player when they came out a couple of years ago. It was so amazing that you just had to have one, but then once you had it, you rapidly discovered the fact that you had no movies to play on it (or at least very few). When I plunked down my hard-earned dollars for a Commodore 64 or an IBM PC, about all I got along with it was a manual. Because of this, one of the most under-appreciated elements of Windows is that the system comes prepackaged with a number of useful—and entertaining—applications. From the Address Book to WordPad, you can find all sorts of good stuff already installed when you first start using a Windows 9*x* or 2000 machine.

For complete coverage of objective 2.4, please also see Chapters 3, 4, and 6.

In most cases, though, users aren't satisfied to only use the tools that are provided with Windows. Either a particular tool they need isn't included (for example, Microsoft didn't put a spreadsheet application into Windows), or they need a more sophisticated version of a particular application—Wordpad and Word 2000 are both word processors, but that's about where the similarity ends. This demand has led to a booming software industry, and there are literally thousands of applications available that users can install and use with Windows. Because of this, installing and maintaining programs on user's computers is a big part of a technician's job. In order to prepare you for this task, we will discuss the following topics in this chapter:

- Comparing Windows 9*x* to Windows 2000 for application support and install methods
- Common application types
- Installing an application with a simple setup routine
- Installing a more complex program using the new Windows Installer
- Repairing and modifying installed applications
- Uninstalling applications
- Dealing with the issue of old DOS applications

Application Basics

In general, any computer program that is not essential to the operation of the operating system can be thought of as an application. *Applications* are program code designed with a particular purpose in mind, and generally fall into one of a few broad categories:

Utilities   These are programs which accomplish certain tasks. The Backup or Task Scheduler programs are good examples of *utilities* that come with Windows. Other common utilities include WinZip (for compressing and uncompressing files) or McAfee's VirusScan software, which helps protect a computer from malicious attack.

Productivity tools   These are applications that help users get their work done. Simple *productivity tools* such as WordPad and the Calculator are included with Windows; we will also be looking at Microsoft Office (the mother of all productivity tools) later in this chapter. Other common applications that fit into this category are the Lotus SmartSuite (which has word processing and spreadsheet components, among others) and Intuit's Quicken for managing finances.

Entertainment   Well, here we have it. As noted, there are thousands of programs available for Windows, and probably 90 percent of them are games or multimedia tools. This category of application provides special challenges and can often be among the most vexing to install and configure. Fortunately, these are also the applications that are the least likely to be brought to a technician to work on, because most service work is done for corporate accounts—and corporations are unlikely to pay you to figure out why Age of Kings won't install properly! Unfortunately, this doesn't mean you are out of the woods, since once you become a "computer geek," every friend and relative will soon be asking you why their new game doesn't work.

Comparing Windows 9*x* to Windows 2000 for Application Support and Install Methods

When you start looking at installing applications on a Windows machine, the first thing to note is that the installation is generally pretty similar regardless of whether the program is installed on Windows 9*x* or Windows 2000. Even so, there are a number of differences in applications, and as such you should take these into account. Here are a few key things to look for.

Application Architecture

One of the first things you will want to look for when getting ready to install a new application is what type of operating systems are supported by the product.

Not all programs install on all operating systems, and the following sections detail the key questions you will want to ask.

Is It a DOS or a Windows Application?

In order to make it easier for third-party vendors to write applications for Windows, Microsoft provides *APIs (application programming interfaces)* for Windows 3.*x*, 9*x*, and 2000. These APIs allow programmers to write applications more easily because Windows itself provides much of the functionality. For instance, when a programmer wants to write a routine that prints out a result, they can simply call printing APIs, instead of writing out the entire print process. This does two things. First, it makes programming more simple and second, it standardizes the way that certain tasks are performed. Almost all print or file save screens in Windows, for example, look about the same because all of them use a standardized API set.

If a program is written for Windows, it should run on either 9*x* or 2000. We will see in the next section that it may not run optimally, but generally, it will work. If the application was written for DOS, though, it could be a different story. Windows 9*x* provides an environment that allows you to use older DOS applications, but Windows 2000 does not. Most non-Windows applications will fail if you attempt to run them on Windows 2000! We will deal with how Windows 9*x* runs DOS applications later in the chapter.

There are, of course, applications written for many operating systems other than Windows and DOS. Most of them will not run on either Windows 9*x* or Windows 2000. Macintosh applications, Linux applications, and C/PM applications, for instance, will all error if you try to use them on a Windows machine.

Is It a 32-Bit or 16-Bit Windows Application?

Windows-based applications that are written for older versions of Windows are referred to as *16-bit applications* or *Windows 3.x applications*. Newer applications written specifically for Windows 9*x* or Windows 2000 are designed for use on more modern hardware and take advantage of the fact that Windows 9*x* and 2000 are 32-bit operating systems. Although both 16-bit and 32-bit Windows applications will generally run on either of the 32-bit Windows platforms, 32-bit applications are faster and more stable and should be used whenever possible.

Does the Application Use Any Non-Standard Windows APIs?

As I just mentioned, most 16-bit and 32-bit Windows applications will run on either Windows 98 or Windows 2000. Unfortunately, though, this is a guideline, not a rule. Because of the fact that there are Windows APIs which are supported by Windows 9*x* but not by Windows 2000, and vice versa, you will occasionally find that a 32-bit Windows application will work only on the 9x or the 2000 platform.

Microsoft has developed a standard for easily identifying whether an application is compatible with a particular version of Windows. Most software written for Windows now comes with a graphic that declares which systems it is verified to run on.

Because they are very similar architecturally, applications written for Windows 95 will work with Windows 98, and those written for Windows NT will work with Windows 2000. Those written for the newer systems, however, are not always backward compatible.

Other Considerations

Aside from architecture, there are a couple of other things you should be aware of when installing applications.

Beta Code

Pioneered by Netscape, which was one of the first companies to use the Internet as its primary software distribution channel, the popularity of *beta* applications has added an entire new chapter to the book of technician headaches. When an application is in development, its *alpha* phase is the time during which the application is being created and tested in-house. Once the application is thought to be ready, a number of companies have taken to releasing a presales version of the application on the Internet as a way of testing consumer response. Later versions of the beta product are generally released as well, and eventually a "release version" of the software is completed. Because beta software is generally released on an as-is basis, you should avoid using this on production systems. Most beta software is not eligible for technical support and is generally less stable than the later release version of the software.

Licensing Issues

As the great Napster controversy of 2000 has shown, the Internet is a place where many of the rules that govern property rights have gone out the window. In your role as a technician, though, you are a part of the computer industry, and protecting the copyrights and intellectual property of software developers is part of that job. As such, you will need to familiarize yourself with licensing issues and make certain that you don't end up installing programs for which you don't have a license.

What you do at home is your own business, but if you are being paid to install a piece of software, the people who wrote it should be getting paid, too. If a user buys one copy of Microsoft Word from you and asks you to install it on 10 machines, that is a clear violation of the licensing agreement. This is a difficult situation, as you don't want to aggravate the customer, but you also can't ethically do what they are asking. Get ready to deal with this issue, by the way, because it almost certainly will come up eventually. Figure 5.1 shows an example of licensing information.

FIGURE 5.1 MS Word licensing info

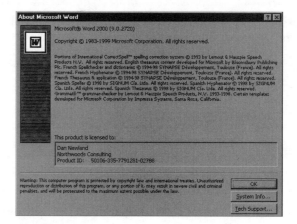

Installing Applications

Once you have determined that an application is able to run on your Windows machine (or you think it will!) you need to transfer the files and settings for that application onto the computer. In Windows, this is generally done through the use of a Setup program, although, as you will see with Windows 2000, Microsoft has debuted a new way of installing and managing applications that could mean the end of setup as we know it. Because of this, the installation information in this chapter is divided into two sections: the first describes a standard application setup, and the second describes a setup using the *Windows Installer* (*MSI*) files. We will not divide this up in a Windows *9x*/Windows 2000 fashion because they are identical in the way they handle each setup.

Because it is the application that controls the setup procedures, both Windows 9*x* and Windows 2000 machines will be able to use the new setup method of Office 2000.

Running a Basic Setup Program

In preparing for the A+ exams, one thing you are nearly certain to need is a copy of the objectives, as laid out on the CompTIA Web site. It isn't just as simple as going out and reading them, though, as the objectives are saved on the site in

Adobe Acrobat format. Acrobat is a great utility that allows you to save documents in exactly the form they are produced and distribute them for viewing. The only disadvantage to this is that in order for a user to see the document, they must have a special piece of software called the Adobe Acrobat Reader. In this first section, I will show you how to obtain the reader installation software and run its setup routine.

Getting the Files

Applications are really nothing more than software code installed onto the hard drive of your machine. Because of this, it shouldn't be a big surprise to know you have to obtain a copy of the software installation files before running setup. The most common installation methods today are as follows:

CD-ROM Most programs are sold on CD-ROM. To install them, you simply put the disk into the disk drive, and an install routine should start up. If it doesn't, you may have to browse to the setup file.

Network In organizations where network installations are available, they are generally preferred to CD-ROM installs because there is no need to carry around the disk (or in my case, to *find* the disk I need). Network installs are also generally faster than CD-ROM installs.

Internet Installing software that is downloaded directly over the Internet is becoming increasingly popular because of its convenience and flexibility.

Installing applications acquired from the Internet can also be dangerous to the health of your machine. Most viruses and other malicious problems are passed on through opening and using executable files, and SETUP.EXE is one such file. Only download and use content direct from vendor sites or respected mirror sites.

For Acrobat Reader, the best place to go is www.adobe.com, the home page of the company that makes the Acrobat software. At Adobe you can download a copy of the Reader for free simply by registering and providing some marketing info; on Adobe's Web site, just look for the icon shown in Figure 5.2.

FIGURE 5.2 The Acrobat icon

The marketing info is, unfortunately, pretty standard, as everyone wants your name, e-mail address, and a short biography before they give you their stuff. Once you get through this, you will come to a screen from which you are able to download a file that has all of the setup information wrapped up inside it, as shown in Figure 5.3.

FIGURE 5.3 The File Download window

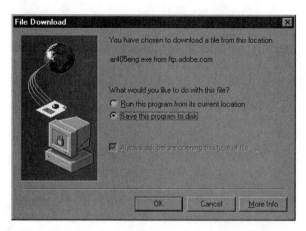

Generally, you will save this file to a directory on your hard drive and then run it from there.

Starting the Install

Once you have the installation CD or have downloaded the files you need, find the installation file—it will usually be SETUP.EXE or INSTALL.EXE. In this case, though, the file is called A40ENG.EXE. Start the setup program by double-clicking A40ENG.EXE. The Acrobat icon will unpack the file and then start the setup program, as shown in Figure 5.4.

FIGURE 5.4 Unpacking the Acrobat files

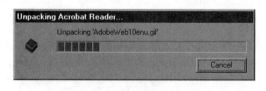

Nonstandard setup filenames are relatively common among software distributed over the Internet. In this case, it simply reflects that this is the Acrobat **4.05 ENG**lish version. As updates become available and the version number changes, so will the filename. If the numbers in the download file are higher than 405, the application has probably been updated, and a newer version is being distributed.

Once setup begins, you will usually be presented with a number of questions given sequentially by a setup Wizard (Figure 5.5). Your answers to one question may determine what pages you see later in setup.

FIGURE 5.5   Choosing a destination for the Acrobat files

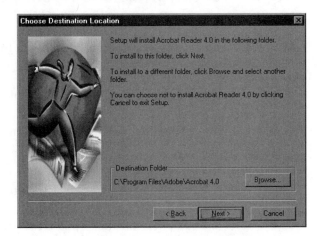

Once the setup routine has completed (Figure 5.6), you will find that a number of changes have been made to your system. First, there are changes to the GUI consisting of a new group of icons in Start ➤ Programs ➤ Adobe Acrobat 4.0, and there is an icon on the Desktop as well.

FIGURE 5.6   A note that the install is done

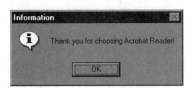

In addition to these changes, the setup file also makes changes under the hood. A number of files are installed onto the hard drive in C:\PROGRAM FILES\ ADOBE\ACROBAT 4.0. These files consist of DLLs (which are code libraries) and other informational and executable files, but there are no configuration files such as INI text files. Rather, configuration elements are set by adding a number of entries to the Registry, which can be found (among other places) in HKEY_LOCAL MACHINE\SOFTWARE\ADOBE.

I have used Acrobat for years and never had to modify its Registry settings (although it *is* technically possible to do so). The same can be said for most other simple programs. Install them and upgrade them when a new version comes out—you are generally best off if you simply leave their innards alone!

Installing Microsoft Office 2000 Using the New Windows Installer

Most programs use a setup program similar to the one we saw with the Acrobat Reader install. There are some significant limitations to these setup programs, though, and Microsoft recently began using a new method of setting up applications called the *Windows Installer*. The installer has the following advantages over traditional installation methods:

- The ability to logically group application elements for installation
- The ability to install components only when they are needed, through the Install on First Use option
- The ability to automatically detect and restore deleted or corrupt files (!)
- Easier customization through the use of MST files, which are used to save customized installation options for reuse

As an example of how these features work, let's run through an upgrade install of one of the most popular application suites, Microsoft Office 2000.

Office has a number of versions—it is not really a program so much as it is a collection of programs, or *suite*. Office Standard includes Word (word processing), Excel (spreadsheet), Outlook (personal information manager), and PowerPoint (presentation). Office Professional adds Access, which is a database, and Office Premium adds the FrontPage Web editor and a number of other tools.

As with other programs, Microsoft Office has a SETUP.EXE file that it uses to start its installation routine. To start the install, simply insert the Office 2000 disk into your disk drive. Setup will begin automatically and will install Windows Installer onto your machine. If you already have a current version of the MS Installer software, the install continues, as in Figure 5.7. If not, an update will occur, and you may need to reboot and restart the install.

FIGURE 5.7 The Installer starting setup

After this, you will be asked for a CD key, and you will need to agree to the license agreement. Once you have typed in the ridiculously long 25-digit key and have signed away your organs to Microsoft, you will be presented with a choice of a standard or a custom install.

Choose the custom choice and leave the default location. On the Selecting Features screen, you will be asked to not only decide which options you want, but also how you want them to be installed. In Figure 5.8, for instance, Microsoft Word Help is selected to run from CD, Wizards and Templates will not be installed, and Text with Layout Converter will be installed only if it is used. The Address Book and Page Border Art are the only optional Word components that will actually be written to the disk as part of this installation. These installation options are available because of the flexibility of the Windows Installer program, which actually stays on your hard drive and can start a small install any time you need it, as when someone wants to use the Text with Layout converter. Not all programs support these options yet, but many more will in the coming years.

FIGURE 5.8 The Selecting Features screen for Office 2000

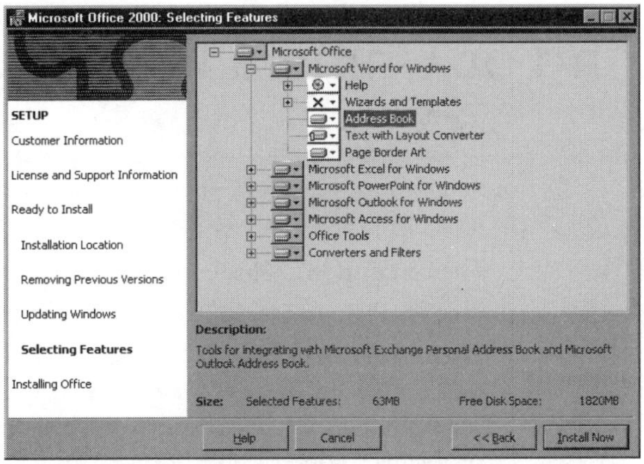

Once you have selected the options you need, click the Install Now button, and the setup program will configure your setup. Figure 5.9 displays the indicator that shows you how the installation is progressing.

FIGURE 5.9 Setup verifying tasks

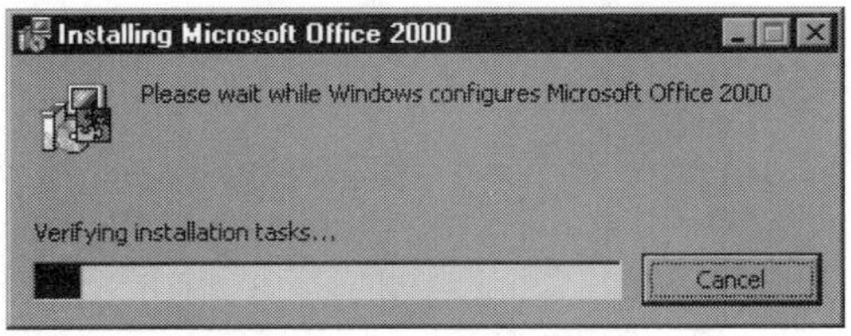

Once setup has completed, the Installer presents you with a parting gift in the form of a restart notification. This is because new information has been written to the Registry and may not be properly read until the system is reinitialized.

Some programs, such as Acrobat, do not need to reboot. Others do, though, and generally it is best to restart immediately if asked (Figure 5.10).

FIGURE 5.10 Windows completing the install and asking if you want to restart

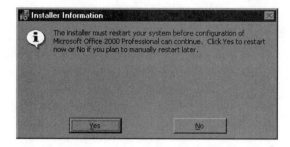

Repairing or Uninstalling Applications

Once an application is installed, it is generally pretty stable as long as one of two things does not happen. The basic categories of application problems can be categorized as follows:

File corruption   This can be caused by failing hard drives, power failures, viruses, or even poorly written programs

User error   Users… You gotta love 'em, because without them we would make a lot less money. Users may delete critical application files, shut down the system improperly, or introduce beta software onto the system that causes problems to other applications, among other things.

Between them, these two problems account for pretty much all problems with software applications. Generally, an application that has gone bad can be dealt with by either repairing or reinstalling it. If an application is badly written or is functioning perfectly but you no longer need it, you can also *uninstall* it, which removes it completely.

Repairing an Application

For most Windows programs, *file corruption* or deletion is best dealt with by running the setup program over again or by using the Add/Remove Programs Control Panel program. In such a case, you normally have to just reinstall the application with the same options as before, and the files will be recopied. Some programs, such as Internet Explorer 5, will even allow you to run a limited recopy that looks at your previous install and repairs it by recopying any files that are missing or corrupt. The IE options are shown in Figure 5.11.

Corrupt files can usually be detected by the repair process because their size changes due to the corruption.

FIGURE 5.11   The Repair Internet Explorer option

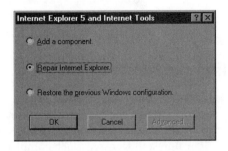

Microsoft Office is able to repair itself as well because it uses the Windows Installer (as does Internet Explorer). If Office or Internet Explorer has a problem, the Installer is able to review the installation and either download the needed replacement files or ask the user to install a CD with the files on it, as in Figure 5.12.

FIGURE 5.12   The Office Maintenance Mode window with Repair, Add, or Remove options

Windows Update

As more and more users are getting online and as bandwidth is becoming cheaper and more available, many software companies are making software updates available online. Some companies send out an e-mail to registered users noting that an updated version of the software is available for download, while others have mechanisms built into the software that can automatically update the software as new versions or patches are available. Because of the security issues involved in having new software installing itself on a PC without user knowledge or consent, this sort of update is currently rather uncommon, but it is definitely on the rise! As part of this, Microsoft now allows users to automatically update Windows OS components, as well as other Microsoft applications using Windows Update. We won't look at this as it is not generally something techs need to deal with, but you may run across it, so it's good to know about.

Uninstalling an Application

Occasionally, you will install an application on a PC and then decide that you no longer need it. In order to free up hard drive space, you may then want to remove that application from the PC. This is done through a process called *uninstalling*. The uninstall feature, which completely removes a program from the computer, also goes into the Registry and other system areas and removes references to the application. To access the uninstall feature for an application in Windows, you generally have one of two options (or sometimes both):

- Use the Uninstall icon from the application's program group
- Use Add/Remove Programs and choose to remove all or uninstall, depending on what terminology the program uses.

It is crucial to the health of your system that you do not simply go into the Windows Explorer and delete the files for an application. Removing the files without performing an uninstall will cause Registry problems and other difficulties, and may even make the system unstable.

We'll use Adobe Acrobat as an example of a program to uninstall.

The Uninstall Option in Its Program Group

Not all applications provide you with this handy tool, but most of the good ones do. On the Start menu, simply click Programs ➤ Adobe Acrobat 4.0 ➤ Uninstall Adobe Acrobat 4.0 (Figure 5.13), and the program removes the software icons and files and cleans up after itself in the Registry as well.

FIGURE 5.13   The Uninstall option for Acrobat

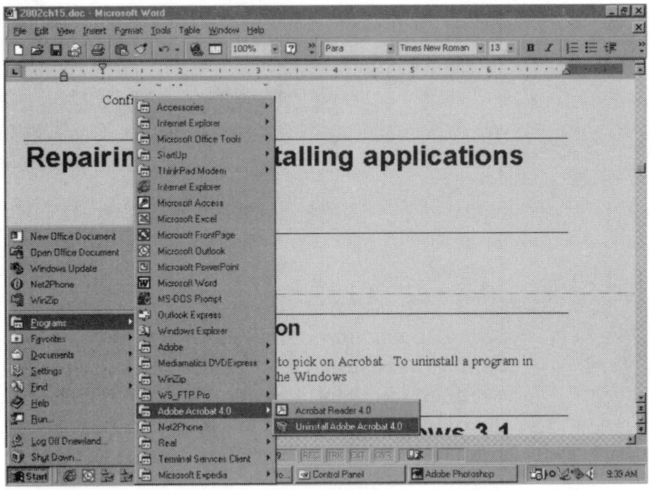

The Add/Remove Programs Control Panel Program

With this Control Panel program, you can add and remove Windows components and third-party software. To uninstall an option, open the Control Panel,
click Add/Remove Programs, select the program you wish to uninstall , and click
the Add/Remove button, as shown in Figure 5.14. Windows will look for uninstall information for the application and begin the uninstall process.

FIGURE 5.14   The Windows Add/Remove Programs Control Panel program

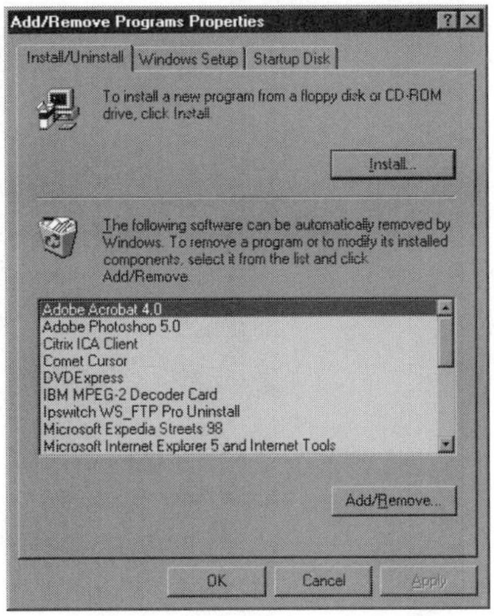

Once you have chosen to uninstall a program, you will be presented with the Confirm File Deletion dialog box as displayed in Figure 5.15.

FIGURE 5.15 The Confirm File Deletion dialog box

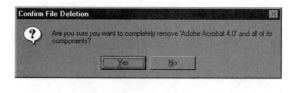

 Some applications, such as Office, have literally hundreds of possible components. These larger applications usually present an intermediate screen asking whether you want to add or remove particular components or whether you wish to completely uninstall the product. Acrobat has very few options and simply starts the uninstall routine immediately.

If you select Yes, the Remove Programs from Your Computer window, as shown in Figure 5.16, shows you which components are being removed, including Registry information. Some programs are better at this than others, but it is important to remember that few programs ever remove all of the files that they install. There are other third-party applications (such as CleanSweep) that go out and find leftover elements of deleted applications, but generally the uninstall feature does a good enough job. Once the uninstall routine completes, you will see the `Uninstall successfully completed` message.

FIGURE 5.16 Completing the uninstall

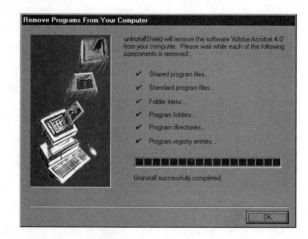

In the case of Acrobat, for instance, a post-uninstall Registry and drive search shows that the files have all been removed properly, but a few references to Acrobat remain in the Registry. If I wanted to, I could manually search and destroy these as well, but it is rarely worth it to be that compulsive. For general intents and purposes, the application is completely uninstalled.

Sometimes you need to uninstall an older (or beta) version of an application before reinstalling a newer or full version of the product. In such cases, the setup routine for the newer application may search the Registry for earlier installations of the product, and you may have to physically delete leftover Registry information before your reinstall will work properly.

Dealing with Older DOS/Windows 3.x Applications

There are two ways to install DOS programs onto a Windows 9x machine. Many older DOS programs can simply be copied; newer, more complex DOS programs will have to be installed with a setup routine specific to that application. In either case, Windows 9x has the ability to let you configure the DOS environment to allow DOS applications to run as well as, well, a DOS application is going to run.

The process for installing and using DOS applications is the same in Windows 2000 as it is in Windows 9x. That said, there is one critical difference: DOS applications generally run pretty well under Windows 9x and generally won't run at all under Windows 2000. If you are thinking of installing a 16-bit DOS application on Windows 2000 Professional, you need to test it carefully to make certain it will function properly.

Windows 3.x 16-bit applications setup routines look similar to the Windows 32-bit applications we looked at earlier except that they use INI and other configuration files and are generally completely ignorant of the Registry.

Installing an Application by Copying

Many years ago, DOS applications were simple executable COM or EXE files that could be run from a floppy. Copying these files to the hard drive was a common practice (if the computer had a hard drive) because programs run faster from a hard drive than they do from a floppy drive. As programs became larger, with many pieces and added-in drivers, it became more than just practical to copy the files to the hard drive; it became necessary.

Figure 5.17 shows a list of files on a floppy disk being copied to a directory on the hard drive. Two of these files are DOS executables, INTERLNK.EXE and INTERSVR.EXE. (These files are required to establish an interlink connection between two computers.)

FIGURE 5.17 Copying DOS program files

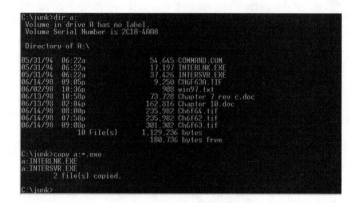

Installing an Application with a Setup Routine

More complex DOS programs need to be installed, rather than just copied, to work properly. One example is PC Tools from Central Point Software. PC Shell is a DOS shell with a bit of a graphical look and feel that can be used for file management. It's made up of a collection of files that fit onto several floppies but can work together only on a larger drive. Some of the utilities included in this suite can be run from the floppy, but others require the presence of overlay files and device drivers that span more than one floppy disk.

Although PC Tools (in its early versions, at least) *can* be copied onto the hard drive, it comes with an installation program that aids in the copying process by locating or creating a subdirectory for the files to be copied to. The install program also prompts you to insert each floppy disk as it is needed.

More complex programs require a more intricate installation procedure, usually meaning that you'll have to make decisions throughout the setup process. DOS programs generally use device drivers that are specific to that program, so when you load WordPerfect for DOS, you'll need to select a printer, even though you may have already selected the printer for Lotus 1-2-3. Likewise, you may have to select a display driver for fitting more text or typed data on a screen.

As shown in Figure 5.18, early installation routines primarily copy files and offer a few options on how to configure the files and computer after the application has been installed. Notice that this screen is a little bit graphical but not to the extent that modern Windows screens are. This PC Tools installation screen is actually built up out of DOS ASCII characters.

FIGURE 5.18   Installing PC Tools version 6

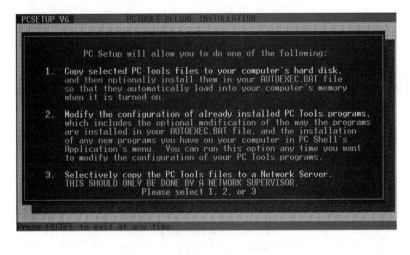

If you have questions about installing a DOS-based programs in a DOS environment, refer to the user guide that comes with the software.

Launching an Application

Launching an application in DOS usually means typing in its name or the name of its main executable file at a DOS command prompt. For example, you could start the Central Point Software program PC Shell by typing **pcshell** at the DOS command prompt. Generally, programs are put into their own subdirectories, so a path must exist pointing to that subdirectory, or you must already be in that subdirectory.

Alternatives include typing the complete path at the command prompt along with the startup command or launching the application with a batch file that has the complete path as part of the startup command. For example, an AUTOEXEC.BAT file could include the following command line in order to start the PC Tools shell when the computer starts up:

    C:\PCTOOLS6\PCSHELL6

The PC Shell utility provides file list and directory tree windows similar to Windows File Manager (in Windows 3.*x*) or Windows Explorer (in Windows 9*x* or 2000).

Uninstalling an Application

With DOS programs, the uninstall process is the reverse of copying: you simply erase all the files associated with the program.

Of course, sometimes an installation will have made modifications to the `CONFIG.SYS` and `AUTOEXEC.BAT` files. Depending on the nature of these configuration modifications, there may be no side effects to the removal of a program, or there may be some error messages about files not being found.

Rarely are these configuration changes harmful if left in, although many times the changes will leave extra and unneeded drivers loaded or memory configurations that are not optimized for the applications left on the hard drive. If you edit the `CONFIG.SYS` and the `AUTOEXEC.BAT` files, remarking out suspicious statements, it will usually fix things up.

Summary

In this chapter, we looked at how you can extend the functionality of a Windows-based computer by installing additional software on it. The installation and configuration of applications and utilities is a big part of a technician's daily work.

We looked at the different types of software available and at the different ways in which that software can be obtained and installed. We also looked at removing programs that are no longer used and examined the increasingly uncommon case of installing DOS/Windows 3.x applications on a Windows 9x or 2000 machine.

Key Terms

Before you take the exam, be certain you are familiar with the following terms:

alpha	productivity tool
beta	uninstall
file corruption	Windows Installer

Review Questions

1. Programs that are used to accomplish certain tasks are referred to as:

    A. Utilities

    B. Productivity tools

    C. Entertainment

    D. Control panels

2. Common examples of a utility program are: (Select all that apply.)

    A. WinZip

    B. Backup

    C. Virus scan software

    D. WordPad

    E. Calculator

3. Applications that help users get their work done are referred to as:

    A. Utilities

    B. Productivity tools

    C. Entertainment

    D. Control panels

4. When purchasing an application, which of the following would be listed as logical questions to ask? (Select all that apply.)

    A. Is the application a DOS or a Windows application?

    B. Is it a 32-bit or 16-bit application?

    C. Is it a third-party or first-party vendor?

    D. Does the application use any nonstandard Windows APIs?

5. If a program is written for Windows it should run on either:

    A. Windows $9x$ or Windows 2000

    B. Windows $2.x$ or Windows 95

    C. Windows $3.x$ or Windows NT

    D. Windows $3.x$ or Windows 98

6. APIs allow programmers to do all of the following except:

    A. Write applications more easily

    B. Accept nonstandard applications

    C. Standardize the way certain tasks are performed

    D. Make programming more simple

7. Windows 9*x* and Windows 2000 are what type of operating systems?

    A. 12-bit operating systems

    B. 8-bit operating systems

    C. 16-bit operating systems

    D. 32-bit operating systems

8. Applications written for Windows 95 will work with which operating systems?

    A. Only Windows 98

    B. Windows 98, Windows NT, Windows 2000

    C. Windows 98 and Windows NT

    D. Windows 98 and Windows 2000

9. Applications written for Windows 2000 are pretty certain to run on which of these operating systems? (Select all that apply.)

    A. Windows 95

    B. Windows 98

    C. Windows NT

    D. Windows 2000

    E. All of the above

10. When an application is in the early stages of development, it's referred to as being in the _____ phase:

    A. Alpha

    B. Beta

    C. Testing

    D. Developmental

11. Protecting the copyrights and intellectual properties of software developers is referred to as:

    A. Coding

    B. Licensing

    C. Copying

    D. Developing

12. Windows Installer files can be easily identified by the extension:

    A. EXE

    B. BAT

    C. MSI

    D. DAT

13. Applications can be installed from all of the following devices except:

- **A.** Backup drives
- **B.** CD-ROM
- **C.** Network
- **D.** Internet

14. In starting the installation you must activate the installation file. Most installation files have which extension? (Select all that apply.)

- **A.** EXE
- **B.** BAT
- **C.** DAT
- **D.** TMP

15. Which of the following is not an advantage of the Windows Installer over traditional installing methods?

- **A.** The ability to individualize application elements for installation
- **B.** The ability to install components only when they are needed
- **C.** The ability to detect and restore deleted or corrupt files
- **D.** Easier customization through the use of MST files

16. Which is the recommended choice for install for new beginners?

- **A.** Custom
- **B.** Typical
- **C.** Express
- **D.** Advanced

17. The basic categories of application problems can be categorized as: (Select all that apply.)

- **A.** File corruption
- **B.** User error
- **C.** Application error
- **D.** Program error

18. How many options are there to uninstall an application?

- **A.** One
- **B.** Two
- **C.** Three
- **D.** Four

19. The Windows 98 Add/Remove Programs icon is located in:

A. Control Panel

B. Network Neighborhood

C. My Computer

D. The Recycle Bin

20. DOS applications generally run under all of the following except:

A. Windows 95

B. Windows 98

C. Windows NT

D. Windows 2000

E. Both C and D

Answers to Review Questions

1. A. Utilities provide a way for a user to control the provisions and use of hardware resources and are a subcategory of system software designed to enhance the operating system.

2. A, B, C. Utility programs, when activated, accomplish specific tasks. For Example, Norton Utilities troubleshoots problems with a computer's disk drives, makes data more secure by encrypting it, and helps to retrieve data from damaged disks.

3. B. A productivity tool is a graphical user interface. Tools help users get their work done by making it easier for users to interact with a software program.

4. A, B, D. Whether it's a first- or third-party vendor usually doesn't matter. The main issue when purchasing an application is compatibility. Most software written for Windows now comes with a graphic declaring which systems it is verified to run on; this is an easy way to identify whether an application is compatible with a particular version of Windows.

5. A. If a program is written for Windows, it should run on either 9*x* or 2000—it may not run optimally, but generally it will work. However, most non-Windows applications will fail if you attempt to run them on Windows 2000.

6. B. APIs allow programmers to write applications more easily because Windows itself provides much of the functionality. For instance, when a programmer wants to write a routine that prints out a result, they can simply call printing APIs, instead of writing out the entire print process. This makes programming simpler and standardizes the way that certain tasks are performed.

7. D. Although both 16-bit and 32-bit Windows application will generally run on either of the 32-bit Windows platforms, 32-bit applications are faster and more stable and should be used whenever possible.

8. A. Because the operating systems are very similar architecturally, applications written for Windows 95 will work with Windows 98. Those written for newer systems, however, are not always backward compatible.

9. D. Although Windows 2000 applications may run well on Windows NT or Windows 9*x* as well as on 2000, this is not always the case and should be verified, not assumed.

10. A. When an application is in development, its *alpha* phase is the time during which the application is being created and tested in-house.

11. B. Protecting the copyrights and intellectual properties of software developers is referred to as licensing. A software license is a legal contract that defines the ways in which you may use a computer program.

12. C. The Windows Installer service has files with the extensions MSI and MST.

13. A. Backup brings back files from an existing install. It cannot be used to perform an initial installation.

14. A, B. Most installation files have the file extension EXE and BAT. EXE stands for execution; BAT stands for *batch*.

15. A. Windows Installer has the ability to logically group application elements for installation, install components only when they are needed though the Install on First Use option, and automatically detect and restore deleted or corrupt files. The Installer also provides easier customization through the use of MST files, which are used to save customized installation options for reuse.

16. B. It is recommended that beginners use the typical install because settings are chosen for them automatically, and the most commonly used options are installed.

17. A, B. File corruption and user error account for almost all of the problems with software applications. File corruption can be caused by failing hard drives, power failures, viruses, or even poorly written programs. Examples of user errors are deleting critical application files, shutting down the system improperly, or introducing beta software onto the system that causes problems with other applications.

18. B. To uninstall an application you can either uninstall from the application's program group or use Add/Remove Programs. It is crucial to the health of your system that you do not go into the Windows Explorer and delete the files for an application by hand. Removing the files without performing an uninstall will cause Registry problems and other difficulties and may even make the system unstable.

19. A. The Windows 98 Add/Remove Programs icon is located in Control Panel, which you can access either by selecting Start ≻ Settings ≻ Control Panel, or opening My Computer and double-clicking Control Panel.

20. E. DOS applications do not generally run under Windows NT and Windows 2000.

Chapter 6

Using and Configuring Additional Peripherals

THE FOLLOWING OBJECTIVES ARE COVERED IN THIS CHAPTER:

✓ **2.4 Identify procedures for loading/adding and configuring application device drivers and the necessary software for certain devices.**

Content may include the following:

- Windows 9*x* Plug and Play and Windows 2000
- Identify the procedures for installing and launching typical Windows and non-Windows applications. (Note: there is no content related to Windows 3.1)
- Procedures for set up and configuring Windows printing subsystem.
  - Setting Default printer
  - Installing/Spool setting
  - Network printing (with help of LAN admin)

Just as there are many different types of peripherals, there are many types of peripheral connection methods. The A+ exam will test your knowledge of these different types of methods, including

- Serial
- Parallel
- SCSI
- USB
- FireWire (IEEE 1394)

For complete coverage of objective 2.4, please also see Chapters 3, 4, and 5.

Peripheral Connection Methods

In this section, you'll learn about the different types of peripheral connection methods. You'll also learn how to differentiate them from one another by their properties.

Serial

Of all the peripheral connection methods, none is as popular as serial. It's a simple, effective way to connect a peripheral to a PC. It is also cheap to manufacture, which is probably the main reason it's so popular. *Serial* connections transfer data one bit at a time, one right after another. The maximum speed of a serial connection is 128Kbps, so it isn't good for large amounts of data transfer, but it works great for synchronizing two data sources. The most popular application of a serial connection is connecting an external modem to a PC.

Parallel

The next most popular peripheral connection method is parallel. *Parallel* connections transfer data 8 bits at a time as opposed to 1 bit at a time (as serial connections do). The most common peripheral connected via a parallel connection is a printer. Hence, parallel ports are often called printer ports. Additionally, newer parallel ports can connect devices like scanners and Zip drives to computers. Unfortunately, this doesn't work as well as other types of connection methods such as USB work because the parallel connection wasn't designed for connecting devices other than printing devices. Parallel was only designed to connect one peripheral at a time.

SCSI

The *Small Computer System Interface (SCSI)* is another method of connecting peripherals. It is the best choice for peripherals that require high-speed connections, as well as those that transfer large amounts of data, because it can transfer data either 16 or 32 bits at a time. For example, you could use a SCSI connection to connect a scanner, which might have to transfer megabytes of image data in a short period of time. The most popular use for SCSI is to connect disk drives to computers.

Although it is most often found in server systems, SCSI can be added to desktop systems through the use of an expansion card.

USB

In the last few years, a high-speed bus has been developed specifically for peripherals. That bus is the *Universal Serial Bus*, or *USB*. The serial bus could only connect a maximum of two external devices to a PC. USB, on the other hand, can connect a maximum of 127 external devices. Also, USB is a much more flexible peripheral bus than either serial or parallel. USB supports connections to printers, scanners, and many other input devices (such as joysticks and mice).

When connecting USB peripherals, you must connect them either directly to one of the USB ports on the PC or to a USB hub that is connected to one of those USB ports. Hubs can be chained together to provide multiple USB connections. Although you can connect up to 127 devices, it is impractical in reality. Most computers with will support around 12 USB devices.

Here are the steps to connect a USB digital camera to a PC to download the images from the camera:

1. With the PC powered on, connect the USB cable from a digital camera to an open USB port, either on a hub or a USB port on the back of the computer. Windows Plug and Play will recognize that there is a new device attached and will automatically start the Add New Hardware Wizard.

2. Follow the prompts on the screen to install the driver for your digital camera.

3. Install the image manipulation software that came with your digital camera.

As you can see, the combination of USB and Windows Plug and Play allows devices to be configured very easily.

FireWire (IEEE 1394)

With the advent of digital video, a new peripheral connection method was needed in order to download large video files into a PC. *IEEE-1394* was the standard developed to meet this need. This standard was developed from work done by Apple and others. The standard is more commonly known as *FireWire*, after the moniker given to it by Apple. FireWire was a leap in technology over USB because it could transfer data at a maximum of 400MB per second. It became the peripheral connection method of choice for connecting digital video cameras to PCs. IEEE 1394 ports can be found on many different types of computers, but they are most commonly found on Apple iMac computers. As a matter of fact, Apple has made a special version of the iMac, called the iMac DV, that is specifically set up for digital video.

Windows Printing Configuration

Probably the most troublesome aspect of a technician's job is configuring Windows printing properly. As such, the A+ exam will test your ability to do so. There are two ways to configure Windows printing: with a local printer or a network printer. In this section, you will learn about topics related to each.

When it comes to configuring a printer, the steps for both Windows 9*x* and 2000 are essentially the same.

Local Printing Configuration

One of the most common devices to add to computer system is a printer. Whether you are installing a dot-matrix printer or laser printer, the configuration is basically the same. In this section, we'll examine how to set up a Windows computer to print to a locally attached printer. Setting a workstation to print to a network printer is covered later in this chapter.

Adding a Printer

Microsoft was thoughtful enough to provide a wizard to help us install printers. The name of this wizard is the Add Printer Wizard (neat, huh?). It will guide you through the basic steps of installing a printer by asking you questions about how you would like the printer configured.

To start the Add Printer Wizard (APW for short), you must first open the PRINTERS folder by either going to Start ➤ Settings ➤ Printers or double-clicking the Printers icon in the Control Panel. Once you get to the PRINTERS folder, you can double-click the Add Printer icon. Doing so will display a screen that tells you the wizard is going to help you install your printer "quickly and easily." Let's hope so. Click Next to begin the configuration.

The first question the APW will ask you is where this printer is (Figure 6.1). If it is connected to the network, click the button next to Network Printer. If the printer is connected to your PC, click Local Printer. We will discuss using network printers later, so for right now, click Local Printer and click Next.

FIGURE 6.1 Telling the APW where the printer is

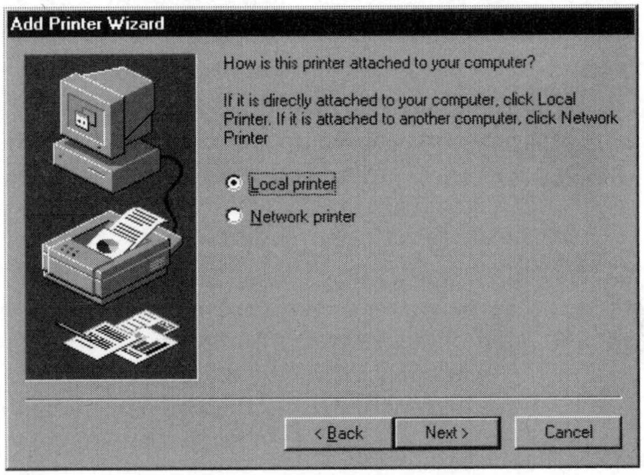

![Add Printer Wizard dialog box titled "How is this printer attached to your computer?" with text "If it is directly attached to your computer, click Local Printer. If it is attached to another computer, click Network Printer" and radio buttons for Local printer (selected) and Network printer, with Back, Next, and Cancel buttons]

In Windows 2000, there is an extra option to allow Windows to automatically detect and install the printer for you. If you want, you can leave this option selected (which is the default), and Windows will automatically install the driver and configure the printer. The rest of these steps will then be moot.

The next screen that the APW presents allows you to choose the driver for your printer by simply selecting the manufacturer from the list on the left and the model from the list that appears on the right (Figure 6.2). You may need to scroll on either side because the lists can get rather long. If your printer is not listed, or if you would like to install a more current driver, you can click the Have Disk button and

APW will prompt you to insert the disk and type in the path to the directory where the driver is located. Either way, select your driver and click Next.

FIGURE 6.2   Selecting a printer driver to install

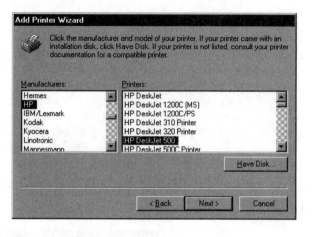

 Make sure you select the correct driver for your model of printer. Most printing problems can be traced to a corrupt or out-of-date printer driver.

 Some printer drivers can't be installed using the Add Printer Wizard. You must run SETUP or INSTALL from the disk to install the printing software. These programs will not only install the correct printer drivers, they will also set up the printer for use with Windows. In this case, you won't have to run the APW (in fact, it won't work because you can't select the right driver).

The next screen (Figure 6.3) allows you to choose which port the printer is hooked to. It will present you with a list of ports that Windows knows about, including parallel (LPT), serial (COM), and infrared (IR) ports, and ask you to choose which port the printer is hooked to. Simply click the port name on the list and click Next. If necessary, you can click Configure Port to configure any special port settings the printer may require.

FIGURE 6.3   Picking the printer port

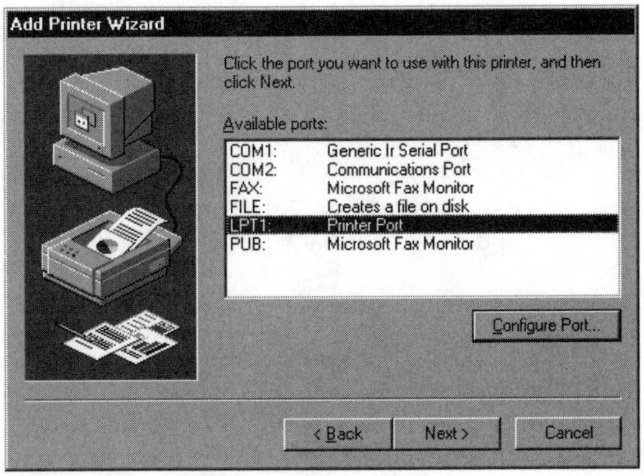

In the next step, APW asks you to give the printer a name (Figure 6.4) so that you can choose the printer by name when you select Print from any program. By default, the APW will supply the name of the print driver in this field. You can change it by simply clicking in the field and typing in a new name. Additionally, you can select whether or not you want this printer to be the default that Windows selects when you don't select a specific printer. If you want this printer to be the default, click the button next to Yes. If not, click No. When you're finished changing these settings, click Next.

FIGURE 6.4   Naming the printer

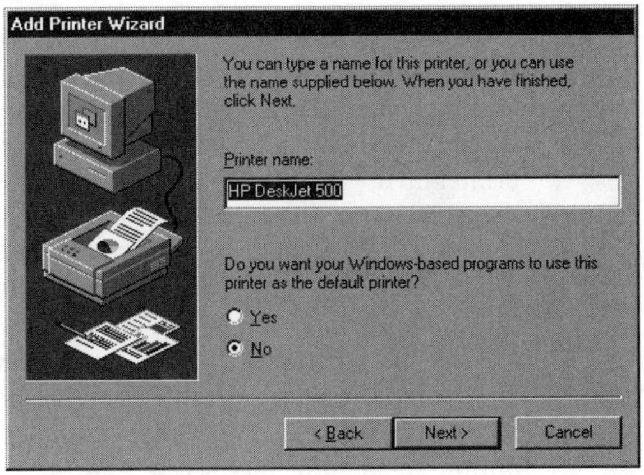

The final step in setting up a new printer is to indicate to the APW whether or not you'd like to print a test page (Figure 6.5). If you say Yes and click Finish, Windows will copy the driver and any support files and then try to print a test page. When the test page is printed, Windows will present you with a screen asking you if the page printed correctly. If you click Yes, the APW is finished and you know the printer works. If you select No, APW will launch Windows Help and bring you to the Printing Troubleshooting page. If you don't want to print a test page, select No (from the APW screen) and APW will simply copy the files and bring you back to the desktop.

FIGURE 6.5   Finishing setting up a printer

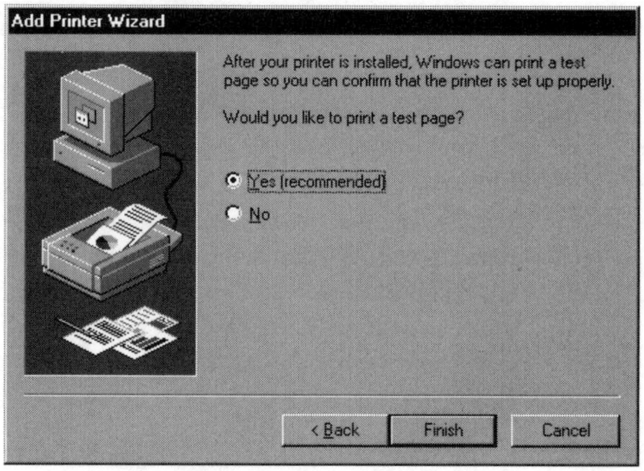

Managing an Existing Printer

If you have a printer installed on your Windows computer, there will be times where you need to change the way the printer functions. For this reason, you should know how to manage an existing printer under Windows. Managing a printer involves knowing how to configure the printer object after you have used the APW to set it up.

First, most of what you need to configure is centered around the printer icon (in the PRINTERS folder) that represents the printer you want to configure. You can configure most items from the property page of the printer by double-clicking the icon of the printer you want to configure.

If you right-click a printer's icon in the PRINTERS folder and choose Properties, you will see a screen similar to the one in Figure 6.6. There may be more options, depending on the type of printer it is. Each tab is used to configure different properties. Table 6.1 lists the tabs and a description of the function of each one.

You can print a test page from this page at any time by simply clicking the Print Test Page button.

FIGURE 6.6 The property page for a printer

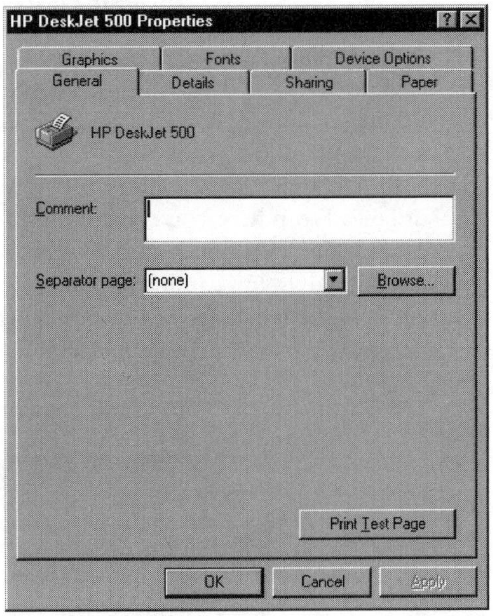

HP DeskJet 500 Properties

| Graphics | Fonts | Device Options |
| General | Details | Sharing | Paper |

HP DeskJet 500

Comment:

Separator page: (none)   Browse...

Print Test Page

OK   Cancel   Apply

TABLE 6.1 Printer Properties Tabs and Functions

Tab	Description
General	Displays the printer's name as well as any comments you want to enter to describe the printer's functions (or eccentricities).
Details	Used to configure how Windows communicates with the printer.
Sharing	Used to share the printer on the network to which the machine is connected.
Paper	Used to configure what kind of paper the printer is using (size-wise) as well as its orientation when printing.

TABLE 6.1   Printer Properties Tabs and Functions *(continued)*

Tab	Description
Graphics	Used to configure the resolution of the printer. Lower resolutions use less toner.
Fonts	Displays the installed fonts. Also used to install other fonts.
Device Options	Changes depending on what kind of printer it is. Used to set the device-specific settings for the printer.

If you select the Details tab, you will see a screen similar to the one in Figure 6.7. From here you can configure how Windows communicates with the printer. For example, you can select a different port to print to for this printer. Additionally, you can install a new or updated driver from this screen. Simply click on the New Driver button. Windows will present you with a driver selection screen (similar to the one shown in Figure 6.2 earlier in this chapter).

FIGURE 6.7   The Details tab of the property page of a Windows 9x printer

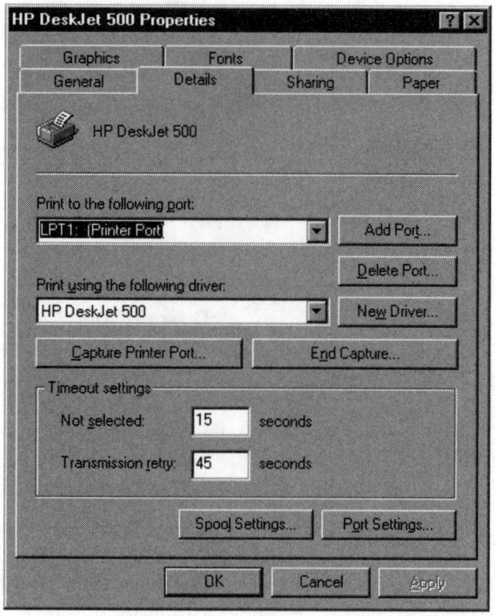

One of the most important options on this screen is the Spool Settings button. This button allows you to configure whether or not Windows will spool print jobs. If print jobs are spooled, every time you click Print in a program, the job is

printed to a spool directory (usually a subdirectory of the C:\WINDOWS\SPOOL directory) by a program called SPOOL32.EXE. Then the job is sent to the printer in the background while you continue to work. If you don't want print jobs to be spooled (it is the default), click the Spool Settings button. From the screen shown in Figure 6.8, you can choose either Spool Print Jobs... or Print Directly to the Printer. Choose the appropriate option and click OK. Once you have made changes to a printer, click OK on the property page to save them.

FIGURE 6.8   Changing a printer's spool settings

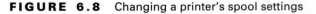

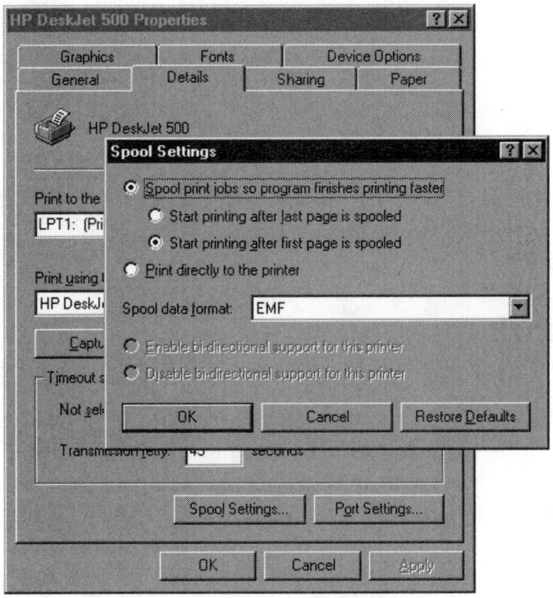

The other way to configure a printer is through the printer item in the System Tray (Figure 6.9). When you print a document, an icon of a printer will appear in the System Tray. By double-clicking it, you can open it so that you can manage the print jobs.

FIGURE 6.9   The printer icon in the System Tray

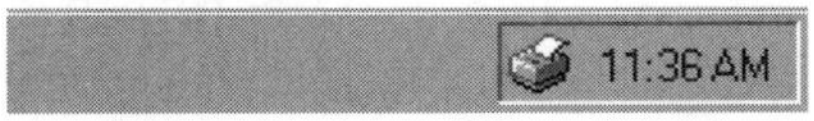

When you double-click the printer icon, you will see the screen shown in Figure 6.10. From here you can see any pending print jobs listed as well as their statistics. Notice that there is one print job currently being printed. If you want to stop the printer, you can choose Printer ➢ Pause Printing and Windows will stop sending print jobs to the printer. If you want to delete a job, click the job in the list of jobs and press the Delete key on your keyboard.

FIGURE 6.10 Printer job list

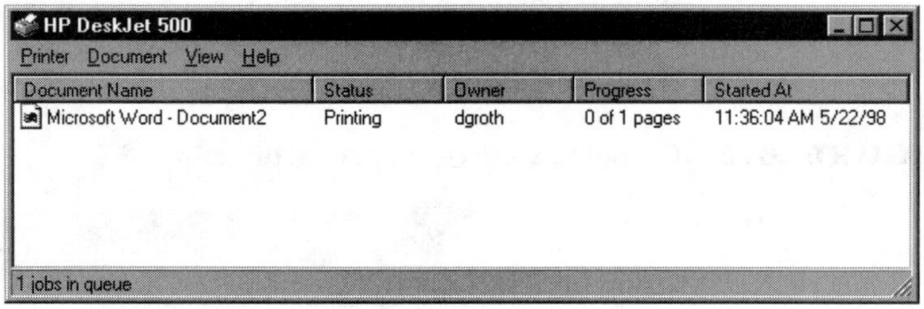

Document Name	Status	Owner	Progress	Started At
Microsoft Word - Document2	Printing	dgroth	0 of 1 pages	11:36:04 AM 5/22/98

HP DeskJet 500 — Printer Document View Help — 1 jobs in queue

If you want to delete all jobs in this list, choose Purge Print Jobs from the Printer menu. All jobs that are currently spooled will be deleted.

Network Printing

Network printing is a lot like local printing except that with network printing, you are introducing a degree of separation between the computer and the printer. That degree of separation is a network. Configuring network printing is very similar to configuring local printing except you must configure the Windows printer driver to print to the network instead of to a local printer port. Usually, this involves installing network software that comes with the printer; the software will make a virtual printer port that points to the specified network printer.

For the A+ exam, you will not be expected to know everything about connecting network printers (after all, that is what the Network+ exam is for). However, you should know the basic steps.

Installing a Network Printer

To set up the printer on your workstation, you most likely will use the Point and Print option for Windows printing. This option allows you to click and drag a printer to the PRINTERS folder and run a shorter version of the Add Printer Wizard, which will set up the printer icon and set up the right drivers on your machine automatically. Follow these steps:

1. Browse to the computer that hosts the printer you want to set up and double-click the computer name. You'll see a window with a list of resources the computer is hosting.

2. Open up the PRINTERS folder (choose Start ➤ Settings ➤ Printers). Arrange these windows so you can see both at the same time (Figure 6.11).

FIGURE 6.11   Preparing for the Point-and-Print process

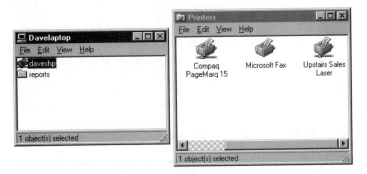

3. To start the Add Printer Wizard, drag the printer you want to set up from the list of resources the computer is hosting to the Printers window. As soon as you release the mouse button, you will see the wizard start, and it will display the window shown in Figure 6.12.

FIGURE 6.12   Starting the Add Printer Wizard

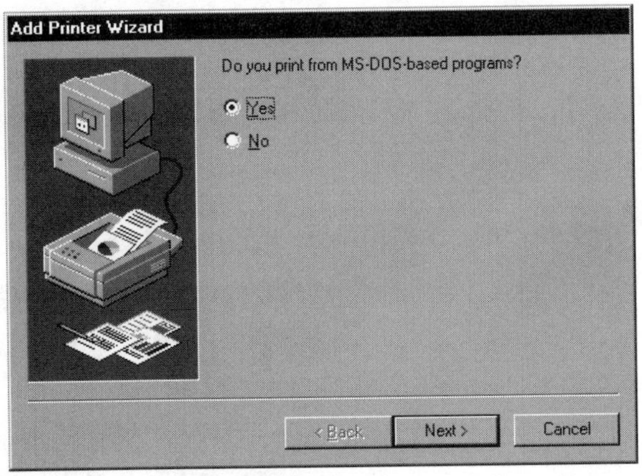

4. The wizard will ask you a series of questions that will help you to configure the printer. The first question it will ask you is "Do you print from MS-DOS–based programs?" The reasoning behind this question is similar to the reason we map drive letters. Most older DOS programs (and to a lesser extent, Windows programs) don't understand the UNC path syntax for access to a shared resource. Instead, they understand a name for a local hardware resource (like LPT1, for the first local parallel port). So, you must point a local printer port name out to the network in a process known as capturing. If you need to capture a printer port, answer "Yes"

to this question; otherwise leave it set to the default ("No"). For our example, click Yes and click Next to move to the next step of the wizard.

5. The next step in the Add Printer Wizard is to capture the printer port, assuming you chose Yes in the preceding step. If you did, you will see the screen in Figure 6.13. This screen allows you to capture a printer port so that DOS programs can print to the network printer. Click the Capture Printer Port button to bring up the screen (shown in Figure 6.14) that allows you to choose which local port you want to capture.

FIGURE 6.13 Capturing a printer port

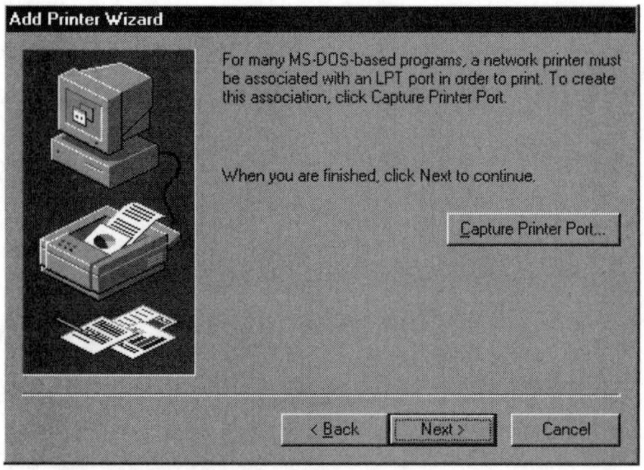

FIGURE 6.14 Picking which local port to capture

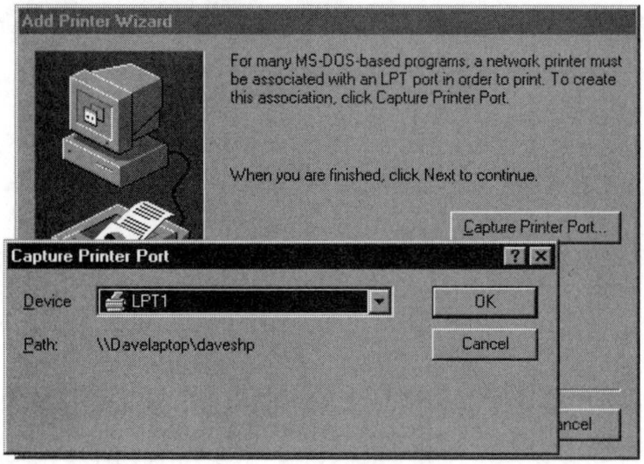

6. From the drop-down list shown, choose the local port you want to capture (any port from LPT1 to LPT9). Remember two things about capturing ports:

   - The port doesn't physically have to be installed in your computer in order to be captured. The capture process just associates a port name with a shared printer.

   - If the port you capture *is* installed in your computer and you capture it, all print jobs sent to that port name will be sent to the network printer, not out the local port (which is the way it is supposed to work). If you have a printer attached to that port, you would not be able to print to it.

7. Pick the LPT port you want to capture and click OK to accept the choice and return to the wizard screen. Then, click Next to continue running the wizard.

8. The next step is to give the printer instance a name. You should give a network printer a name that reflects what kind of printer it is and which machine is hosting it. In this example, the printer is labeled HP LaserJet III (the default name of the driver), but it could have been named Laser on Bob's PC. Type in the name that makes sense to you in the screen that the wizard presents (Figure 6.15). You also have the choice as to whether or not you want the printer to be the default printer that gets used by all Windows applications.

FIGURE 6.15   Naming the printer

From here on, printer installation is exactly the same as installing a local printer. We covered this earlier, so we won't discuss it further here.

Installing and Configuring Peripheral Drivers

In order to make Windows recognize a particular piece of hardware, you must install a driver for it. Each driver is written for the hardware it supports. Not only do you need to install the driver for it, it must be the correct driver. It *is* possible to install a similar driver that may function but is not the correct one. In this section, you will learn how to install a piece of hardware in both Windows 9*x* and 2000.

Windows 95/98

Adding new hardware devices is very simple under Windows. When you start Windows after installing a new hardware device, it will normally detect the new device using Plug and Play and automatically install the software for it. If not, you need to run the Add New Hardware Wizard.

To start adding the new device, double-click the My Computer icon. Then double-click the Control Panel. To start the wizard, double-click Add New Hardware icon in the Control Panel window (Figure 6.16).

FIGURE 6.16 The Control Panel window

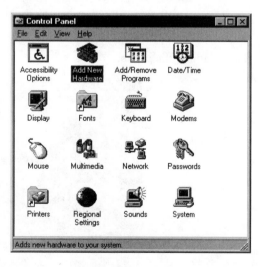

 You can also bring up this window by choosing clicking the Start ➢ Settings ➢ Control Panel.

Once you have started the Add New Hardware Wizard, you will see a screen similar to the one in Figure 6.17. This is the introduction to the wizard. To start the configuration of the new hardware, click Next.

FIGURE 6.17   Add New Hardware Wizard

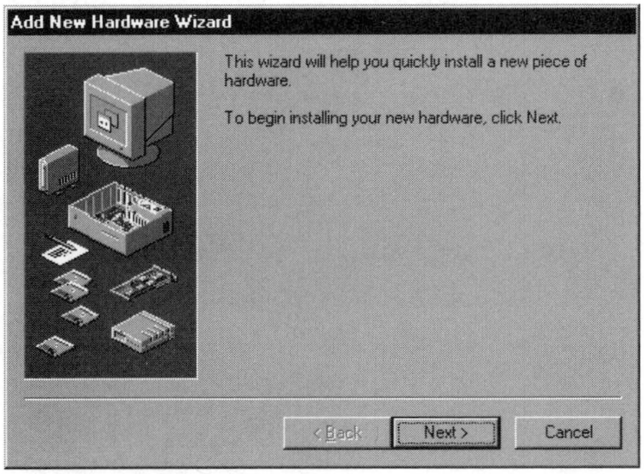

The next screen that is presented (Figure 6.18) allows you to select whether the wizard will search for the hardware. If you choose Yes, then in the next step, Windows will search for the hardware and install the drivers for it automatically. It is the easiest method (especially if the hardware is Plug and Play compliant) and is the least complex. If you choose No, the wizard will present a screen from which you will have to select the type, brand, and settings for the new hardware. For our example, choose Yes and click Next.

FIGURE 6.18   Telling Windows to search for the new hardware

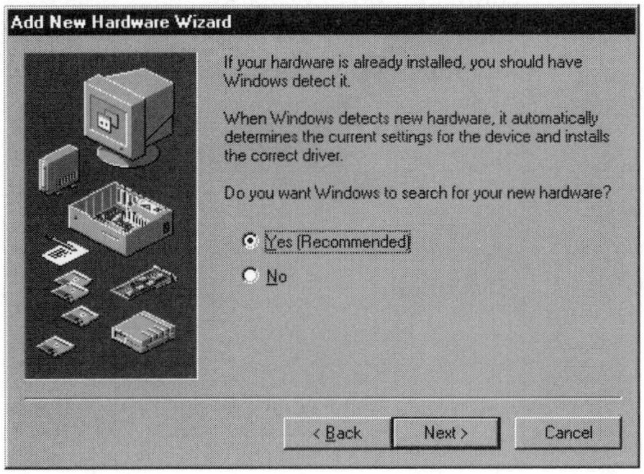

The next screen will tell you that Windows is ready to search for the new hardware. To begin the detection, click Next again. Windows will make an intensive scan of the hardware (you should notice that the hard disk light will be on almost constantly and you will hear the hard disk thrashing away during the detection). During this scan, you will see a progress bar at the bottom of the screen (Figure 6.19) that indicates Windows's progress with the detection. You can stop the detection at any time by clicking the Cancel button.

FIGURE 6.19 Detecting new hardware

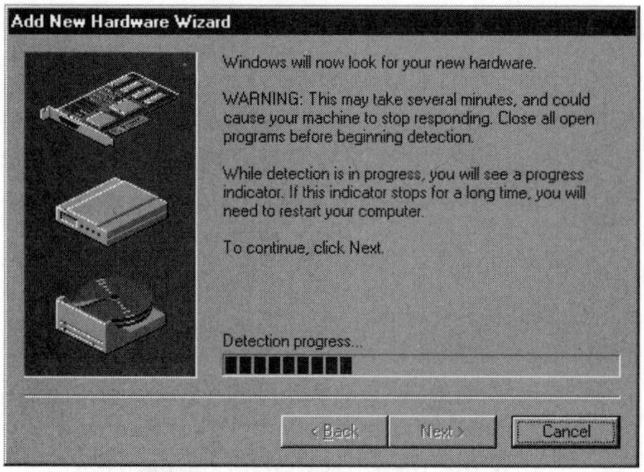

When the progress indicator gets all the way to the right, Windows will tell you that it found some hardware that it can install (Figure 6.20). You can see which hardware it found by clicking the Details button. To finish the setup of the new hardware, click the Finish button. Windows will copy the drivers from the installation disks or CD for the device. Once it has done that, it may ask you for configuration information, if necessary. To finish the hardware setup, it will ask you to reboot Windows so that the changes take effect and Windows can recognize (and use) the new hardware.

FIGURE 6.20 Finishing new hardware installation

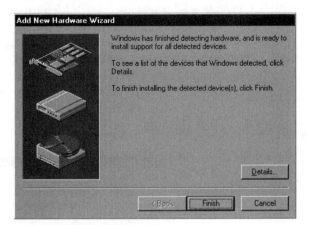

Windows 2000

Again, just like adding printers, there are very few differences between adding a new piece of hardware in Windows 9x and in Windows 2000. However subtle the differences, though, they are important to note. First, Windows 2000 relies very heavily on Plug and Play. Installing a piece of hardware in a Windows 2000 computer basically involves physically installing the device, booting the computer, and letting Windows 2000 automatically install the driver for that device. If it can't find the driver, it will ask you for the location. Additionally, the screens have the Windows 2000 "look and feel." Finally, you can use the Add New Hardware Wizard to both add new hardware and update drivers for existing hardware.

Just as with Windows 9x, you can begin the by double-clicking the Add New Hardware icon (found in Start ➤ Settings ➤ Control Panel). This will start the Add New Hardware Wizard, which is similar to the one in Windows 9x. However, after clicking Next past the first screen, you will be asked if you want to either add/troubleshoot a device or uninstall/unplug a device. The latter choice will allow you to prepare Windows to completely remove a device or temporarily disable a device. To continue adding a hardware device, choose Add/Troubleshoot a Device and click Next.

At this point, Windows 2000 will try to search for any uninstalled Plug and Play devices. It will also search for a list of currently installed devices that may or may not need new drivers. The wizard will then present you with a list of devices so that you can choose which device you want to install a new driver for (either a new device or an existing one), as shown in Figure 6.21. If you are installing a new device, choose Add a New Device. If you are updating a driver for an existing device, choose the device you want to update the driver for. When you've made your choice, click Next.

FIGURE 6.21 Choosing a device to install a driver for

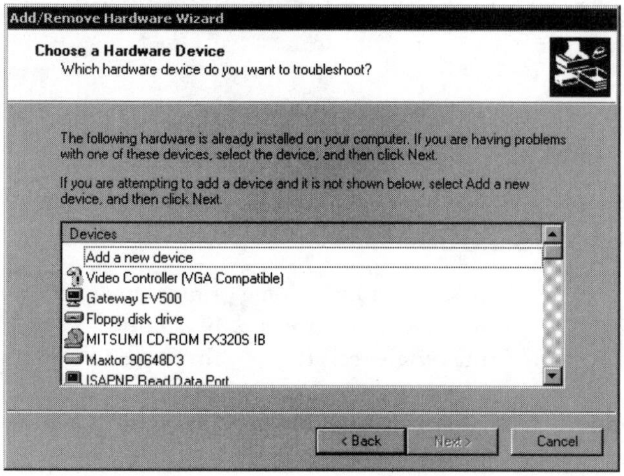

From this point on, the Add New Hardware Wizard works almost exactly the same as the Windows 9*x* wizard. You choose whether you want Windows to search for the hardware or whether you'll select from a list. The wizard will then install the hardware driver or ask you for the appropriate driver and the installation will be finished.

One final difference between installing new hardware on 9*x* and installing it on 2000 is that, if the device driver can't be found or won't install correctly, Windows 2000 will start a troubleshooting wizard to help you finish installing the new hardware.

Summary

In this chapter, you learned how to use and configure additional peripherals. A peripheral is any device that is not part of the computer itself. Examples of peripherals include modems, printers, scanners, and so on.

In the first section of this chapter, you learned about the most popular methods of connecting peripherals to host computers. These methods include serial, parallel, USB, FireWire, and SCSI. We discussed the advantages and disadvantages of each connection method as well as the best application for each.

In the final section, you learned about the proper methods of setting up Windows printing for both locally connected printers and network-connected printers. We showed you how to use the Add Printer Wizard to connect both of these types of printers as well as how to add printer drivers and configure printing properties for each type of printer.

Key Terms

Before you take the exam, be certain you are familiar with the following terms:

FireWire

IEEE-1394

Small Computer System Interface (SCSI)

Universal Serial Bus (USB)

Review Questions

1. You've successfully completed an upgrade to Windows 2000 Professional. Several days later, you add your old printer, using the driver that originally came with it. Now the printer, which has never had a problem, won't print. What do you need to do to fix the problem?

   A. Older printers are often not compatible with Windows 2000. You may need to replace the printer.

   B. Your printer driver is out-of-date. Contact the vendor or visit its Web site for an updated driver.

   C. Uninstall, then reinstall the printer using the original driver.

   D. None of the above.

2. You've set up a network printer. However, you cannot print from your DOS-based programs. What did you do wrong during printer setup?

   A. Nothing. You cannot print from DOS-based programs within Windows 2000.

   B. You have an incorrect printer driver and need an update.

   C. During setup, you did not "capture" the printer port. Rerun the Add Printer Wizard and make the appropriate changes.

   D. Run the Add Printer Wizard again and accept all defaults.

3. When you print in Windows 2000, you cannot perform any other task until the print job is complete. What can you do?

   A. Your printer driver is corrupt. Replace it.

   B. There is nothing you can do. That is the normal printing mode.

   C. Change your printer settings back to the default mode.

   D. Your computer needs more RAM.

4. Which of the following methods correctly adds new hardware to a Windows 9x system if Plug and Play does not work? (Select all that apply.)

   A. Choose Start ➢ Settings ➢ Control Panel and then click the Add New Hardware icon.

   B. Exit to DOS and use the software that came with the device to run the installation.

   C. If Plug and Play does not work, there is no way to get the hardware working in the Windows 9x environment.

   D. On the desktop, double-click the My Computer icon, double-click the Control Panel icon, then double-click the Add New Hardware icon.

5. The most popular connection method is serial. Which of the following are characteristics of a serial connection? (Select all that apply.)

   A. Transfer rate of one data bit at a time.

   B. Maximum speed of 128Kbps.

   C. Though popular, it is expensive to manufacture.

   D. All of the above.

6. Which of the following is a difference between installing new hardware on a Windows 9x system versus a Windows 2000 system?

   A. There is no difference.

   B. With Windows 9x, if the proper device driver cannot be found or won't install properly, a troubleshooting wizard helps finish the task.

   C. With Windows 2000, if the proper device driver cannot be found or won't install properly, a troubleshooting wizard helps finish the task.

   D. With Windows 9x, if the proper device driver cannot be found or won't install properly, then the device cannot be installed at all.

7. The Small Computer System Interface (commonly known as SCSI) is yet another method for connecting peripherals. Which of the following are characteristics of SCSI? (Select all that apply.)

   A. SCSI is the best choice for high-speed connectivity.

   B. SCSI, when properly linked, can support up to 127 peripheral devices.

   C. SCSI can transfer either 16 or 32 bits of data at a time.

   D. SCSI can be added to desktop systems with an expansion card.

8. Which of the following are peripheral connection methods for Windows 9x and Windows 2000? (Select all that apply.)

   A. Parallel

   B. Serial

   C. SCSI

   D. USB

   E. IEEE 1394

9. You're using your USB port for your scanner. What is the preferred method for swapping your scanner with a previously configured digital camera?

    A. Shut the computer down, disconnect the scanner, connect the digital camera, and then turn your computer back on.

    B. With USB, you can hot-swap devices. Therefore, just disconnect the scanner, hook up the digital camera, and you're done.

    C. Turn off the scanner and disconnect it. Connect the digital camera. Reboot. You can now use your digital camera.

    D. None of the above. Digital cameras will not work on a USB port.

10. Which of the following are accepted methods for initiating the Add Printer Wizard (APW, for short)? (Select all that apply.)

    A. Choose Start ➤ Settings ➤ Printers and double-click the Add Printer icon.

    B. Type **APW.EXE** at the DOS prompt.

    C. Double-click the Printers icon in the Control Panel and double-click the Add Printer icon.

    D. Choose Start ➤ Run, type **APW.EXE**, and click OK.

11. Serial connections are very popular. One of the most popular applications of a serial connection is _____ .

    A. Synchronize two data sources

    B. Link multiple peripherals

    C. Transfer large amounts of data at high speeds

    D. All of the above

12. What is the final step in setting up a newly installed printer?

    A. Configure the port settings.

    B. Create a unique printer identification name.

    C. Configure the Graphics setting.

    D. Print a test page.

13. FireWire, or IEEE 1394, is a relatively new peripheral connection method. What is FireWire used for?

    A. It is primarily used to download large video files to a PC.

    B. It is the preferred method for linking multiple peripherals.

    C. It provides direct access to the Internet, bypassing the modem.

    D. It is used to activate explosives via computer.

14. A previously installed Windows 9x printer needs to be modified for higher resolution. How can this be accomplished?

    A. Uninstall, then reinstall the printer, making your changes during the installation process.

    B. Right-click the printer icon, choose Properties, click the Graphics tab, and make your changes.

    C. Right-click the printer icon, choose Change Graphics, and make your changes.

    D. Right-click the printer icon, choose Properties, click Change Graphics, click Resolution, and make your changes.

15. One of the most popular connection methods is parallel. Which of the following are characteristics of a parallel connection? (Select all that apply.)

    A. Transfer rate of 8 data bits at a time

    B. Usually used to connect printers

    C. New parallel ports can connect scanners and Zip drives

    D. Can connect multiple devices at the same time

16. Plug and Play includes a troubleshooting wizard on which operating system?

    A. Windows 95

    B. Windows 98

    C. Windows NT

    D. Windows 2000

17. Which icon will allow you to manage print jobs as well as printer properties?

    A. PRINTERS folder

    B. Printer icon in PRINTERS folder

    C. Printer icon in System Tray

    D. Spooler control panel

18. In addition to the Add Printer Wizard, which other method(s) can be used to configure a printer?

    A. Copy the new driver to the C:\WINDOWS\PRINTERS directory

    B. INSTALL on manufacturer's disk

    C. PSETUP in C:\WINDOWS directory

    D. SETUP on manufacturer's disk

19. The Universal Serial Bus, or USB, is a relatively new connection device. Which of the following are characteristics of USB?

A. Can connect a maximum of 127 external devices

B. Supports printers, scanners, joysticks, digital cameras, and mice

C. Faster data transfer rate than a serial port

D. All of the above

20. You've installed a printer for network use, but no one on the network is able to print to it. Which of the following would be a viable solution to fixing the problem?

A. Right-click the Printer icon, click Network, and configure the printer as needed.

B. Right-click the Printer icon, click Properties, click the Sharing tab, and configure the printer as needed.

C. Open the Control Panel, double-click the Printer icon, click Network, and configure the printer as needed.

D. Only a reinstall of the printer will enable it for network use.

Answers to Review Questions

1. B. When installing a printer, you must always be sure to have an updated driver. Many printing problems originate with out-of-date printer drivers.

2. C. During setup, you must point a local printer port name out to the network. This process is known as capturing. During normal setup, the default to capture a printer port is No. If the Add Printer Wizard is run again and the answer to the Capture Printer Port question is changed to Yes, your printer should then be able to print from DOS-based programs.

3. C. The default setting for printing enables a program called SPOOL32.EXE. That program allows your printing to be done in the background while you can work on other tasks. Spool Print Jobs is a property of most printers.

4. A, D. Plug and Play will automatically detect new hardware and install the proper software. If it is not successful, the Add New Hardware program can be used. That program can be accessed by the methods indicated in answers A and D.

5. A, B. Serial connections have a transfer rate of one data bit at a time, a maximum speed of 128Kbps, and are very inexpensive to manufacture.

6. C. One major difference between installing new hardware on a Windows 9x system versus a Windows 2000 system is that, if the proper device driver cannot be found or won't install properly, a Windows 2000 troubleshooting wizard helps to finish the task.

7. A, C, D. SCSI offers an array of benefits, including high speeds, 16- or 32-bit data transfer rates, and ease of use via an expansion card, but it cannot support 127 peripheral devices. Only USB can do that.

8. A, B, C, D, E. All of the options are peripheral connection methods.

9. B. With USB, you can hot-swap devices. With the PC powered on, disconnect the scanner from the USB cable and connect the cable to the digital camera. There is no need to shut the computer down or reboot.

10. A, C. As with most functions within Windows, there is more than one way to accomplish a task. To initiate the Add Printer Wizard, options A and C are equally correct.

11. A. Serial connections are popular because they are so inexpensive to manufacture. But their transfer rate is slow and only one peripheral can be connected to a serial port. They are, however, an excellent way to synchronize two data sources.

12. D. Option D, print a test page, is the final step in setting up a new printer.

13. A. With a maximum data transfer rate of 400MB per second, FireWire is primarily used to download large video files.

14. B. It is relatively easy to make changes to installed printers. Right-clicking the printer icon and choosing Properties opens a series of printer property pages and functions. Thus, B is the correct answer.

15. A, B, C. Parallel connections have a transfer rate of 8 data bits, they are primarily used to connect printers, and new parallel ports can connect other devices. However, they can connect only one device at a time.

16. D. When Plug and Play does not work, Windows 2000 has a troubleshooting wizard to assist the user. Also, the Add New Hardware Wizard in Windows 2000 can be used to add new hardware and update drivers for existing hardware.

17. C. While a document is printing, a printer icon will appear in the System Tray. By double-clicking it, you can open it and manage your print jobs as well as the printer properties from menus within it.

18. B, D. There are printers for which the APW does not work. In such instances, you will need to run SETUP or INSTALL from the vendor printer disk to install the appropriate printing software.

19. D. The Universal Serial Bus (USB) connects up to 127 external devices, supports most peripherals (including printers, scanners, digital cameras, mice, etc), and provides a high data transfer rate.

20. B. One of the tabs on the printer property page is Sharing. That tab is used to share the printer on the network. The Sharing function can be accessed as indicated in option B.

Chapter

7

Preventative Maintenance

THE FOLLOWING OBJECTIVES ARE COVERED IN THIS CHAPTER:

✓ **2.3 Identify the basic system boot sequences and boot methods, including the steps to create an emergency boot disk with utilities installed for Windows 9x, Windows NT, and Windows 2000.**

Content may include the following:

- Startup disk
- Safe Mode
- MS-DOS mode
- NTLDR (NT Loader), BOOT.INI
- Files required to boot
- Creating emergency repair disk (ERD)

✓ **3.2 Recognize common problems and determine how to resolve them.**

Content may include the following:

- Eliciting problem symptoms from customers
- Having customer reproduce error as part of the diagnostic process
- Identifying recent changes to the computer environment from the user
- Troubleshooting Windows-specific printing problems
  - Print spool is stalled
  - Incorrect/incompatible driver for print
  - Incorrect parameter

Other Common problems

- General Protection Faults
- Illegal operation
- Invalid working directory
- System lock up

- Option (Sound card, modem, input device) or will not function
- Application will not start or load
- Cannot log on to network (option—NIC not functioning)
- TSR (Terminate Stay Resident) programs and virus
- Applications don't install
- Network connection

Viruses and virus types

- What they are
- Sources (floppy, e-mails, etc.)
- How to determine presence

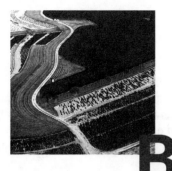

Because of their very nature, computers can and do fail. *Preventative maintenance* involves performing certain practices on a computer so that the computer will function reliably and not fail as often.

NOTE For complete coverage of objective 2.3, please also see Chapters 3 and 4. For complete coverage of objective 3.2, please also see Chapter 9.

Thankfully, Microsoft has included a few pieces of software with their operating systems that allow us to perform preventative maintenance fairly easily. No fuss, no muss. The three preventative maintenance procedures we're going to discuss in this chapter are:

- Backing up your data
- Guarding against virus attacks
- Creating and using an emergency disk

With these procedures, you should be able to recover most of the common problems.

Backing Up Your Data

A *backup* is a duplicate copy of all the files and software on your hard disk. This copy is usually stored in a safe place (like a safe) in case of a system failure. When a system failure occurs, the backup can be copied back onto the system, restoring the system to the state it was in at the time of the last backup. This process of restoring the system is known as a *restore*.

Most backups are done the same way: select what you want to back up, then select where you want to back up to, then finally begin the backup. The files and directories you want to back up (and, subsequently, the drive they are stored on) are called the *backup source*. The device that you are backing up to is called the *backup target*. Once you have selected these items, some backup software will let you save these selections in a file known as a *backup set* so that you can reselect them later for restore by simply retrieving the backup set file from the backup media.

Backup Devices

There are several pieces of backup hardware that are currently available. You can back up your information to magnetic tape, Digital Audio Tape (DAT), Digital Linear Tape (DLT), optical disk, removable hard disk, and many other removable media. The key here is that all of these media can be removed from the drive and stored in a safe place.

It's a common misconception that if you back up your data to a second, non-removable hard disk in your computer, your data is safe. But what happens if your computer is in a fire? What happens is that you lose your data. On the other hand, if the backup media are stored in a fireproof safe, you can purchase a new computer (assuming you have insurance), restore the data from the backup, and be working again in a short time.

Of all the backup media that are available, the most popular is magnetic tape (including reel-to-reel, DAT, DLT, and any backup system that uses a magnetic tape in a cartridge). There are a few reasons it is the most popular:

- First, it's inexpensive. Magnetic tape costs around $.01 to $.02 per MB (around $30 to $40 to back up 2GB), and the price is going down.
- Second, magnetic tapes are small and each holds several hundred MB of data.
- Finally, it's reliable. Magnetic tape is a proven technology that has been around for several years and will continue to expand in capacity and speed in the future.

Backup Types

There are four major types of backup that most backup software will use when backing up files. The four types are Full, Differential, Incremental, and Custom. Each type differs in the amount that it backs up, the time it takes to perform the backup and the time it takes to restore the system to its pre-backup condition.

Full Backup

A Full backup, as its name suggests, backs up everything on the entire disk at once. It simply copies everything from the disk being backed up to the backup device. The backup takes a long time to perform (relative to the other types of backup), but the advantage is that the backup (and, subsequently, the restore) will use only one tape (assuming the tape capacity is large enough to handle backing up the hard disk in one shot).

Full backups are most often performed on systems that require that there be very little down time. Insurance computer systems are one such example. Their administrators will perform a Full backup every night so that if there is a failure, the system can be brought up quickly and the data will be as current as the time of the last backup.

Differential

A Differential backup backs up the files on a disk that have changed since the last Full backup, regardless of whether a Differential or Incremental backup has been done since the last Full backup. The Full backup is done usually once a week (i.e., on Friday) and copies all the files from the disk to the backup device. The Differential backup is done every day.

The size of a Differential backup increases every day following the Full backup. For example, if you do a Full backup on Friday night, then start your Differential backups on Monday, the Monday Differential tape will only have a small amount of information on it. When you get to Thursday, the Thursday tape will have all of the information on the disk that has changed since last Friday (including Monday, Tuesday, Wednesday, and Thursday's information).

The advantage to a Differential backup style is that during the week, the backups don't take very long (although the time it takes to back up increases as the week goes on). In addition, you don't have to buy many backup tapes or media. You can use the same backup media you use for the Differential backup (not the one for the Full backup) over and over again each day.

When you restore from a Differential backup, you will need two tapes: the Full backup from the previous week and the current Differential backup. You will need to restore the Full backup first, then restore the Differential backup to restore the changes made since the last Full backup.

Incremental

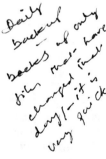

What kind of backup strategy would you use with a terabyte (1,024 gigabytes) of data? A Full backup every day would be impractical because it would take too long and use several tapes. A Differential backup would use even more tapes. Given these limitations, an Incremental backup would be the best choice.

The Incremental backup works similarly to the Differential backup but uses fewer tapes in a large backup situation. An Incremental backup does a Full backup once a week, then the backup software backs up all the files that have changed since the *previous* backup (not necessarily the last *Full* backup). Each day the backup software backs up a different amount of data, depending on the amount of data that was created that day.

The upside to the Incremental backup is that only the files that have changed that day will be backed up. If only three files changed today, then only three files will be backed up. Incremental backups tend to be very quick. Additionally, there is very little wasted effort because you aren't backing up files that haven't changed since you last backed them up. The downside to Incremental backups is the number of tapes needed for a restore. To restore from an Incremental backup, you need the last Full backup tape and all the Incremental backup tapes from the day of the failure back to the day of the last Full backup.

Custom

The last type of backup that is performed is the Custom backup. A Custom backup is any combination of the above three types. A Custom backup involves selecting the files you want backed up as well as when you want them backed up. Most backup software programs have the ability to perform this type of backup. An example of a time when you might need to perform a Custom backup is the end of the year. Accountants will need to back up the previous year's accounting data before finishing the year's accounting, just in case they make any mistakes and need to restore and start over.

And Now for the Real World...

There are some computer systems that can't afford any "down time" (i.e., banking, flight control, and certain high-volume sales systems). These systems back up all the data in real time and are called "high-availability data solutions." They will use various techniques to ensure that as soon as the data is written to disk, another copy is written to a second disk. If the system goes down, the backup system takes over automatically.

As you can imagine, these systems are usually impractical for home users, but they are found quite commonly in the network world on servers.

Backing Up in MS-DOS: Using MSBACKUP.EXE

Because of the importance of backing up your data, there are many different backup programs to choose from. Microsoft has ensured that you will have one to use by including one with each of its major operating systems: DOS, Windows 3.x and Windows 95 (a backup utility is also included with Windows 98, NT, and 2000).

 We will assume that you will be backing up to floppy for these examples, but it should be noted that most computers can be fitted with tape drives that can be used by some of these programs (the Windows 9x/NT/2000 Backup, for example). If you have a tape drive in your computer and want to use the following guidelines to back up your data, just ignore the steps where you need to swap disks.

The MS-DOS backup program MSBACKUP is a very simple, very powerful program. It can be run in either command line mode or with a menu-driven interface. In either mode it can copy files to any DOS device (including floppy drives and redirected network drives—tape drives aren't supported). It can perform any of the types of backups including Full, Incremental, and Differential (and Custom is an option if you select specific files to back up).

MSBACKUP uses special settings files called SET files to store the settings for how it should run. The default SET file is called DEFAULT.SET and, if unmodified by the user, will allow a user to back up their entire hard drive by simply starting the backup program and pressing *B* for Backup and *S* for Start Backup.

To start MSBACKUP, simply type **C:\>MSBACKUP** at the DOS command line and press Enter. MSBACKUP will start and present you with a menu giving you five choices: Backup, Restore, Compare, Configure, or Quit. Because the A+ Exam doesn't have too many questions about this menu, we'll just give a summary of each of these options.

If you have never run MSBACKUP before, it will present you with a screen that asks you to configure it. You will need to enter some settings and test MSBACKUP to make sure that backups are reliable.

Configure

Because MSBACKUP is a DOS program, you may need to configure the hardware it's using. When you select the Configure button from the main menu, you will be presented with a screen where you can configure the video settings (like what resolution and which colors you want to use), mouse settings (important if you want the mouse to work properly in this program), and which backup devices MS Backup is going to use (not really necessarily if you are backing up to floppy).

The final option on this screen is the Compatibility Test. This test ensures that your system is able to backup files reliably. The test is automated (you must specify which drive you are using to back up to), but you will need to have a disk available so that it can do a test backup. Click the button to perform this compatibility test. If it finishes with no errors, you can begin your backup.

You cannot perform a backup until you run a compatibility test!

Backup

To use the Backup option:

1. Click the Backup button (assuming your mouse is set up to work under DOS) or type **B**. When you select this option, a menu will appear.

2. At the top of this menu, you will see a file name under "Setup File." This is the name of the SET file that MSBACKUP gets its settings from. If you

have saved previously configured settings, choose this option and pick the SET file that contains the details of how backup should run. Otherwise, leave this option set to DEFAULT.SET.

3. You can then click the Backup From box and choose which files you want to back up. Click the drive(s) that you want to back up or use the Select Files button underneath this window to pick specific files you want to back up. Remember that the more you choose to back up, the longer the backup will take and the more media (disks) you will use.

4. Choose the drop-down list under Backup To to pick which drive letter you want to back the files up to. If you pick a floppy disk drive (A or B in most systems), MSBACKUP will copy as many files as it can to the disk, then ask for a new, blank disk when it is full.

As you remove disks or other backup media that are full from a drive, label them immediately. That way you won't lose them or get them out of order.

5. After you have chosen where you are backing up to, you should choose whether to do a Full, Differential, or Incremental backup. (Custom backups simply involve changing the settings for any of the other types.) The default type is Full, but you can change this option by clicking on the drop-down menu and selecting Differential or Incremental.

6. When you have finished setting up the backup, you can click Start Backup. During the backup, MSBACKUP will display how long the backup will take, how many disks it will take, and how much data is being backed up. When the backup is complete, it will display a screen telling you all the statistics about the backup that was performed, including any files that were skipped and the speed (in KB per minute) at which the backup took place.

Compare

Once you have performed a backup, you should use the Compare option on the MS Backup main menu to compare the files you just backed up to the originals that are currently on the disk. This option, when selected, will allow you to perform one of two operations:

- You can check the integrity of the current backup.

- You can check to see how many files have changed on your computer since the backup was performed.

The second of these two operations is useful before performing an Incremental or Differential backup because it will give you an idea of how many files have changed and thus of how many will be backed up during either an Incremental or Differential.

Restore

Hopefully, you will never need to restore. If you have to restore, that usually means there was a disk failure of some kind and you've lost some (or all) of your data. Before you can restore, you must have DOS, as well as the MSBACKUP program installed on the computer. Then, follow these steps:

1. Run MSBACKUP and select Main ➢ Restore.

2. Place the backup media that contains the files you want restored into its appropriate drive.

3. Choose the location you want to restore from by clicking Restore From and choosing the drive letter of the disk you are restoring from.

4. Select Restore To ➢ Original Locations so that the files will be restored along with the directories they came from.

5. Next, you *must* choose which files to restore (you can't proceed with the restore otherwise):

   - To restore the entire backup of the drive, just make sure that [-C-] All Files is selected in the Restore Files window.

   - If you want to restore a particular file or files, choose Select Files and pick the file(s) you want to restore.

6. When you are finished with your selections, click the Start Restore button to begin the restoration. During the restoration, MS Backup will ask you for several disks, in the same order it did when you performed the backup. Insert each disk when MS Backup asks for it.

When the restore is finished, you will see a status screen informing you of how long it took and how many files were restored.

Quit

Select this option when you have finished performing your backup, configure, or restore. When selected, this option will exit the program and leave you at a DOS prompt.

Backing Up in Windows 3.*x*: Using MWBACKUP.EXE

Now that we have discussed the MSBACKUP program for DOS, we need to discuss the available, built-in backup for Windows 3.*x*. There is a Windows version of MSBACKUP.EXE that comes with MS-DOS. It is called MWBACKUP.EXE, and it runs basically the same as the MS-DOS version, except all screens now have the Windows "look and feel" to them. Additionally, the main menu has been replaced by a menu bar at the top of the Microsoft Backup window. The four buttons are the same choices you have with the DOS version, and they perform the same functions.

Using the Microsoft Backup for Windows is basically the same as using the DOS version. This is mainly because they are based on the same backup engine. Generally speaking, you can follow the same steps to back up with Microsoft Backup for Windows that you did with MSBACKUP.EXE for DOS. The only difference is that you will see Windows windows and menus instead of DOS windows and menus.

Backing Up in Windows 95: Using Backup for Windows 95

The third backup utility we're going to discuss is Microsoft Backup for Windows 95. It is basically the old Microsoft Backup, with a new interface and a few new features. It can support backing up to both floppies and other types of backup devices (like tape drives). However, the types of tape drives it can use are somewhat limited. Table 7.1 lists the tape drives that are compatible with Windows 95 and the ones that aren't.

TABLE 7.1 Windows 95 Backup Tape Drive Compatibility Chart

Tape Drive	Compatible
Archive (any)	No
QIC 40	Yes
QIC 80	Yes
QIC 3010	Yes
QIC 40, 80, and 3010	Yes
Irwin (any)	No
Mountain (any)	No
QIC Wide	No
QIC 3020	No
SCSI tape drives (any)	No
Summit (any)	No
Travan (any)	No
Wangtek (QIC 40, 80, and 3010)	Yes

As you can see, basically only a QIC 40, 80, or 3010 tape drive will really work properly with Backup for Windows 95 (as well as any floppy drive).

Installing Windows 95 Backup

In Windows 95, Backup can sometimes be found under Start ➢ Programs ➢ Accessories ➢ System Tools. I say "sometimes" because it is not installed by default. You must specifically install it (either after Windows 95 has been installed or during a custom install) in order to use it.

To install Backup after Windows 95 has been installed, follow these steps:

1. Proceed to the Windows 95 Control Panel under Start ➢ Settings ➢ Control Panel.

2. Select Add/Remove Programs and choose the Windows Setup tab (Figure 7.1).

3. Click the check box next to Disk Tools. Doing so will tell the Windows 95 Setup program that you want to install the disk tools (including Backup).

4. To finish the installation, click OK.

Windows will copy the files from the installation location (either floppy or CD-ROM) and update the System Tools program group with an icon for Backup.

FIGURE 7.1   Installing Windows 95 Backup using Add/Remove Programs

Starting Backup

To start the Windows 95 Backup, choose Start ➤ Programs ➤ Accessories ➤ System Tools ➤ Backup. The first time you run Backup, you will see a screen similar to the one shown in Figure 7.2. As you can see, this window explains, in a very broad sense, how to use Backup to back up your files. If you haven't used Backup before, you might want to click the Help button. This will bring up a Windows Help screen that will allow you to browse and search for help on how to use Backup. Once you have read the help file, or if you already know how to use Backup, you can click OK.

FIGURE 7.2 You will see this screen the first time you run Backup.

 If you don't want to see this screen again, check the box next to Don't Show This Again.

The nice thing about the Windows 95 Backup program is that it automatically makes a backup set for you, to get you started. This backup set is a full backup of the hard disk, including the Registry files (which some backup programs can't back up). After you click OK to the screen in Figure 7.2, Backup will present you with the screen shown in Figure 7.3, which tells you it has made this backup set and what you can use it for.

 Do not use this backup set (called Full System Backup) to base your Incremental or Differential backups on. They may not work correctly if based on this particular backup set.

FIGURE 7.3   Backup automatically creates a backup set called Full System Backup for you the first time you run it.

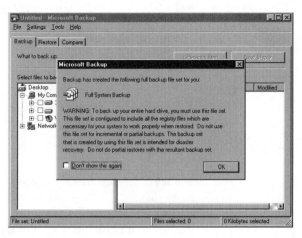

To start using Backup, mark the check box (if you don't want to see this warning again) and click OK.

Layout of Backup

Backup is a rather simple yet powerful program. There are two panes in the main window (Figure 7.4). These two panes work very similarly to the Windows Explorer program. If you double-click on an item in the right pane, it will open and allow you to see what's inside. You can also use the right pane and click on the + signs next to items to "tree them out" and show the directory structure. These two panes allow you to select items to be backed up or restored depending on which tab is selected above. In Figure 7.4, the Backup tab is forward, meaning that selections you make will be for files and directories to be backed up.

FIGURE 7.4   The Windows 95 Backup main window

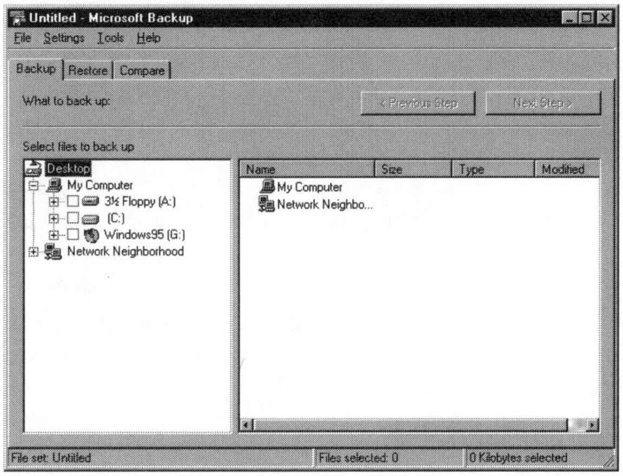

In addition to the two panes, you will notice that there are menus at the top of the screen. The most important of these menus is Help. If you don't understand how to do something in Backup, press the F1 key or choose Help ➢ Help Topics. Doing so will open the Windows 95 Help topics for Backup.

Backing Up Files

Backing up files in Windows 95 Backup works very similarly to the Windows MWBACKUP.EXE program. First you select what you want to back up, then where to want to back up those files and directories to, and then you initiate the backup:

1. To start the backup process, select the Backup tab (if it's not already selected).

2. Then select the directories you want to back up by clicking the check boxes next to them (you may need to click the + sign next to a directory if the subdirectory you want is inside it). If you want to back up the entire C drive, simply click the check box next to the drive icon labeled "C:" When you make a selection, a window will appear that shows you it is counting the files and determining how much space they will take up (Figure 7.5).

FIGURE 7.5 Selecting files to back up

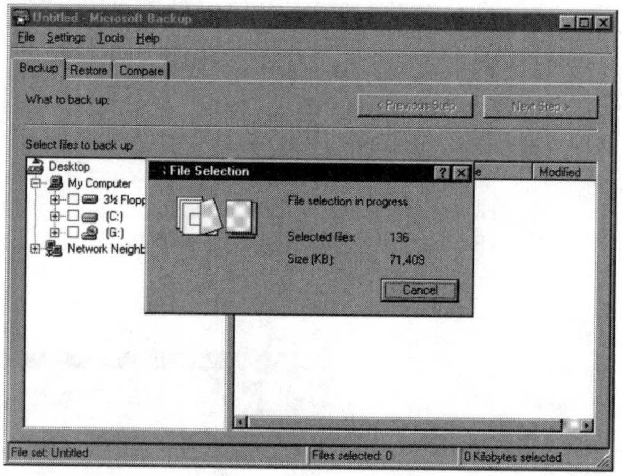

3. Once Backup finishes counting files, you will be able to click the button marked Next Step to start the Backup Wizard.

If you make an icon on your desktop for Backup and you have a preconfigured backup set (SET file), you can start the backup by dragging the SET file onto the Backup icon.

4. The next step in the backup process involves selecting where you want to back the files up to (Figure 7.6).

- If you have a compatible tape drive installed, it will show up in the list on the left. You can then select it as the target device and click Start Backup to begin the backup.

- If you don't have a tape drive (or don't want to use it), you can select one of the floppy drives as the target device by clicking on its name. The name of the device will appear under Selected Device or Location as the device that has been specified as the target. In either case, select the device you want to back up to and click Start Backup to continue.

FIGURE 7.6   Selecting a backup target device

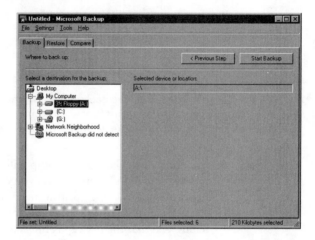

5. Now that you have selected what you want to back up, chosen the target backup device, and begun the backup, Backup will ask you what you want to call the backup set (Figure 7.7). Type in a name that describes what you are backing up. You can use any character except \, /, :, or > in the backup set name. For example, if you are backing up the entire C drive, you might call the backup of the C drive "Full Backup." To start the backup, type the name of the backup set, then click OK.

FIGURE 7.7 Entering a backup set name

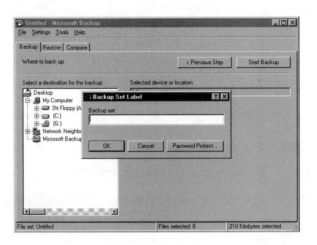

 You can protect sensitive backup data by entering a password for the backup set. Simply click the Password Protect button to enter a password. This password will be required during the restore process in order to restore the data.

6. As soon as you click OK, Backup will present you with a screen similar to the one shown in Figure 7.8. As you can see, this screen shows you how many files it is backing up, how much space they occupy, and how far along the backup is. When the backup is finished, it will present you with a screen telling you that the backup is finished (Figure 7.9). Click OK to acknowledge this screen, and you will see the backup statistics screen that shows you how many files were backed up, how much data (in KB) was backed up, and how long it took. Click OK and you are finished with the backup.

FIGURE 7.8 Backup progress screen

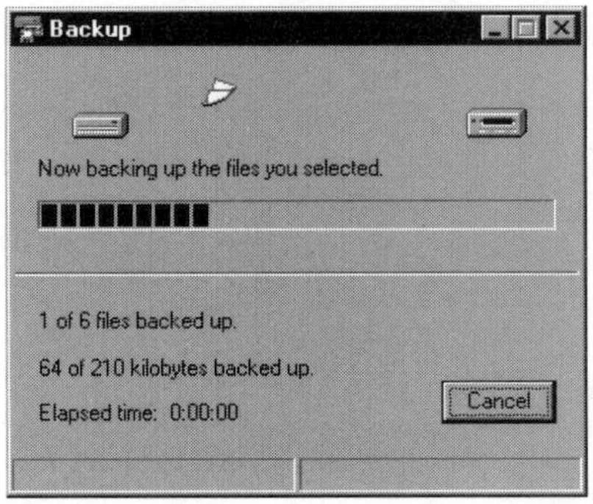

FIGURE 7.9   The Backup Finished window

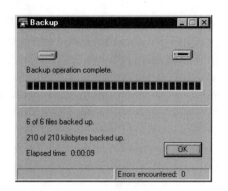

Restoring Files

It's amazing: There are some customers I've done work for who have had a computer company come in, set up their backup system for them, and only show them how to change tapes! When the customers have a problem, they feel helpless and don't know if their backup is any good until the computer company comes in and does their restore for them.

In order to ensure that your backups are good, you should perform a test restore every once in a while. If you used the Windows 95 backup program to back up your files, you will need to know how to use it to restore, as well:

1. To begin a restore, run Backup and insert the first disk (or tape) of the backup into the drive.

2. Once Backup is up and running, you must click on the Restore tab to start the restore process.

3. In the screen that appears (Figure 7.10), you will see a list of the possible backup devices on the left. From this list, you must select the device you want to restore from by clicking on it.

4. Once you select a backup device, a list of the backup sets on that device will appear in the right-hand window. To continue, you must select the backup set that contains the files you want to restore and click Next Step.

5. If there is a password on the backup set, Backup will prompt for it. You must enter the correct password before Backup will let you continue with the restore.

FIGURE 7.10 The Windows 95 Backup Restore window

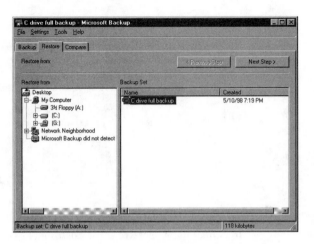

6. The next step in the restore is to select the files and directories you want to restore. The screen shown in Figure 7.11 works the same as the file selection screen for backing up files earlier in the chapter: simply place a check mark next to the file(s) you want to restore and click Start Restore. On the other hand, if you want to restore the whole backup set, click the check box next to the name of the backup set in this window. All files from the backup set will be restored with this selection.

FIGURE 7.11 Selecting files to restore

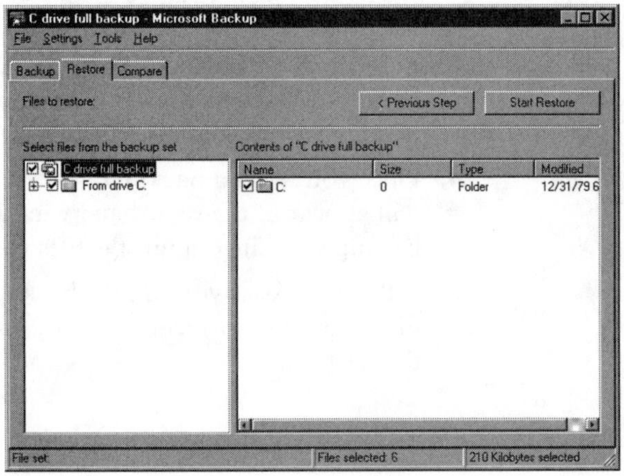

Once you have clicked Start Restore, Backup will review the backup set and count how many files there are to restore. It will then display a status window (very similar to the backup progress window in Figure 7.8) that will show how far along the backup is. (See Figure 7.12.) This screen will display how many files have been restored (out of the total number of files to be restored), how long you have been restoring files, and how much data has been restored (in KB).

FIGURE 7.12 Restore progress screen

When Backup finishes restoring all the files you have selected, it will present you with a summary of the restore (Figure 7.13) detailing how much data was restored and how long it took. Click OK to complete the restore and return to the Backup main screen.

FIGURE 7.13 Restore summary screen

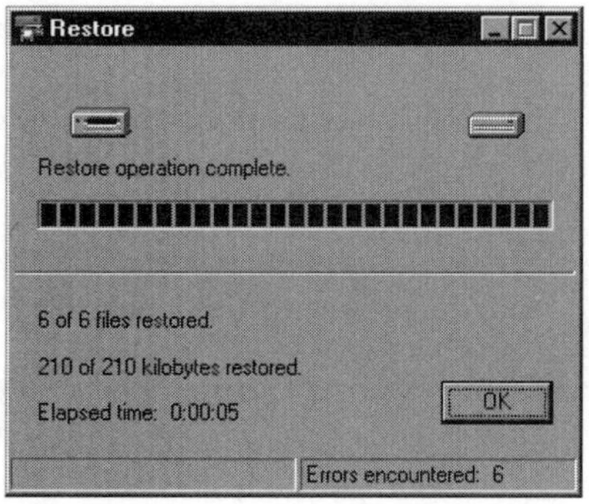

And Now for the Real World...

In most situations, the backup software that comes with most operating systems is adequate. However, you can buy backup software that has more features than the included software. Some of those features include data compression, backup scheduling, and greater hardware device support.

For home computers, the Microsoft backup products are more than adequate. However, for business users, I would recommend looking at products like Norton Backup or Central Point backup. The features they add will make a computer administrator much happier in the end.

Guarding against Virus Attacks

A computer *virus* is a small, deviously genius program that replicates itself to other computers, generally causing the computers to behave abnormally. Generally speaking, a virus's main function is to reproduce. A virus attaches itself to files on a hard disk and modifies the files. When these files are accessed by a program, the virus can "infect" the program with its own code. The program may then, in turn, replicate the virus code to other files and other programs. In this manner, a virus may infect an entire computer.

When an infected file is transferred to another computer (via disk or modem download), the process begins on the other computer. Because of the frequency of downloads from the Internet, viruses can run rampant if left unchecked. For this reason, anti-virus programs were developed. They check files and programs for any program code that shouldn't be there and either eradicate it or prevent the virus from replicating. An anti-virus program is generally run in the background on a computer and examines all the file activity on that computer. When it detects a suspicious activity, it will notify the user of a potential problem and ask them what to do about it. Some anti-virus programs can also make intelligent decisions about what to do as well. The process of running an anti-virus program on a computer is known as *inoculating* the computer against a virus.

For a listing of most of the viruses that are currently out there, refer to Symantec's Anti-Virus Research Center (SARC) at www.symantec.com/avcenter/index.html.

There are two real categories of viruses, benign and malicious. The benign viruses don't do much besides replicate themselves and exist. They may cause the occasional problem, but it is usually an unintentional side effect. Malicious viruses, on the other hand, are designed to destroy things. Once a malicious virus (i.e., the Michelangelo virus) infects your machine, you can usually kiss the contents of your hard drive goodbye.

> ### But Where Do I Stick the Needle?
>
> You may notice that a lot of the language surrounding computer viruses sounds like language we use to discuss human illness. The moniker "virus" was given to these programs because a computer virus functions much like a human virus, and the term helped to anthropomorphize the computer a bit. Somehow, if people can think of a computer as getting "sick," it breaks down the computer phobia that many people have.

Anti-Virus Software

Wouldn't it be nice if Microsoft included an anti-virus program with their operating systems? They did, but only with MS-DOS. MS-DOS 6.22 comes with anti-virus software that lets you detect viruses on your computer as well as clean any infected files. This software is called Microsoft Anti-Virus and has been included with DOS since version 6.0. The same program contains files to allow it to work with Windows.

Using Microsoft Anti-Virus for DOS

To use Microsoft Anti-Virus for DOS:

1. Type **C:\>MSAV** at the MS-DOS command line. From the main menu on the screen that appears, you can check for viruses on any disk drive as well as remove them if any are present. In the lower-right corner of this screen, you can see which drive you are currently scanning for viruses.

2. From the main menu, you have five options: Detect, Detect & Clean, Select New Drive, Options, and Exit. Choose Select New Drive. This option allows you to pick which drive you want to scan. You can select from any of the disk drives you have installed in your system.

You don't necessarily have to scan the drive letters for CD-ROM drives. CD-ROMs are read-only so viruses can't be transferred to them from your machine. On the other hand, you may want to scan them anyway because viruses can be burned onto CDs if the machine doing the burning has a virus.

3. Back at the Main menu, you have two options if you want to see if you have a virus on your computer. You can use the Detect option or the Detect & Clean option. Choose either one and MS Anti-Virus will check the entire disk to find any viruses that it knows about.

   - If it detects a virus and you have Detect & Clean selected, it will present you with a screen that allows you to choose whether or not you want MS Anti-Virus to try and clean the virus from the disk or to ignore it (Figure 7.14).

- If MS Anti-Virus finds a virus and you have Detect selected, the program will simply tell you which files are afflicted.

FIGURE 7.14 MS Anti-Virus finds a virus

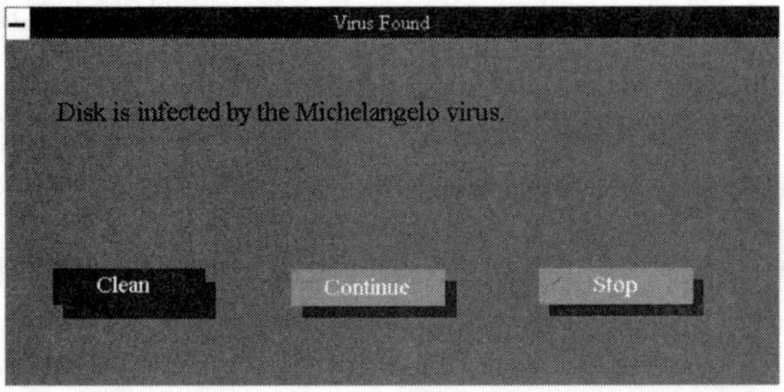

4. When it has finished scanning the disk, MSAV will present you with a list of the disks it has scanned, the file types it has scanned, the number of viruses found on the disks, and the number of files cleaned. If it hasn't found any viruses, select OK to return to the main menu. Then select Exit to quit MSAV. If it did find a virus or two, select OK and return to the main menu, then re-run the Detect & Clean process just to make sure the virus is gone.

There are two options left on the main menu to discuss: Options and Exit. Both are pretty much self-explanatory. The Options menu allows you to change how aggressively MSAV checks for viruses. The Exit menu completely exits you from the MSAV program.

Using Microsoft Anti-Virus for Windows

If you want to use Microsoft Anti-Virus for Windows, simply open the Microsoft Tools program group and double-click the Microsoft Anti-Virus icon. In the window that appears, select which disk (or disks) you want to scan from the list at the left side, then click the Detect button or the Detect & Clean button to start the scanning for viruses.

During detection MSAV will display a screen showing which files it's scanning and the progress. If it finds a file infected with a virus, it will display a warning and give you the same options it does under MS-DOS.

Finally, once MSAV is finished running, it will present you with a status screen that gives you a list of the number of files it scanned, the number that were infected, and the time it took the scan (similar to the status screen for the DOS version).

> **And Now for the Real World...**
>
> There are several commercial anti-virus programs available. One of the best and most widely used is Symantec Anti-Virus (SAM). It has a memory resident component to constantly look for viruses, as well as an executable component for scanning for viruses. SAM is available for Macintosh, Windows 3.*x*, Windows 9*x*, Windows NT, Windows 2000, UNIX, and a few other platforms.
>
> There are also programs like Norton Anti-Virus and Central Point Anti-Virus available if the Symantec product isn't your bag. And you can always just use the ones that come with DOS and Windows (unless you have Windows 95, which doesn't come with one).

Creating and Using an Emergency Disk

What happens when your Windows computer has a problem so severe the computer won't boot? Often times, if the Registry is corrupt, the Windows interface won't come up—not even in Safe Mode. All versions of Windows after 95 come with a utility that allows you to create a disk that can be used to fix Windows. This disk is often called the Windows Emergency Repair Disk (ERD). It contains enough of the Windows startup files to boot the computer. The disk also contains files and utilities to examine (and possibly fix) the machine, utilities like FDISK, SCANDISK, EDIT, ATTRIB, FORMAT, DEBUG, CHKDSK, and UNINSTAL.EXE.

Windows 9*x* Startup Disk

The Windows 9*x* emergency disk is a simple bootable disk that contains some basic utilities, like FDISK, ATTRIB, CHKDSK, DEBUG, EDIT, FORMAT, RESTART, SCANDISK, and SYS. These files are used to correct basic disk problems as well as file boot problems. However, the Windows 9*x* emergency disk CANNOT be used to restore a corrupt Registry (apart from copying the USER.DAT and SYSTEM.DAT files from their backup locations).

Creating a Windows 9*x* Startup Disk

To create a Windows 9*x* startup disk, select Start ➢ Settings ➢ Control Panel, double-click Add/Remove Programs, and select the Startup Disk tab (see Figure 7.15). When you are ready to create a startup disk, insert a blank floppy disk in your A drive and click the Create Disk icon. Windows 9*x* will format the disk and make it bootable (see Figure 7.16). It will then copy the aforementioned utilities to it so that you can use them to fix Windows 9*x*.

When Windows 9*x* finishes copying files to the disk, remove the disk from the drive, label it "Windows 9*x* Emergency Startup Disk," and put it in a safe place so that you can get to it easily if there is ever a problem.

FIGURE 7.15 The Startup Disk tab of the Add/Remove Programs control panel

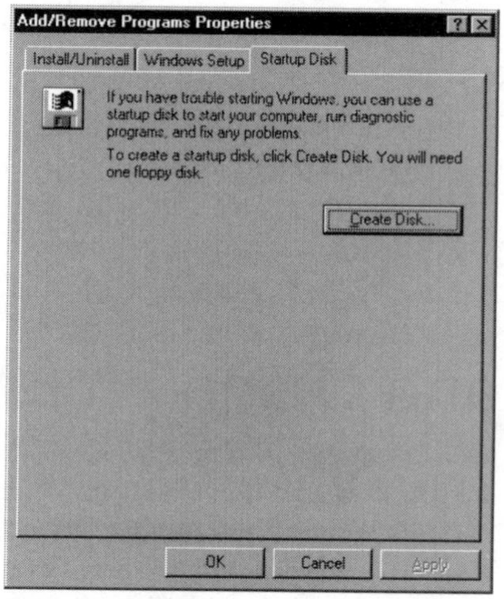

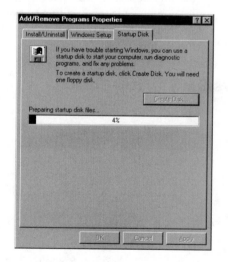

FIGURE 7.16 Creating a new startup disk

Using the Windows 9*x* Repair Disk

If you have a problem with your Windows installation and you suspect the disk has a problem, you can boot to the repair disk and try to repair the hard disk.

Simply insert the floppy you made into your floppy drive and boot to it. This startup disk will create a small, virtual disk drive (usually labeled D or something similar) with all the repair utilities installed on it. You can then use these utilities to repair the disk or files. Additionally, since you are booted up to a command line, you can copy new files over old, corrupt ones, if necessary.

Windows NT Emergency Repair Disk (ERD)

When compared to Windows 9*x*, Windows NT is a much more advanced operating system that relies much more on the Registry than any of its predecessors did. The Windows NT Emergency Repair Disk (ERD) is a special disk you can create in Windows NT that can be used to repair the Registry as well as startup files. One important difference between the NT ERD and the Windows 9*x* Startup Disk is that the NT ERD contains only information—it is NOT a bootable disk. You must use some other method of booting NT (usually a startup disk set or the NT installation CD itself).

The Windows NT ERD typically contains the following files:

- System Registry hive (SYSTEM._)
- Software Registry hive (SOFTWARE._)
- The Security Account Manager (SAM) and Security database Registry hives (SAM._ and SECURITY._)
- Default user profile (default._)
- New user profile (ntuser.da_) Windows NT version 4.0 only
- The SETUP.LOG file
- The AUTOEXEC.NT file
- The CONFIG.NT file

These files can be used to restore a Windows NT system to proper operation.

An explanation of these files can be found in Chapter 4, "Windows 2000."

Creating a Windows NT ERD

To create a Windows NT Emergency Repair Disk, you must use the RDISK utility. This utility is installed with the default installation of Windows NT and by default is installed to the C drive in the WINNT\SYSTEM32 directory. To create the NT ERD using RDISK, follow these steps:

1. Go to Start ➢ Run and type **RDISK**.

2. The graphic below will display. At this screen, click the Create Repair Disk button.

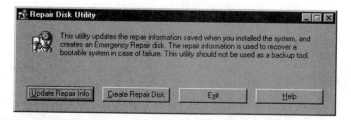

3. RDISK will prompt you to insert a disk. Insert a blank diskette (or one that is okay to format) and click OK.

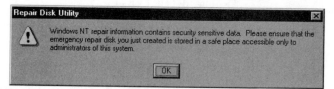

4. RDISK will format the diskette and copy the configuration files to it. RDISK will present progress bars as it does so to let you know how far along the process is.

5. When it has finished creating the disk and copying files to it, it will present a screen telling you that this disk contains security sensitive data and to store it only in a safe location. Click OK to finish creating the disk.

```
Repair Disk Utility                                         [×]

   ⚠️   Windows NT repair information contains security sensitive data. Please ensure that the
        emergency repair disk you just created is stored in a safe place accessible only to
        administrators of this system.

                          [  OK  ]
```

6. When RDISK returns to the initial screen, click the Exit button to exit the program. Remove the diskette from your floppy drive and label it as Windows NT ERD. You will also want to label that disk as being only for that particular Windows NT machine.

Using the Windows NT ERD

To use the ERD, you must first boot the NT computer using either an NT Setup Boot Disk set or the Windows NT CD-ROM. Once you get to the screen that asks you to "Press Enter to install Windows NT or press R to repair a damaged installation", go ahead and press R. Insert the ERD in your floppy drive when prompted by the setup program. Once you have started the emergency repair, you will have four options:

- Inspect Registry files
- Inspect startup environment
- Verify Windows NT system files
- Inspect Boot Sector

Which option(s) you choose will depend on what you suspect is wrong with your computer. To choose an option, navigate to it using the arrow keys and select or clear the check boxes using the Enter key.

Windows 2000

In Windows 2000, if your system won't start and either Safe Mode or the Recovery Console hasn't helped, you may need to use the emergency repair disk option. Unlike previous versions of Windows, the "Create Emergency Repair Disk" option is part of the Windows 2000 backup program. This program includes a wizard to help you create a disk to repair your system. Then, like with Windows NT, you can start the machine with either the startup disks or Setup CD-ROM and use the ERD to restore the system files.

Creating a Windows 2000 ERD

To create an emergency repair disk in Windows 2000, use the following steps:

1. Insert a blank, formatted 1.44MB floppy disk into your floppy disk drive.
2. Select Start ➤ Programs ➤ Accessories ➤ System Tools ➤ Backup.
3. From the Welcome tab, click Emergency Repair Disk.

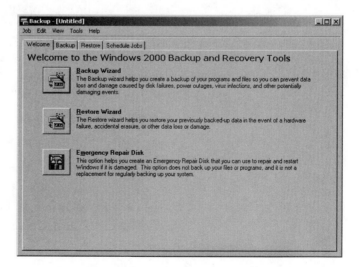

4. Backup prompts you to insert a disk, which you have already done. There is a check box on this screen that, when selected, will put a copy of the Registry in the C:\WINNT\REPAIR directory (assuming Windows 2000 was installed to C:\WINNT).

> **Emergency Repair Diskette**
>
> Insert a blank, formatted floppy disk into drive A: and click OK.
>
> ☑ Also backup the registry to the repair directory. This backup can be used to help recover your system if the registry is damaged.
>
> OK
> Cancel

WARNING When you finish installing Windows 2000 successfully, information about the setup is stored in the *systemroot*\Repair folder on the system partition. DO NOT DELETE THIS FOLDER. It contains the information necessary to use the ERD to restore your system to its original state.

5. Click OK to start copying ERD files. Backup will display a progress bar as the files copy.

> **Emergency Repair Diskette**
>
> Please wait while the system data is copied.
>
> Progress:
> ▮▮▮▮
>
> OK
> Cancel

6. When finished, Backup will display a message that the disk was created successfully. Remove the disk, label it as your Windows 2000 ERD and include the name of the computer it was created for. Put it in a safe place so it will be available when your computer has a problem.

> **Emergency Repair Diskette**
>
> The emergency repair diskette was saved successfully.
>
> Please label the diskette "Emergency Repair Disk" and note the current date. Place it in a safe location in case it is needed at a later date.
>
> OK
> Cancel

Using a Windows 2000 ERD

If you want to use or test your newly created ERD, follow the following steps:

1. Boot to either the Windows 2000 Startup floppy disks or the Windows 2000 CD-ROM.

2. When prompted, choose the Repair option by pressing R.

3. When prompted, choose the emergency repair process by pressing R. You can additionally choose to either run a manual repair (by selecting M) or a fast repair (by selecting F).

4. Follow the prompts. During this process, the backup files of the C:\WINNT\Repair directory are restored to the setup of Windows 2000.

5. The system will restart automatically when the repair is successfully completed.

Summary

Preventative maintenance is a set of practices that you do to prevent problems from happening (or to prevent them from happening frequently). In this chapter, you learned several preventative maintenance techniques to aid you in keeping your computer functional. Some of these techniques include backing up, anti-virus software use and installation, and making an emergency repair disk.

In this first section, you learned about the proper procedures for protecting your data by copying it to a backup media. You learned about the different methods of backing up (Full, Differential, and Incremental) as well as how to perform these backups using the built-in backup software of DOS, Windows, and Windows 9x.

In addition to protecting your data by backing up, you learned how to protect your computer from malicious programs known as viruses. In the next section, you learned about the built-virus protection programs, how to use them to protect against viruses, and how to eliminate any existing virus.

On occasion, your Windows software will become damaged so badly that it can't be booted. When that happens, you can fixed your damaged Windows installation by booting an Emergency Repair Disk (ERD). This disk will allow you to boot your machine. Additionally, it contains utilities to help you fix these problems. Some of these utilities include FDISK, FORMAT, COPY, and ATTRIB.

Key Terms

Before you take the exam, be certain you are familiar with the following terms:

backup	preventative maintenance
backup set	restore
backup source	target
inoculating	virus

Review Questions

1. Which type of backup copies all files that have changed since the last full backup, regardless if they have been backed up since then?

   A. Full

   B. Incremental

   C. Differential

   D. Custom

2. A computer virus is _____.

   A. A small program

   B. A small living organism

   C. Something that makes you sick

   D. A type of word processing software

3. What is one of the main functions of all viruses?

   A. Party

   B. Reproduce

   C. Destroy files

   D. Make strange things happen to your computer

4. To start the Windows 95 backup program the correct sequence is_____.

   A. Choose Start ➤ Programs ➤ Accessories ➤ System Tools ➤ Backup.

   B. Choose Programs ➤ Start ➤ Accessories ➤ System Tools ➤ Backup.

   C. Choose Backup ➤ Start ➤ Programs ➤ Accessories ➤ System Tools.

   D. Choose Accessories ➤ Start ➤ Programs ➤ System Tools ➤ Backup.

5. If you backed up 60MB of data using the full backup technique, how many tapes are required to restore from a full backup (generally speaking)?

   A. 4

   B. 2

   C. 7

   D. 1

6. What is the name of the executable for Microsoft Backup for DOS?

   A. MSBKUP.EXE

   B. MSBACKUP.EXE

   C. BACKUP.EXE

   D. MWBACKUP.EXE

7. What is the name of the executable for Microsoft Backup for Windows 3.*x*?

   A. MSBKUP.EXE

   B. MSBACKUP.EXE

   C. BACKUP.EXE

   D. MWBACKUP.EXE

8. What kind of backup strategy would you use with a terabyte of data?

   A. Full

   B. Differential

   C. Incremental

   D. Custom

9. What would you type at a DOS command line to start the Microsoft Anti-Virus?

   A. AV

   B. MSANTIVI

   C. MSAV

   D. ANTIVIRU

10. Which program in the Control Panel can be used to create a startup disk?

    A. System

    B. Add New Hardware

    C. Add/Remove Programs

    D. Startup

11. Which type of backup involves selecting the files you want backed up as well as when you want them backed up?

    A. Full

    B. Differential

    C. Incremental

    D. Custom

12. There are several pieces of backup hardware that are currently available. Of the following, which are NOT valid backup hardware?

    A. Digital audio tape

    B. Digital linear tape

    C. Optical disk

    D. Stationary hard disk

13. Which type of backup backs up files on a disk that has changed since the last full backup?

    A. Differential

    B. Incremental

    C. Full

    D. Custom

14. The final option in the Configure Screens menu is _____.

    A. Selecting the type of backup

    B. Selecting the device you are backing up to

    C. The compatibility test

    D. Selecting the backup option

15. The MSBACKUP program in DOS receives its settings from what file?

    A. DAT file

    B. BAK file

    C. TDR file

    D. SET file

16. Once the backup has been performed, what is the next step?

    A. Compare

    B. Restore

    C. Quit

    D. Reboot

17. The main menu of the Microsoft Anti-Virus program has how many options?

    A. One

    B. Two

    C. Five

    D. Three

18. The five options on the main menu for the Microsoft Anti-Virus program contain all of the following except _____.

    A. Detect

    B. Detect & Clean

    C. Erase

    D. Select New drive

    E. Exit

19. The Windows 95 Emergency Repair Disk should contain all of the following files and utilities except:

    A. CHKDSK

    B. UNINSTALL.EXE

    C. REGEDIT

    D. MSAV

20. What is the company most readily identified with anti-virus software?

    A. Symantec

    B. Microsoft

    C. Macintosh

    D. Novell

Answers to Review Questions

1. C. The differential type of backup copies all files that have changed since the last full backup, regardless if they have been backed up since then.

2. A. A computer virus is a small program that, if left unattended, can destroy an entire hard drive and all files on the hard drive.

3. B. One of the main functions of all viruses is to reproduce and that means to duplicate all files on the hard drive, thus taking up all hard drive space. Although some viruses do destroy files, that is not their main function.

4. A. To start the Windows 95 backup program the correct sequence is: Start ➤ Programs ➤ Accessories ➤ System Tools ➤ Backup.

5. D. To back up 60MB of data, one tape is required to restore from a Full backup, as opposed to Differential or Incremental backups, which require multiple tapes.

6. B. The name of the executable for Microsoft Backup for DOS is MSBACKUP.EXE.

7. D. The name of the executable for Microsoft Backup for Windows 3.x is MWBACKUP.EXE.

8. C. The Incremental backup is best suited for this situation because an Incremental only backs up the daily changed information. A Full backup every day would be impractical, because it would take too long and use several tapes. A Differential backup would use even more tapes. Given these situations, an Incremental backup would be the best choice.

9. C. The command to type at a DOS command line to start the Microsoft Anti-Virus is MSAV.

10. C. The Add/Remove Programs in the Control Panel can be used to create a Startup Disk.

11. D. Custom is the type of backup that involves selecting the files you want backed up as well as when you want them backed up.

12. D. Of the items listed, the following are valid backup hardware: digital audio tape, digital linear tape, and optical disk. Because hard disks are more failure-prone than the other types listed, they make a poor backup medium.

13. A. The Differential type of backup backs up files on a disk that have changed since the last Full backup.

14. C. The final option in the Configure Screens menu is the compatibility test.

15. D. The MSBACKUP program in DOS receives its settings from the SET file.

16. A. Once the backup has been performed, the next step is to select the Compare option to compare the files you just backed up to the originals that are currently on the disk. That way, you know if the ones backed up are the same as the ones on the disk and that the backup was successful.

17. C. The main menu of the Microsoft Anti-Virus program has five options.

18. C. The five options on the main menu for the Microsoft Anti-Virus program contain all of the options listed except Erase.

19. D. To have an effective emergency repair disk, the ERD should contain all of the files listed above except MSAV.

20. A. The company most readily identified with anti-virus software is Symantec.

Chapter

8

Configuring Network Software

THE FOLLOWING OBJECTIVES ARE COVERED IN THIS CHAPTER:

✓ **4.1 Identify the networking capabilities of Windows, including procedures for connecting to the network.**

> **Content may include the following:**

- Protocols
- IPCONFIG.EXE
- WINIPCFG.EXE
- Sharing disk drives
- Sharing print and file services
- Network type and network card
- Installing and Configuring browsers
- Configure OS for network connection

✓ **4.2 Identify concepts and capabilities relating to the Internet and basic procedures for setting up a system for Internet access.**

> **Content may include the following:**
>
> **Concepts and terminology**

- ISP
- TCP/IP
- IPX/SPX
- NetBEUI
- E-mail
- PING.EXE
- HTML
- HTTP://
- FTP
- Domain Names (Web sites)
- Dial-up networking
- TRACERT.EXE

When the first version of this book appeared, we noted, "It seems that everywhere you look today, someone is talking about the Internet." Well, we hadn't seen anything at that point. Having toppled into the new millennium, we really need to modify that statement to "It seems that everywhere you look today, someone is *using* the Internet."

In the space of just a few years, computer networking has gone from an obscure technology to a part of everyday life. Computers are being connected to networks and to each other at a flabbergasting rate, and as a computer professional, one of your primary jobs over the next decade may be to connect your clients' PCs to a network or to manage their access resources on their local network or the Internet.

Just look at the preponderance of Web site addresses on radio and television commercials today. The Web has become a "hot button" that advertising companies love to exploit. But very few people realize what the Internet actually is. Some people think it's a public thoroughfare for information (hence the moniker "information superhighway"). Others believe it to be some kind of new high-tech toy. In reality, however, the *Internet* is just a mesh of interconnected private networks that spans the globe. Whether it is the Internet or a local network at your school or place of work, the basic concepts remain the same. Because of this, to understand the Internet, you really must understand its underlying infrastructures: networks.

Simply put, a *network* is a number of devices (not just computers) connected together for the purpose of sharing resources, such as printers or disk space. Networks provide the physical path upon which computers communicate. When two networks connect to each other, they then form a single larger network called an *internetwork*. The largest of these internetworks is the Internet, which spans the globe and reaches into nearly every major business in the world, as well as into millions of homes. Networking software is written to be used by several people at once and to perform a variety of functions such as e-mail, collaboration, and business management, whereas networking hardware includes the machines that make that collaboration possible.

The A+ exam includes information about basic networking concepts, the Internet, and setting up computers to access both regular business networks and the Internet. We will discuss the installation and configuration of connecting to local area networks (LANs) and to the Internet from both Windows 9*x* and Windows 2000. Luckily, much of this information is similar in both systems, but as always, there are some significant differences.

In the networking software business, there are quite a few major players (like Novell, Microsoft, IBM, and Seagate). However, there are clearly two leaders in the game: Novell (whose company headquarters is in Provo, UT) and Microsoft (headquartered in Redmond, WA). Each company produces several software products for networks, but in the following sections, we'll focus on the different ways that Windows 98 and Windows 2000 connect to the networking operating systems (NOSs) made by these two companies.

Even as Microsoft was creating both clients and servers, other companies were specializing in one or the other. One of the most successful was Novell (www.novell.com), who has been a market leader in providing networking and network management software for the last decade. Novell has developed a NOS called NetWare (currently at version 5.1). NetWare has been the 800-pound gorilla of the networking world for over a decade, but Microsoft's Windows 2000 Server is following on the heels of the immensely successful Windows NT 4 Server and has made substantial gains over the last few years. Both NetWare and Windows 2000 Server are extremely common at this time. Other systems, such as Sun's Solaris or the open-source Linux variants, will not be specifically discussed.

The Internet is still very much a Unix world, though, so in fact our discussion of how to access the Internet is in some ways a look at how to attach to everything that isn't NetWare or Windows.

Except that you have to know what they are, we won't be dealing with the NOS servers themselves. Rather, we will be looking at how Windows 98 and Windows 2000 implement various networking elements and examine their networking capabilities when they're hooked up to other systems. Also, because the A+ exam deals only with the client side of networking (i.e., getting to resources that are already on the network), we won't be dealing extensively with how Windows 98 or Windows 2000 works as a network server. Nonetheless, both operating systems can act as servers, and if you are interested in learning more about this refer to *Network+ Study Guide* (Sybex, 2001).

Microsoft Networking Basics

When MS-DOS was developed, it was designed to be a simple, standalone, operating system. To that end, it didn't contain any network software, except SHARE.EXE. SHARE.EXE was designed as an add-on to popular networking software that allowed two users to edit the same file at the same time on a network. Without SHARE.EXE, when a second user tried to open a file that the first user had opened, they got an error message. With SHARE.EXE installed, when the second user tried to open the file, they received a message saying that the file was being used by someone else and offering to provide a copy of the file.

Another aspect of networking with MS-DOS is that DOS can run client software for Novell and Microsoft networks. Most client software for DOS (and Windows 3.*x*) falls into the category of redirection software. This software redirects requests bound for *local resources* out to network resources (Figure 8.1). For example, with network client software installed, you could point a DOS drive letter to some disk space on the network. When you saved a file to that drive letter, you were really saving that file to a server. But, as far as DOS was concerned, it was accessing a local drive letter.

FIGURE 8.1 Network client software redirects local requests to the network.

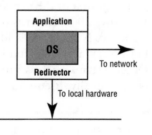

With *client software*, a computer can connect to a server and access the network resources hosted by that server.

As discussed earlier, Windows 3.1 was little more than a pretty face sitting on top of the MS-DOS OS, and because of this, Windows 3.1 networking was every bit as limited as DOS networking. In an effort to help, Microsoft brought out Windows 3.11, which has an add-on called Windows for Workgroups. This add-on allows a machine running DOS and Windows 3.11 to participate in a peer-to-peer network and share its files and any local printers with the rest of the network. Windows for Workgroups also allowed a user to add 32-bit TCP/IP networking. While far better than before, though, even Windows 3.11 was relatively limited in its networking capacities.

Microsoft was not only working on its clients, though. The Redmond Fun Bunch had also released Microsoft LAN Manager, a relatively primitive network server that would allow users to access centralized resources on the network. LAN Manager then evolved into Windows NT, and as part of that evolution, the LAN Manager networking software was integrated into the Windows NT Workstation client as well, giving Microsoft its first really effective network client.

Servers are computers that offer up resources (files, printers) or services (name resolution, time synchronization) to other machines on the network. They use special software to detect and respond to client requests.

Windows 95 and Beyond

When Windows 95 was released in late 1995, it wasn't the first Microsoft operating system to contain built-in networking. Both the Windows NT operating system and, to a lesser extent, Windows for Workgroups already had provided networking functionality. However, Windows 95 was similar to the "Monolith" of 2001 in that it issued in a new age of PC networking by providing easy-to-use-and-configure built-in networking. Suddenly, normal people could actually get their modems to work, corporate users could actually use the network without constantly getting sharing errors (SHARE.EXE was no more!), and improved support for all phases of the networking process rounded out the package.

Installing Networking Hardware and Software

Before you can begin with the configuration of your network, you must have a network card installed in the machine. Installing a network card is a fairly simple task if you have installed any expansion card before; a network interface card (NIC) is just a special type of expansion card. To install an NIC, follow these steps:

1. First move jumpers or flip DIP switches on the expansion card to set it to the correct IRQ/DMA/IO port settings as per the factory instructions. If the card uses a software set program, you can ignore this step. Most newer NICs do not have jumpers and are entirely software configured.

2. Next, power off the PC, remove the case, and insert the expansion card into an open slot.

3. Secure the expansion card with the screw provided.

4. Put the case back on the computer and power it up (you can run software configuration at this step, if necessary). If there are conflicts, change any parameters so that the NIC doesn't conflict with any existing hardware.

5. The final step in installing an NIC is to install a driver for the NIC for the type of operating system that you have. Windows should auto-detect the NIC and install the driver automatically. It may also ask you to provide a

copy of the necessary driver if it does not recognize what type of NIC you have installed. If the card is not detected at all, run the Add New Hardware Wizard by double-clicking Add New Hardware in the Control Panel.

6. After installing an NIC, you must hook the card up to the network using the cable supplied by your network administrator. You will need to attach this "patch cable" to the connector on the NIC and to a port in the wall, thus connecting your PC to the rest of the network.

Sometimes older NICs can conflict with newer Plug-and-Play (PnP) hardware. Additionally, some newer NICs with PnP capability don't like some kinds of networking software. To resolve a PnP conflict of the latter type, disable PnP on the NIC either with a jumper or with the software setup program. In this chapter, we will assume that your NIC is installed and the drivers are loaded. For more information on resolving hardware issues, refer to Chapter 6.

Configuring Windows 9x as a Network Client

The configuration of Windows 9x networking centers on the Control Panel's Network program. From this one interface, you configure client software, protocols, network interface cards (NICs), and the network services you want this machine to perform. To access the Network program, select Start ➤ Settings ➤ Control Panel and double-click Network in the Control Panel window that appears. Windows 9x will display the Network window. The Network window has three areas of interest: the components list, the primary logon list, and the File and Print Sharing button.

If you already have some networking components installed, you can simply right-click the Network Neighborhood icon on your desktop and choose Properties from the pop-up menu.

Network Components

First, let's review the four basic types of networking components that can be added in the Network panel, as shown in Figure 8.2. This screen can be reached by clicking Add on the Configuration tab.

FIGURE 8.2   The Select Network Component Type window

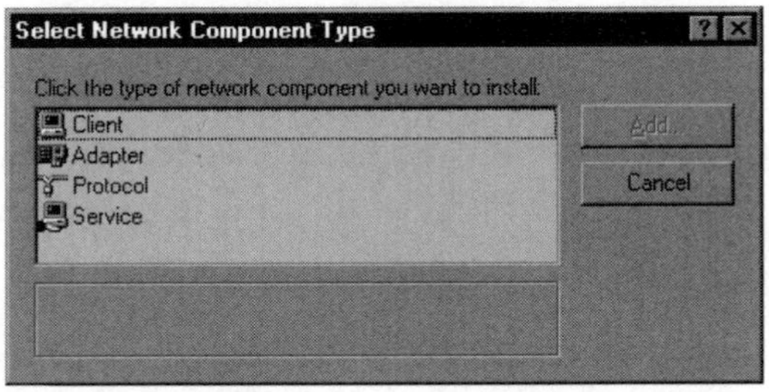

The networking components are as follows:

Client   As mentioned before, the client is software that allows your machine to talk to servers on the network. Each server vendor uses a different way of designing its network access, though, so if a computer needs to get to both a Novell and a Microsoft network, the computer must have two pieces of client software installed, one for each type of server. The three network client groups supported by Windows 9*x* are for Microsoft, Novell, and Banyan servers.

Adapter   The *adapter* is technically the peripheral hardware that installs into your computer, but in this case, it refers to the software that defines how the computer talks to that hardware. If you do not have the proper adapter software installed, your PC will not be able to talk properly to the NIC and you will not be able to access the network until you change the adapter to one that is compatible with the hardware. It is often best to simply think of an adapter as a network driver, which is what it is. A long list of adapters are supported by Windows 95, and Windows 98 supports even more, with support for more recent hardware. Adapter drivers can also be downloaded from most NIC vendors' Web sites.

Protocol   Once the client service and the adapter are installed, you have cleared a path for communication from your machine to network servers. The *protocol* is the computer language that you use to facilitate communication between the machines. If you want to talk to someone, you have to speak their language. Computers are no different. Among the languages available to Windows 98 are NetBEUI, NWLink, and *TCP/IP*.

Service   A *service* is a component that gives a bit back to the network that gives it so much. Services add functionality to the network by providing resources or doing tasks for other computers. In Windows 98, services include file and printer sharing for Microsoft or Novell networks.

Installing Components

Let's suppose you want to connect to Microsoft servers on your network (including Windows 2000 Server, 2000 Professional, or Windows 9x with sharing enabled). To connect to this network, you must have at least three components (no services, the fourth component, are required at this point):

- A client, such as Client for Microsoft Networks
- A protocol (whichever protocol is in use on the network; generally TCP/IP)
- An adapter (whatever is in the PC)

To install a client and protocol for use with your network adapter, follow these steps:

1. Click the Add button toward the bottom of the Network window. This will display the screen shown in Figure 8.2.

2. In this screen you can choose what type of item you are going to install. In this example, we're installing the Client for Microsoft Networks, so click Client and then click Add.

3. You will see a screen similar to the one in Figure 8.3. This screen is the standard "pick your component" screen that Windows 95 uses. On the left, select the company whose software (or driver) you want to install (in this example, Microsoft). When you have selected a manufacturer, a list of the software that Windows 95 can install from that company appears on the right.

FIGURE 8.3 Selecting the software you want to install

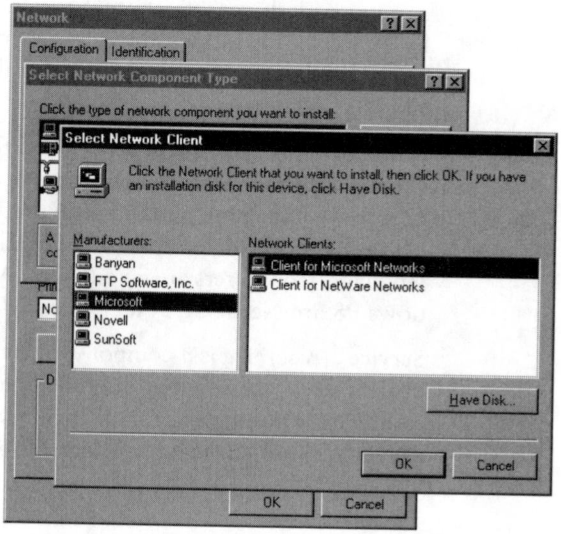

4. Click Client for Microsoft Networks when it appears in the right pane, then click OK. Windows 9x will bring you back to the Configuration tab of the Network program.

5. Once you have a client installed, you can verify that the protocol you need is present. TCP/IP generally installs by default, but this is not always so. If it is not present, click Add on the Configuration tab. In the Select Network Component Type window, select Protocol and then click Add. In the Select Network Client window, select Microsoft in the Manufacturers list and TCP/IP in the Network Protocols list. Click OK to complete the installation.

When it is first installed, TCP/IP is configured to expect that a special server, called a *Dynamic Host Configuration Protocol (DHCP)* server, is available on the network to provide it with information about the network. If a DHCP server is not available, the protocol will not function properly. Consult your administrator to see whether the network uses DHCP or static addressing. In static addressing, all TCP/IP settings must be manually added, and in this case, you will need additional information from the administrator. TCP/IP will be discussed in more detail later in this chapter.

The list of components should reflect your additions and show which network components are currently installed on this machine. If there are a number of components, a scroll bar appears on the right-hand side. The scroll bar allows you to see all the clients, network adapters, protocols, and services that might be installed. Once the client and protocol are installed, you will have all the software you need to connect to the network. At that point, just a few choices remain. Don't close that Network program yet!

Primary Logon

A Windows 9x workstation can support multiple simultaneous network types. For example, a user can log in to both Novell and Microsoft networks, assuming they have both network clients installed and configured correctly. The Primary Network *Logon* drop-down list determines which network type you will log on to first. If you have not yet installed a network client, this list will only give you one option: Windows Logon.

We have installed a Microsoft network client, so select the Client for Microsoft Networks as the primary logon, as displayed in Figure 8.4.

FIGURE 8.4 Choosing a Primary Network Logon

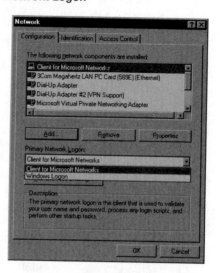

Once you have made this selection, click the OK button. The Network program will close, and you will be asked to restart the computer so that the new settings can take effect. Until you reboot, the network will not function. When the machine restarts, the network should be available.

Configuring Windows 2000 Professional as a Network Client

For the most part, the concepts behind configuring Windows 9x are the same as the concepts for configuring in Windows 2000. You still need a client, a protocol, and an adapter, for instance. The difference is in how they are configured because Microsoft has changed a few things in Windows 2000.

First, the Network program is now called Network and Dial-up Connections (NDC hereafter) and is organized differently. When you first access the NDC window, you will see that instead of a list of all components, you are greeted simply by a Make New Connection icon and a Local Area Connection icon, as shown in Figure 8.5.

FIGURE 8.5 The Network and Dial-up Connections window

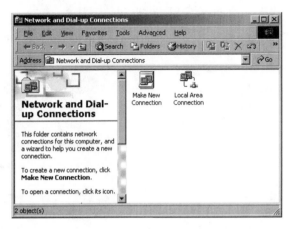

 If you do not see a local area connection, your NIC or modem is not present or is not functioning properly. If you see more than one LAN connection, it means you have multiple NICs installed (Windows 2000 can support multiple NICs).

To add client software and protocols, right-click the LAN connection and select Properties. You should find that everything you need is in place because the MS client and IP are installed by default on the LAN adapter.

 File and Printer Sharing for Microsoft Networks is also installed by default. To disable it, click the check mark next to the service. To remove it completely, click Uninstall.

You can also add additional clients, protocols, and services. Windows 2000 supports the same components Windows 9*x* supports, plus some new additions (the only component not supported in 2000 that is in 9*x* is the Banyan client). Once you have verified that the Client for Microsoft Networks and TCP/IP are installed, click OK. You should not have to reboot after making changes to the network settings in Windows 2000.

Configuring Clients for NetWare Network Access

Both Windows 9*x* and Windows 2000 handle the addition of a network client for NetWare in similar ways. Add (9*x*) or install (2000) the client, and it will automatically install the NetWare-compatible NWLink protocol for you as well (Figure 8.6). Once you have these, you will be presented with a NetWare logon option screen on startup, where you can choose which NetWare servér or tree you wish to log on to (Figure 8.7).

FIGURE 8.6 NDC with the NetWare client and NWLink installed

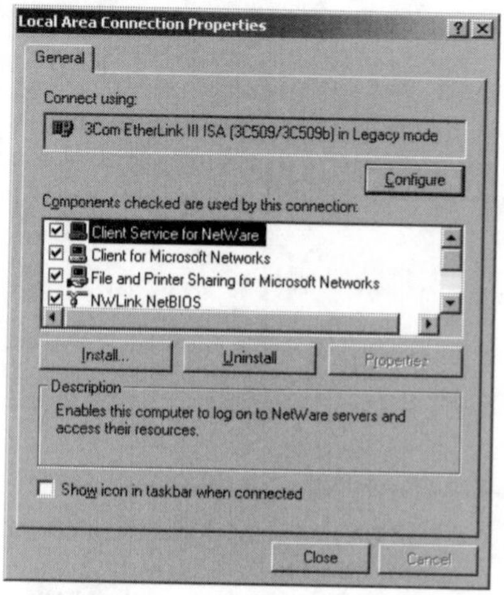

FIGURE 8.7 The NetWare default server/tree option screen

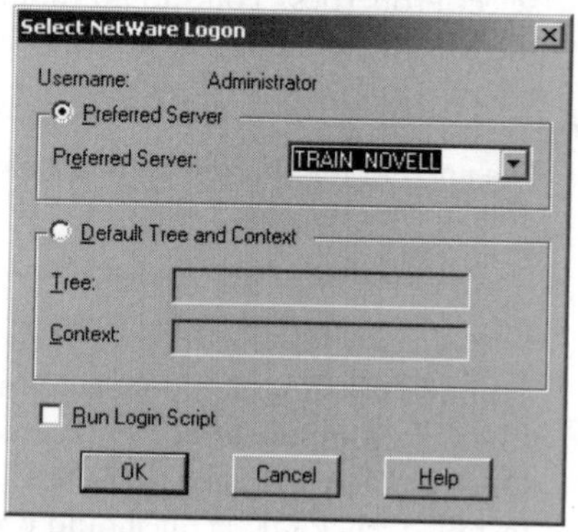

The tree is a group of machines that share security and configuration information. Both Novell's NetWare and Microsoft's Active Directory use tree structures to store information and authenticate users. To access the NetWare tree more efficiently, frequent NetWare users should download the newest version of NetWare's own client software for 9x/2000. It is available at www.novell.com/download/index.htm.

Configuring Windows to Share Files and Printers

As noted before, it is possible to set up both Windows 9*x* and Windows 2000 Professional to share files and printers with other users on the network. Networking in which users share each other's resources is called *peer-to-peer networking*, where each computer acts as both a client and a server.

We have already completed the client configuration. This is a must, actually, because file and printer sharing is only possible if the proper client and protocol are already set up. Now they are, so all you need to do is turn on file and print sharing and then specify which resources you wish to share. Even after file and printer sharing is enabled, you must specifically share any directory or printer that you want to make available on the network.

Enabling File and Printer Sharing on Windows 9*x*

To add file and printer sharing services, perform the following steps:

1. Open the Network program and click the File and Print Sharing button. You will see a screen that will allow you to select which services you want to share (Figure 8.8).

FIGURE 8.8   Enabling file and printer sharing

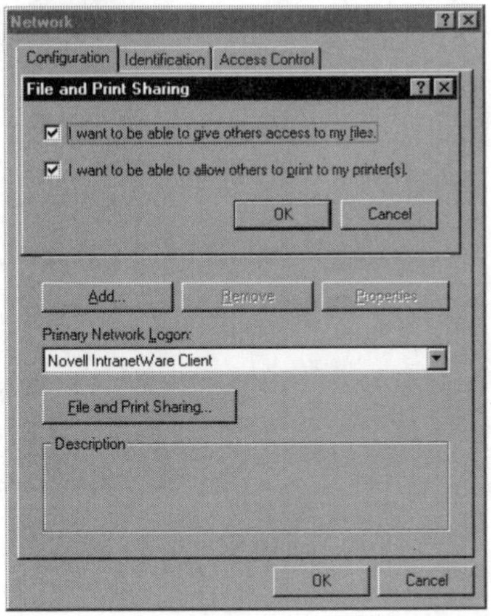

2. Click the box next to the top option (I Want to Be Able to Give Others Access to My Files) if you want to share files on your machine with someone

else on the network. If you want others to be able to print to a printer hooked to your machine, click the box next to the bottom option, I Want to Be Able to Allow Others to Print to My Printer(s). A check mark will appear in the box next to an option when it is enabled. To disable an option, simply click in the box again and the check mark will disappear.

3. Once you have enabled file and printer sharing, the service called File and Printer Sharing for Microsoft Networks will appear in the list of installed network components. In addition to specifying what you are going to share, you must specify how security is going to be handled. There are two options: Share-Level Access Control and User-Level Access Control. With share-level control, you supply a username, password, and security settings for each resource that you share. With user-level control, there is a central database of users (usually administrated by the network administrator) that Windows 9x can use to specify security settings for each shared resource. Most of the time, share-level access control is fine. There are only a few cases where user-level control is needed (such as in a network where the administrator has said you will do it this way). To specify these settings, choose the Access Control tab in the Network window (Figure 8.9) and choose the appropriate option.

FIGURE 8.9 Specifying the access control method

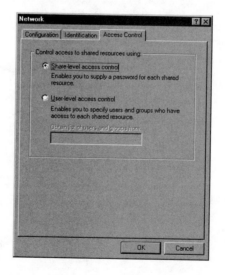

4. Click OK to save all of these new settings.

5. Windows *9x* will copy some files and ask you to reboot (big surprise, huh?). Reboot your computer to start sharing files and printers.

As described earlier, Windows 2000 automatically starts and installs File and Printer Sharing when a network connection is created. Unless you have disabled it, no additional configuration is required to begin sharing resources!

Sharing Folders

If you have a folder on your machine that contains information that everyone should be able to see, you will need to enable *file sharing*. Sharing is generally enabled through Windows Explorer.

Any folder can be shared (including the root of the C: drive). When you share a folder, the person you share it with will be able to see not only the folder you've shared but also any folders inside that folder. Therefore, you should be certain that all subfolders under a share are intended to be shared as well. If they are not, move them out of the share path.

Once you have decided what to share, simply right-click the folder that will be the start of the share and choose Sharing from the menu that pops up. This option will bring up the Properties window of that folder with the Sharing tab in front.

You can also access the Sharing tab by right-clicking a folder, choosing Properties, and clicking the tab.

To start the share, click the Shared As radio button. Two previously grayed-out fields will become visible (Figure 8.10). The first field is Share Name. The name you enter here will be used to access this folder. It should be something that accurately represents what you are sharing. The second field allows you to enter a description of the share as a comment that will help identify the contents of the share to users. The share name is required, and the comment is optional.

FIGURE 8.10 Enabling a share

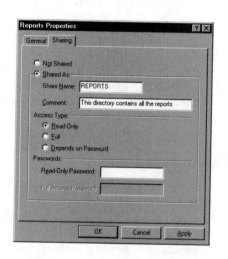

Finally, you may specify the access rights and password(s) for the share. There are three options for access rights when you're using the share-level security scheme. Click the radio button next to the option you want to use:

Read-Only   With this option selected, anyone accessing the share will only be able to open and read the files inside the folder and any subfolders. You must specify a password that users can use to access the share in read-only mode.

Full   In full access mode, everyone accessing the share has the ability to do anything to the files in the folder as well as any subfolders. This includes being able to delete those files. You must specify a password that the users will use to access this share.

Depends on Password   This option is probably the best option of the three. With this option, users can use one password to access the share in read-only mode and a different password to access it in full access mode. You can give everyone the read-only password so they can view the files and give the full access password only to users who need to change the files.

By default, the share is a full control share in Windows NT/2000. This means that anyone on the network can come in and view, modify, or even delete the files in the share. Often this is just a bit too dangerous, and as such, you will probably want to use a read-only or a depends-on password security setting. (A Windows 9x share is read-only by default. Anyone on the network can view files in the share.)

Once you have specified the share name, comments, and access rights, click OK to share the folder. Notice that the folder now has a hand underneath it, indicating that it is being shared (Figure 8.11).

FIGURE 8.11 The REPORTS folder after being shared

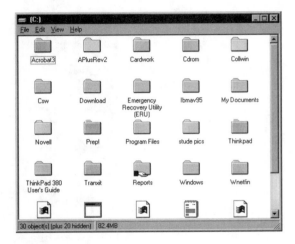

In Windows 2000, sharing is enabled in exactly the same way as in Windows 9x. The only difference is that in 2000, you can enable the NTFS file system and use it to secure files and folders. At that point, all you have to do is create a share on Windows 2000 Professional to the directories you wish to allow the network access to and the permissions set at the file level will be enforced.

Sharing Printers

Sharing printers is similar to sharing folders. First, you must have the printer correctly set up to print on the machine that will be "hosting" it. Second, you need to right-click on a printer in the PRINTERS folder and click Sharing. The printer property page will appear with the Sharing tab selected to allow you to share the printer.

To share the printer, simply click Shared As and specify a name for the share (Figure 8.12). The name will default to a truncated version of the printer name you gave it when you installed it. Notice in Figure 8.12 that Windows 95 truncated the name HP LaserJet III to HP. The name you give this share (called the *share name*) should be something that everyone will recognize when they see it on the network and that accurately describes the printer. This one is called DavesHP so people will know that it's next to Dave's workstation and that it's an HP printer.

FIGURE 8.12 Sharing a printer

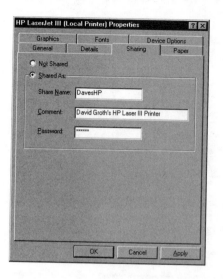

In addition to specifying the name of the printer share, you can enter a comment that describes the printer accurately. Finally, you should specify a password that users must enter in order to install this printer on their workstations (they won't have to enter it every time they print).

To finish sharing the printer, click OK. Windows 95 will prompt you for the password again, just to verify that you know what it is and that you didn't misspell it. Retype the password in the box that appears and click OK and the share will be active. Notice that the printer in the PRINTERS folder in Figure 8.13 has a hand under it, indicating that it is shared.

FIGURE 8.13 The printer is now shared.

Using Shared Resources

To access shared folders and printers, we'll turn to the Network Neighborhood icon. When you double-click this icon, you can browse the network for resources. Figure 8.14 shows an example of a Network Neighborhood browse window. As you can see, there are several entities on this network. The little icons that look like computers are just that, computers on the network. However, there isn't a different icon for a Novell server, an NT server, or a Windows 95 machine sharing out part of its hard disk. They all look the same to Windows 95. The one that looks like a tree is in fact an NDS tree for a Novell network.

FIGURE 8.14   A sample Network Neighborhood window

Through this screen, you can double-click any computer to see the resources that are hosted by that computer. Once you have found the share you require, using a shared folder is just like using any other folder on your computer, with one or two exceptions: First, the folder exists on the network, so you have to be connected to the network to use it. Second, for some programs to work properly, you must map a local drive letter to the network folder. This is because the Windows 9*x* reference to a share on the network uses the Universal Naming Convention path (or UNC path). The UNC path uses the format *machinename**share**path*\. So, a directory called JULY98 underneath a share called REPORTS on a machine called DAVELAPTOP would be written as \\DAVELAPTOP\REPORTS\JULY98.

In Windows 9*x*, if you do know the name of the computer that hosts the resource you are looking for, you can use the Find command instead of browsing. Just go to Start ➤ Find ➤ Computer and type in the name of the computer preceded by two backslashes (the beginning of a UNC path).

If there is a space in the name of any item, be careful. Some DOS utilities can't interpret spaces.

To connect to a network folder share, simply double-click the computer that's hosting it to view the list of shares (Figure 8.15). Notice that both the folder and printer that were shared in the previous examples are there. Because we want to use the folder share, we can just double-click it to see its contents (and copy files to and from it if necessary). Or, we can map a drive letter so that all our applications will be able to use it.

FIGURE 8.15   Viewing the resources a computer is hosting

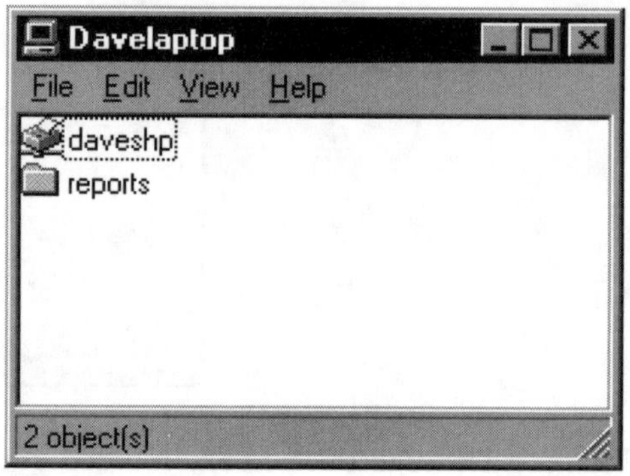

```
┌────────────────────────────────────┐
│ 🖥 Davelaptop              _ □ ✕    │
├────────────────────────────────────┤
│  File  Edit  View  Help             │
│ 🖨 daveshp                           │
│ 📁 reports                           │
│                                      │
│                                      │
│                                      │
├────────────────────────────────────┤
│ 2 object(s)                          │
└────────────────────────────────────┘
```

Now that you see all the resources the computer is hosting, you can map a drive letter to it by right-clicking the folder (REPORTS in this case) and choosing Map Network Drive. This will cause the screen shown in Figure 8.16 to appear. You must pick a drive letter (one that is not being used) and click OK to map the drive. Remember that most Windows applications can use UNC paths and don't need drive mappings, but even some newer applications still require a drive letter.

FIGURE 8.16   Mapping a drive letter to a network share

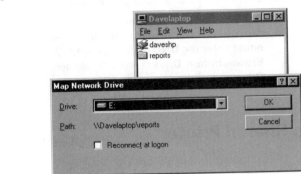

Now that you have a drive mapped, you can use the files and directories in the share that you mapped to.

Sharing Options with Windows 2000

Windows 2000 is very similar to Windows 9*x* when it comes to accessing network resources, but there are just a few modifications. First, Network Neighborhood is renamed My Network Places in Windows 2000. Second, to search for computers by name, you no longer go to the Find menu (now renamed Search, anyhow). Instead, when you double-click My Network Places, you will have the Search for Computers and Search for Files or Folders options in the left part of the window (Figure 8.17). Click the Entire Contents link on the left, and the network contents will be displayed. At that point, everything will be displayed as it is in Windows 9*x* and you can view and map network drives.

FIGURE 8.17   The initial Entire Network window

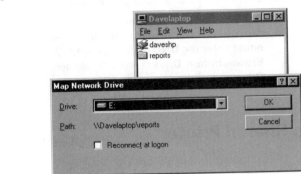

Another option for mapping a drive in 9x and 2000 is to use the Windows Explorer. In Explorer, click the Tools menu, and select Map Network Drive. You will need to either enter the UNC path (\\server\share) or navigate to the folder using the Browse button. Drives can be disconnected using the Tools ➢ Disconnect Network Drive option.

Using a Shared Printer

In this section, we'll discuss the way to set up a Windows 9x or 2000 client to print to a shared printer. Accessing shared printers is very similar to accessing shared resources; in both cases, you are accessing a resource that has been shared on the host computer. Additionally, in both cases, you are pointing a local resource (in this case a printer icon) to a network resource (a shared printer).

To set up the printer on your workstation, you most likely will use the Point and Print option for Windows 9x and 2000 printing. This option allows you to click and drag a printer to the PRINTERS folder and run the Add Printer Wizard, which will set up the printer icon and set up the right drivers on your machine. Follow these steps:

1. Browse to the computer that hosts the printer you want to set up and double-click the computer name so you can see the printer you want to install.

2. Open up the PRINTERS folder under Start ➢ Settings ➢ Printers. Arrange these windows so you can see both at the same time (Figure 8.18).

FIGURE 8.18 Preparing to configure the Point and Print option

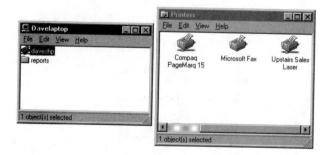

3. To start the Add Printer Wizard, drag the printer you want to set up from the list of resources the computer is hosting to the Printers window. As soon as you release the mouse button, you will see the wizard start, and it will display the window shown in Figure 8.19.

FIGURE 8.19 Starting the Add Printer Wizard

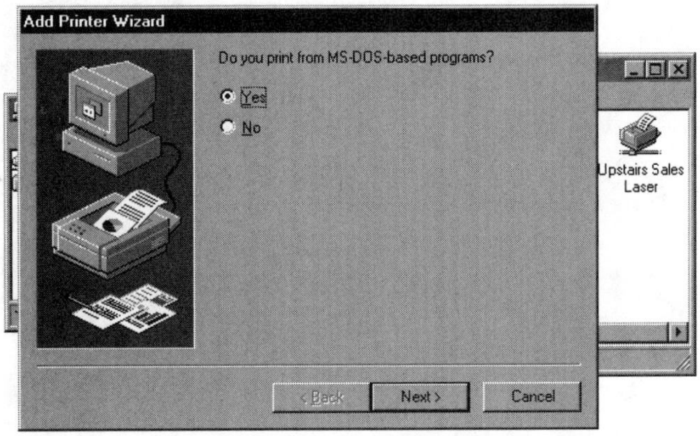

Add Printer Wizard

Do you print from MS-DOS-based programs?

○ Yes
○ No

Upstairs Sales Laser

< Back   Next >   Cancel

4. The wizard will ask you a series of questions that will help you to configure the printer. If you are using Windows 9x, the wizard will ask "Do you print from MS-DOS–based programs?" The reasoning behind this question is similar to the reason we map drive letters. Most older DOS programs (and to a lesser extent, Windows programs) don't understand the UNC path syntax for access to a shared resource. Instead, they understand a name for a local hardware resource (like LPT1: for the first local parallel port). So, you must point a local printer port name out to the network in a process known as capturing. If you need to capture a printer port, answer "Yes" to this question, otherwise leave it set to the default ("No"). For our example, click Yes and click Next to move to the next step of the wizard.

Although Windows 2000 allows you to map LPT: ports, 2000 does not have much interest in DOS, and so it does not make any special mention of it.

5. If you chose Yes in the preceding step, the next step is to capture the printer port. You will see the screen in Figure 8.20. This screen allows you to capture a printer port so that DOS programs can print to the network printer. Click the Capture Printer Port button to bring up the screen (Figure 8.21) that allows you to choose which local port you want to capture. Select a port (generally LPT:1).

FIGURE 8.20 Capturing a Printer port

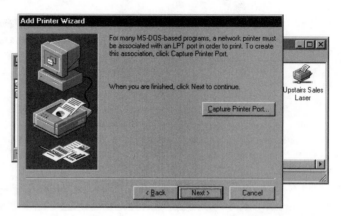

FIGURE 8.21 Picking which local port to capture

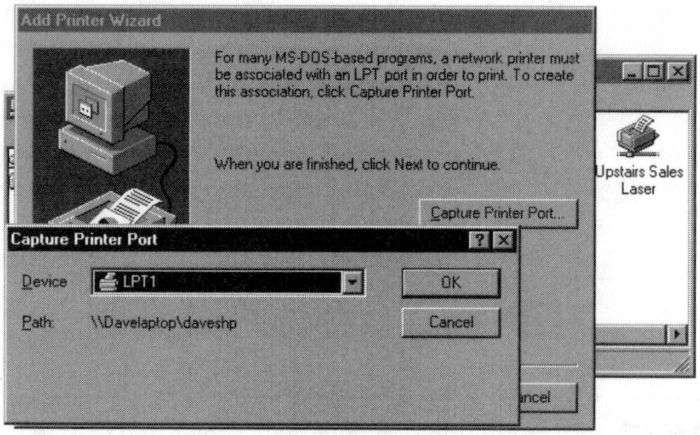

6. The next step is to give the printer instance a name. You should give a network printer a name that reflects what kind of printer it is and which machine is hosting it. In this example, the printer is labeled HP LaserJet III (the default name of the driver), but we could have named it Laser on Bob's PC. Whatever name makes sense to you, type in the name that you want to call the printer in the screen that the wizard presents (Figure 8.22). You also have the choice as to whether or not you want the printer to be the default printer that gets used by all Windows applications.

FIGURE 8.22   Naming the printer

From here on, printer installation is exactly the same as installing a local printer (covered in Chapter 6).

Networking and the Internet

One of the most oft-performed procedures by today's technicians is setting up a computer to connect to the Internet. The Internet is no longer just a buzzword, it's a reality. It has been estimated that over 50 percent of the homes in America have computers and that over 50 percent of those computers are connected to the Internet. It's is no wonder that most computers come with software to connect them to the Internet.

Before we can discuss connecting Windows to the Internet, we need to discuss the Internet itself. There are some common terms and concepts every technician must understand about the Internet. First of all, the Internet is really just a bunch of private networks connected together using public telephone lines. These private networks are the access points to the Internet and are run by companies called Internet Service Providers (ISPs). They will sell you a connection to the Internet for a monthly service charge (kind of like your cable bill or phone bill). Your computer talks to the ISP using public phone lines, or even using new technologies such as cable or wireless.

Types of Connections

There are several designations and types of public phone lines that range in speeds from 56Kbps to several Megabits per second (Mbps) and that your computer might use to talk to an ISP. Remember that these same types of phone lines connect the ISPs to each other to form the Internet. Table 8.1 details a few of the more common connection types and speeds.

TABLE 8.1 Common Connection Types and Speeds

Designation	Speed Range	Description
POTS	2400bps to 115Kbps	Plain Old Telephone System. Your regular analog phone line.
ISDN	64Kbps to 1.554Mbps	Integrated Services Digital Network. Popular for home office Internet connection.
Frame Relay	56Kbps to 1.554Mbps	Cheap, simple connection where you share bandwidth with several other people.
56K Point-to-Point	56Kbps	A direct connection between two points at a guaranteed bandwidth.
T1	1.554Mbps	A direct connection between two points at a guaranteed bandwidth.
T3	44Mbps	A direct connection between two points at a guaranteed bandwidth. Extremely fast.
DSL	256Kbps to ?	Digital Subscriber Line. Shares existing phone wires with voice service.
ATM	155Mbps	Asynchronous Transfer Mode. Fiber-optic ring network. Extremely fast.

The majority of home Internet connections use POTS (Plain Old Telephone System) and a modem. Most ISPs connect with each other using phone lines of T1 speeds (1.554Mbps) or faster. Certain ISPs that make up the backbone of the Internet use technologies like SONET that can get the data moving at gigabit speeds.

Connection Protocols

Whichever connection type is used, there must be a plan for how to transmit data across a network's lines. Network connection types also use different protocols to communicate, just as computers do, and because of this we also need to mention these connection protocols. For instance, TCP/IP Internet traffic runs over

like voltage in a circuit, fluid pressure, depends level etc.

two different analog connection protocols: Serial Line Internet Protocol (SLIP) and Point-to-Point Protocol (PPP). Both work to get you on the Internet, but PPP is more commonly used because it is more easily configured; it's also more stable because it includes enhanced error-checking capabilities. Other common connection protocols include X.25 and ATM (the name is used for both the network and the connection protocol controlling traffic across it).

A TCP/IP Primer

Regardless of which network type you choose, you will probably be running Transmission Control Protocol/Internet Protocol (TCP/IP) over the top of it. Because the Internet is a network, everyone on it needs to be running the same protocol in order to communicate. The protocol of the Internet is TCP/IP, and increasingly, the protocol of the Internet is becoming the primary protocol of all networks. Named for two of its most commonly used components, TCP/IP is actually a suite of protocols rather than just being a single monolithic creation.

Created in 1969 as a part of DARPAnet (the Defense Advanced Research Projects Administration Network), TCP/IP evolved over time. The DARPAnet evolved also, eventually moving out of government hands and becoming the Internet that we know and love. Currently the Internet is managed by the Internet Society (`www.isoc.org`), which develops new standards for the Internet and for the TCP/IP suite.

When starting to work with TCP/IP, the first thing to note is that it is generally managed by using two independent hierarchical structures. The first is the IP-address hierarchy. Each computer that runs TCP/IP must have a unique IP address assigned to it, and that address must fall within a specific range. IP addresses are composed of a set of four numbers, each of which must be from 0 to 255. The IP address can either be automatically assigned to the machine or an administrator can specifically assign it. Aside from its IP address, a machine will also have a *host name*, which identifies it on the network. Host names are friendly names by which computers can be more easily located, and they are managed using a worldwide naming system called the *Domain Name System (DNS)*. DNS allows a user to type in http://www.yahoo.com and be taken directly to a computer hundreds or thousands of miles away. The same user could have used an IP address such as http://200.50.172.14, (not Yahoo!'s actual address), but most people find that the domain name (yahoo.com) is far easier to remember! Table 8.2 includes a list of other common Internet terms with which you will want to be familiar.

TABLE 8.2 Internet Terminology

Term	What It does
ISP	Internet Service Provider. A company that provides access to the Internet.
Host	A computer on a TCP/IP network such as the Internet.
WWW	A graphical extension of the Internet, the World Wide Web (or just the Web) allows users to search for and view information easily through the use of a browser. Users navigate the Web by jumping from one page to the next through hyperlinks.
Hyperlink	Text or an image on a Web page that, when clicked, takes the user to another place on the page or to a different page.
Browser	Software made to understand and interpret HTTP content.
HTTP	A TCP/IP protocol which defines how World Wide Web content is downloaded and displayed in your browser. HTTP stands for Hypertext Transfer Protocol.
FTP	Another TCP/IP protocol. The File Transfer Protocol is used to transfer large files over the Internet. Users can use either a graphical client or a command line.
E-mail	Electronic mail is a way of sending and receiving messages over the Internet.
DHCP	The Dynamic Host Configuration Protocol. This is used to automatically configure TCP/IP information for hosts on the network.
WINS	Windows Internet Name Service. Manages Microsoft NetBIOS-based names and makes It easier to find resources on a Microsoft network.
DNS	The Domain Name System manages Internet host and domain names and makes it easier to find resources on TCP/IP networks.

Computer Name Resolution

This isn't something that is in the objectives, so you can take it or leave it, but it is incredibly important to understanding how machines communicate on Microsoft networks. When Microsoft first started producing network-capable operating systems, such as DOS with networking, LanManager and Windows NT 3.1, the

Internet was nothing but a group of mainframe computers connecting selected military and university campuses. At that time, it seemed that the thing to do when you created network software was to also create your own proprietary protocol and assume that no one would ever connect to any network but yours. Novell had IPX/SPX, Apple had AppleTalk, and Microsoft, sadly, came up with NetBEUI.

The NetBEUI protocol is insufficient on so many levels that discussing its faults is too big a job for this chapter. Nonetheless, it is an extremely fast protocol for allowing a few computers on a single network to communicate. It just doesn't scale very well, which has doomed it as networks grew and started to interconnect.

The death knell of NetBEUI wasn't a problem, because TCP/IP and other protocols were ready to take over. The one thing that has continued to cause confusion and trouble, though, is that NetBEUI was based on another Microsoft protocol called NetBIOS, which has been far more difficult to replace.

NetBEUI and NetBIOS

NetBEUI and NetBIOS are obviously similar-looking terms, and unfortunately, there has been a certain amount of confusion surrounding them. Here is a brief explanation of what each does:

- NetBEUI is a transport protocol. It is responsible for how data is transmitted between two computers. It is not routable and is rarely used in modern computing.

- NetBIOS is a name resolution system. It allows a computer to search for another computer on the network by its Microsoft computer name. It must be used on every Microsoft-based network up to Windows 2000.

Computer Names and Host Names

The continuing presence of NetBIOS makes for some interesting confusion in that a Microsoft *9x* machine with TCP/IP installed actually has two distinct names. Its NetBIOS computer name is set in the Identification tab of the Network program (Figure 8.23), whereas its host name is set in the TCP/IP DNS Configuration tab (Figure 8.24). In the figures, both names are set to COYOTE, and usually the computer and host name will be the same because they are set that way by default. If you are having trouble reaching a *9x* or NT machine, though, you may want to check this setting.

FIGURE 8.23 The NetBIOS computer name

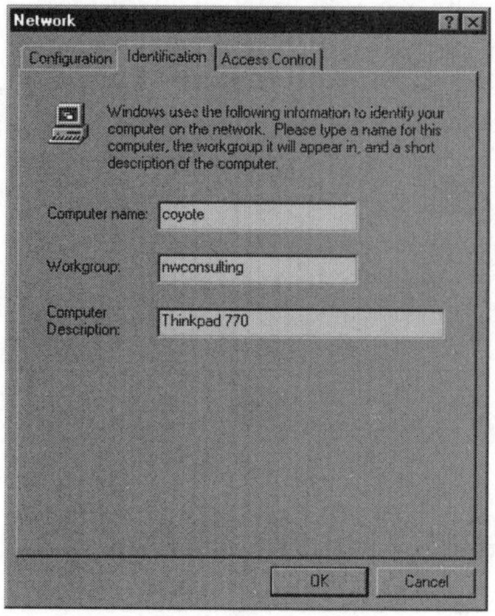

FIGURE 8.24 The TCP/IP host name

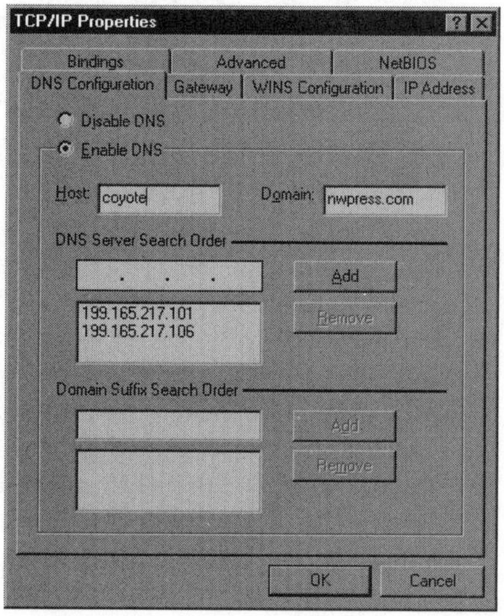

In Windows 2000, Microsoft has finally started to make a break from this nonsense. Computer and host names in 2000 must be the same, and NetBIOS name resolution has largely been replaced with DNS naming resolution.

So What Is Resolution?

In order for a computer to talk to another computer, it must be able to access it using an IP address. Computers speak in numbers, not letters! Because of this, the "friendly" names that we use to make computers easy to remember and find must be *resolved* to find out what IP address the machine is using. There are a number of methods of doing this, but WINS servers and DNS servers are the most common. WINS resolves NetBIOS computer names to IP addresses, and DNS does so for host names. More on this in a minute.

Another way of resolving names is to use either the LMHOSTS file (computer names) or the HOSTS file (host names). These are text files into which you can put entries that specifically tell your machine what the address of another machine is, as in the following line:

        192.168.1.250   NTSERVER

Although these files work fine, they require a lot of maintenance and are not used regularly in modern networking.

Configuring TCP/IP

NetBEUI and NWLink are protocols that need little tuning. You can pretty much install them and go, without needing to configure anything. Not so with TCP/IP, which has a number of settings that must be configured so you can access network resources.

First, there are two settings that are absolutely crucial. Without an IP address and a subnet mask, TCP/IP will not function. In addition, a number of other settings may also be needed, depending on what you are planning to access. The settings are listed in Table 8.3 (settings needed for Internet access are marked with an asterisk).

TABLE 8.3   TCP/IP Configuration Settings

Setting	Example	Purpose
IP address*	192.168.1.75	Uniquely identifies the computer on the network.

TABLE 8.3 TCP/IP Configuration Settings *(continued)*

Setting	Example	Purpose
Subnet mask*	255.255.255.0	Used to determine whether other IP addresses are on the same network or on another network. Sadly, there is no easy explanation for subnet masks. Suffice it to say that you need it, and it has to be right! The network administrator should give you the subnet mask setting (and all other necessary info).
Default gateway*	192.168.1.1	The address of the router your machine will use to access the outside world.
Host	Coyote	The name that the machine is referred to in DNS.
Domain	Sybex.com	The name of the organization you are in. Similar to a workgroup, but for TCP/IP.
DNS server*	192.168.1.250	The machine that resolves names for the network. This machine will answer a question such as "What IP address does coyote.sybex.com have?" with an answer of "192.168.1.75."
WINS server	192.168.1.250	Serves the same purpose as DNS, but deals with computer names, not host names. Answers questions such as "What IP address does COYOTE have?"

Managing TCP/IP

There are two ways to manage TCP/IP. The manual way involves going to each machine and setting upward of 10 separate values for TCP/IP. This would also be known as the "hard way" of configuring IP. Another possibility is the use of DHCP. If your network is using DHCP, all you have to do is install IP and reboot. A special server called a DHCP server will then provide your machine with all the values it needs when it starts up again. Machines are given "leases" to the IP addresses that the server manages and must periodically renew these leases. If you are using DHCP, your TCP/IP settings in the Network program should be grayed out, as shown in Figure 8.25.

FIGURE 8.25 TCP/IP auto-configured by DHCP

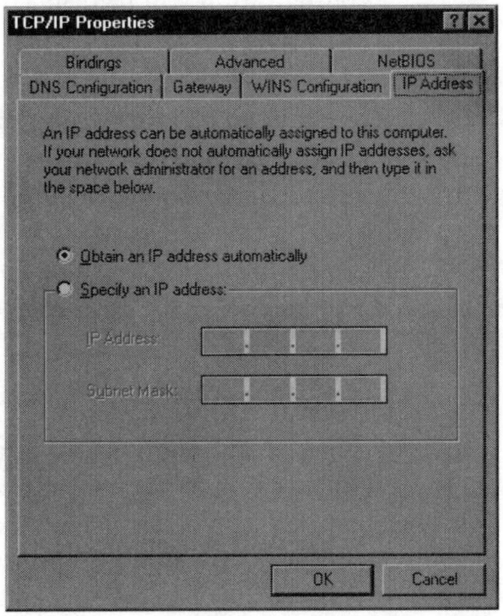

If you are wondering what the IP settings for a machine are, there are a number of utilities you can use. The primary options, though, are listed in Table 8.4.

TABLE 8.4 TCP/IP Utilities

Protocol	Function
WINIPCFG	A graphical utility on Windows 9x that allows you to get information about your IP configuration. It also allows you to release a DHCP lease and request a new one.
IPCONFIG	Does the same thing as WINIPCFG, but for Windows NT and 2000. IPCONFIG is also different in that it is a command-line utility.
PING	The PING command allows you to test connectivity with another host by just typing **PING www.sybex.com** or **PING 192.168.1.250**.
Tracert	This trace route utility allows you to watch the path that information takes getting from your machine to another one.

Using these utilities is pretty straightforward. For an example, follow these steps to view TCP/IP information on Windows 2000:

1. Choose Start ➢ Run.

2. Type **CMD** and press Enter. This will bring up a command prompt.

3. At the prompt, type **IPCONFIG**. Basic information about your TCP/IP configuration will be displayed.

4. Type **IPCONFIG** again, this time adding the /A switch: **IPCONFIG /A**. The /A switch tells the system to display additional information. Other options can be found using the IPCONFIG /? Command. The additional options are also run using switches, and are run in the same fashion as the /A switch, by typing them in after the command.

Configuring Internet Access Software

If you want to connect your Windows 95 machine to the Internet, the first step is to get an account with an Internet Service Provider. They will give you a sheet with all the information you need to connect your machine, or in some cases, they will give you a disk with a preconfigured connection and browser so all you have to do is install the software and you'll be ready to connect to the Internet. A browser is a piece of software used to access the World Wide Web, and a Dial-Up Networking (DUN) connection holds the settings needed to access an ISP. In this section, we will look at how to install and use each of these.

Although in most cases you need to make a Dial-Up Networking connection to use the Internet, it is important to note that some service providers, such as AOL or Prodigy, create their own connections. Don't try to make the connection for them, and don't delete them!

Some connections, such as cable or DSL, do not use a modem and as such are configured through the use of network cards and standard network clients. Configuring Internet access for DSL is very similar to configuring access on a company network. You simply install TCP/IP, configure it properly, and then skip ahead to "Connecting to the Internet." You will need information from the ISP when configuring these systems.

Creating a Windows 9x DUN Connection

To create a new DUN connection, open the Dial-Up Networking folder under Start ➤ Programs ➤ Accessories. This will open a window that shows all the DUN connections that are configured. You must create a new one to connect to the

Internet. To do so, double-click the item in this folder called Make New Connection. This will bring up the screen shown in Figure 8.26. From this screen, you can give the connection a name. As with other names in Windows 9x, use one that reflects what it is (in this case, a connection to the Internet). Additionally, this screen will allow you to select which modem you want to use to dial this connection (if you only have one configured in Windows 9x, it will default to that one).

FIGURE 8.26   Making a new connection and naming it

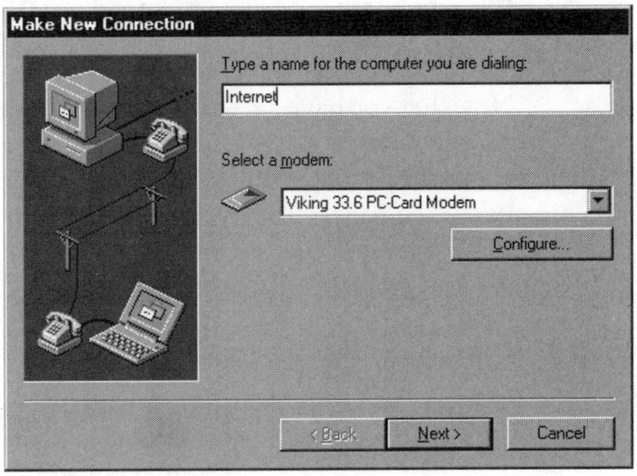

The next step is to enter the phone number of the system you are dialing (Figure 8.27). Simply type in the area code and phone number of your ISP and click Next to continue. When it dials, Windows 9x will determine if it's a long-distance number automatically and either add or omit the 1 plus the area code.

FIGURE 8.27   Entering the ISP's phone number

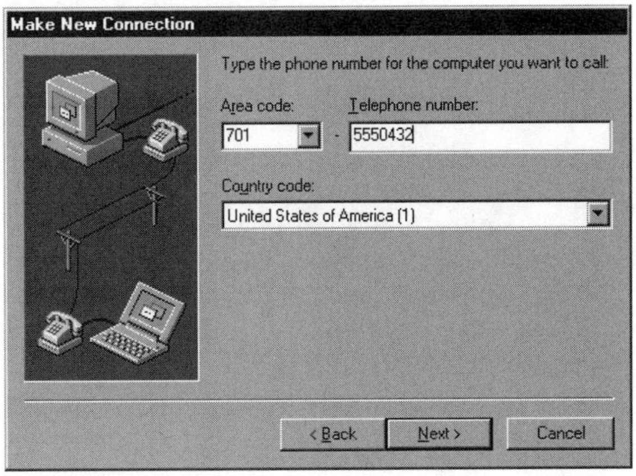

11

Chapter 8 · Configuring Network Software

 If you live in another country, select your country under Country Code to change how Windows 95 interprets phone number syntax.

Finally, you are presented with the final screen that tells you that you are basically finished setting up the connection. All you have to do is click the Finish button to finish creating the connection.

Configuring the Properties of a Windows 9*x* DUN Connection

Now that you have a DUN connection, you need to configure the settings specific to your Internet connection. Simply right-click the connection in the Dial-Up Networking folder (Figure 8.28). From the menu that appears, you can choose to use the connection to connect (the Connect option), or you can choose the Properties option to configure it. Because you aren't ready to connect yet, choose the Properties item from the menu.

FIGURE 8.28 Choosing the DUN connection to configure

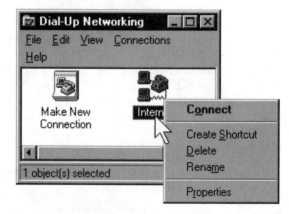

You should now see a screen similar to the one in Figure 8.29. From this screen, you can configure the same properties you configure in the Make New Connection Wizard (i.e., telephone number, connection name, and modem). This screen has two more tabs that you can use to configure the other properties (such as protocol settings).

FIGURE 8.29   Properties of the Internet DUN connection

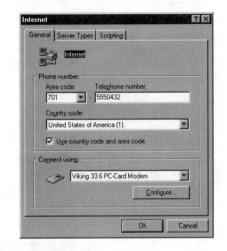

If you click the Server Types tab, you will see the settings for the type of server you are dialing in to (Figure 8.30). For an Internet connection, this is usually set to PPP: Windows 95, Windows NT 3.5, Internet (unless your ISP instructs you to use another setting). Notice also that there are check boxes for several other settings, including which protocol(s) this dial-up connection will use. TCP/IP must be selected in order for an Internet connection to work. Configure these settings according to your ISP's instructions and click OK to accept them.

FIGURE 8.30   Configuring the Server Types parameter

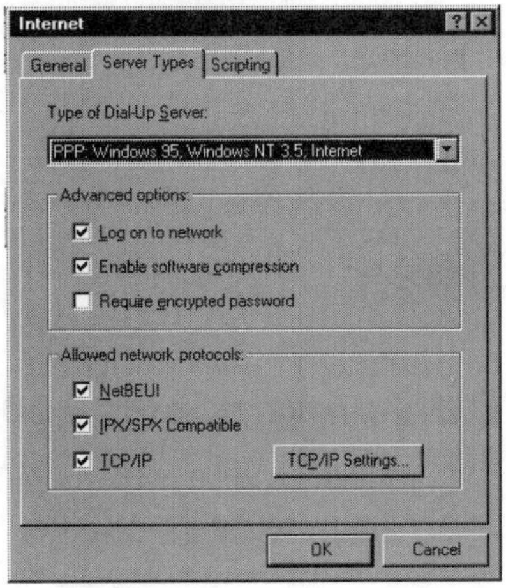

The Scripting tab is used if your ISP doesn't support any type of automatic user-name and password authentication protocol like *Password Authentication Protocol (PAP)* or *Challenge Handshake Authentication Protocol (CHAP)*. If in doubt, ask your ISP. This tab allows you to specify a file that will automatically enter your username and password. The Windows 95 Help file documents how to use this feature.

You can also configure DUN parameters in the Connect screen of the Internet connection. To access this area, double-click the connection. You will see a screen similar to the one in Figure 8.31. In this screen, you enter the username and password that your ISP has assigned you. Additionally, double-check the phone number you entered to make sure it's correct. Once you've finished configuring the phone number, you're ready to connect to the Internet.

FIGURE 8.31 The Connect screen

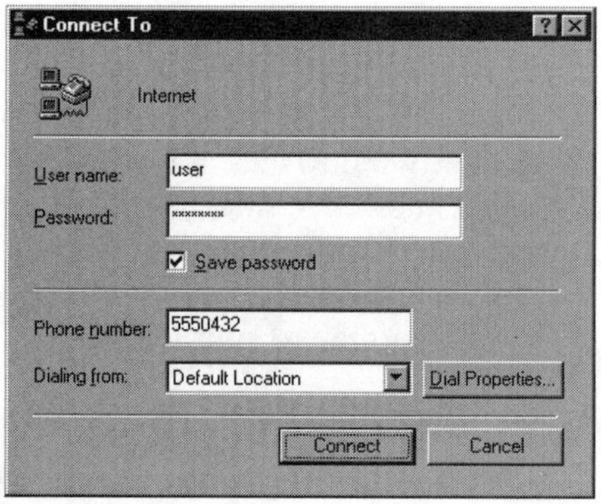

If you want to save the password so you don't have to type it in every time, click the check box next to Save Password. Be careful, though. If you save your password, anyone can get onto the Internet from your computer (using your username) without having to enter a password.

Installing DUN on Windows 2000

With Windows 2000, wizards are used everywhere, including the creation of a dial-up networking connection:

1. Choose Start ≻ Settings≻ Network and Dial-up Connections.

2. In the window that appears, double-click Make New Connection.

3. If this is the first time you have created a network connection, the Location Information window appears. You cannot escape this window without entering an area code, so enter it and click OK. You will get another location screen as well. Click OK again and the Network Connection Wizard appears.

4. In the Network Connection Wizard, choose Dial Up to the Internet and the Welcome to the Internet Connection Wizard (ICW) window appears (Figure 8.32). That makes three nested wizards. A bit extreme, no?

FIGURE 8.32 The first screen of the Internet Connection Wizard

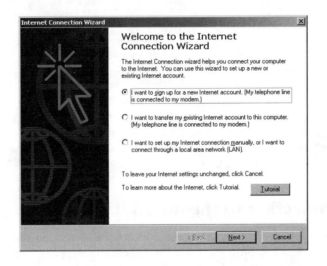

5. In the ICW, you will be led through a long series of choices. Click through and enter the values that apply to your Internet setup. You will be asked what type of device (modem or network) you are using, what number you need to dial, and what your username and password are. At the end, you can even set up your mail account, and the wizard offers to connect you when you are finished.

6. A new icon will appear in the Network and Dial-Up Connections window showing that your new connection has been added (Figure 8.33). You can view the status of a connection by double-clicking it or change its settings by right-clicking and selecting Properties.

FIGURE 8.33 The finished dial-up connection

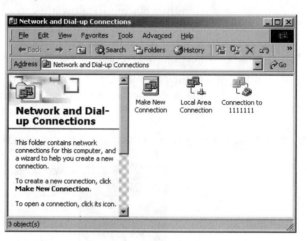

 The Windows 2000 Internet setup is typical of the sort of straightforward, easy-to-use tools that we as technicians have to hope do not become common. If everything gets this easy, it's going to be tough to make a living in this business!

Connecting to the Internet

Connecting to the Internet is simple once you get the connection configured. Simply double-click the connection, enter the password (unless you chose the Save Password button previously), and click Connect. A window will appear that allows you to follow the status of the connection (Figure 8.34). You should hear the modem dial and then connect. When it connects, the status screen will say, "Verifying Username and Password," and then "Connected." Once you are connected, the status screen will go away and you will see an icon on the taskbar (the same icon that's on the status screen). At this point, you are connected to your ISP and, through it, to the rest of the world. You can then fire up your favorite Web browser and start surfin'.

FIGURE 8.34 Connection status screen

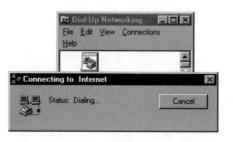

If you are configuring the system for someone who just wants to click and go, you can also right-click the Internet Explorer icon on the desktop and use the Connection tab of the Internet Settings window to configure auto-dial. Set the connection you have created as the default and specify that the system should "Always dial my default connection." Any time an application needs to access the Internet, it can simply initiate the DUN connection automatically.

Browsers

The first, and probably the most important, thing you'll need is a Web browser. This piece of software will allow you to view Web pages from the Internet. The two browsers with the largest market share are Netscape Navigator and Microsoft Internet Explorer (also known as IE). Both work equally well for browsing the Internet. Microsoft includes its browser, IE (Figure 8.35), with both Windows 98 and Windows 2000, whereas Netscape Navigator (Figure 8.36), which is free, must be downloaded separately.

FIGURE 8.35 The main window of Microsoft Internet Explorer

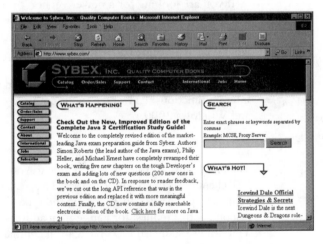

FIGURE 8.36 The main window of Netscape Navigator

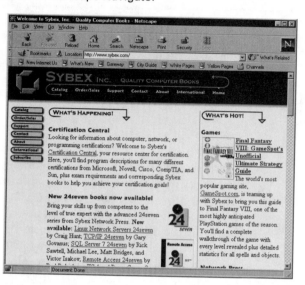

If you are looking for a newer version of Internet Explorer, you can go to Microsoft's Web site, www.microsoft.com/windows/ie. For Navigator, go to www.netscape.com. Once you are there, select the version you want and specify what type of machine you will be using it on. You can then download and install the software.

Besides a browser, you will probably need to use at least two other critical Internet functions: FTP and e-mail. Both are supported natively in Windows *9x* and Windows 2000.

FTP

The File Transfer Protocol is available to you either through the command-line FTP client or through your browser. To access the Microsoft FTP site through the command prompt, open a prompt and type **FTP ftp.microsoft.com**. The site will respond with a request for your e-mail address, and you will then be given access. You can use standard DOS navigation commands to move between directories, and you can retrieve or send files using the GET *<filename>* or PUT *<filename>* commands. When you are finished with your session, simply type **QUIT**.

Internet Explorer also supports FTP. To go to Microsoft's Web site, you can simply type in **http://www.microsoft.com** and you will be taken to a Web page.

If you change the first part of the name to ftp://, though, the system knows to look for an FTP resource instead. Typing **ftp://ftp.microsoft.com** will also take you to the Microsoft Web site, and you can then use all of the standard Explorer GUI file management techniques, just as you would if you were connecting to any other network drive.

Because Microsoft's FTP site is a public site, it allows you to use a special anonymous account that provides access. If you go to a site where that account has been disabled, you will need to provide another username and password, which should be provided by the site's administrator, or you will not be allowed into the site. Also, most FTP sites only allow visitors to download data, so PUT commands generally will be rejected unless you have a real (non-anonymous) account on the server.

E-Mail

Another common use of the Internet is to send and receive electronic mail. E-mail allows you to quickly and inexpensively transfer messages to other people. To send and receive e-mail, you need to have only two things: an e-mail account and an e-mail client. The account can be provided by a company, or it can be associated with your ISP account. Either way, you will have an address that looks like username@domain.com.

The last part of this address (after the @) identifies the domain name of the company or ISP that provides you with your e-mail account. The part before the @ is your username. A username must be unique on each domain. Two Bill the Cat users on a single network, for instance, might be billthecat@domain.com and billthecat1@domain.com.

As with other TCP/IP services, e-mail needs to be configured. Nothing in TCP/IP networking ever just works, it seems. Still, Windows provides a service called *Messaging Application Programming Interface (MAPI)* to make configuring e-mail easier, and overall, configuring e-mail is relatively straightforward.

Your MAPI settings can be defined in Control Panel's Mail program. Figure 8.37 shows just a few of the many Internet e-mail settings you can define. Among these are the *Post Office Protocol v 3 (POP3)* and *Simple Mail Transport Protocol (SMTP)* server settings, which you will need to be given by an administrator. A POP3 server is a machine on the Internet that accepts and stores Internet e-mail and allows you to retrieve that mail when you are online. An SMTP server is a server that accepts mail you want to send, and forwards it to the proper user. In order to send and receive mail, you need both!

FIGURE 8.37   Internet E-mail properties

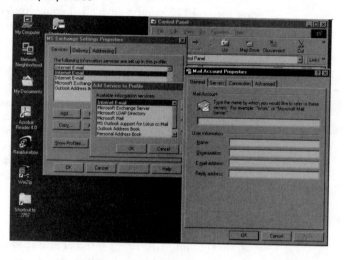

Once you have the settings configured, you will need to simply install an e-mail client or use the built-in client included with Windows 98 and 2000. That client is called Outlook Express, and it's a good basic e-mail application.

Monitoring and Disconnecting from the Internet

To see information (such as speed and quantity) about the data you have transferred during your Internet session, you can double-click the connection icon in the system tray (lower-right portion of the screen) to bring up a status window. From this window, you can see the number of bytes sent and received, and you can disconnect from the Internet. You can also do disconnect by simply right-clicking the connection icon itself and choosing Disconnect.

Summary

At one time, computer repair technicians and computer network engineers had distinctly different job descriptions, and techs rarely needed to deal with network issues at all. As documents become larger, and networking and the Internet become a more basic part of both home and office computer use, understanding networking is no longer an optional part of a computer technician's job description. Whether you need to access drivers on the Internet or set up a client's machine to share files on the network, PC techs now need to learn about networking.

In this chapter, we looked at a number of the basic issues you may come across, including how to set up a Windows machine to use a particular protocol and client software. We also looked at how a Windows client can access file or print resources on the network and how a Windows 9x or 2000 machine can also be configured to provide file or print services to other machines on the network.

Last, we looked at the special case of the TCP/IP protocol, and the Internet, because configuring TCP/IP and installing and using Internet applications are crucial tasks for both network and Internet configurations.

Key Terms

Before you take the exam, be certain you are familiar with the following terms.

browser	Logon
client software	Messaging Application Programming Interface (MAPI)
default gateway	network
domain	network adapter
Domain Name System (DNS)	peer-to-peer networking
Dynamic Host Configuration Protocol (DHCP)	PING
e-mail	Post Office Protocol v 3 (POP3)
file sharing	protocol
File Transfer Protocol (FTP)	Servers
host	share name
host name	Simple Mail Transport Protocol (SMTP)
Hypertext Transfer Protocol (HTTP)	subnet mask
Internet	TCP/IP
Internet Service Provider (ISP)	Tracert
internetwork	Windows Internet Name Service (WINS)
IP address	WINIPCFG
IPCONFIG	World Wide Web (WWW)
local resources	

Review Questions

1. Using either a Windows 9*x* or Windows 2000 workstation, which of the following components do you need to connect to a Microsoft network server? (Select all that apply.)

    A. Protocol

    B. Client

    C. Adapter

    D. Sharing

2. Which of the following are common Internet connection types. (Select all that apply.)

    A. ISDN

    B. POTS

    C. T1

    D. DSL

    E. All of the above

3. Transmission Control Protocol/Internet Protocol (TCP/IP) is a collection of protocols that help manage Internet communication. Each computer running TCP/IP must have a unique IP address assigned to it. Which of the following statements best describes an IP address?

    A. An IP address is no more than your dial-up telephone number.

    B. An IP address is a set of four numbers, each of which must be from 0 to 255. These numbers can be automatically provided or assigned by a system administrator.

    C. An IP address is a set of three numbers, each of which must be from 0 to 255. An IP address is a unique name that identifies the computer within a network. This name can be automatically provided or assigned by a system administrator.

    D. IP addresses are composed of four numbers, each of which is between 1 and 256. These numbers can be automatically provided or assigned by a system administrator.

4. You've enabled file and printer sharing on your Windows 9*x* system. You must now specify how security will be handled. What are your options? (Select all that apply.)

    A. Share-Level Access Control

    B. System-Wide Access Control

    C. Remote-Access Control

    D. User-Level Access Control

5. TCP/IP is installed on each PC within a network. You can communicate within the network but are unable to access the Internet. Which of the following TCP/IP settings must be properly configured for Internet access? (Select all that apply.)

   A. IP Address

   B. Subnet Mask

   C. Default Gateway

   D. DNS Server

6. A Windows 9x workstation includes default support for which of the following network types? (Select all that apply.)

   A. Microsoft's Windows Networking

   B. Sun's Solaris

   C. Novell's NetWare

   D. Apple's Macintosh Networking

7. You've installed an older NIC in a Windows 9x system. During the Plug-and-Play (PnP) process, you encounter a conflict. Which of the following methods would you use to resolve the conflict?

   A. Disable PnP on the NIC either with a jumper or with the software setup program.

   B. Run PnP again. The conflict should be resolved the second time around.

   C. Older NICs are prone to this problem. Remove the older NIC and buy a new one.

   D. None of the above.

8. Configuring a Windows 2000 system as a network client requires three elements: a client, an adapter, and _____ .

   A. A host name

   B. An IP address

   C. A protocol

   D. A gateway

9. You've set up a network whereby each computer acts as a client and a server and in which each user shares each other's resources, including printers. What is the correct term for such an arrangement?

   A. Enterprise Services

   B. Sharing & Caring

   C. Server-client linking

   D. Peer-to-peer networking

10. In a Windows 9*x* system, which of the following statements involving NetBEUI and NetBIOS is true?

    A. NetBEUI is a name resolution system, whereas NetBIOS is a transport protocol.

    B. NetBEUI and NetBIOS are subprotocols of TCP/IP.

    C. NetBEUI is a transport protocol, and NetBIOS is a name resolution system.

    D. NetBEUI and NetBIOS are not used within a Windows 9*x* system.

11. Sending and receiving electronic mail (e-mail) is a common benefit of the Internet. Assuming a user has access to the Internet on a properly configured PC, which of the following items are required before a user can begin using e-mail?

    A. An e-mail account and a domain

    B. An e-mail account and an e-mail client

    C. An e-mail account and e-mail permissions

    D. None of the above

12. You can map a network drive in both Windows 9*x* and 2000 using which of the following commands?

    A. Map Network Drive

    B. Connect to Network Share

    C. Connect Network Share

    D. Map Network Share

13. You've been granted the right to use a shared folder and printer in a Windows 9*x* system. What do you need to do to gain access to them?

    A. From the desktop, double-click the Network icon. Click the Shared Resources tab. Any resources you have access to will be listed.

    B. Double-click the My Computer icon on your desktop. Click Web Folders. Your shared resources will be listed.

    C. From the desktop, double-click the Network Neighborhood icon, which will allow you to browse for shared resources.

    D. Open the Control Panel and click on the Network Neighborhood icon. Browse for shared resources.

14. Computers communicate using IP addresses. The address can be a series of numbers or a host name such as Bob's PC. Obviously, it is easier for humans to remember the host name, but computers communicate with numbers. Which of the following methods help locate a computer's numeric IP address when a human searches for it using only the host name? (Select all that apply.)

    A. NRP (Name Resolution Protocol)

    B. WINS (Windows Internet Name Service)

    C. DNS (Domain Name System)

    D. None of the above

15. Which of the following types of networking components can be added in the Network program on a Windows 9x system? (Select all that apply.)

    A. Protocol

    B. Adapter

    C. Client

    D. Service

16. Which of the following is the correct way to use the protocol utility IPCONFIG in a Windows 2000 environment?

    A. IPCONFIG does not work with Windows 2000.

    B. Choose Start ➤ Run and type **IPCONFIG**.

    C. Open a browser window and type **IPCONFIG** in the address line.

    D. Choose Start ➤ Run, type **CMD**, and press Enter. At the command prompt, type **IPCONFIG**.

17. What would you need to do to create a new Dial-Up Networking (DUN) connection within a Windows 9x system?

    A. Open the Control Panel and click the Dial-Up Networking icon. Click Make New Connection. Choose a name for your connection. Select which modem you are using. Enter the dial-in telephone number. Click the Finish button.

    B. Choose Start ➤ Programs ➤ Accessories. Choose Dial-Up Networking. This will open a window that shows all current DUN connections. Double-click Make New Connection. Choose a name for your connection. Select which modem you are using. Enter the dial-in telephone number. Click the Finish button.

    C. Open the Control Panel and click the Make New Connection icon. Choose a name for your connection. Select which modem you are using. Enter the dial-in telephone number. Click the Finish button.

    D. None of the above.

18. Networks that transmit data use protocols to make communication possible. TCP/IP, for example, uses two different analog connection protocols: Serial Line Internet Protocol (SLIP) and Point-to-Point Protocol (PPP). PPP is the more common of the two protocols for which of the following reasons? (Select all that apply.)

    A. PPP is easier to configure.

    B. PPP broadcasts all data requests, increasing the chances of a response.

    C. PPP uses enhanced error-checking, making it more stable.

    D. All of the above.

19. In a Windows 9x environment, if you don't know the name of the computer that is acting as the host for a resource you are looking for, you can use the _____ command.

    A. Map

    B. Run

    C. Find

    D. Search

20. You have just granted someone share-level access to a folder in your Windows 9x system. What are the three access rights available? (Select all that apply.)

    A. Full Access

    B. Depends on Password

    C. Depends on IP Address

    D. Read-Only

Answers to Review Questions

1. A, B, C. Using either Windows *9x* or 2000, three initial components—Adapter, Client, and Sharing—are required to connect to a Microsoft network server.

2. E. Most home Internet connections use POTS (Plain Old Telephone System). Other options include fiber optics (ATM), digital phone technology (DSL), T1 and T3, digital phone line (ISDN), Frame Relay, and 56K point-to-point.

3. B. Every computer running TCP/IP must have a unique IP address, and that address is in the format *x.x.x.x*, where *x* is a number from 0 to 255. These numbers can be automatically provided or assigned by a system administrator. The machine will also have a host name, which identifies the machine on the network.

4. A, D. There are two security options in a Windows *9x* system. Share-Level Access Control involves supplying a username, password, and security setting for each shared resource. User-Level Access Control means there is a central database of users that Windows *9x* uses to specify security settings for each shared resource.

5. A, B, C, D. A proper IP address and subnet mask are essential for any sort of network communication. However, to reach the Internet, a default gateway, which is the IP address of the router your machine uses to access the Internet, must be configured. You also need the Domain Name System (DNS) server, so you can type **www.yahoo.com** instead of having to remember the numeric IP address.

6. A, C. Within a Windows *9x* workstation, clients are provided for both Microsoft and Novell networks.

7. A. Conflicts between older NICs and the Plug-and-Play installation process can occur. However, as indicated in option A, if PnP is disabled either with a jumper or with the software program, the device can be successfully installed.

8. C. Both Windows 2000 and Windows *9x* require three elements: a client, an adapter, and a protocol. How each element is configured is slightly different between the two operating systems, however. Host names, IP addresses, and gateways may also be necessary, but only if the chosen protocol is TCP/IP.

9. D. Networking in which users share each other's resources, is called peer-to-peer networking.

10. C. NetBEUI is a transport protocol, managing data transmission between two computers. NetBIOS is a name resolution system, allowing a computer to search for another computer on a network by its Microsoft computer name.

11. B. To send and receive e-mail, all that is required is an e-mail account and an e-mail client.

12. A. This is one of those "technicality" questions, but knowing proper terminology is important when taking technical exams, and questions like this crop up regularly.

13. C. The Network Neighborhood icon, located on the Desktop, provides easy access to any shared resources. Network Neighborhood is not accessible from the Control Panel or from My Computer.

14. B, C. Although there are a number of services available for resolving names, the most common are WINS and DNS. WINS resolves NetBIOS computer names to the appropriate IP address, while DNS does the same for host names.

15. A, B, C, D. There are four basic types of networking components in a Windows 9*x* system. They are protocol, adapter, client, and service.

16. D. As indicated in option D, the IPCONFIG protocol utility is a good way to find basic information about your TCP/IP configuration. It can be used at the command prompt. If you type **IPCONFIG /A**, the system will display additional information.

17. B. You can create a new DUN as indicated in option B. The Dial-Up Networking icon can also be accessed by double-clicking My Computer from the desktop.

18. A, C. As indicated, what makes Point-to-Point the more popular analog connection protocol is the fact that it is easy to configure, and due to its error-checking capabilities, it is more stable.

19. C. The Find command can be used to search your machine for files or the network for other machines. Search is used on Windows 2000 to do the same tasks.

20. A, B, D. Read-Only, Full Access, and Depends on Password are the three options for access rights. These options are accessible by right-clicking the shared folder and choosing Sharing.

Windows and Application Troubleshooting

THE FOLLOWING OBJECTIVES ARE COVERED IN THIS CHAPTER:

✓ **1.2 Identify basic concepts and procedures for creating, viewing, and managing files, directories, and disks. This includes procedures for changing file attributes and the ramifications of those changes (for example, security issues).**

Content may include the following:

- File attributes—Read Only, Hidden, System, and Archive attributes
- File naming conventions (most common extensions)
- IDE/SCSI
- Internal/External
- Backup/Restore
- Partitioning/Formatting/File System
    - FAT
    - FAT16
    - FAT32
    - NTFS4
    - NTFS5
    - HPFS

Windows-based utilties:

- SCANDISK
- Device Manager
- System Manager
- Computer Manager

- MSCONFIG.EXE
- REGEDIT.EXE (View information/Backup registry)
- REGEDT32.EXE
- ATTRIB.EXE
- EXTRACT.EXE
- DEFRAG.EXE
- EDIT.COM
- FDISK.EXE
- SYSEDIT.EXE
- SCANREG
- WSCRIPT.EXE
- HWINFO.EXE
- ASD.EXE (Automatic Skip Driver)
- Cvt1.EXE (Drive Converter FAT16 to FAT32)

✓ **3.1 Recognize and interpret the meaning of common error codes and startup messages from the boot sequence, and identify steps to correct the problems.**

Content may include the following:

- Safe Mode
- No operating system found
- Error in CONFIG.SYS line XX
- Bad or missing COMMAND.COM
- HIMEM.SYS not loaded
- Missing or corrupt HIMEM.SYS
- SCSI
- Swap file
- NT boot issues
- Dr. Watson
- Failure to start GUI
- Windows Protection Error
- Event Viewer—Event log is full
- A device referenced in SYSTEM.INI, WIN.INI, Registry is not found

✓ **3.2 Recognize common problems and determine how to resolve them.**

> **Content may include the following:**

- Eliciting problem symptoms from customers
- Having customer reproduce error as part of the diagnostic process
- Identifying recent changes to the computer environment from the user
- Troubleshooting Windows-specific printing problems
  - Print spool is stalled
  - Incorrect/incompatible driver for print
  - Incorrect parameter

> **Other common problems:**

- General Protection Faults
- Illegal operation
- Invalid working directory
- System lock up
- Option (sound card, modem, or input device) will not function
- Application will not start or load
- Cannot log on to network (option—NIC not functioning)
- TSR (Terminate Stay Resident) programs and virus
- Applications don't install
- Network connection

> **Viruses and virus types:**

- What they are
- Sources (floppy, e-mails, etc.)
- How to determine presence

roubleshooting involves asking a lot of questions of yourself and of other people. Beginners (and yes, I was a beginner once upon a time) like the trial and error method of fixing things, but in the long run, a methodological approach will work better. The reason that beginners often choose a trial and error approach is that they don't yet have a good enough background to analyze the problem.

For complete coverage of objective 1.2, please also see Chapter 4. For complete coverage of objective 3.2, please also see Chapter 7.

Analysis is the act of breaking down a structure or system into its component parts and their relationships.

More than occasionally, a technician will unwittingly create new problems in an attempt to fix a real problem. For example, if a program will not run and displays an Out of Memory error, it might seem logical to add more memory.

But certain types of memory currently on the market will not work in older 486 computers—what happens if the memory the technician installs is the wrong type for the computer? Now there are two problems.

And what if the computer with the mismatched memory actually starts up but eventually locks up because of the memory problem? The lock-ups could create an interruption in writing information to the hard drive, and a program could become corrupted. That would make three problems total.

Once the technician has sorted out all the problems, it's time to actually repair whatever went wrong. In the above example, it is quite likely that the source of the original Out of Memory error was really some corrupted program code. Many times, a Windows program with some damage to one or more components will cause exactly that error to be displayed.

Troubleshooting Steps

In a computer system, there are at least four main parts to be considered, each of which is in turn made up of many pieces:

1. There is a collection of hardware pieces that are integrated into a working system. As you know, the hardware can be quite complex, what with motherboards, hard drives, video cards, etc. Software can be equally perplexing.

2. There is an operating system that in turn is dependent on the hardware. Remember that the DOS and Windows operating systems have kernels, internal commands, and external commands, which may interact with the hardware in different ways.

3. There is an application or a software program that is supposed to do something. Programs such as Microsoft Word and Excel are now bundled with a great many features.

4. There is a computer user, ready to take the computer system to its limits (and beyond). A technician can often forget that the customer user is a very complex and important part of the puzzle.

Effective troubleshooting will require some experience just for the background required to analyze the problem at hand, but there are also some other logical steps that need to be remembered. Ask yourself the question, "Is there a problem?" Perhaps it is as simple as a customer expecting too much from the computer. If there is a problem, is it just one problem?

Step 1: Talk to the Customer

Talking to the user is an important first step. Your first contact with the computer that has a problem will usually be through the customer, either directly or by way of a work order that contains the user's complaint. Often, the complaint will be something straightforward, such as, "There's a disk stuck in the floppy drive." At other times, the problem will be complex and the customer will not have mentioned everything that has been going wrong.

The act of diagnosis starts with the art of customer relations. Go to the customer with an attitude of trust: *believe* what the customer is saying. At the same time, go to the customer with an attitude of hidden skepticism, meaning *don't* believe that the customer has told you everything. This attitude of hidden skepticism is not the same as distrust. Most customers are not going to lie, but they may inadvertently forget to give some crucial detail.

For example, a customer once complained that his CD-ROM drive didn't work. What he failed to say was that it had never worked and that he had installed it himself. It turned out that he had mounted it with screws that were too long and that these prevented the tray from ejecting properly.

The most important part of this step is to have the customer show you what the problem is. The best method I've seen of doing this is to ask them, "Show me what 'not working' looks like." That way, you see the conditions and methods under which the problem occurs. The problem may be a simple matter of an improper method. The user may be doing an operation incorrectly or doing the steps in the wrong order. During this step, you have the opportunity to observe how the problem occurs, so pay attention.

Step 2: Gather Information

The user can give you vital information. The most important question is "what changed?" Problems don't usually come out of nowhere. Was a new piece of hardware or software added? Did the user drop some equipment? Was there a power outage or a storm? These are the types of questions that you can ask a user in trying to find out what is different.

If nothing changed, at least outwardly, then what was going on at the time of failure? Can the problem be reproduced? Can the problem be worked around? The point here is to ask as many questions as you need to in order to pinpoint the trouble.

Step 3: Eliminate Possibilities

Once the problem or problems have been clearly identified, your next step is to isolate possible causes. If the problem cannot be clearly identified, then further tests will be necessary. A common technique for hardware and software problems alike is to strip the system down to bare-bones basics. In a hardware situation, this could mean removing all interface cards except those absolutely required for the system to operate. In a software situation, this may mean booting up with the CONFIG.SYS and AUTOEXEC.BAT files disabled.

Generally, then, you can gradually rebuild the system toward the point where it started. When you reintroduce a component and the problem reappears, then you know that component is the one causing the problem.

Step 4: Document Your Work

One last point needs to be made in this brief introduction to troubleshooting: you should document your work. If the process of elimination or the process of questioning the user goes beyond two or three crucial elements, start writing it down. Nothing is more infuriating than knowing you did something to make the system work but not being able to remember what it was.

Windows File-Related Problems

Many problems in Windows can be traced to missing, corrupt, or misconfigured files. They can cause consternation to no end because they can be troublesome to fix. Thankfully, they usually give indications of which file is the problem in the error message.

In this section, you will learn about some of the various file-related problems that can be found in Windows as well as their solutions. The problems you will learn about in this section can be categorized into four main areas:

- System files not found
- Config file issues
- Swap file issues
- NT boot issues

Since the most easily fixed problems are related to missing system files, that's the next topic we'll cover.

System Files Not Found

Every operating system or operating environment (such as Windows 9*x* or Windows NT) has certain key system files that must be present in order for it to function. If these files are missing or corrupt, the operating system will cease to function properly. Files can be deleted by accident rather easily, so it's important to know what these system files are, where they are located, and how to replace them.

Windows 9*x* system files are covered in Chapter 3, "Windows 95/98," and Windows 2000 system files are covered in Chapter 4, "Windows 2000."

When you boot Windows 9*x* or Windows NT, the presence of the system files (e.g., HIMEM.SYS, COMMAND.COM, etc.) is checked, and each file is loaded. If you'll remember, the computer's BIOS first checks the hardware of the PC, then looks for a boot sector on one of the disks and loads the operating system found in that boot sector. However, if the computer can't find a boot sector with an operating system installed on any of the disks, it will display an error similar to the following:

```
No operating system found
```

This error means that the computer's BIOS checked all the drives it knew about and couldn't find any disk with a bootable sector. This could be for any number of reasons, including:

- An operating system wasn't installed.
- The boot sector has been corrupted.
- The boot files have been corrupted.

Thankfully, there are a couple of solutions to these problems. First of all, if the file or files are simply missing, just copy them from the original setup diskettes or CD-ROM, or copy them from a backup (assuming you have one). The same holds true if you have a corrupt file, except you must delete the corrupt file(s) first, then replace them with new copies.

 When deleting and/or replacing system files, you must use the ATTRIB command to remove the hidden, system, and read-only attributes before you replace these files.

These same concepts hold true for other system file–related problems, such as:

Bad or missing COMMAND.COM
HIMEM.SYS not loaded
Missing or corrupt HIMEM.SYS

These errors just mean that the specified (e.g., COMMAND.COM, HIMEM.SYS) files are either missing or corrupt. Just replace them with fresh copies. The error should go away, and the computer will function properly.

Configuration File Issues

As discussed in Chapters 3 and 4, Windows 9x and Windows NT contain several files that hold configuration data for the Windows, such as the Registry, SYSTEM.INI, WIN.INI, and the CONFIG.SYS. Because these files can be edited by a user, the possibility for introduction of invalid configurations is more likely. Additionally, most of the software installation programs modify these files when a new program is installed. These files are modified so often, in fact, that it is a wonder they aren't corrupted more often.

Some of the more commonly seen errors in Windows that are related to configuration files are:

A device referenced in SYSTEM.INI can not be found
A device referenced in WIN.INI can not be found
A device referenced in the Registry can not be found
Error in CONFIG.SYS line XX

These errors are basically the same error and mean that an item that refers to a piece of hardware or software that wasn't installed was placed into a configuration file. The difference is which file the error is contained in. Again, with missing stuff, the solution is very simple: just add the missing item. In fact, in `Error in CONFIG.SYS line xx`, the error message actually tells you which line has the error in it. You can then go directly to that line and fix the problem. With the `SYSTEM.INI` and `WIN.INI` file errors, you must search through the files using your favorite text editor to try and find the invalid line. It may be something as hard to find as an additional backslash put in the wrong place, or as easy to find as a string of corrupt characters.

That process is the same for the Registry except that you must use the Registry Editor (`REGEDIT.EXE` or `REGEDT32.EXE`, for Windows *9x* and Windows NT/2000, respectively) to search for corrupt or invalid entries. You will learn more about the Registry later in this chapter.

Swap File Issues

As mentioned in earlier chapters, Windows uses swap files (called page files in Windows NT) to increase the amount of usable memory it has by using hard disk space as memory. However, sometimes problems can occur when a computer doesn't have enough disk space to make a proper swap file. Because Windows relies on swap files for proper operation, if a swap file isn't big enough, Windows will slow down and start running out of usable memory. All sorts of memory-related problems can stem from incorrect or too small swap files. Symptoms of swap file problems include an extremely slow system speed and a disk that is constantly being accessed. This condition is known as hard disk *thrashing* and occurs because Windows doesn't have enough memory to contain all the programs that are running, and there isn't enough disk space for a swap file to contain them all. This causes Windows to swap between memory and hard disk.

The solution to this problem is to first free up some disk space. With IDE hard disk sizes at tens of gigabytes for around $100, the easiest thing to do is install a bigger hard disk. If that solution isn't practical, you must delete enough unused files so that the swap file can be made large enough to be functional.

Windows NT Boot Issues

Troubleshooting Windows NT boot issues is another type of Windows troubleshooting that is commonly performed. To understand Windows NT boot issues, you must first understand the NT boot process, which is as follows:

1. The POST routine examines the boot sector and loads the Master Boot Record (MBR).
2. The boot sector is loaded from the active partition.
3. NTLDR is loaded from the boot sector and initialized.
4. NTLDR loads the appropriate minifile drives for the type of file system on the boot partition (e.g., FAT or NTFS).

5. NTLDR reads the BOOT.INI file and looks for the list of operating systems installed on the computer. Windows NT is one of the choices, along with any other operating system that was installed over when Windows NT was installed.

6. A user selects an operating system to boot to.

7. If Windows NT is selected, NTLDR runs NTDETECT.COM to detect new hardware.

8. NTLDR then loads the kernel file (NTOSKRNL.EXE), hardware abstraction layer (HAL), and the Registry, as well as any device drivers found there.

9. NTLDR finally passes control to NTOSKRNL.EXE. At this point, the boot process is finished and NTOSKRNL can start loading other files.

As you can see, NTLDR is heavily relied upon during the boot process. If it is missing or corrupted, Windows NT will not be able to boot and you'll get an error similar to Can't find NTLDR.

On the other hand, if you get an error such as NTOSKRNL.EXE missing or corrupt on bootup, it may be an error in the BOOT.INI file. This is a common occurrence if you have improperly used the multi(0)disk(0)rdisk(0)partition(1)\WINNT="Windows NT Server" syntax entries. If these entries are correct, the NTOSKRNL.EXE file may be corrupt or missing. Boot to a startup disk and replace the file from the setup disks or CD-ROM.

Windows Printing Problems

If a printer is not printing at all, then you should start with the DOS troubleshooting method. First, reboot the computer in Safe Mode DOS Prompt. (See the section "Windows-Based Utilities" for more information on Safe Mode.) Then copy a file or a directory listing to the printer port. If the file or directory listing doesn't print, the cause is most likely a hardware failure or loose cable. If it *does* print, then you can assume the printing problems are associated with the Windows printer drivers.

One common source of printer driver errors is corruption of the driver. If a printer doesn't work, you can delete the printer from the printer settings window and reinstall it. If this method fails, the problem may be that related printer files were not replaced. Delete all printers from the computer and reinstall them. If this second method fails, then the printer driver is not compatible with Windows 9*x* or with the printer, and you will need to obtain an updated driver.

A quick way to test the printer functionality is to use the Print Test Page option. This option is presented to you as the last step when setting up a new printer in Windows. Always select this option when you're setting up a new printer so you can test its functionality. To print a test page for a printer that's already set up, look for the option on the Properties menu for the particular printer.

After the test page is sent to the printer, the computer will ask if it printed correctly. For the first few times, you'll probably want to answer No and use the troubleshooting Wizard that appears, but after you have troubleshot a few printer problems, you may prefer to answer Yes and bypass the Wizard, which is rather simplistic and annoying.

Other Common Problems

Some common Windows problems don't fall into any great category other than "common Windows problems". Some of these problems include:

General Protection Faults (GPFs)   Probably the most common and most frustrating error. A *General Protection Fault (GPF)* happens in Windows when a program accesses memory that another program is using or when a program accesses a memory address that doesn't exist. Generally, GPFs are the result of sloppy programming. To fix this type of problem, a simple reboot will usually clear memory. If they keep occurring, check to see which software is causing the GPF. Then, find out if the manufacturer of the software has a patch to prevent it from GPFing.

Windows protection error   A Windows protection error is a condition that usually happens on either startup or shutdown. Protection errors occur because Windows 9x could not load or unload a virtual device driver (VxD) properly. Thankfully, this error usually tells which VxD is experiencing the problem so you can check to see if the specified VxD is missing or corrupt. If it is, you can replace it with a new copy. If it is one of the Windows 9x built-in VxDs, you must re-run Windows 9x SETUP.EXE with the /p I option.

Illegal operation   Occasionally, a program will quit for apparently no reason and present you with a window that says This program has performed an illegal operation and will be shut down. If the problem persists, contact the program vendor. An *illegal operation error* usually means that a program was forced to quit because it did something Windows didn't like. It then displays this error window. The name of the program that quit will appear at the top of the window along with three buttons: OK, Cancel, and Details. The OK and Cancel buttons do the same thing: they both dismiss the window. The Details button will open the window a little farther and show the details of the error. The details of the error include which module experienced the problem, the memory location being accessed at the time, and the registers and flags of the processor at the time of the error.

System lock-up   It is obvious when a system lock-up occurs. The system simply stops responding to commands and stops processing completely. System lock-ups can occur when a computer is asked to process too many instructions at once with too little memory. Usually, the cure for a system lock-up is to simply reboot. If the lock-ups are persistent, it may be a hardware-related problem instead of a software problem.

Dr. Watson   Windows NT 4 includes a special utility known as Dr. Watson. This utility intercepts all error conditions and, instead of presenting the user with a cryptic Windows error, presents the user with a slew of information that can be used to troubleshoot the problem. Additionally, Dr. Watson logs all errors to log files stored in the WINDOWS\DRWATSON directory.

Failure to start GUI   Occasionally, the GUI of Windows won't appear. The system will hang just before the GUI appears. Or, in the case of Windows NT, the *Blue Screen of Death (BSOD)*—not a technical term, by the way—will appear. The BSOD is another way of describing the blue screen error condition that occurs when Windows NT fails to boot properly or quits unexpectedly. In Windows 9x, instead of a BSOD, you will simply get a black screen (usually with a blinking cursor in the upper left corner) that indicates there is a problem. Because it is at this stage that the device drivers for the various pieces of hardware are installed, if your Windows GUI fails to start properly, more than likely the problem is related to a misconfigured driver or misconfigured hardware. Try booting Windows in Safe Mode to bypass this problem. (See the section "Windows-Based Utilities" for more information on Safe Mode.)

If you happen to get a Blue Screen of Death (BSOD) with a "Fatal Exception error 0D," chances are that the culprit is a problem relating to the video card.

Option (sound card, modem, SCSI card, or input device) will not function   When you are using Windows, you are constantly interacting with some piece of hardware. Each piece of hardware has a Windows driver that must be loaded in order for Windows to be able to use it. Additionally, the hardware has to be installed and functioning properly. If the device driver is not installed properly or the hardware is misconfigured, the device won't function properly.

TSR (Terminate and Stay Resident) programs and viruses   In the days of DOS, there was no easy way of running a utility program in the background while you ran an application. Because necessity is the mother of invention, programmers came up with Terminate and Stay Resident (TSR) programs. These programs were loaded from the AUTOEXEC.BAT and stayed resident in memory until called for by some key combination. Unfortunately, while that worked for DOS, Windows 95 had its own method for using background utilities. If any DOS TSR programs are in memory when Windows 9x is running, the TSR(s) can interfere with the proper operation of Windows programs. Before you install Windows 9x, make sure that any DOS TSRs are disabled in the AUTOEXEC.BAT.

Cannot log on to network (option—NIC not functioning)   If your computer is hooked up to a network (and more and more computers today are), you need to know when your computer is not functioning on the network properly and what to do about it. In most cases, the problem can be attributed to either a malfunctioning Network Interface Card (NIC) or improperly installed network software. The biggest indicator in Windows that some component of the network software is nonfunctional is that you can't log on to the network or access any network service. To fix this problem, you must first fix the underlying hardware problem (if one exists), then properly install or configure the network software.

 Networking software is covered in Chapter 8, "Configuring Network Software."

Applications don't install   We've all experienced this frustration. You are trying to install the coolest new program and, for whatever reason, it just won't install properly. It may give you one of the above-mentioned errors or a cryptic installation error. If a software program won't install and it gives you any previously mentioned errors (e.g., GPF or Illegal Operation), use the solutions for those errors first. If the error that occurs during install is unique to the application being installed, check the application manufacturer's Web site for an explanation or update. These errors generally occur when you're trying to install over an application that already exists, or when you're trying to replace a file that already exists but that another application has in use. When installing an application, it is extremely important that you quit all running programs before installing so that the installer can replace any files it needs to.

Application will not start   Once you have an application successfully installed, you may run across a problem getting the application to start properly. This problem can come from any number of sources, including an improper installation, software conflict, and system instability. If your application was installed incorrectly, the files required to properly run the program may not be present and the program can't function without them. If a shared file that's used by other programs is installed, it could be a different version from what should be installed that causes conflicts with other already-installed programs. Finally, if one program GPFs, it can cause memory problems that can destabilize the system and cause other programs to crash. The solution to these problems is to reinstall the offending application, first making sure that all programs are closed.

Invalid working directory   Some Windows programs are extremely processing intensive. These programs require an area on the hard disk to store their temporary files while they work. This area is commonly known as a *working directory*, and the location of it is usually specified during that program's installation. However, if that directory changes after installation and the program still thinks its working directory is in the same location, the program will receive an error that says something such as `Invalid working directory`. The solution is to reinstall the program with the correct parameters for the working directory.

It is for this reason that many programs use the Windows TEMP directory as their working directory. You will only see this error if the programmer chose to use a user-settable working directory.

Bad Network Connection   When troubleshooting network problems, as with other problems, never fail to check the simple stuff. Although it could be something difficult like weird driver conflicts, more often than not, problems sending and receiving data with the network can often be attributed to bad physical connections. Bad network connections are the result of some problem with the cabling system and its connections. Things to check when looking for cable problems include:

- Broken or loose connectors
- Wires pulled free from connector
- Kinked wires
- Unplugged patch cables

Remember that there are two universal solutions to Windows problems: rebooting and obtaining an update from the software manufacturer.

Windows-Based Utilities

In addition to learning about the many common problems and troubleshooting techniques for Windows, you should know about the different resources that Microsoft provides with Windows to troubleshoot Windows. These resources are the best to use if you have no other troubleshooting tools available. They can also be used as a starting point for troubleshooting a computer. The built-in Windows tools that the A+ exam tests you on, include:

- Safe Mode
- SCANDISK
- Device Manager
- System Manager

- Computer Manager
- `MSCONFIG.EXE`
- `REGEDIT.EXE` (view information/back up Registry)
- `REGEDT32.EXE`
- `ATTRIB.EXE`
- `EXTRACT.EXE`
- `DEFRAG.EXE`
- `EDIT.COM`
- `FDISK.EXE`
- `SYSEDIT.EXE`
- `SCANREG`
- `WSCRIPT.EXE`
- `HWINFO.EXE`
- `ASD.EXE` (Automatic Skip Driver)
- `CVT1.EXE` (Drive Converter FAT16 to FAT32)
- Event Viewer—Event log is full

Safe Mode

When Windows won't start properly, it is probably due to a driver or some piece of software that's not loading correctly. To fix problems of this nature, you should boot Windows in *Safe Mode*. In Safe Mode, Windows loads a minimal set of drivers (including a VGA-only video driver) so that you can disable an offending driver. To start Windows in Safe Mode, press the F8 key when you see the Starting Windows display during Windows bootup. This will bring up a menu that will allow you to choose to start Windows in Safe Mode. Once booted in Safe Mode, you can uninstall any driver you suspect is causing a Windows boot problem. Upon reboot, the system should go back to normal operation (non-Safe Mode).

 NOTE You can also use the F8 menu to select other boot options, such as logging all messages to a log file during boot, booting to a command prompt, or starting Windows in Safe Mode with network support.

SCANDISK

You can use the Windows SCANDISK utility to correct corrupt file problems or disk errors, like cross-linked files (which CHKDSK can't do). There are two ways you can use SCANDISK. First, if you suspect a particular hard disk is having problems or you have a corrupt file on a particular disk, you can manually start SCANDISK by right-clicking the problem disk and selecting Properties. This will bring up the Properties window for that disk, which shows the current status of the selected disk drive, as shown here.

Click the Tools tab at the top of the screen, then click the Check Now button in the Error-Checking Status section to start SCANDISK, as shown here.

Once you start SCANDISK, you start the scanning process by selecting the type of scan you want to perform (Standard or Thorough) and clicking Start.

SCANDISK will scan the disk looking for corrupt files and fix or delete them, as shown here. Additionally, if you choose the Thorough option, SCANDISK will scan the surface of the disk for defects and mark them as unusable.

You can also run SCANDISK automatically. When you turn off a Windows computer without choosing the Shut Down command, Windows 95 OSR2 and Windows 98 will automatically run SCANDISK when the computer is restarted. SCANDISK will check to see if any of the Windows files are corrupt so that Windows can be started.

Device Manager

With Windows 9x, Microsoft provides the Device Manager, a tool that will analyze hardware-related problems. The Device Manager displays all of the devices installed in a computer (as shown in Figure 9.1). If a device is malfunctioning, a yellow triangle with an exclamation point inside it is displayed (as with the Iomega Parallel Port Interface in Figure 9.1).

FIGURE 9.1 The Windows 9*x* Device Manager

With this utility, you can not only view the devices installed in a system and any of those devices that are failing, but you can also double-click on a device and view and set its properties (as shown in Figure 9.2). On the General tab, you will see the status of the device (i.e., whether its working or not). The other tabs are used for configuring the individual devices, adding or updating drivers, and verifying the version of drivers installed.

FIGURE 9.2 Properties of a network card

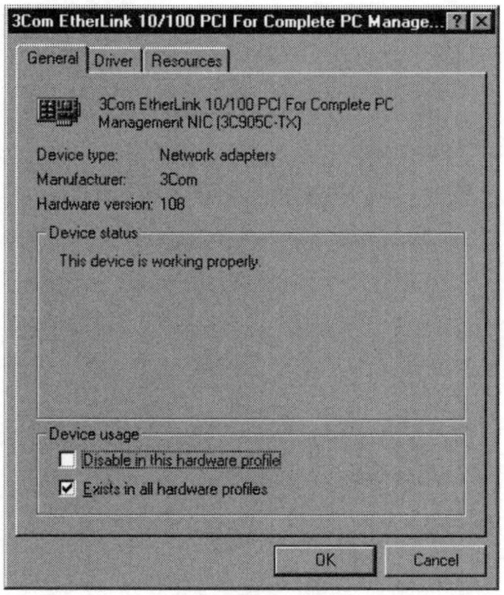

When troubleshooting a specific Windows-related hardware problem, you can access the Device Manager in two different ways. First and quickest, you can right-click on the My Computer icon and choose Properties. This brings up the General tab by default. To access the Device Manager from here, click on the Device Manager tab. You can then use the Device Manager to troubleshoot your system.

System Manager

You may be asking yourself, what is a System Manager? We asked ourselves the same question when we looked at the CompTIA A+ objectives. There are several options, but at the time of this writing we could find none that referred to Windows 9x, NT, or 2000. As the A+ operating system technology evolves, perhaps we will see a more definitive explanation as to why CompTIA included System Manager in their objectives.

Computer Manager

Windows 2000 includes a new piece of software to manage computer settings, the Computer Manager. Since Windows 2000 is more advanced as a platform, the Computer Manager can manage more than just the installed hardware devices. In addition to a Device Manager that functions almost identically to the one in Windows 9x, Computer Manager can also manage all the services running on that computer. It contains an Event Viewer to show all the system errors and events that show up, as well as methods to configure the software components of all the computer's hardware. Figure 9.3 shows an example of the Computer Manager running on Windows 2000.

FIGURE 9.3   Windows 2000 Computer Manager

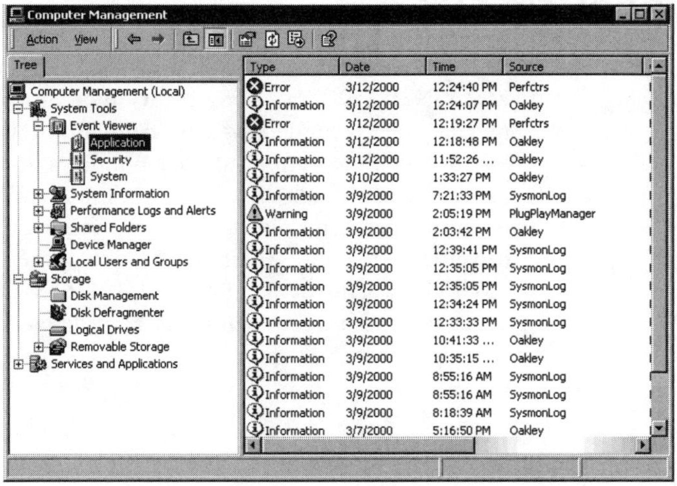

To access the Computer Manager, go to Start ➤ Programs ➤ Administrative Tools ➤ Computer Manager. You will see all of the computer management tools, including the Device Manager. You can then use Computer Manager to manage hardware devices and software services.

Event Viewer

Windows NT, like other network operating systems, employs comprehensive error and informational logging routines. Every program and process theoretically could have its own logging utility, but Microsoft has come up with a rather slick utility, Event Viewer, which, through log files, tracks all events on a particular Windows NT computer. Normally, though, you must be an administrator or a member of the Administrators group to have access to Event Viewer.

To start Event Viewer, log in as an administrator (or equivalent) and go to Start ➤ Programs ➤ Administrative Tools ➤ Event Viewer. From here you can view the System, Application, and Security log files. The System log file displays alerts that pertain to the general operation of Windows. The Application log file logs server application errors. The Security log file logs security events such as login successes and failures. These log files can give a general indication of a Windows computer's health.

One situation that does occur with the Event Viewer is that the Event Viewer log files get full. Although it isn't really a problem, it can make viewing log files confusing because there are many entries. Even though each event is time- and date-stamped, you should clear the Event Viewer every so often. To do this, open the Event Viewer and choose Clear All Events from the log menu. This will erase all events in the current log file, allowing you to see new events easier when they occur.

MSCONFIG.EXE

With the introduction of Windows 98, a new utility was introduced, MSCONFIG.EXE (a.k.a. System Configuration Utility) that allows a user to manage their computer system's configuration. MSCONFIG.EXE (shown in Figure 9.4) allows a user to boot Windows 98 in diagnostic mode, in which a user can select which drivers to load interactively. If you suspect a certain driver is causing problems during boot, you can use MSCONFIG.EXE to prevent that driver from loading. Additionally, each of the major configuration files (CONFIG.SYS, AUTOEXEC.BAT, WIN.INI, SYSTEM.INI) and the programs loaded at startup can be reconfigured and reordered using a graphical interface.

FIGURE 9.4   MSCONFIG.EXE Screen

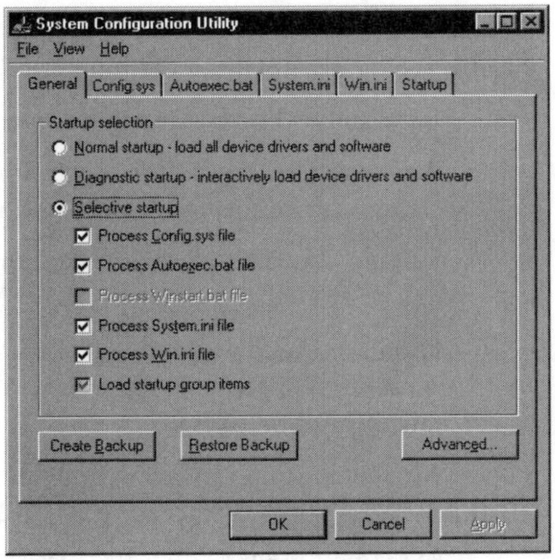

If you want to prevent a particular driver from loading, you can go to the tab that represents the file from which the driver is loaded and uncheck the box in front of the driver you want to eliminate. Or, from the General tab, you can check Diagnostic Startup in the Startup Selection area and then reboot the computer. Upon reboot, as each driver loads, you will be able to choose whether or not a particular driver loads or not during this boot cycle.

REGEDIT.EXE

The most flexible (and possibly the most dangerous) utility in the Windows troubleshooting arsenal is the Registry Editor, also known by its executable names REGEDIT.EXE (for Windows 9*x*) and REGEDT32.EXE (for Windows NT and 2000). The Registry stores all Windows configuration information. If you edit the Registry, you are essentially changing the configuration of Windows. The Registry Editor is used to manually change settings that are usually changed by other means (such as through Setup programs and other Windows utilities).

In addition to changing Windows settings, you can use REGEDIT to back up and restore the Registry. To back up the Registry, choose the Export Registry File command under the Registry menu. This command will allow you to save the Registry file to some kind of backup media. You can restore it later by choosing the Import Registry File command under the Registry menu.

ATTRIB.EXE

Every operating system since DOS provides four attributes that can be set for files to modify their interaction with the system. These attributes are as follows:

Read-only   Prevents a file from being modified, deleted, or overwritten.

Archive   Used by backup programs to determine whether the file has changed since the last backup and needs to be backed up.

System   Used to tell the OS that this file is needed by the system and should not be deleted.

Hidden   Used to keep files from being seen in a normal directory search. This is useful to prevent system files and other important files from being accidentally moved or deleted.

Attributes are set for files using an external DOS command called ATTRIB.EXE, which uses using the following syntax:

ATTRIB <filename> [+ or -][attribute]

To set the read-only attribute on the file TESTFILE.DOC, use the following series of commands:

ATTRIB TESTFILE.DOC +r

Occasionally, it is necessary to remove various attributes and replace them again. To do this, use the ATTRIB command.

EXTRACT.EXE

All Windows setup files come compressed in Cabinet (CAB) files. These files are extracted during the Windows Setup process by the EXTRACT.EXE utility. This utility can also be used to extract one or multiple files from a CAB file to replace a corrupt file. If you have one Windows file that is corrupt, you can extract a replacement from the Windows setup CAB files. If you don't know which CAB file a particular Windows system file is contained in, you can look it up in the CABS.TXT file

For example, to extract the UNIDRV.DLL file from the Win95_10.CAB file on a CD-ROM in drive D: to the C:\WINDOWS\SYSTEM directory, use the following command syntax:

EXTRACT D:\WIN95_10.CAB UNIDRV.DLL /L C:\WINDOWS\SYSTEM

The new file will be extracted to the new location and replace the old corrupt version in that location.

DEFRAG.EXE

When Windows is installed on a new disk, all the full clusters are contiguous. That is, they are located one after another rotationally on the disk. However, as files and programs get installed and deleted, the blocks of disk space get less and less contiguous. This can hinder Windows performance as it has to constantly go looking for more sections of different files.

To solve this problem, Microsoft has included a utility with Windows known as DEFRAG.EXE that is used to reorganize, or *defragment* the hard disk. You can access this program from the properties of the disk drive you want to fragment (it's found on the same option page as SCANDISK). Or, you can run it using the Start ➤ Run command and type in DEFRAG. Finally, you can run it by going to Start ➤ Programs ➤ Accessories➤ System Tools ➤ Disk Defragmenter.

The utility will ask you which disk you want to defragment. Choose the appropriate disk from the drop-down list and click OK. Defrag will start defragmenting the drive. This process may take several minutes or several hours, depending on how badly the drive is fragmented.

Defragmenting a drive will increase the system's performance because file access times will be faster.

EDIT.COM

Occasionally, you need to quickly edit a configuration file or other text file (such as the CONFIG.SYS or AUTOEXEC.BAT). For this, a simple editor named EDIT.COM has been included with all Microsoft operating systems since DOS version 6. To edit a file, start a command line session and type in the following:

    EDIT <filename>

Replace <filename> with the name of the file you wish to edit. Once EDIT comes up, it works like any other word processor or text editor. When you are finished editing the file, save it, and it will be saved as a standard ASCII text file.

FDISK.EXE

If you have already installed the disk drives and now need to configure unused space on your drive for use, you will need to use the FDISK command. FDISK.EXE is a DOS program that allows you to access and modify information about your fixed disks (hence the name). It is used for four major tasks:

- Viewing the current partition configuration
- Creating DOS partitions or logical DOS drives
- Setting active partitions
- Deleting partitions or logical DOS drives

These functions can be used on any of the physical disks in your machine, as long as those disks are considered to be permanent, that is, fixed, drives. Hard drives, whether they are SCSI, IDE, or EIDE, are all fixed. Once installed, they are expected to be permanently attached to the system, and if one is removed, extensive reconfiguration may need to be done on the system. Floppy drives and

CD-ROM drives are designed to support removable, interchangeable media, and as such are not configurable under FDISK.

To run the FDISK utility, boot to a bootable disk and type **FDISK**.

WARNING You must run FDISK from a bootable disk, NOT from within a command prompt within Windows. This is because Windows may not represent the disk drives correctly.

Following the prompts on screen, you can then view, add, or delete partitions.

SYSEDIT.EXE

The System Editor (SYSEDIT.EXE) is a holdover from Windows 3.*x*. With this utility, you can view and edit the CONFIG.SYS, AUTOEXEC.BAT, WIN.INI, SYSTEM.INI, PROTOCOL.INI, and MSMAIL.INI. Although it is not as efficient as MSCONFIG.EXE, you can still use SYSEDIT to edit these files quickly and to easily remove an offending driver entry or software configuration. To run this program in Windows 9*x*, go to Start ➢ Run and type in SYSEDIT. This will bring up the window shown in Figure 9.5 from which you can click on a window and edit any of the particular files just as if you were using EDIT.COM. You can then save the changes and restart the computer to make them take effect.

FIGURE 9.5 SYSEDIT screen

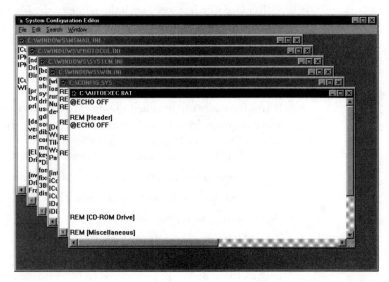

SCANREG.EXE

The Windows Registry Checker, SCANREG.EXE is a quick and simple utility that you can use to check the Registry for consistency and to make a backup of the Registry. To start SCANREG, go to Start ➤ Run, type **SCANREG**, and click OK. This will start SCANREG, which will initiate an immediate scan and fix the Registry (Figure 9.6).

FIGURE 9.6   SCANREG.EXE screen

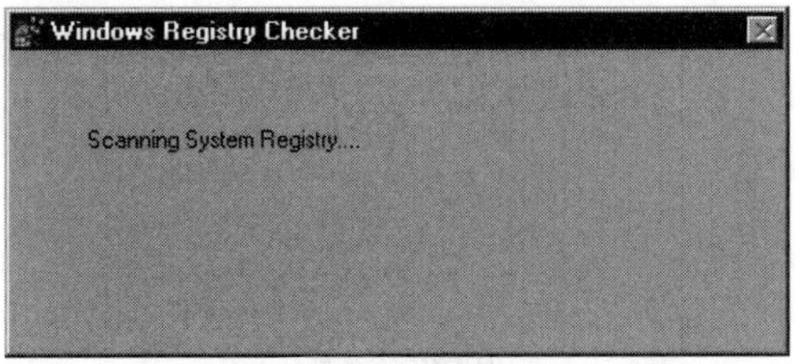

After the Registry scan is complete, SCANREG will prompt you to back up your Registry. You can use this backup to restore the Registry in case of a problem.

WSCRIPT.EXE

The Windows Scripting Host (WSCRIPT.EXE) is a service that allows programmers to write Windows scripts that can perform any number of automated tasks. Unfortunately, because WSCRIPT can also work with Internet Explorer, if it's allowed to run unchecked it is a major security hole that can potentially allow malicious scripts to be run without the user's knowledge.

This tool is responsible for the propagation of weird Microsoft-only bugs such as the fairly recent I Love You virus. If you see WSCRIPT present in the task list on Windows NT, make sure it is supposed to running. Or, if you are sure you won't need it for any scripts of any kind, completely delete it.

HWINFO.EXE

Windows $9x$ and above includes a utility that can give a text report of all the hardware configuration information for Windows. It includes the driver name, version, company name, Registry information, and other file-related information for the driver. You can then save or print this text report for later reference on this system.

To view this file, you must start the HWINFO.EXE utility by selecting Start ➤ Run, typing **HWINFO /UI**, and clicking OK. This will run the HWINFO utility and produce a report similar to the one in Figure 9.7. You can then either save this file as an ASCII text file or print the file to a printer by using either the Save or Print command, respectively, under the File menu.

FIGURE 9.7 The HWINFO Screen

This utility is useful when trying to track down a hardware problem you suspect may be due to an outdated driver. You can examine the file this utility produces for the versions of all drivers and compare them to the newest possible drivers on the hardware vendors' Web sites.

ASD.EXE (Automatic Skip Driver)

It never fails: eventually, you will have a driver that hangs the system on bootup. We've already discussed several methods for troubleshooting this problem, and this is yet another one. The Automatic Skip Driver (ASD.EXE) utility is used to automatically skip loading a driver during boot that failed to load at the last boot.

To use ASD, go to Start ➤ Run, type **ASD**, and click OK. This will bring up the ASD utility (Figure 9.8). From this screen, you can see which tasks failed to respond. If you check a box next to a particular task, the next time you boot Windows, that task won't load. In this way, ASD can prevent lockups during boot.

FIGURE 9.8   ASD.EXE main screen

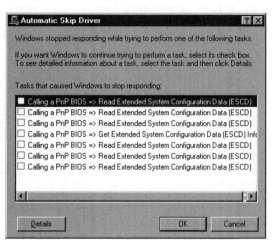

CVT1.EXE

With the release of Windows 95 OSR2 came a new feature: a new 32-bit FAT table, also known as FAT32. Up until that point, the FAT system was a 16-bit system (now known as FAT16). The new FAT32 system allowed for faster access and larger drive sizes. With newly installed systems, FAT32 was the FAT type of choice. However, older systems still used FAT16. The FAT32 Upgrade Wizard, also known as CVT1.EXE, allows you to convert a FAT16 disk system to a FAT32 system. To do this, you must first run the Drive Converter by clicking Start ➢ Run, typing in **CVT1.EXE**, and clicking OK. This will start the Driver Converter Wizard (Figure 9.9). From this Wizard, you follow the prompts and continue clicking Next to convert your drive from FAT16 to FAT32.

FIGURE 9.9   FAT32 Convert Wizard

A Few Warnings about Converting to FAT32

- Once you convert to FAT32, you can't go back to FAT16.

- You may not be able to convert a compressed drive.

- Removable disks formatted with FAT32 may not work with other systems.

- Dual-boot to older systems will not be possible after a conversion to FAT32.

Summary

In this chapter, you were given some tips for troubleshooting the Windows environment. Just as with troubleshooting hardware, it is important that you know how to troubleshoot software problems. However, troubleshooting software is actually more difficult because the problems can appear to be more "phantom."

In the first section, you learned the basic steps to troubleshooting software problems. You also learned how to apply these troubleshooting steps to problems. These steps are:

1. Talk to the customer.
2. Gather information.
3. Eliminate possibilities.
4. Document the solution.

In the next section, you learned how to troubleshoot file-related problems. You learned some of the more common file-related problems and their solutions. Some of the problems you learned about include missing or corrupt system files, missing application DLL files, Windows NT boot problems, and swap file issues.

In the next section, you learned about some of the printing problems that are commonly found in the Windows environment (e.g., wrong driver installed). You learned how to use the Windows printing troubleshooting utilities (Print Test Page and the Troubleshooting Wizard) to troubleshoot these problems.

Because Windows has some problems that don't fall into any particular category, you learned in the next section how to troubleshoot problems that don't fall into any particular category. Some of these problems include General Protection Faults, Invalid Page Faults, and applications that won't install. You learned how to recognize the symptoms of each of these problems and how to solve them when they occur.

Finally, you learned how to use the various built-in Windows troubleshooting utilities. You learned what each utility is for and how to use it. You also learned when to apply a particular utility to a problem and when NOT to use a utility.

Key Terms

Before you take the exam, be certain you are familiar with the following terms:

Blue Screen of Death (BSOD)	Safe Mode
defragmentation	thrashing
General Protection Fault (GPF)	working directory
illegal operation error	

Review Questions

1. All of the following are considered to be Windows-based utilities except:

   A. SYSEDIT

   B. PSCRIPT

   C. HWINFO.EXE

   D. ASD.EXE

   E. CVT1.EXE

2. Some of the common problems faced in troubleshooting Windows and applications are all of the following except:

   A. General Protection Faults

   B. Valid working directory

   C. System lock-up

   D. Application will not start or load

3. The first step in the troubleshooting process is:

   A. Talk to the customer

   B. Gather information

   C. Eliminate possibilities

   D. Document your work

4. Windows file-related problems include all of the following except:

   A. System files not found

   B. Config file issues

   C. AUTOEXEC.BAT issues

   D. Swap file issues

   E. NT boot issues

5. The files that are checked upon bootup of Windows *9x* or Windows NT are:

   A. Config files

   B. AUTOEXEC.BAT files

   C. System files

   D. Swap files

6. The No Operating System Found error message means that the computer's BIOS checked all the drives it knew about and couldn't find any disk with a bootable sector. This could occur because of all of the following reasons except:

   A. An operating system wasn't installed

   B. There is no problem with the boot sector

   C. The boot files have been corrupted

   D. The boot sector has been corrupted

7. Some of the commonly seen errors in Windows that are related to configuration files include all of the following except:

   A. Device referenced in Info.INI file cannot be found

   B. Device referenced in WIN.INI cannot be found

   C. Device referenced in the Registry cannot be found

   D. Error in CONFIG.SYS line XX

8. In order to delete and/or replace system files, which command must you use to remove the hidden, system, and read-only attributes on the file before you replace the file?

   A. UNDELETE

   B. ERASE

   C. ATTRIB

   D. DELETE

9. Symptoms of swap file problems include extremely slow system speed and a disk that is constantly being accessed, which is referred to as:

   A. Clocking

   B. Thrashing

   C. Booting

   D. Filtering

10. The solution to thrashing is: (Select all that apply.)

    A. Formatting the disk

    B. Buying a new hard disk

    C. Freeing up disk space

    D. Deleting all files

11. All of the following are a part of the NT boot process except:

    A. The POST routine examines the boot sector and loads the MBR.

    B. The boot sector is loaded from the extended partition.

    C. NTLOADER is loaded from the boot sector and initialized.

    D. NTLDR reads the BOOT.INI file and looks for the list of operating systems installed on the computer.

12. The solution to a corrupt `NTOSKRNL.EXE` file is to:

    A. Reinstall Windows NT

    B. Replace the corrupt file with a new one

    C. Delete the `NTOSKRNL.EXE` file and modify the `BOOT.INI` file

    D. Boot to a startup disk and replace the file from the setup disks or CD-ROM

13. After connecting to a printer and installing the print drivers, what is the best way to test its functionality? (Select all that apply.)

    A. Go to Word and print a document

    B. Print a test page from Printer Properties

    C. Go to the printer and run diagnostics

    D. Wait until someone prints a document and complains

14. One of the most frustrating sets of problems for Windows is:

    A. Hardware problems

    B. Software problems

    C. Printing problems

    D. Windows operating system problems

15. The most common Windows printing problems are: (Select all that apply.)

    A. Print spool is stalled

    B. Incompatible printer model

    C. Incorrect/incompatible driver for print

    D. Incorrect parameter

16. A condition that usually happens on either startup or shutdown and results because Windows 9*x* could not load or unload a virtual device driver properly is called:

    A. General Protection Fault (GPF)

    B. Windows protection error

    C. Illegal operation

    D. System lock-up

17. The most common error that happens in Windows when a program accesses memory that another program is using or when a program accesses a memory address that doesn't exist is called:

    A. General Protection Fault

    B. Windows protection error

    C. Illegal operation

    D. System lock-up

18. Which Windows error message is displayed when a program is forced to quit because it did something Windows didn't like?

    A. General Protection Fault

    B. Windows protection error

    C. Illegal operation

    D. System lock-up

19. What error occurs when the system stops responding to commands and stops processing completely?

    A. General Protection Fault

    B. Windows protection error

    C. Illegal operation

    D. System lock-up

20. What error occurs when the GUI of Windows won't appear?

    A. Illegal operation

    B. Dr. Watson

    C. Failure to start GUI

    D. Option sound card, modem, SCSI card, or input device will not function

Answers to Review Questions

1. B. PSCRIPT is not considered to be a Windows-based utility. SYSEDIT, HWINFO.EXE, ASD.EXE, and CVT1.EXE are all utilities used to troubleshoot Windows.

2. B. Valid working directory is not a common problem faced in troubleshooting Windows and applications.

3. A. The first step in the troubleshooting process is to talk to the customer. It is best to obtain as much information as possible from the user so you have an idea of where to begin your troubleshooting.

4. C. Windows file-related problems do not include AUTOEXEC.BAT issues. AUTOEXEC.BAT is a DOS batch file that is automatically executed during boot-up if the file is present.

5. C. The files that are checked upon bootup of Windows 9*x* and Windows NT are the system files. Every operating system or operating environment has certain key system files that must be present in order for it to function.

6. B. The No Operating System Found error means that an operating system wasn't installed, the boot sector has been corrupted, or the boot files have been corrupted.

7. A. Some of the commonly seen errors in Windows that are related to configuration files include all of the following except Device referenced in Info.INI file cannot be found.

8. C. In order to delete and/or replace system files you must use the ATTRIB command to remove the hidden, system, and read-only attributes on the file.

9. B. Thrashing means an extremely slow system speed and a disk that is constantly being accessed. This condition occurs because Windows doesn't have enough memory to contain all the programs that are running.

10. B, C. The solution to thrashing is to free up some disk space. However, with IDE hard disk sizes at tens of gigabytes available for around $100, the easiest thing to do is install a bigger hard disk. If that solution isn't practical, you must delete enough unused files so that the swap file can be made large enough to be functional.

11. B. The boot sector is always loaded from the active partition, not the extended partition.

12. D. The solution to a corrupt NTOSKRNL.EXE file is to boot to a startup disk and replace the file from the setup disks or CD-ROM.

13. A, B, D.   You should go to Word and print a document, print a test page in Printer Properties, or wait until someone prints a document and complains. Printing diagnostics only tests whether the printer is able to print if it is connected to a device with the correct drivers.

14. C.   One of the most frustrating set of problems for Windows is printing problems.

15. A, C, D.   The most common Windows printing problems are that the print spool is stalled, there's an incorrect/incompatible driver for print, or there's an incorrect parameter. Windows will support almost any type of printer model.

16. B.   A condition that usually happens on either startup or shutdown and results because Windows 9*x* could not load or unload a virtual device driver properly is called a Windows protection error.

17. A.   The most common error that happens in Windows when a program accesses memory that another program is using or when a program accesses a memory address that doesn't exist is called a General Protection Fault. Generally, GPFs are the result of sloppy programming and can often be fixed by clearing the memory with a simple reboot.

18. C.   Illegal operation is the Windows error message displayed when a program is forced to quit because it did something Windows didn't like. The details of the error include which module experienced the problem, the memory location being accessed at the time, and the registers and flags of the processor at the time of the error.

19. D.   The system lock-up error occurs when the system stops responding to commands and stops processing completely. System lock-ups can occur when a computer is asked to process too many instructions at once with too little memory. Usually, the cure for a system lock up is to simply reboot. If the lock-ups are persistent, it may be a hardware-related problem.

20. C.   If your Windows GUI fails to start properly, more than likely the problem is related to a misconfigured driver or misconfigured hardware.

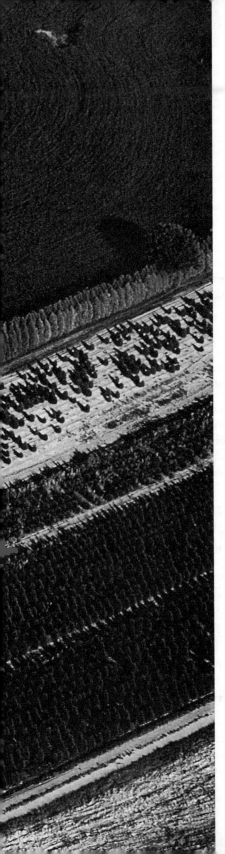

A+ Complete Glossary

386 enhanced mode   In Microsoft Windows, the most advanced and complex of the different operating modes, 386 enhanced mode lets Windows access the protected mode of the *80386* (or higher) processor for extended memory management and multitasking for both Windows and non-Windows application programs.

802.3   An IEEE standard that defines a bus topology network that uses a 50-ohm coaxial baseband cable and carries transmissions at 10Mbps. This standard groups data bits into frames and uses the Carrier Sense Multiple Access with Collision Detection (CSMA/CD) cable access method to put data on the cable.

802.5   The IEEE 802.5 standard specifies a physical star, logical ring topology that uses a token-passing technology to put the data on the cable. IBM developed this technology for their mainframe and minicomputer networks. IBM's name for it was Token Ring. The name stuck, and any network using this type of technology is called a Token Ring network.

80286   Also called the 286. A 16-bit microprocessor from Intel, first released in February 1982 and used by IBM in the IBM PC/AT computer. Since then it has been used in many other IBM-compatible computers. The 80286 uses a 16-bit data word and a 16-bit data bus, and it uses 24 bits to address memory.

80287   Also called the 287. A floating-point processor from Intel, designed for use with the 80286 CPU chip. When supported by application programs, a floating-point processor can speed up floating-point and transcendental math operations by 10 to 50 times. The 80287 conforms to the IEEE 754-1985 standard for binary floating-point operations, and it is available in clock speeds of 6, 8, 10, and 12MHz.

80386DX   Also called the 80386, the 386DX, and the 386. A full 32-bit microprocessor introduced by Intel in October 1985 and used in many IBM and IBM-compatible computers. Available in 16-, 20-, 25-, and 33MHz versions, the 80386 has a 32-bit data word, can transfer information 32 bits at a time over the data bus, and can use 32 bits in addressing memory. The 80386 is equivalent to about 275,000 transistors, and can perform 6 million instructions per second. The floating-point processor for the 80386DX is the 80387.

80386SX   Also called the 386SX. A lower-cost alternative to the 80386DX microprocessor, 80386SX was introduced by Intel in 1988. Available in 16-, 20-, 25-, and 33MHz versions, the 80386SX is an 80386DX with a 16-bit data bus. This design allows systems to be configured using cheaper 16-bit components, leading to a lower overall cost. The floating-point processor for the 80386SX is the 80387SX.

80387   Also called the 387. A floating-point processor from Intel, 80387 was designed for use with the 80386 CPU chip. When supported by application programs, a floating-point processor can speed up floating-point and transcendental math operations by 10 to 50 times. The 80387 conforms to the IEEE 754-1985 standard for binary floating-point operations and is available in speeds of 16, 20, 25, and 33MHz.

80486DX   Also called the 486 or i486. 80486DX is a 32-bit microprocessor introduced by Intel in April 1989. The 80486 represents the continuing evolution of the 80386 family of microprocessors and adds several notable features, including on-board cache, built-in floating-point processor and memory management unit, as well as certain advanced provisions for multiprocessing. Available in 25-, 33-, and 50MHz versions, the 80486 is equivalent to 1.25 million transistors and can perform 20 million instructions per second.

80486DX2   Also known as the 486DX2. A 32-bit microprocessor introduced by Intel in 1992. It is functionally identical to and 100 percent compatible with the 80486DX, but it has one major difference: the DX2 chip adds what Intel calls speed-doubling technology—meaning that it runs twice as fast internally as it does with components external to the chip. For example, the DX2-50 operates at 50MHz internally but at 25MHz while communicating with other system components, including memory and the other chips on the motherboard, thus maintaining its overall system compatibility. 50- and 66MHz versions of the DX2 are available. The 486DX2 contains 1.2 million transistors and is capable of 40 million instructions per second.

80486SX   Also called the 486SX. A 32-bit microprocessor introduced by Intel in April 1991. The 80486SX can be described as an 80486DX with the floating-point processor circuitry disabled. Available in 16-, 20-, and 25MHz versions, the 80486SX contains the equivalent of 1.185 million transistors and can execute 16.5 million instructions per second.

80487   Also called the 487. A floating-point processor from Intel, designed for use with the 80486SX CPU chip. When supported by application programs, a floating-point processor can speed up floating-point and transcendental math operations by 10 to 50 times. The 80487 is essentially a 20MHz 80486 with the floating-point circuitry still enabled. When an 80487 is added into the coprocessor socket of a motherboard running the 80486SX, it effectively becomes the main processor, shutting down the 80486SX and taking over all operations. The 80487 conforms to the IEEE 754-1985 standard for binary floating-point operations.

8086   This 16-bit microprocessor from Intel was first released in June 1978, and it is available in speeds of 4.77MHz, 8MHz, and 10MHz. The 8086 was used in a variety of early IBM-compatible computers as well as the IBM PS/2 Model 25 and Model 30. The 8086 uses a 16-bit data word and a 16-bit data bus. The 8086 contains the equivalent of 29,000 transistors and can execute 0.33 million instructions per second.

8088　This 16-bit microprocessor from Intel was released in June 1978, and it was used in the first IBM PC, as well as the IBM PC/XT, Portable PC, PCjr, and a large number of IBM-compatible computers. The 8088 uses a 16-bit data word, but transfers information along an 8-bit data bus. Available in speeds of 4.77MHz and 8MHz, the 8088 is approximately equivalent to 29,000 transistors and can execute 0.33 million instructions per second.

8-bit bus　The type of expansion bus that was used with the original IBM PC. The bus can transmit 8 bits at a time.

Accelerated Graphics Port (AGP) bus　A type of 32-bit expansion bus that runs at 66MHz. It is a very high-speed bus that is used primarily for video expansion cards and can transfer data at a maximum throughput 508.6MBps.

access time　The period of time that elapses between a request for information from disk or memory and the information arriving at the requesting device. Memory access time refers to the time it takes to transfer a character from memory to or from the processor, while disk access time refers to the time it takes to place the read/write heads over the requested data.

Active Directory　The Active Directory, a new feature of Windows 2000, stores information about users, computers, and network resources. The Active Directory is stored in databases on special Windows 2000 Server computers called Domain Controllers.

Active hubs　A type of hub that uses electronics to amplify and clean up the signal before it is broadcast to the other ports.

active matrix　A type of liquid crystal display that has a transistor for each pixel in the screen.

active-matrix screen　An LCD display mechanism that uses an individual transistor to control every pixel on the screen. Active-matrix screens are characterized by high contrast, a wide viewing angle, vivid colors, and fast screen refresh rates, and they do not show the streaking or shadowing that is common with cheaper LCD technology.

actuator arm　The device inside a hard disk drive that moves the read/write heads as a group in the fixed disk.

address bus　The internal processor bus used for accessing memory. The width of this bus determines how much physical memory a processor can access.

address　The precise location in memory or on disk where a piece of information is stored. Every byte in memory and every sector on a disk have their own unique addresses.

Administrative Tools　In Windows 2000 Professional, this is the group of utilities used to manage many common configuration and maintenance tasks.

allocation unit   An allocation unit is a portion of the hard drive that is used by the computer when saving information to the drive. Smaller allocation units are generally more efficient, because they result in less wasted space.

alpha   Extremely early versions of computer software are called "alpha code." Alpha code is generally incomplete and unusable, and it is almost never released to the public.

analog   Describes any device that represents changing values by a continuously variable physical property such as voltage in a circuit, fluid pressure, liquid level, and so on. An analog device can handle an infinite number of values within its range.

anti-static bag   A bag designed to keep static charges from building up on the outside of a computer component during shipping. The bag will collect some of the charges, but does not drain them away as ESD mats do.

anti-static wrist strap (ESD strap)   A specially constructed strap worn as a preventive measure to guard against the damages of ESD. One end of the strap is attached to an earth ground and the other is wrapped around the technician's wrist.

anti-virus program   An application program you run to detect or eliminate a computer virus or infection. Some anti-virus programs are terminate-and-stay-resident programs that can detect suspicious activity on your computer as it happens, while others must be run periodically as part of your normal housekeeping activities.

Application layer   The seventh, or highest, layer in the International Organization for Standardization's Open Systems Interconnection (ISO/OSI) model for computer-to-computer communications. This layer uses services provided by the lower layers, but is completely insulated from the details of the network hardware. It describes how application programs interact with the network operating system, including database management, e-mail, and terminal emulation programs.

ASCII   Acronym for American Standard Code for Information Interchange. A standard coding scheme that assigns numeric values to letters, numbers, punctuation marks, and control characters, to achieve compatibility among different computers and peripherals.

asynchronous   Describes a type of communication that adds special signaling bits to each end of the data. The bit at the beginning of the information signals the start of the data and is known as the start bit. The next few bits are the actual data that needs to be sent. Those bits are known as the data bits. Stop bits indicate that the data is finished. Asynchronous communications have no timing signal.

AT bus   Another name for the ISA bus. See also *ISA*.

ATA version 2 (ATA-2)   The second version of the original IDE (ATA) specification that allowed drive sizes of several gigabtyes and overcame the limitation of 528MB. It is also sometimes generically known as Enhanced IDE (EIDE).

Attached Resource Computer Network (ARCNet)   A network technology that uses a physical star, logical ring and token passing access method. It is typically wired with coaxial cable.

AUTOEXEC.BAT   A contraction of AUTOmatically EXECuted BATch. AUTOEXEC.BAT is a special DOS batch file, located in the root directory of a startup disk, and it runs automatically every time the computer is started or restarted.

auto-ranging multimeters   A multimeter that automatically sets its upper and lower ranges depending on the input signal. These multimeters are more difficult to damage by choosing the wrong range setting. See also *multimeter*.

Autorun   On a CD-ROM, the Autorun option allows the CD to automatically start an installation program or a menu screen when it is inserted into the CD-ROM drive.

"baby" AT   A type of motherboard form factor where the motherboard is smaller than the original AT form factor.

backup   A duplicate copy made to be able to recover from an accidental loss of data.

backup set   A related collection of backup media.

backup software   Program that is used to back up a small amount of data.

backup source   The device or data being backed up.

bandwidth   In communications, the difference between the highest and the lowest frequencies available for transmission in any given range. In networking, the transmission capacity of a computer or a communications channel stated in megabits or megabytes per second; the higher the number, the faster the data transmission takes place.

basis weight   A measurement of the "heaviness" of paper. The number is the weight, in pounds, of 500 11" × 17" sheets of that type of paper.

batch file   File with a .bat extension that contains other DOS commands. By typing the name of the batch file and pressing Enter, DOS will process all of the batch file commands, one at a time, without need for any additional user input.

baud rate   In communications equipment, a measurement of the number of state changes (from 0 to 1 or vice versa) per second on an asynchronous communications channel.

Berg connector   A type of connector most commonly used in PC floppy drive power cables; it has four conductors arranged in a row.

Berg connectors   A type of power connector that is used on floppy drives.

beta   Beta code is software that has reached the stage where is usable and generally stable, but it is not completely finished. Beta code is often released to the public for testing on an "as is" basis, and user comments are then used to finish the release version of the product.

bias voltage   The high-voltage charge applied to the developing roller inside an EP cartridge.

binary   Any scheme that uses two different states, components, conditions, or conclusions. In mathematics, the binary (base-2) numbering system uses combinations of the digits 0 and 1 to represent all values.

BIOS (basic input/output system)   The ROM-based software on a motherboard that acts as a kind of "interpreter" between an operating system and a computer's hardware.

BIOS CMOS setup program   Program that modifies BIOS settings in the CMOS memory. This program is available at system startup time by pressing a key combination such as Alt+F1 or Ctrl+F2.

BIOS shadow   A copy of the BIOS in memory.

bit   Contraction of BInary digiT. A bit is the basic unit of information in the binary numbering system, representing either 0 (for off) or 1 (for on). Bits can be grouped together to make up larger storage units, the most common being the 8-bit byte. A byte can represent all kinds of information including the letters of the alphabet, the numbers 0 through 9, and common punctuation symbols.

bit-mapped font   A set of characters in a specific style and size, in which each character is defined by a pattern of dots. The computer must keep a complete set of bitmaps for every font you use on your system, and these bitmaps can consume large amounts of disk space.

Blue Screen of Death (BSOD)   A typical way of describing the blue screen error condition that occurs when Windows NT fails to boot properly or quits unexpectedly.

boot   The loading of an operating system into memory, usually from a hard disk, although occasionally from a floppy disk. This is an automatic procedure begun when you first turn on or reset your computer. A set of instructions contained in ROM begin executing, first running a series of power on self-tests (POSTs) to check that devices, such as hard disks, are in working order, then locating and loading the operating system, and finally passing control of the computer over to that operating system.

bootable disk   Any disk capable of loading and starting the operating system, although most often used when referring to a floppy disk. In these days of larger and larger operating systems, it is less common to boot from a floppy disk. In some cases, all of the files needed to start the operating system will not fit on a single floppy disk, which makes it impossible to boot from a floppy.

BPS (bits per second)   A measurement of how much data (how many bits) is being transmitted in one second. Typically used to describe the speed of asynchronous communications (modems).

bridge   This type of connectivity device operates in the Data Link layer of the OSI model. It is used to join similar topologies (Ethernet to Ethernet, Token Ring to Token Ring) and to divide traffic on network segments. This device will pass information destined for one particular workstation to that segment, but it will not pass broadcast traffic.

broadcasting   Sending a signal to all entities that can listen to it. In networking, it refers to sending a signal to all entities connected to that network.

brouter   In networking, a device that combines the attributes of a bridge and a router. A brouter can route one or more specific protocols, such as TCP/IP, and bridge all others.

brownout   A short period of low voltage often caused by an unusually heavy demand for power.

browser   A piece of software used to access the Internet. Common browsers are Netscape's Navigator and Microsoft's Internet Explorer.

bubble-jet printer   A type of sprayed ink printer, this type uses an electric signal that energizes a heating element, causing ink to vaporize and get pushed out of the pinhole and onto the paper.

bug   A logical or programming error in hardware or software that causes a malfunction of some sort. If the problem is in software, it can be fixed by changes to the program. If the fault is in hardware, new circuits must be designed and constructed. Some bugs are fatal and cause the program to hang or cause data loss, others are just annoying, and many are never even noticed.

bug-fix   A release of hardware or software that corrects known bugs but does not contain additional new features. Such releases are usually designated only by an increase in the decimal portion of the version number; for example, the revision level may advance from 2 to 2.01 or 2.1, rather than from 2 to 3.

bus   A set of pathways that allow information and signals to travel between components inside or outside of a computer.

bus clock   A chip on the motherboard that produces a type of signal (called a clock signal) that indicates how fast the bus can transmit information.

bus connector slot   A slot made up of several small copper channels that grab the matching "fingers" of the expansion circuit boards. The fingers connect to copper pathways on the motherboard.

bus mastering   A technique that allows certain advanced bus architectures to delegate control of data transfers between the Central Processing Unit (CPU) and associated peripheral devices to an add-in board.

bus mouse   A mouse connected to the computer using an expansion board plugged into an expansion slot, instead of simply connected to a serial port as in the case of a serial mouse.

bus topology   Type of physical topology that consists of a single cable that runs to every workstation on the network. Each computer shares that same data and address path. As messages pass through the trunk, each workstation checks to see if the message is addressed for itself. This topology is very difficult to reconfigure, since reconfiguration requires you to disconnect and reconnect a portion of the network (thus bringing the whole network down).

byte   Contraction of BinarY digiT Eight. A group of 8 bits that, in computer storage terms, usually holds a single character, such as a number, letter, or other symbol.

cable access methods   Methods by which stations on a network get permission to transmit their data.

cache   Pronounced "cash." A special area of memory, managed by a cache controller, that improves performance by storing the contents of frequently accessed memory locations and their addresses. When the processor references a memory address, the cache checks to see if it holds that address. If it does, the information is passed directly to the processor; if not, a normal memory access takes place instead. A cache can speed up operations in a computer in which RAM access is slow compared with its processor speed, because the cache memory is always faster than normal RAM.

cache memory   Fast SRAM memory used to store, or cache, frequently used instructions and data.

capacitive keyboard   Keyboard designed with two sheets of semi-conductive material separated by a thin sheet of Mylar inside the keyboard. When a key is pressed, the plunger presses down and a paddle connected to the plunger presses the two sheets of semi-conductive material together, changing the total capacitance of the two sheets. The controller can tell by the capacitance value returned which key was pressed.

capacitive touch screen   Type of display monitor that has two clear plastic coatings over the screen, separated by air. When the user presses the screen in a particular spot, the coatings are pressed together and the controller registers a change in the total capacitance of the two layers. The controller then determines where the screen was pressed by the capacitance values and sends that information to the computer in the form of x,y coordinates.

capacitor   An electrical component, normally found in power supplies and timing circuits, used to store electrical charge.

card services   Part of the software support needed for PCMCIA (PC Card) hardware devices in a portable computer, controlling the use of system interrupts, memory, or power management. When an application wants to access a PC Card, it always goes through the card services software and never communicates directly with the underlying hardware.

carpal tunnel syndrome   A form of wrist injury caused by holding the hands in an awkward position for long periods of time.

carriage motor   Stepper motor used to move the print head back and forth on a dot-matrix printer.

cathode-ray tube   See *CRT*.

CCD (charge-coupled device)   A device that allows light to be converted into electrical pulses.

CCITT   Acronym for Comité Consultatif Internationale de Téléphonie et de Télégraphie. An organization, based in Geneva, that develops worldwide data communications standards. CCITT is part of the ITU (International Telecommunications Union). The organization has been renamed ITU-T (ITU Telecommunications Standardization Sector).

CD-ROM   Acronym for compact disc read-only memory. A high-capacity, optical storage device that uses compact disc technology to store large amounts of information, up to 650MB (the equivalent of approximately 300,000 pages of text), on a single 4.72" disk.

Central Processing Unit (CPU)   The computing and control part of the computer. The CPU in a mainframe computer may be contained on many printed circuit boards, the CPU in a mini computer may be contained on several boards, and the CPU in a PC is contained in a single extremely powerful microprocessor.

centralized processing   A network processing scheme in which all "intelligence" is found in one computer and all other computers send requests to the central computer to be processed. Mainframe networks use centralized processing.

Centronics parallel interface   A standard 36-pin interface in the PC world for the exchange of information between the PC and a peripheral, such as a printer, originally developed by the printer manufacturer Centronics, Inc. The standard defines eight parallel data lines, plus additional lines for status and control information.

CGA   Acronym for Color/Graphics Adapter. CGA is a video adapter that provided low-resolution text and graphics. CGA provided several different text and graphics modes, including 40- or 80-column by 25-line, 16-color text mode, and graphics modes of 640 horizontal pixels by 200 vertical pixels with 2 colors, or 320 horizontal pixels by 200 vertical pixels with 4 colors. CGA has been superseded by later video standards, including EGA, VGA, SuperVGA, and XGA.

Charge-coupled device   See *CCD (charge-coupled device)*.

charging corona   The wire or roller that is used to put a uniform charge on the EP drum inside a toner cartridge.

checksum   A method of providing information for error detection, usually calculated by summing a set of values.

checksumming   An error checking routine the runs a mathematical equation against a set of data and comes up with a result, called a checksum. The data is then transmitted, and the receiver then runs the same formula against the data transmitted and compares the result to the checksum. If they are the same, the transmission is considered successful.

chip creep   The slow self-loosening of chips from their sockets on the system board as a result of the frequent heating and cooling of the board (which causes parts of the board—significantly, the chip connector slots—to alternately expand and shrink).

chip puller   A tool that is used on older (pre-386) systems to remove the chips without damaging them.

cleaning step   The step in the EP print process where excess toner is scraped from the EP drum with a rubber blade.

client   A network entity that can request resources from the network or server.

client computers   A computer that requests resources from a network.

client software   Software that allows a device to request resources from a network.

clock doubling   Technology that allows a chip to run at the bus's rated speed externally, but still be able to run the processor's internal clock at twice the speed of the bus. This technology improves computer performance.

clock rate See *clock speed.*

clock signal Built-in metronome-like signal that indicates how fast the components can operate.

clock speed Also known as clock rate. The internal speed of a computer or processor, normally expressed in MHz. The faster the clock speed, the faster the computer will perform a specific operation, assuming the other components in the system, such as disk drives, can keep up with the increased speed.

clock tripling A type of processor design where the processor runs at one speed externally and at triple that speed internally.

cluster The smallest unit of hard disk space that DOS can allocate to a file, consisting of one or more contiguous sectors. The number of sectors contained in a cluster depends on the hard disk type.

CMOS Acronym for Complementary Metal Oxide Semiconductor. An area of nonvolatile memory that contains settings that determine how a computer is configured.

CMOS battery A battery used to power CMOS memory so that the computer won't lose its settings when powered down.

COMMAND.COM Takes commands issued by the user through text strings or click actions and translates them back into calls that can be understood by the lower layers of DOS. It is the vital command interpreter for DOS.

Complementary Metal Oxide Semiconductor See *CMOS.*

computer name The name by which a Microsoft computer is known on the network. This is a NetBIOS name (up to 15 characters in length) which must be unique on the network. In Windows 2000, the computer name is always the same as the machine's host name, while in Windows 9*x* the two can be different.

conditioning step The step in the EP print process where a uniform charge is applied to the EP drum by the charging corona or charging roller.

conductor Any item that permits the flow of electricity between two entities.

CONFIG.SYS In DOS and OS/2, a special text file containing settings that control the way that the operating system works. CONFIG.SYS must be located in the root directory of the default boot disk, normally drive C, and is read by the operating system only once as the system starts running. Some application programs and peripheral devices require you to include special statements in CONFIG.SYS, while other commands may specify the number of disk-read buffers or open files on your system, specify how the disk cache should be configured, or load any special device drivers your system may need.

connectivity devices   Any device that facilitates connections between network devices. Some examples include hubs, routers, switches, and gateways.

Control Program for Microcomputer (CP/M)   A computer operating system that was an early competitor of Microsoft's DOS system. CP/M was a command-line system that was developed by Gary Kildall.

conventional memory   The amount of memory accessible by DOS in PCs using an Intel processor operating in real mode, normally the first 640K.

cooperative multitasking   A form of multitasking in which all running applications must work together to share system resources.

corona roller   Type of transfer corona assembly that uses a charged roller to apply charge to the paper.

corona wire   Type of transfer corona assembly. Also, the wire in that assembly that is charged by the high voltage supply. It is narrow in diameter and located in a special notch under the EP print cartridge.

CPU (Central Processing Unit)   See *Central Processing Unit (CPU)*.

CPU clock   Type of clock signal that dictates how fast the CPU can run.

crosstalk   Problem related to electromagnetic fields when two wires carrying electrical signals run parallel and one of the wires induces a signal in the second wire. If these wires are carrying data, the extra, unintended signal can cause errors in the communication. Crosstalk is especially a problem in unshielded parallel cables that are longer than 10 feet.

CRT   Acronym for cathode-ray tube. A display device used in computer monitors and television sets. A CRT display consists of a glass vacuum tube that contains one electron gun for a monochrome display, or three (red, green, and blue) electron guns for a color display. Electron beams from these guns sweep rapidly across the inside of the screen from the upper-left to the lower-right of the screen. The inside of the screen is coated with thousands of phosphor dots that glow when they are struck by the electron beam. To stop the image from flickering, the beams sweep at a rate of between 43 and 87 times per second, depending on the phosphor persistence and the scanning mode used—interlaced or non-interlaced. This is known as the refresh rate and is measured in Hz. The Video Electronics Standards Association (VESA) recommends a vertical refresh rate of 72Hz, non-interlaced, at a resolution of 800 by 600 pixels.

cylinder   A hard disk consists of two or more platters, each with two sides. Each side is further divided into concentric circles known as tracks, and all the tracks at the same concentric position on a disk are known collectively as a cylinder.

daisy-chaining   Pattern of cabling where the cables run from the first device to the second, second to the third, and so on. If the devices have both an "in" and an "out," the in of the first device of each pair is connected to the out of the second device of each pair.

daisy-wheel printer   An impact printer that uses a plastic or metal print mechanism with a different character on the end of each spoke of the wheel. As the print mechanism rotates to the correct letter, a small hammer strikes the character against the ribbon, transferring the image onto the paper.

DAT   See *digital audio tape (DAT)*.

data bits   In asynchronous transmissions, the bits that actually comprise the data; usually 7 or 8 data bits make up the data word.

data bus   Bus used to send and receive data to the microprocessor.

data compression   Any method of encoding data so that it occupies less space than in its original form.

data encoding scheme (DES)   The method used by a disk controller to store digital information onto a hard disk or floppy disk. DES has remained unbroken despite years of use; it completely randomizes the information so that it is impossible to determine the encryption key even if some of the original text is known.

Data Link layer   The second of seven layers of the International Standards Organization's Open Systems Interconnection (ISO/OSI) model for computer-to-computer communications. The Data Link layer validates the integrity of the flow of data from one node to another by synchronizing blocks of data and by controlling the flow of data.

data set ready   See *DSR*.

data terminal equipment   See *DTE*.

data terminal ready   See *DTR*.

data transfer rate   The speed at which a disk drive can transfer information from the drive to the processor, usually measured in megabits or megabytes per second.

daughter board   A printed circuit board that attaches to another board to provide additional functions.

DB connector   Any of several types of cable connectors used for parallel or serial cables. The number following the letters DB (for data bus) indicates the number of pins that the connector usually has.

de facto   Latin translation for "by fact". Any standard that is a standard because everyone is using it.

de jure Latin translation for "by law". Any standard that is a standard because a standards body decided it should be so.

debouncing A keyboard feature that eliminates unintended triggering of keystrokes. It works by having the keyboard controller constantly scan the keyboard for keystrokes. Only keystrokes that are pressed for more than two scans are considered keystrokes. This prevents spurious electronic signals from generating input.

decimal The base-10 numbering system that uses the familiar numbers 0–9.

dedicated server The server that is assigned to perform a specific application or service.

default gateway If a user needs to communicate by TCP/IP with a computer that is not on their subnet (the local network segment) the computer needs to use a gateway to access this remote network. The default gateway is simply the path that is taken by all outgoing traffic unless another path is specified.

defragmentation The process of reorganizing and rewriting files so that they occupy one large continuous area on your hard disk rather than several smaller areas.

DES See *data encoding scheme (DES)*.

Desktop Contains the visible elements of Windows and defines the limits of the graphic environment.

Desktop Control Panel Windows panel that is used to configure the system so it is more easily usable. This control panel contains the settings for the background color and pattern as well as screen saver settings.

developing roller The roller inside a toner cartridge that presents a uniform line of toner to help apply the toner to the image written on the EP drum.

developing step The step in the EP print process where the image written on the EP drum by the laser is developed, that is, it has toner stuck to it.

device driver A small program that allows a computer to communicate with and control a device.

Device Manager A utility in Windows 9*x* and Windows 2000 that allows the user to view and modify hardware settings. Device drivers can be installed or upgraded, and problems with devices can be found and dealt with here.

DEVICE= Command found in the DOS CONFIG.SYS that tells DOS which driver to find and load into memory at boot time.

DEVICEHIGH= Command that is used to load the device drivers into upper memory blocks, thereby freeing up space in conventional memory.

diagnostic program   A program that tests computer hardware and peripherals for correct operation. In the PC, some faults are easy to find, and these are known as "hard faults"; the diagnostic program will diagnose them correctly every time. Others, such as memory faults, can be difficult to find; these are called "soft faults" because they do not occur every time the memory location is tested, but only under very specific circumstances.

differential backup   Backs up files that have changed since the last full backup.

digital audio tape (DAT)   A method of recording information in digital form on a small audio tape cassette. Many gigabytes of information can be recorded on a cassette, and so a DAT can be used as a backup medium. Like all tape devices, however, DATs are relatively slow.

digital signal   A signal that consists of discrete values. These values do not change over time; in effect, they change instantly from one value to another.

DIMM (Dual Inline Memory Module)   Memory module that is similar to a SIMM (Single Inline Memory Module), except that a DIMM is double-sided. There are memory chips on both sides of the memory module.

DIN-*n*   Circular type of connector used with computers. (The *n* represents the number of connectors.)

DIP (Dual Inline Package)   A standard housing constructed of hard plastic commonly used to hold an integrated circuit. The circuit's leads are connected to two parallel rows of pins designed to fit snugly into a socket; these pins may also be soldered directly to a printed-circuit board. If you try to install or remove dual inline packages, be careful not to bend or damage their pins.

DIP switch   A small switch used to select the operating mode of a device, mounted as a Dual Inline Package. DIP switches can be either sliding or rocker switches and are often grouped together for convenience. They are used on printed circuit boards, dot-matrix printers, modems, and other peripherals.

direct memory access   See *DMA (direct memory access)*.

directory   Directories are used to organize files on the hard drive. Another name for a directory is a folder. Directories created inside or below others are called "subfolders" or "subdirectories."

Direct Rambus   A memory bus that transfers data at 800MHz over a 16-bit memory bus. Direct Rambus memory models (often called *RIMMs*), like DDR SDRAM, can transfer data on both the rising and falling edges of a clock cycle.

direct-solder method   A method of attaching chips to the motherboard where the chip is soldered directly to the motherboard.

disk cache   An area of computer memory where data is temporarily stored on its way to or from a disk. A disk cache mediates between the application and the hard disk, and when an application asks for information from the hard disk, the cache program first checks to see if that data is already in the cache memory. If it is, the disk cache program loads the information from the cache memory rather than from the hard disk. If the information is not in memory, the cache program reads the data from the disk, copies it into the cache memory for future reference, and then passes the data to the requesting application.

disk-caching program   A program that reads the most commonly accessed data from disk and keeps it in memory for faster access.

disk controller   The electronic circuitry that controls and manages the operation of floppy or hard disks installed in the computer. A single disk controller may manage more than one hard disk; many disk controllers also manage floppy disks and compatible tape drives.

disk drive   A peripheral storage device that reads and writes to magnetic or optical disks. When more than one disk drive is installed on a computer, the operating system assigns each drive a unique name—for example A and C in DOS, Windows, and OS/2.

disk duplexing   In networking, a fault-tolerant technique that writes the same information simultaneously onto two different hard disks. Disk duplexing is offered by most of the major network operating systems and is designed to protect the system against a single disk failure; it is not designed to protect against multiple disk failures and is no substitute for a well-planned series of disk backups.

diskette   An easily removable and portable "floppy" disk that is 3.5" in diameter and enclosed in a durable plastic case that has a metal shutter over the media access window.

diskless workstation   A networked computer that does not have any local disk storage capability.

disk mirroring   In networking, a fault-tolerant technique that writes the same information simultaneously onto two different hard disks, using the same disk controller. In the event of one disk failing, information from the other can be used to continue operations. Disk mirroring is offered by most of the major network operating systems and is designed to protect the system against a single disk failure; it is not designed to protect against multiple disk failures and is no substitute for a well-planned series of disk backups.

Disk Operating System   See *DOS*.

distributed processing   A computer system in which processing is performed by several separate computers linked by a communications network. The term often refers to any computer system supported by a network, but more properly refers to a system in which each computer is chosen to handle a specific workload and the network supports the system as a whole.

DIX Ethernet   The original name for the Ethernet network technology. Named after the original developer companies, Digital, Intel, and Xerox.

DMA (direct memory access)   A method of transferring information directly from a mass-storage device such as a hard disk or from an adapter card into memory (or vice versa), without the information passing through the processor.

DMA channels   Dedicated circuit pathways on the motherboard that make DMA possible.

docking station   A hardware system into which a portable computer fits so that it can be used as a full-fledged desktop computer. Docking stations vary from simple port replicators (that allow you access to parallel and serial ports and a mouse) to complete systems (that give you access to network connections, CD-ROMs, even a tape backup system or PCMCIA ports).

domain   1. The security structure for Windows NT Server and Windows 2000 Active Directory.
2. The namespace structure of TCP/IP's DNS structure.

Domain Name System (DNS)   DNS allows TCP/IP-capable users anywhere in the world to find resources in other companies or countries by using their domain name. Each domain is an independent namespace for a particular organization, and DNS servers manage requests for information about the IP addresses of particular DNS entries. DNS is used to manage all names on the Internet.

dongle   A special cable that provides a connector to a circuit board that doesn't have one. For example, a motherboard may use a dongle to provide a serial port when there is a ribbon cable connector for the dongle on the motherboard, but there is no serial port.

dongle connection   A connector on a motherboard where a dongle will connect.

DOS   1. Acronym for Disk Operating System, an operating system originally developed by Microsoft for the IBM PC. DOS exists in two very similar versions; MS-DOS, developed and marketed by Microsoft for use with IBM-compatible computers, and PC-DOS, supported and sold by IBM for use only on computers manufactured by IBM.
2. A DOS CONFIG.SYS command that loads the operating system into conventional memory, extended memory, or into upper memory blocks on computers using the Intel 80386 or later processor. To use this command, you must

have previously loaded the HIMEM.SYS device driver with the DEVICE command in CONFIG.SYS.

DOS Environment Variables   Variables that specify global things like the path that DOS searches to find executables.

DOS extender   A small program that extends the range of DOS memory. For example, HIMEM.SYS allows DOS access to the memory ranges about 1024K.

DOS prompt   A visual confirmation that DOS is ready to receive input from the keyboard. The default prompt includes the current drive letter followed by a right angle bracket (for example, C>). You can create your own custom prompt with the PROMPT command.

DOS shell   An early graphic user interface for DOS that allowed users to manage files and run programs through a simple text interface and even use a mouse. It was soon replaced by Windows.

dot-matrix printer   An impact printer that uses columns of small pins and an inked ribbon to create the tiny pattern of dots that form the characters. Dot-matrix printers are available in 9-, 18-, or 24-pin configurations.

dot pitch   In a monitor, the vertical distance between the centers of like-colored phosphors on the screen of a color monitor, measured in millimeters (mm).

dots per inch (dpi)   A measure of resolution expressed by the number of dots that a device can print or display in one inch.

double-density disk   A floppy disk with a storage capacity of 360KB.

DRAM   See *dynamic RAM (DRAM)*.

drawing tablet   Pointing device that includes a pencil-like device (called a stylus) for drawing on its flat rubber-coated sheet of plastic.

drive bay   An opening in the system unit into which you can install a floppy disk drive, hard disk drive, or tape drive.

drive geometry   Term used to describe the number of cylinders, read/write heads, and sectors in a hard disk.

drive hole   Hole in a floppy disk that allows the motor in the disk drive to spin the disk. Also known as the hub hole.

drive letter   In DOS, Windows, and OS/2, the drive letter is a designation used to specify a particular hard or floppy disk. For example, the first floppy disk is usually referred to as drive A, and the first hard disk as drive C.

driver   See *device driver*.

driver signing   In order to prevent viruses and poorly written drivers from damaging your system, Windows 2000 uses a process called driver signing that allows companies to digitally sign their device software, and it also allows administrators to block the installation of unsigned drivers.

driver software   See *device driver*.

D-Shell   See *DB connector*.

DSR   Abbreviation for data set ready. A hardware signal defined by the RS-232-C standard to indicate that the device is ready.

D-Sub   See *DB connector*.

DTE   Abbreviation for data terminal equipment. In communications, any device, such as a terminal or a computer, connected to a communications channel or public network.

DTR   Abbreviation for data terminal ready. A hardware signal defined by the RS-232-C standard to indicate that the computer is ready to accept a transmission.

dual-booting   If a single machine must be used for many tasks, it may be necessary for it to have multiple operating systems installed simultaneously. To do this a boot manager presents the user with a choice of which operating system to use at startup. To use a different OS the user would have to shut down the system, restart it, and select the other OS.

Dual Inline Memory Module   See *DIMM (Dual Inline Memory Module)*.

Dual Inline Package   See *DIP (Dual Inline Package)*.

dumb terminal   A combination of keyboard and screen that has no local computing power, used to input information to a large, remote computer, often a minicomputer or a mainframe. This remote computer provides all the processing power for the system.

duplex   In asynchronous transmissions, the ability to transmit and receive on the same channel at the same time; also referred to as full duplex. Half-duplex channels can transmit only or receive only. Most dial-up services available to PC users take advantage of full-duplex capabilities, but if you cannot see what you are typing, switch to half duplex. If you are using half duplex and you can see two of every character you type, change to full duplex.

duplex printing   Printing a document on both sides of the page so that the appropriate pages face each other when the document is bound.

dynamic electricity   See *electricity*.

Dynamic Host Configuration Protocol (DHCP)   DHCP manages the automatic assignment of TCP/IP addressing information (such as the IP address, subnet mask, default gateway and DNS server). This can save a great deal of time when configuring and maintaining a TCP/IP network.

Dynamic Link Library (DLL) files   Windows component files that contain small pieces of executable code that are shared between multiple Windows programs. They are used to eliminate redundant programming in certain Windows applications. DLLs are used extensively in Microsoft Windows, OS/2, and in Windows NT. DLLs may have filename extensions of `.dll`, `.drv`, or `.fon`.

dynamic RAM (DRAM)   A common type of computer memory that uses capacitors and transistors storing electrical charges to represent memory states. These capacitors lose their electrical charge, and so they need to be refreshed every millisecond, during which time they cannot be read by the processor. DRAM chips are small, simple, cheap, easy to make, and hold approximately four times as much information as a static RAM (SRAM) chip of similar complexity. However, they are slower than static RAM. Processors operating at clock speeds of 25MHz or more need DRAM with access times of faster than 80 nanoseconds (80 billionths of a second), while SRAM chips can be read in as little as 15 to 30 nanoseconds.

Each operating system contains a standard set of device drivers for the keyboard, the monitor, and so on, but if you add specialized peripherals (such as a CD-ROM disk drive) or a network interface card, you will probably have to add the appropriate device driver so that the operating system knows how to manage the device. In DOS, device drivers are loaded by the DEVICE or DEVICEHIGH commands in CONFIG.SYS.

edge connector   A form of connector consisting of a row of etched contacts along the edge of a printed circuit board that is inserted into an expansion slot in the computer.

EDO (Extended Data Out) RAM   A type of DRAM that increases memory performance by eliminating wait states.

EEPROM   Acronym for Electrically Erasable Programmable Read-Only Memory. A memory chip that maintains its contents without electrical power, and whose contents can be erased and reprogrammed either within the computer or from an external source. EEPROMs are used where the application requires stable storage without power but may have to be reprogrammed.

EGA   Acronym for Enhanced Graphics Adapter. A video adapter standard that provides medium-resolution text and graphics. EGA can display 16 colors at the same time from a choice of 64, with a horizontal resolution of 640 pixels and a vertical resolution of 350 pixels. EGA has been superseded by VGA and SVGA.

EISA   Acronym for Extended Industry Standard Architecture. A PC bus standard that extends the traditional AT-bus to 32 bits and allows more than one processor to share the bus. EISA has a 32-bit data path and, at a bus speed of 8MHz, can achieve a maximum throughput of 33 megabytes per second.

EISA Configuration Utility (EISA Config)   The utility used to configure an EISA bus expansion card.

Electrically Erasable Programmable Read-Only Memory   See *EEPROM*.

electricity   The flow of free electrons from one molecule of substance to another. This flow of electrons is used to do work.

electromagnetic drawing tablets   Type of drawing tablet that has grids of wires underneath the rubberized surface. The stylus contains a small sensor that is sensitive to electromagnetic fields. At timed intervals, an electromagnetic pulse is sent across the grid. The sensor in the stylus picks up these pulses.

electromagnetic interference (EMI)   Any electromagnetic radiation released by an electronic device that disrupts the operation or performance of any other device.

electron gun   The component of a monitor that fires electrons at the back of the phosphor-coated screen.

electrostatic discharge (ESD)   When two objects of dissimilar charge come in contact with one another, they will exchange electrons in order to standardize the electrostatic charge between the two objects. This exchange, or discharge, can sometimes be seen as a spark or arc of electricity. Even when it cannot be seen it is damaging to electronic components.

e-mail   Electronic mail is generally sent across the Internet using protocols named SMTP (for sending) and POP3 (for receiving).

EMI   See *electromagnetic interference (EMI)*.

EMM386.EXE   Reserved memory manager that emulates Expanded Memory in the Extended Memory area (XMS) and provides DOS with the ability to utilize upper memory blocks to load programs and device drivers.

encoding   Process by which binary information is changed into flux transition patterns on a disk surface.

Enhanced Graphics Adapter   See *EGA*.

enhanced keyboard   A 101- or 102-key keyboard introduced by IBM that has become the accepted standard for PC keyboard layout. Unlike earlier keyboards, it has 12 function keys across the top, rather than 10 function keys in a block on the left side, has extra Ctrl and Alt keys, and has a set of cursor control keys between the main keyboard and the numeric keypad.

Enhanced Small Device Interface (ESDI)   A popular hard-disk, floppy-disk, and tape-drive interface standard, capable of a data transfer rate of 10 to 20 megabits per second. ESDI is most often used with large hard disks.

environment variables   These are used to set certain system-wide parameters that can then be used by applications running on the system. For instance, a system's temporary directory can be set to a specific location using an environment variable.

EP drum   Device that is coated with a photosensitive material that can hold a static charge when not exposed to light. The drum contains a cleaning blade that continuously scrapes the used toner off the photosensitive drum to keep it clean.

EP print process   Six-step process an EP laser printer uses to form images on paper. In order, the steps are charging, exposing, developing, transferring, fusing, and cleaning.

EP printer (electrophotographic printer)   Printer that uses high voltage, a laser, and a black carbon toner to form an image on a page.

EPROM   Acronym for erasable programmable read-only memory. A memory chip that maintains its contents without electrical power, and whose contents can be erased and reprogrammed by removing a protective cover and exposing the chip to ultraviolet light.

ergonomics   Standards that define the positioning and use of the body to promote a healthy work environment.

ESD   See *electrostatic discharge (ESD)*.

ESD mat   Preventive measure to guard against the effects of ESD. The excess charge is drained away from any item that comes in contact with it.

Ethernet   A network technology based on the IEEE 802.3 CSMA/CD standard. The original Ethernet implementation specified 10MBps, baseband signaling, coaxial cable, and CSMA/CD media access.

even parity   A technique that counts the number of 1s in a binary number and, if the number of 1s total is not an even number, adds a digit to make it even. (See also *parity*).

exit roller   Found on laser and page printers, the mechanism that guides the paper out of the printer into the paper-receiving tray.

expanded memory page frame   See *page frame*.

expanded memory specification (EMS)   The original version of the Lotus-Intel-Microsoft Expanded Memory Specification (LIM EMS) that lets DOS applications use more than 640KB of memory space.

expansion bus   An extension of the main computer bus that includes expansion slots for use by compatible adapters, such as memory boards, video adapters, hard disk controllers, and SCSI interface cards.

expansion card   A device that can be installed into a computer's expansion bus.

expansion slot   One of the connectors on the expansion bus that gives an adapter access to the system bus. You can add as many additional adapters as there are expansion slots inside your computer.

extended DOS partition   A further optional division of a hard disk, after the primary DOS partition, that functions as one or more additional logical drives. A logical drive is simply an area of a larger disk that acts as though it were a separate disk with its own drive letter.

Extended Graphics Array   See *XGA*.

Extended Industry Standard Architecture   See *EISA*.

extended memory manager   A device driver that supports the software portion of the extended memory specification in an IBM-compatible computer.

Extended Memory System (XMS)   Memory above 1,024KB that is used by Windows and Windows-based programs. This type of memory cannot be accessed unless the HIMEM.SYS memory manager is loaded in the DOS CONFIG.SYS with a line like DEVICE=HIMEM.SYS.

extended partition   If all of the space on a drive is not used in the creation of the drive's primary partition, a second partition can be created out of the remaining space. Called the extended partition, this second partition can hold one or more logical drives.

external bus   An external component connected through expansion cards and slots allows the processor to talk to other devices. This component allows the CPU to talk to the other devices in the computer and vice versa.

external cache memory   Separate expansion board that installs in a special processor-direct bus that contains cache memory.

external commands   Commands that are not contained within COMMAND .COM. They are represented by a `.COM` or `.EXE` extension.

external hard disk   A hard disk packaged in its own case with cables and an independent power supply rather than a disk drive housed inside and integrated with the computer's system unit.

external modem   A stand-alone modem, separate from the computer and connected by a serial cable. LEDs on the front of the chassis indicate the current modem status and can be useful in troubleshooting communications problems.

An external modem is a good buy if you want to use a modem with different computers at different times or with different types of computer.

FAQ   Acronym for Frequently Asked Question. A document that lists some of the more commonly asked questions about a product or component. When researching a problem, the FAQ is usually the best place to start.

FAT   See *file allocation table (FAT)*.

fax modem   An adapter that fits into a PC expansion slot and provides many of the capabilities of a full-sized fax machine, but at a fraction of the cost.

FDDI   See *fiber distributed data interface (FDDI)*.

FDISK.EXE   The DOS utility that is used to partition hard disks for use with DOS.

feed roller   The rubber roller in a laser printer that feeds the paper into the printer.

fiber distributed data interface (FDDI)   A specification for fiber-optic networks transmitting at a speed of up to 100 megabits per second over a dual, counter-rotating, Token Ring topology. FDDI is suited to systems that require the transfer of very large amounts of information, such as medical imaging, 3D seismic processing, oil reservoir simulation, and full-motion video.

fiber optic cable   A transmission technology that sends pulses of light along specially manufactured optical fibers. Each fiber consists of a core, thinner than a human hair, surrounded by a sheath with a much lower refractive index. Light signals introduced at one end of the cable are conducted along the cable as the signals are reflected from the sheath.

field replacement unit   See *FRU (field replacement unit)*.

file allocation table (FAT)   A table maintained by DOS or OS/2 that lists all the clusters available on a disk. The FAT includes the location of each cluster, as well as whether it is in use, available for use, or damaged in some way and therefore unavailable. FAT also keeps track of which pieces belong to which file.

file compression program   An application program that shrinks program or data files, so that they occupy less disk space. The file must then be extracted or decompressed before you can use it. Many of the most popular file compression programs are shareware, like WinZIP, PKZIP, LHA, and StuffIt for the Macintosh, although utility packages like PC Tools from Central Point Software also contain file compression programs.

file corruption   Occasionally an improper shutdown, a virus, or a random problem will cause a file's information to become unreadable. This unreadable file is referred to as "corrupt" and it must be either repaired or replaced.

file locking   A feature of many network operating systems that prevents more than one person from updating a file at the same time by "locking" the file.

File Manager   Windows utility that allows the user to accomplish a number of important file-related tasks from a single interface. This is a Windows 3.*x* feature only; Window 9*x* uses Explorer.

file server   A networked computer used to store files for access by other client computers on the network. On larger networks, the file server may run a special network operating system; on smaller installations, the file server may run a PC operating system supplemented by peer-to-peer networking software.

file sharing   In networking, the sharing of files via the network file server. Shared files can be read, reviewed, and updated by more than one individual. Access to the file or files is often regulated by password protection, account or security clearance, or file locking, to prevent simultaneous changes from being made by more than one person at a time.

File Transfer Protocol (FTP)   FTP is used to transfer large files across the Internet or any TCP/IP network. Special servers, called FTP servers, store information and then transfer it back to FTP clients as needed. FTP servers can also be secured with a username and password to prevent unauthorized downloading (retrieval of a file from the server) or uploading (placing of a file on the server).

FireWire   See *IEEE-1394*.

firmware   Any software stored in a form of read-only memory—ROM, EPROM, or EEPROM—that maintains its contents when power is removed.

fixed disk   A disk drive that contain several disks (also known as platters) stacked together and mounted through their centers on a small rod. The disks rotate as read/write heads float above the disks that make, modify, or sense changes in the magnetic positions of the coatings on the disk.

fixed resistor   Type of resistor that is used to reduce the current by a certain amount. Fixed resistors are color coded to identify their resistance values and tolerance bands.

flash memory   A special form of non-volatile EEPROM that can be erased at signal levels normally found inside the PC, so that you can reprogram the contents with whatever you like without pulling the chips out of your computer. Also, once flash memory has been programmed, you can remove the expansion board it is mounted on and plug it into another computer if you wish.

flatbed scanner   An optical device used to digitize a whole page or a large image.

flat-panel display   In laptop and notebook computers, a very narrow display that uses one of several technologies, such as electroluminescence, LCD, or thin film transistors.

floating-point calculation   A calculation of numbers whose decimal point is not fixed but moves or floats to provide the best degree of accuracy. Floating-point calculations can be implemented in software, or they can be performed much faster by a separate floating-point processor.

floating-point processor   A special-purpose, secondary processor designed to perform floating-point calculations much faster than the main processor.

floppy disk   A flat, round, magnetically coated plastic disk enclosed in a protective jacket. Data is written onto the floppy disk by the disk drive's read/write heads as the disk rotates inside the jacket. It can be used to distribute commercial software, to transfer programs from one computer to another, or to back up files from a hard disk. Floppy disks in personal computing are of two physical sizes, 5.25" or 3.5", and a variety of storage capacities. The 5.25" floppy disk has a stiff plastic external cover, while the 3.5" floppy disk is enclosed in a hard plastic case. IBM-compatibles use 5.25" and 3.5" disks, and the Macintosh uses 3.5" disks.

floppy disk controller   The circuit board that is installed in a computer to translate signals from the CPU into signals that the floppy disk drive can understand. Often it is integrated into the same circuit board that houses the hard disk controller; it can, however, be integrated into the motherboard in the PC.

floppy disk drive   A device used to read and write data to and from a floppy disk. Floppy disk drives may be full-height drives, but more commonly these days they are half-height drives.

floppy drive cable   A cable that connects the floppy drive(s) to the floppy drive controller. The cable is a 34-wire ribbon cable that usually has three connectors.

floppy drive interfaces   A connector on a motherboard used to connect floppy drives to the motherboard.

floptical disk   A removable optical disk with a recording capacity of between 20 and 25 megabytes.

flux transition   Presence or absence of a magnetic field in a particle of the coating on the disk. As the disk passes over an area the electromagnet is energized to cause the material to be magnetized in a small area.

footprint   The amount of desktop or floor space occupied by a computer or display terminal. By extension, also refers to the size of software items such as applications or operating systems.

FORMAT.COM   External DOS command that prepares the partition to store information using the FAT system as required by DOS and Windows 9*x*.

formatter board   Type of circuit board that takes the information the printer receives from the computer and turns it into commands for the various components in the printer.

formatting   1. To apply the page-layout commands and font specifications to a document and produce the final printed output.
2. The process of initializing a new, blank floppy disk or hard disk so that it can be used to store information.

form factors   Physical characteristics and dimensions of drive styles.

form feed (FF)   A printer command that advances the paper in the printer to the top of the next page by pressing the FF button on the printer.

fragmentation   A disk storage problem that exists after several smaller files have been deleted from a hard disk. The deletion of files leaves the disk with areas of free disk space scattered throughout the disk. The fact that these areas of disk space are located so far apart on the disk causes slower performance because the disk read/write heads have to move all around the disk's surface to find the pieces of one file.

free memory   An area of memory not currently in use.

Frequently Asked Question   See *FAQ*.

friction feed   A paper-feed mechanism that uses pinch rollers to move the paper through a printer, one page at a time.

FRU (field replacement unit)   The individual parts or whole assemblies that can be replaced to repair a computer.

"full" AT   A type of motherboard form factor where the motherboard is the same size as the original IBM AT computer's motherboard.

full-duplex communications   Communications where both entities can send and receive simultaneously.

function keys   The set of programmable keys on the keyboard that can perform special tasks assigned by the current application program.

fuser   Device on an EP Printer that uses two rollers to heat the toner particles and melt them to the paper. The fuser is made up of a halogen heating lamp, a Teflon-coated aluminum fusing roller, and a rubberized pressure roller. The lamp heats the aluminum roller. As the paper passes between the two rollers, the rubber roller presses the paper against the heated roller. This causes the toner to melt and become a permanent image on the paper.

fusing assembly   See *fuser*.

fusing step   The step in the EP process where the toner image on the paper is fused to the paper using heat and pressure. The heat melts the toner and the pressure helps fuse the image permanently to the paper.

game port   A DB-15 connector used to connect game devices (like joysticks) to a computer.

gateway   In networking, a shared connection between a local area network and a larger system, such as a mainframe computer or a large packet-switching network. Usually slower than a bridge or router, a gateway typically has its own processor and memory and can perform protocol conversions. Protocol conversion allows a gateway to connect two dissimilar networks; data is converted and reformatted before it is forwarded to the new network.

GDI.EXE   Windows core component that is responsible for drawing icons and windows in Windows 3.*x*.

General Protection Fault (GPF)   A Windows error that typically occurs when a Windows program tries to access memory currently in use by another program.

gigabyte   One billion bytes; however, bytes are most often counted in powers of 2, and so a gigabyte becomes 2 to the 30th power, or 1,073,741,824 bytes.

GPF   See *General Protection Fault (GPF)*.

graphical user interface (GUI)   A graphics-based user interface that allows users to select files, programs, or commands by pointing to pictorial representations on the screen rather than by typing long, complex commands from a command prompt. Application programs execute in windows, using a consistent set of pull-down menus, dialog boxes, and other graphical elements such as scroll bars and icons.

graphics accelerator board   A specialized expansion board containing a graphics coprocessor as well as all the other circuitry found on a video adapter.

graphics mode   A mode of a video card that allows the video card to display graphics.

group icons   A type of Windows icon that groups Windows program icons together in the Program Manager.

GUI   See *graphical user interface (GUI)*.

half-duplex communications   Communications that occur when only one entity can transmit or receive at any one instant.

half-height drive   A space-saving drive bay that is half the height of the 3" drive bays used in the original IBM PC. Most of today's drives are half-height drives.

hand-held scanner   Type of scanner that is small enough to be held in your hand. Used to digitize a relatively small image or artwork, it consists of the controller, CCD, and light source contained in a small enclosure with wheels on it.

hard disk controller   An expansion board that contains the necessary circuitry to control and coordinate a hard disk drive. Many hard disk controllers are capable of managing more than one hard disk, as well as floppy disks and even tape drives.

hard disk drive   A storage device that uses a set of rotating, magnetically coated disks called platters to store data or programs. A typical hard disk platter rotates at up to 7200rpm, and the read/write heads float on a cushion of air from 10 to 25 millionths of an inch thick so that the heads never come into contact with the recording surface. The whole unit is hermetically sealed to prevent airborne contaminants from entering and interfering with these close tolerances. Hard disks range in capacity from a few tens of megabytes to several gigabytes of storage space; the bigger the disk, the more important a well thought out backup strategy becomes.

hard disk interfaces   A connector on a motherboard that makes it possible to connect a hard disk to the motherboard.

hard disk system   A disk storage system containing the following components: the hard disk controller, hard disk, and host adapter.

hard memory error   A reproducible memory error that is related to hardware failure.

hard reset   A system reset made by pressing the computer's reset button or by turning the power off and then on again.

hardware   All the physical electronic components of a computer system, including peripherals, printed-circuit boards, displays, and printers.

Hardware Compatibility List (HCL)   An HCL is a list (that is maintained and regularly updated by Microsoft for each of its Windows OSs) of all hardware currently known to be compatible with a particular operating system. Windows 98, NT, and 2000 all have their own HCL.

hardware interrupt   An interrupt or request for service generated by a hardware device such as a keystroke from the keyboard or a tick from the clock. Because the processor may receive several such signals simultaneously, hardware interrupts are usually assigned a priority level and processed according to that priority.

hardware ports   See *I/O address*.

head   The electromagnetic device used to read from and write to magnetic media such as hard and floppy disks, tape drives, and compact discs. The head converts the information read into electrical pulses sent to the computer for processing.

header   Information that is attached to the beginning of a network data frame.

heat sink   A device that is attached to an electronic component that removes heat from the component by induction. It is often a plate of aluminum or metal with several vertical fingers.

hertz   Abbreviated Hz. A unit of frequency measurement; 1 hertz equals one cycle per second.

hexadecimal   Abbreviated hex. The base-16 numbering system that uses the digits 0 to 9, followed by the letters A to F (equivalent to the decimal numbers 10 through 15). Hex is a very convenient way to represent the binary numbers computers use internally, because it fits neatly into the 8-bit byte. All of the 16 hex digits 0 to F can be represented in 4 bits, and so two hex digits (one digit for each set of 4 bits) can be stored in a single byte. This means that 1 byte can contain any one of 256 different hex numbers, from 0 through FF. Hex numbers are often labeled with a lowercase *h* (for example, 1234h) to distinguish them from decimal numbers.

high-density disk   A floppy disk with more recording density and storage capacity than a double-density disk.

high-level format   The process of preparing a floppy disk or a hard disk partition for use by the operating system. In the case of DOS, a high-level format creates the boot sector, the file allocation table (FAT), and the root directory.

high memory area (HMA)   In an IBM-compatible computer, the first 64K of extended memory above the 1MB limit of 8086 and 8088 addresses. Programs that conform to the extended memory specification can use this memory as an extension of conventional memory although only one program can use or control HMA at a time.

high-voltage power supply (HVPS)   Provides the high voltages that are used during the EP print process. This component converts house AC currents into higher voltages that the two corona assemblies can use.

high-voltage probe   A device used to drain away voltage from a monitor before testing. It is a pencil shaped device with a metal point and a wire lead with a clip.

HIMEM.SYS   The DOS and Microsoft Windows device driver that manages the use of extended memory and the high memory area on IBM-compatible computers. HIMEM.SYS not only allows your application programs to access extended memory, it oversees that area to prevent other programs from trying to use the same space at the same time. HIMEM.SYS must be loaded by a DEVICE command in your CONFIG.SYS file; you cannot use DEVICEHIGH.

HMA   See *high memory area (HMA)*.

home page   On the Internet, an initial starting page. A home page may be related to a single person, a specific subject, or a corporation and is a convenient jumping-off point to other pages or resources.

host   The central or controlling computer in a networked or distributed processing environment, providing services that other computers or terminals can access via the network. Computers connected to the Internet are also described as hosts, and can be accessed using FTP, Telnet, Gopher, or a browser.

host adapter   Translates signals from the hard drive and controller to signals the computer's bus can understand.

host name   The name by which a computer is known on a TCP/IP network. This name must be unique within the domain that the machine is in. In Windows 2000 the computer name is always the same as the machine's host name, while in Windows 9*x* the two can be different.

hub   A connectivity device used to link several computers together into a physical star topology. They repeat any signal that comes in on one port and copies it to the other ports.

HVPS   See *high-voltage power supply (HVPS)*.

hybrid topology   A mix of more than one topology type used on a network.

Hypertext Transfer Protocol (HTTP)   HTTP is the protocol of the World Wide Web, and is used to send and receive Web pages and other content from an HTTP server (Web server). HTTP makes use of linked pages, accessed via hyperlinks, which are words or pictures that, when clicked on, take you to another page.

I/O address   Lines on a bus used to allow the CPU to send instructions to the devices installed in the bus slots. Each device is given its own communication line to the CPU. These lines function like one-way (unidirectional) mailboxes.

I/O ports   See *I/O address*.

laser printer   A generic name for a printer that uses the electrophotographic (EP) print process.

IBM-compatible computer   Originally, any personal computer compatible with the IBM line of personal computers. With the launch of IBM's proprietary micro channel architecture in the PS/2 line of computers, which replaced the AT bus, two incompatible standards emerged, and so the term became misleading. Now, it is becoming more common to use the term "industry-standard computer" when referring to a computer that uses the AT or ISA bus, and the term "DOS computer" to describe any PC that runs DOS and is based on one of the Intel family of chips.

IBM PC   A series of personal computers based on the Intel 8088 processor, introduced by IBM in mid-1981. The PC was released containing 16K of memory, expandable to 64K on the motherboard, and a monochrome video adapter incapable of displaying bit-mapped graphics. The floppy disk drive held 160K of data and programs. There was no hard disk on the original IBM PC; that came later with the release of the IBM PC/XT.

IBM PS/2   A series of personal computers using several different Intel processors, introduced by IBM in 1987. The main difference between the PS/2 line and earlier IBM personal computers was a major change to the internal bus. Previous computers used the AT bus, also known as industry-standard architecture, but IBM used the proprietary micro channel architecture in the PS/2 line instead. Micro channel architecture expansion boards will not work in a computer using ISA. See *IBM-compatible computer*.

IC   See *integrated circuit (IC)*.

Icons   On-screen graphics that act as doors through which programs are started and therefore used to spawn windows. They are shortcuts that allow a user to open a program or a utility without knowing where that program is or how it needs to be configured.

IDE   Acronym for integrated drive electronics. A hard disk technology that can connect multiple drives together. These drives integrate the controller and drive into one assembly. This makes them very inexpensive. Because of this, IDE drives are the most commonly used disk technology installed in computers today.

IEEE-1394   A high-speed digital interface most commonly used to transfer data between computers and digital video cameras. It has a maximum data transfer rate of over 400MBps.

illegal operation error   A Windows error that occurs when a program does something that Windows wasn't expecting or doesn't know how to do.

impact printer   Any printer that forms an image on paper by forcing a character image against an inked ribbon. Dot-matrix, daisy-wheel, and line printers are all impact printers, whereas laser printers are not.

In a virtual memory system, programs and their data are divided up into smaller pieces called pages. At the point where more memory is needed, the operating system decides which pages are least likely to be needed soon (using an algorithm based on frequency of use, most recent use, and program priority), and it writes these pages out to disk. The memory space that they used is now available to the rest of the system for other application programs. When these pages are needed again, they are loaded back into real memory, displacing other pages.

incremental backup   A backup of a hard disk that consists of only those files created or modified since the last backup was performed.

industry-standard architecture   See *ISA*.

INI file   Text file that is created by an installation program when a new Windows application is installed. INI files contain settings for individual Windows applications as well as for Windows itself.

initialization commands   A set of commands sent to a modem to prepare it to function.

inoculating   The process of protecting a computer system against virus attacks by installing antivirus software.

input/output addresses   See *I/O address*.

integrated circuit (IC)   Also known as a chip. A small semiconductor circuit that contains many electronic components.

integrated drive electronics   See *IDE*.

Integrated Services Digital Network   See *ISDN*.

integrated system boards   A system board that has most of the computer's circuitry attached, as opposed to having been installed as expansion cards.

Intel OverDrive   OverDrive chips boost system performance by using the same clock multiplying technology found in the Intel 80486DX-2 and DX4 chips. Once installed, an OverDrive processor can increase application performance by an estimated 40 to 70 percent.

intelligent hub   A class of hub that can be remotely managed on the network.

interface   Any port or opening that is specifically designed to facilitate communication between two entities.

interface software   The software for a particular interface that translates software commands into commands that the printer can understand.

interlacing   A display technique that uses two passes over the monitor screen, painting every other line on the screen the first time and then filling in the rest of the lines on the second pass. It relies on the physiological phenomenon known as persistence of vision to produce the effect of a continuous image.

interleaving   Interleaving involves skipping sectors to write the data, instead of writing sequentially to every sector. This evens out the data flow and allows the drive to keep pace with the rest of the system. Interleaving is given in ratios. If the interleave is 2:1, the disk skips 2 minus 1, or 1 sector, between each sector it writes (it writes to one sector, skips one sector, then writes to the next sector following). Most drives today use a 1:1 interleave, because today's drives are very efficient at transferring information.

International Standards Organization (ISO) An international standard-making body, based in Geneva, that establishes global standards for communications and information exchange.

Internet The Internet (Net) is the global TCP/IP network that now extends into nearly every office and school. The World Wide Web is the most visible part of the Internet, but e-mail, newsgroups, and FTP (to name just a few) are also important parts of the Internet.

Internet address An IP or domain address which identifies a specific node on the Internet.

Internet Protocol See *IP*.

Internet Service Provider (ISP) An ISP is a company that provides Internet access for users. Generally ISPs are local or regional companies that provide Internet access and e-mail addresses to users.

internetwork Any TCP/IP network that spans router interfaces is considered to be an internetwork. This means that anything from a small office with two subnets to the Internet itself can be described as an internetwork.

interrupt A signal to the processor generated by a device under its control (such as the system clock) that interrupts normal processing. An interrupt indicates that an event requiring the processor's attention has occurred, causing the processor to suspend and save its current activity and then branch to an interrupt service routine. This service routine processes the interrupt (whether it was generated by the system clock, a keystroke, or a mouse click) and when it's complete, returns control to the suspended process. In the PC, interrupts are often divided into three classes: internal hardware, external hardware, and software interrupts. The Intel 80x86 family of processors supports 256 prioritized interrupts, of which the first 64 are reserved for use by the system hardware or by DOS.

interrupt request (IRQ) A hardware interrupt signals that an event has taken place that requires the processor's attention, and may come from the keyboard, the input/output ports, or the system's disk drives. In the PC, the main processor does not accept interrupts from hardware devices directly; instead interrupts are routed to an Intel 8259A Programmable Interrupt Controller. This chip responds to each hardware interrupt, assigns a priority, and forwards it to the main processor.

interrupt request (IRQ) lines Hardware lines that carry a signal from a device to the processor.

IP Abbreviation for Internet Protocol. The underlying communications protocol on which the Internet is based. IP allows a data packet to travel across many networks before reaching its final destination.

IP address   In order to communicate on a TCP/IP network, each machine must have a unique IP address. This address is in the form $x.x.x.x$ where x is a number from 0 to 255.

IPCONFIG   Used on Windows 2000 to view current IP configuration information and to manually request updated information from a DHCP server.

IRQ   See *interrupt request (IRQ)*.

ISA   Abbreviation for industry-standard architecture. The 16-bit bus design was first used in IBM's PC/AT computer in 1984. ISA has a bus speed of 8MHz and a maximum throughput of 8 megabytes per second. EISA is a 32-bit extension to this standard bus.

ISDN   Abbreviation for Integrated Services Digital Network. A worldwide digital communications network emerging from existing telephone services, intended to replace all current systems with a completely digital transmission system. Computers and other devices connect to ISDN via simple, standardized interfaces, and when complete, ISDN systems will be capable of transmitting voice, video, music, and data.

joystick port   See *game port*.

jumper   A small plastic and metal connector that completes a circuit, usually to select one option from a set of several user-definable options. Jumpers are often used to select one particular hardware configuration rather than another.

kernel file   Windows core component that is responsible for managing Windows resources and running applications.

kilobit   Abbreviated Kb or Kbit. 1024 bits (binary digits).

kilobits per second   Abbreviated Kbps. The number of bits, or binary digits, transmitted every second, measured in multiples of 1024 bits per second. Used as an indicator of communications transmission rate.

kilobyte   Abbreviated K, KB, or Kbyte. 1024 bytes.

L1 Cache   Any cache memory that is integrated into the CPU.

L2 Cache   Any cache memory that is external to the CPU.

LAN   See *local area network (LAN)*.

laser scanner   The assembly in an EP process printer that contains the laser. This component is responsible for writing the image to the EP drum.

latency   The time that elapses between issuing a request for data and actually starting the data transfer. In a hard disk, this translates into the time it takes to position the disk's read/write head and rotate the disk so that the required sector or cluster is under the head. Latency is just one of many factors that influence disk access speeds.

LCD   See *liquid crystal display (LCD)*.

LCD monitor   A monitor that uses liquid crystal display technology. Many laptop and notebook computers use LCD displays because of their low power requirements.

least significant bit (LSB)   In a binary number, the lowest-order bit. That is, the rightmost bit. So, in the binary number 0001, the 1 is the least significant bit.

LED page printer   A type of EP process printer that uses a row of LEDs instead of a laser to expose the EP drum.

legacy   A component that is still functional but is out of date.

letter quality (LQ)   A category of dot-matrix printer that can print characters that look very close to the quality a laser printer might produce.

liquid crystal display (LCD)   A display technology common in portable computers that uses electric current to align crystals in a special liquid. The rod-shaped crystals are contained between two parallel transparent electrodes, and when current is applied, they change their orientation, creating a darker area. Many LCD screens are also backlit or side-lit to increase visibility and reduce the possibility of eyestrain.

local area network (LAN)   A group of computers and associated peripherals connected by a communications channel capable of sharing files and other resources between several users.

local bus   A PC bus specification that allows peripherals to exchange data at a rate faster than the 8 megabytes per second allowed by the ISA (Industry Standard Architecture) and the 32 megabytes per second allowed by the EISA (Extended Industry Standard Architecture) definitions. Local bus can achieve a maximum data rate of 133 megabytes per second with a 33MHz bus speed, 148 megabytes per second with a 40MHz bus, or 267 megabytes per second with a 50MHz bus.

local resources   Files or folders that are physically located on the machine the user is sitting at are referred to as local to that user. Windows 2000 has the ability to enforce local security, while Windows 9*x* does not.

logic board   The sturdy sheet or board to which all other components on the computer are attached. These components consist of the CPU, underlying circuitry, expansion slots, video components, and RAM slots, just to name a few. Also known as a motherboard or planar board.

logical drive   Created within an extended partition, a logical drive is used to organize space within the partition, which can be accessed through the use of a drive letter.

logical memory   The way memory is organized so it can be accessed by an operating system.

logical topology   Topology that defines how the data flows in a network.

logon   The process of logging on submits your username and password to the network and gives you the network credentials you will use for the rest of that session. Users can either log on to a workgroup or to a network security entity (such as the Active Directory).

low-level format   The process that creates the tracks and sectors on a blank hard disk or floppy disk; sometimes called the physical format. Most hard disks are already low-level formatted; however, floppy disks receive both a low- and a high-level format (or logical format) when you use the DOS or OS/2 command FORMAT.

LPTx ports   In DOS, the device name used to denote a parallel communications port, often used with a printer. DOS supports three parallel ports: LPT1, LPT2, and LPT3, and OS/2 adds support for network ports LPT4 through LPT9.

magneto-optical (MO) drives   An erasable, high-capacity, removable storage device similar to a CD-ROM drive. Magneto-optical drives use both magnetic and laser technology to write data to the disk and use the laser to read that data back again. Writing data takes two passes over the disk, an erase pass followed by the write pass, but reading can be done in just one pass and, as a result, is much faster.

main motor   A printer stepper motor that is used to advance the paper.

master drive   The primary drive in an IDE master/slave configuration.

math coprocessor   A processor that speeds up the floating decimal point calculations that are needed in algebra and statistical calculations.

MCA   MCA is incompatible with expansion boards that follow the earlier 16-bit AT bus standard, physically because the boards are about 50 percent smaller and electronically as the bus depends on more proprietary integrated circuits. MCA was designed for multiprocessing, and it also allows expansion boards to identify themselves, thus eliminating many of the conflicts that arose through the use of manual settings in the original bus.

Megabit (Mbit)   Usually 1,048,576 binary digits or bits of data. Often used as equivalent to 1 million bits.

megabits per second (Mbps) A measurement of the amount of information moving across a network or communications link in 1 second, measured in multiples of 1,048,576 bits.

Megabyte (MB) Usually 1,048,576 bytes. Megabytes are a common way of representing computer memory or hard-disk capacity.

Megahertz (MHz) One million cycles per second. A processor's clock speed is often expressed in MHz. The original IBM PC operated an 8088 running at 4.77MHz, while the more modern Pentium processor runs at speeds of up to 1000MHz and higher.

memory The primary random access memory (RAM) installed in the computer. The operating system copies application programs from disk into memory, where all program execution and data processing takes place; results are written back out to disk again. The amount of memory installed in the computer can determine the size and number of programs that it can run, as well as the size of the largest data file.

memory address The exact location in memory that stores a particular data item or program instruction.

memory map The organization and allocation of memory in a computer. A memory map will give an indication of the amount of memory used by the operating system and the amount remaining for use by applications.

memory optimization The process of making the most possible conventional memory available to run DOS programs.

memory refresh An electrical signal that keeps the data stored in memory from degrading.

mesh topology Type of logical topology where each device on a network is connected to every other device on the network. This topology uses routers to search multiple paths and determine the best path.

Messaging Application Programming Interface (MAPI) The MAPI interface is used to control how Windows interacts with messaging applications such as e-mail programs. MAPI makes most of the functions of e-mail transparent and allows programmers to just write the application, not the whole messaging system.

MFM encoding See *modified frequency modulation (MFM) encoding.*

Microsoft Diagnostics See *MSD (Microsoft Diagnostics).*

Microsoft Disk Operating System See *MS-DOS.*

modem   Contraction of modulator/demodulator, a device that allows a computer to transmit information over a telephone line. The modem translates between the digital signals that the computer uses and analog signals suitable for transmission over telephone lines. When transmitting, the modem modulates the digital data onto a carrier signal on the telephone line. When receiving, the modem performs the reverse process and demodulates the data from the carrier signal.

modified frequency modulation (MFM) encoding   The most widely used method of storing data on a hard disk. Based on an earlier technique known as frequency modulation (FM) encoding, MFM achieves a two-fold increase in data storage density over standard FM recording, but it is not as efficient a space saver as run-length limited encoding.

Molex connector   See *standard peripheral power connector*.

monitor   A video output device capable of displaying text and graphics, often in color.

monochrome monitor   A monitor that can display text and graphics in one color only. For example, white text on a green background or black text on a white background.

most significant bit (MSB)   In a binary number, the highest-order bit. That is, the leftmost bit. In the binary number 10000000, the 1 is the most significant bit.

motherboard   The main printed circuit board in a computer that contains the central processing unit, appropriate coprocessor and support chips, device controllers, memory, and also expansion slots to give access to the computer's internal bus. Also known as a logic board or system board.

mouse   A small input device with one or more buttons used as for pointing or drawing. As you move the mouse in any direction, an on-screen mouse cursor follows the mouse movements; all movements are relative. Once the mouse pointer is in the correct position on the screen, you can press one of the mouse buttons to initiate an action or operation; different user interfaces and file programs interpret mouse clicks in different ways.

MSBACKUP   A DOS program that allows the user to make backup copies of all the programs and data stored on the hard disk. This program is menu-driven and allows the user to set up options that can be used each time you back up the hard drive.

MSD (Microsoft Diagnostics)   Program that allows the user to examine many different aspects of a system's hardware and software setup.

MS-DOS   Acronym for Microsoft Disk Operating System. MS-DOS, like other operating systems, allocates system resources (such as hard and floppy disks, the monitor, and the printer) to the applications programs that need them. MS-DOS is a single-user, single-tasking operating system, with either a command-line interface or a shell interface.

multimedia   A computer technology that displays information by using a combination of full-motion video, animation, sound, graphics, and text with a high degree of user interaction.

multimeter   Electronic device used to measure and test ohms, amperes, and volts.

multiplexer   A network device that combines multiple data streams into a single stream for transmission. Multiplexers can also break out the original data streams from a single, multiplexed stream.

multipurpose server   A server that has more than one use. For example, a multi-purpose server can be both a file server and a print server.

multistation access unit (MAU)   The central device in a Token Ring network that provides both the physical and logical connections to the stations.

multisync monitor   A monitor designed to detect and adjust to a variety of different input signals. By contrast, a fixed-frequency monitor must receive a signal at one specific frequency.

multitasking   A feature of an operating system that allows more than one program to run simultaneously.

multithreading   The ability of a program to send multiple tasks to the processor at the same time. This allows an application to execute more quickly, but it requires the support of a multithreaded operating system.

near letter quality (NLQ)   A category of dot-matrix printer that can come close to the quality of a laser printer, but still is lacking somewhat in print quality.

NetBEUI   Abbreviation for NetBIOS Extended User Interface. A network device driver for the transport layer supplied with Microsoft's LAN Manager.

NetBIOS   Acronym for Network Basic Input/Output System. In networking, a layer of software, originally developed in 1984 by IBM and Sytek, that links a network operating system with specific network hardware. NetBIOS provides an application program interface (API) with a consistent set of commands for requesting lower-level network services to transmit information from node to node.

NetBIOS Extended User Interface   See *NetBEUI*.

network   A group of computers and associated peripherals connected by a communications channel capable of sharing files and other resources between several users. A network can range from a peer-to-peer network (that connects a small number of users in an office or department) to a local area network (that connects many users over permanently installed cables and dial-up lines) or to a wide area network (that connects users on several different networks spread over a wide geographic area).

network adapter   In order to access network resources, a physical connection to the network must be made. This is generally done through the network adapter, which is expansion hardware designed to interface with the network.

Network Basic Input/Output System   See *NetBIOS*.

network client software   The software that enables a computer to communicate on the network.

network interface card (NIC)   In networking, the PC expansion board that plugs into a personal computer or server and works with the network operating system to control the flow of information over the network. The network interface card is connected to the network cabling (twisted-pair, coaxial or fiber-optic cable), which in turn connects all the network interface cards in the network.

Network layer   The third of seven layers of the International Standards Organization's Open Systems Interconnection (ISO/OSI) model for computer-to-computer communications. The Network layer defines protocols for data routing to ensure that the information arrives at the correct destination node.

network security provider   In a network environment, it is often easier to manage the network by having centralized user ID and password storage. Examples of this type of centralized system are Windows 2000's Active Directory or NetWare's NDS.

NIC   See *network interface card (NIC)*.

node   In communications, any device attached to the network.

noncoductor   Any material that does not conduct electricity.

nondedicated server   A computer that can be both a server and a workstation. In practice, by performing the functions of both server and workstation, this type of server does neither function very well. Nondedicated servers are typically used in peer-to-peer networks.

nonintegrated system boards   A type of motherboard where the various subsystems (video, disk access, etc.) are not integrated into the motherboard, but rather placed on expansion cards that can be removed and upgraded.

non-interlaced   Describes a monitor in which the display is updated (refreshed) in a single pass, painting every line on the screen. Interlacing takes two passes to paint the screen, painting every other line on the first pass, and then sequentially filling in the other lines on the second pass. Non-interlaced scanning, while more expensive to implement, reduces unwanted flicker and eyestrain.

NOS (Network Operating System)   Software that runs on the server and controls and manages the network. The NOS controls the communication with resources and the flow of data across the network.

notebook computer   A small portable computer, about the size of a computer book, with a flat screen and a keyboard that fold together. A notebook computer is lighter and smaller than a laptop computer. Some models use flash memory rather than conventional hard disks for program and data storage, while other models offer a range of business applications in ROM. Many offer PCMCIA expansion slots for additional peripherals such as modems, fax modems, or network connections.

NTFS   The NT File System was created to provide enhanced security and performance for the Windows NT operating system, and it has been adopted and improved upon by Windows 2000. NTFS provides Windows 2000 with local file security, file auditing, compression, and encryption options. It is not compatible with Windows 9*x* or DOS.

null modem   A short RS-232-C cable that connects two personal computers so that they can communicate without the use of modems. The cable connects the two computers' serial ports, and certain lines in the cable are crossed over so that the wires used for sending data by one computer are used for receiving data by the other computer and vice versa.

numeric keypad   A set of keys to the right of the main part of the keyboard, used for numeric data entry.

odd parity   A technique that counts the number of *1*s in a binary number and, if the number of *1*s total is not an odd number, adds a digit to make it odd. See also *parity*.

ohm   Unit of electrical resistance.

Open Systems Interconnection (OSI) model   See *OSI (Open Systems Interconnection) model*.

operating system (OS)   The software responsible for allocating system resources, including memory, processor time, disk space, and peripheral devices such as printers, modems, and the monitor. All application programs use the operating system to gain access to these system resources as they are needed. The operating system is the first program loaded into the computer as it boots, and it remains in memory at all times thereafter.

optical disk A disk that can be read from and written to, like a fixed disk but, like a CD, is read with a laser.

optical drive A type of storage drive that uses a laser to read from and write to the storage medium.

optical mouse A mouse that uses a special mouse pad and a beam of laser light. The beam of light shines onto the mouse pad and reflects back to a sensor in the mouse. Special small lines crossing the mouse pad reflect the light into the sensor in different ways to signal the position of the mouse.

optical scanner See *scanner*.

optical touch screen A type of touch screen that uses light beams on the top and left side and optical sensors on the bottom and right side to detect the position of your finger when you touch the screen.

option diskette A diskette that contains the device-specific configuration files for the device being installed into a MCA bus computer.

opto-mechanical mouse Type of mouse that contains a round ball that makes contact with two rollers. Each roller is connected to a wheel that has small holes in it. The wheel rotates between the arms of a U-shaped mechanism that holds a light on one arm and an optical sensor on the other. As the wheels rotate, the light flashes coming through the holes indicate the speed and direction of the mouse, and these values are transmitted to the computer and the mouse control software.

OSI (Open Systems Interconnection) model A protocol model, developed by the International Standards Organization (ISO), that was intended to provide a common way of describing network protocols. This model describes a seven-layered relationship between the stages of communication. Not every protocol maps perfectly to the OSI model, as there is some overlap within some the layers of some protocols.

page description language Describes the whole page being printed. The controller in the printer interprets these commands and turns them into laser pulses or firing print wires.

page frame The special area reserved in upper memory that is used to swap pages of memory into and out of expanded memory.

page printers Type of printer that handles print jobs one page at a time instead of one line at a time.

pages 16K chunks of memory used in expanded memory.

paging The process of swapping memory to an alternate location, such as to and from a page frame in expanded memory or to and from a swap file.

paper pickup roller A D-shaped roller that rotates against the paper and pushes one sheet into the printer.

paper registration roller A roller in an EP process printer that keeps paper movement in sync with the EP image formation process.

paper transport assembly The set of devices that moves the paper through the printer. It consists of a motor and several rubberized rollers that each perform a different function.

parallel port An input/output port that manages information 8 bits at a time, often used to connect a parallel printer.

parallel processing A processor architecture where a processor essentially contains two processors in one. The processor can then execute more than one instruction per clock cycle.

parity Parity is a simple form of error checking used in computers and tele-communications. Parity works by adding an additional bit to a binary number and using it to indicate any changes in that number during transmission.

partition A portion of a hard disk that the operating system treats as if it were a separate drive.

partition table In DOS, an area of the hard disk containing information on how the disk is organized. The partition table also contains information that tells the computer which operating system to load; most disks will contain DOS, but some users may divide their hard disk into different partitions, or areas, each containing a different operating system. The partition table indicates which of these partitions is the active partition, the partition that should be used to start the computer.

passive hub Type of hub that electrically connects all network ports together. This type of hub is not powered.

passive-matrix screen An LCD display mechanism that uses a transistor to control every row of pixels on the screen. This is in sharp contrast to active-matrix screens, where each individual pixel is controlled by its own transistor.

password In order to identify themselves on the network, each user must provide two credentials—a username and a password. The username says, "This is who I am," and the password says, "And here's proof!" Passwords are case sensitive and should be kept secret from other users on the network.

path When referring to a file on a computer's hard drive, the path is used to describe where it exists within the directory structure. If a file is on the D drive in a folder named TEST, its path is d:\test\.

PC Card   A PC Card, also known as a PCMCIA card or a "credit card adapter" is a peripheral device that uses the PCMCIA specification. These have the advantage of being small, easy to use and fully plug-and-play compliant.

PC Card slot   An opening in the case of a portable computer intended to receive a PC Card; also known as a PCMCIA slot.

PC Card Socket Services   See *socket services*.

PCB   See *printed-circuit board (PCB)*.

PC-DOS 1.0   Microsoft's Disk Operating System is generally referred to as MS-DOS. When it was packaged with IBM's personal computers, though, DOS was modified slightly and was called PC-DOS.

PCI   Abbreviation for Peripheral Component Interconnect. A specification introduced by Intel that defines a local bus that allows up to 10 PCI-compliant expansion cards to be plugged into the computer. One of these 10 cards must be the PCI controller card, but the others can include a video card, network interface card, SCSI interface, or any other basic input/output function. The PCI controller exchanges information with the computer's processor as 32- or 64-bits and allows intelligent PCI adapters to perform certain tasks concurrently with the main processor by using bus mastering techniques.

PCMCIA   Abbreviation for PC Memory Card International Association. Expansion cards developed for this standard are now called PC Cards.

peer-to-peer network   Network where the computers act as both workstations and servers and where there is no centralized administration or control.

Pentium   The Pentium represents the evolution of the 80486 family of microprocessors and adds several notable features, including 8K instruction code and data caches, built-in floating-point processor and memory management unit, as well as a superscalar design and dual pipelining that allow the Pentium to execute more than one instruction per clock cycle.

Pentium Pro   The 32-bit Pentium Pro (also known as the P6) has a 64-bit data path between the processor and cache and is capable of running at clock speeds up to 200MHz. Unlike the Pentium, the Pentium Pro has its secondary cache built into the CPU itself, rather than on the motherboard, meaning that it accesses cache at internal speed, not bus speed.

peripheral   Any hardware device attached to and controlled by a computer, such as a monitor, keyboard, hard disk, floppy disk, CD-ROM drives, printer, mouse, tape drive, and joystick.

Peripheral Component Interconnect   See *PCI*.

permanent swap file   A permanent swap file allows Microsoft Windows to write information to a known place on the hard disk, which enhances performance over using conventional methods with a temporary swap file. The Windows permanent swap file consists of a large number of consecutive contiguous clusters; it is often the largest single file on the hard disk, and of course this disk space cannot be used by any other application.

PGA (Pin Grid Array)   A type of IC package that consists of a grid of pins connected to a square, flat package.

photosensitive drum   See *EP drum.*

Physical layer   The first and lowest of the seven layers in the International Standards Organization's Open Systems Interconnection (ISO/OSI) model for computer-to-computer communications. The Physical layer defines the physical, electrical, mechanical, and functional procedures used to connect the equipment.

physical topology   A description that identifies how the cables on a network are physically arranged.

pickup roller   See *paper pickup roller.*

Pin Grid Array   See *PGA (Pin Grid Array).*

PING   PING is a utility used to send a short message to another computer on a TCP/IP network. PING can be useful to test connectivity between networks or to see if a particular machine is communicating with the network.

pixel   Contraction of picture element. The smallest element that display software can use to create text or graphics. A display resolution described as being 640×480 has 640 pixels across the screen and 480 down the screen, for a total of 307,200 pixels. The higher the number of pixels, the higher the screen resolution. A monochrome pixel can have two values, black or white, and this can be represented by 1 bit as either 0 or 1. At the other end of the scale, true color, capable of displaying approximately 16.7 million colors, requires 24 bits of information for each pixel.

planar board   See *motherboard.*

platform   An operating system (OS) is the basic software that runs on a computer, and it is the base on which all other software sits. As such the OS is the "platform" that applications and utilities run on.

Plug and Play (PnP)   A standard that defines automatic techniques designed to make PC configuration simple and straightforward.

POST   See *power on self-test (POST).*

Post Office Protocol v 3 (POP3)   POP3 is used to accept and store e-mail and to allow users to connect to their mailbox and access their mail. SMTP is used to send mail to the POP3 server.

PostScript   A page-description language used when printing high-quality text and graphics. Desktop publishing or illustration programs that create PostScript output can print on any PostScript printer or imagesetter, because PostScript is hardware-independent. An interpreter in the printer translates the PostScript commands into commands that the printer can understand.

potentiometer   See *variable resistor*.

power on self-test (POST)   A set of diagnostic programs, loaded automatically from ROM BIOS during startup, designed to ensure that the major system components are present and operating. If a problem is found, the POST software writes an error message in the screen, sometimes with a diagnostic code number indicating the type of fault located. These POST tests execute before any attempt is made to load the operating system.

power supply   A part of the computer that converts the power from a wall outlet into the lower voltages, typically 5 to 12 volts DC, required internally in the computer.

power surge   A brief but sudden increase in line voltage, often destructive, usually caused by a nearby electrical appliance (such as a photocopier or elevator) or when power is reapplied after an outage.

power users   A power user is someone who either does administrative-level tasks on their machine or needs to have additional access to the system to do their work. The Power Users group on a Windows 2000 Professional station has abilities somewhere between normal users and administrators.

preemptive multitasking   A form of multitasking where the operating system executes an application for a specific period of time, according to its assigned priority and need. At that time, it is preempted and another task is given access to the CPU for its allocated time. Although an application can give up control before its time is up, such as during input/output waits, no task is ever allowed to execute for longer than its allotted time period.

Presentation layer   The sixth of seven layers of the International Standards Organization's Open Systems Interconnection (ISO/OSI) model for computer-to-computer communications. The Presentation layer defines the way that data is formatted, presented, converted, and encoded.

preventative maintenance   The process of performing various procedures on a computer to prevent future data loss or system downtime.

primary DOS partition   In DOS, a division of the hard disk that contains important operating system files. A DOS hard disk can be divided into two partitions, or areas: the primary DOS partition and the extended DOS partition. If you want to start your computer from the hard disk, the disk must contain an active primary DOS partition that includes the three DOS system files: MSDOS.SYS, IO.SYS, and COMMAND.COM. The primary DOS partition on the first hard disk in the system is referred to as drive C. Disk partitions are displayed, created, and changed using the FDISK command.

print consumables   Products that a printer uses in the print process that must be replaced occasionally. Examples include toner, ink, ribbons, and paper.

printed-circuit board (PCB)   Any flat board made of plastic or fiberglass that contains chips and other electronic components. Many PCBs are multilayer boards with several different sets of copper traces connecting components together.

printer control assembly   Large circuit board in the printer that converts signals from the computer into signals for the various parts in the laser printer.

printer ribbon   A fabric strip that is impregnated with ink and wrapped around two spools encased in a cartridge. This cartridge is used in dot-matrix printers to provide the ink for the print process.

printhead   That part of a printer that creates the printed image. In a dot-matrix printer, the printhead contains the small pins that strike the ribbon to create the image, and in an ink-jet printer, the printhead contains the jets used to create the ink droplets as well as the ink reservoirs. A laser printer creates images using an electrophotographic method similar to that found in photocopiers and does not have a printhead.

print media   Another name for the mediums being printed on. Examples include paper, transparencies, and labels.

product key   Software piracy is a serious problem in the industry, so many programs include a product key that must be typed in for the software to install properly. This key is then submitted if the user registers for technical support.

productivity tools   Any of a number of applications users depend on to do job-related tasks. Word processors and spreadsheets are common examples, but most companies have additional productivity tools as well.

Program Groups   See *group icons*.

Program Manager Group (GRP) Files   Files in the Windows 3.*x* directories that store information about which application icons are contained in which group icons.

Program Manager   The primary interface to Windows that allows you to organize and execute numerous programs by double-clicking an icon in a single graphical window.

proprietary design   A motherboard design that is unique to a particular manufacturer and is not licensed to other manufacturers.

protected mode   A processor operating mode where every program's memory is protected from every other program so that if one program crashes, it doesn't bring down the other programs.

protocol   In networking and communications, the specification that defines the procedures to follow when transmitting and receiving data. Protocols define the format, timing, sequence, and error-checking systems used.

protocol stack   In networking and communications, the several layers of software that define the computer-to-computer or computer-to-network protocol. The protocol stack on a Novell NetWare system will be different from that used on a Banyan VINES network or on a Microsoft LAN Manager system.

PS/2 mouse interface   A type of mouse interface that uses a round, DIN-6 connector that gets its name from the first computer it was introduced on, the IBM PS/2.

puck   The proper name for the mouse-like device used with drawing tablets.

QSOP (Quad Small Outline Package)   A type of IC package that has all leads soldered directly to the circuit board. Also called a "surface mount" chip.

Quick-and-Dirty Disk Operating System (QDOS)   Created by Tim Patterson of Seattle Computer Products, QDOS was the basis of MS-DOS. QDOS was purchased by Microsoft and renamed MS-DOS.

radio frequency interference (RFI)   Many electronic devices, including computers and peripherals, can interfere with other signals in the radio-frequency range by producing electromagnetic radiation; this is normally regulated by government agencies in each country.

RAM   Acronym for random access memory. The main system memory in a computer, used for the operating system, application programs, and data.

RAM disk   An area of memory managed by a special device driver and used as a simulated disk. Anything stored on a RAM disk will be erased when the computer is turned off; therefore, the contents must be saved onto a real disk.

Rambus Inline Memory Modules (RIMMs)   A type of memory module that uses Rambus memory. See *Direct Rambus*.

random access memory   See *RAM*.

rasterizing   The process of converting signals from the computer into signals for the various assemblies in the laser printer.

read-only memory   See *ROM (read-only memory)*.

read/write head   That part of a floppy- or hard-disk system that reads and writes data to and from a magnetic disk.

real mode   A processor operating mode whereby a processor emulates an 8086 processor.

reference disk   A special disk that is bootable and contains a program that is able to send special commands to MCA bus devices to configure their parameters.

refresh rate   In a monitor, the rate at which the phosphors that create the image on the screen are recharged.

registration roller   See *paper registration roller*.

Registry   The Registry is used in Windows 9*x*, NT, and 2000 to store configuration information about the machine. This includes information about both individual user settings and global system settings.

REM statement   A command placed in the beginning of a line in a DOS batch file to prevent that line from executing.

removable mass storage   Any high-capacity storage device inserted into a drive for reading and writing, then removed for storage and safekeeping.

removable media   Any storage media that can be removed from the system.

repeater   In networking, a simple hardware device that moves all packets from one local area network segment to another.

reserved memory   In DOS, a term used to describe that area of memory between 640K and 1MB, also known as upper memory. Reserved memory is used by DOS to store system and video information.

resistor   An electronic device used to resist the flow of current in an electrical circuit. See also *fixed resistor* and *variable resistor*.

resistor pack   A combination of multiple resistors in a single package. Often used for terminating SCSI buses.

resource   Anything on a network that clients might want to access or use.

restore   The process of getting data from a backup restored to the computer it originally came from.

RFI   See *radio frequency interference (RFI)*.

rheostat   See *variable resistor*.

ribbon cartridge   The container that holds the printer ribbon.

ring topology   Type of physical topology in which each computer connects to two other computers, joining them in a circle and creating a unidirectional path where messages move from workstation to workstation. Each entity participating in the ring reads a message, regenerates it, and then hands it to its neighbor.

RJ-11/RJ-45   A commonly used modular telephone connector. RJ-11 is a four- or six-pin connector used in most connections destined for voice use; it is the connector used on phone cords. RJ-45 is the eight-pin connector used for data transmission over twisted-pair wiring and can be used for networking; RJ-45 is the connector used on 10Base-T Ethernet cables.

RLL encoding   See *run-length limited (RLL) encoding.*

ROM (read-only memory)   A type of computer memory that retains its data permanently, even when power is removed. Once the data is written to this type of memory, it cannot be changed.

root directory   In a hierarchical directory structure, the directory from which all other directories must branch. The root directory is created by the FORMAT command and can contain files as well as other directories. This directory cannot be deleted.

router   In networking, an intelligent connecting device that can send packets to the correct local area network segment to take them to their destination. Routers link local area network segments at the network layer of the International Standards Organization's Open Systems Interconnect (ISO/OSI) model for computer-to-computer communications.

RS-232-C   In asynchronous transmissions, a recommended standard interface established by the Electrical Industries Association. The standard defines the specific lines, timing, and signal characteristics used between the computer and the peripheral device and uses a 25-pin or 9-pin DB connector. RS-232-C is used for serial communications between a computer and a peripheral such as a printer, modem, digitizing tablet, or mouse.

RS-232 cables   See *serial cables.*

RS-422/423/449   In asynchronous transmissions, a recommended standard interface established by the Electrical Industries Association for distances greater than 50 feet but less than 1000 feet. The standard defines the specific lines, timing, and signal characteristics used between the computer and the peripheral device.

RTS   Abbreviation for request to send. A hardware signal defined by the RS-232-C standard to request permission to transmit.

run-length limited (RLL) encoding An efficient method of storing information on a hard disk that effectively doubles the storage capacity of a disk when compared to older, less efficient methods such as modified frequency modulation encoding (MFM).

Safe Mode A Windows 9*x* operating mode that only loads a basic set of drivers and a basic screen resolution. It can be activated using the F8 key at boot time.

scanner An optical device used to digitize images such as line art or photographs, so that they can be merged with text by a page-layout or desktop publishing program or incorporated into a CAD drawing.

screen saver Program originally designed to prevent damage to a computer monitor from being left on too long. These programs usually include moving graphics so that no one pixel is left on all the time. Screen savers detect computer inactivity and activate after a certain period.

SCSI Acronym for small computer system interface. A high-speed, system-level parallel interface defined by the ANSI X3T9.2 committee. SCSI is used to connect a personal computer to several peripheral devices using just one port. Devices connected in this way are said to be "daisy-chained" together, and each device must have a unique identifier or priority number.

SCSI adapter Device that is used to manage all the devices on the SCSI bus as well as to send and retrieve data from the devices.

SCSI address A unique address given to each SCSI device.

SCSI bus Another name for the SCSI interface and communications protocol.

SCSI chain All the devices connected to a single SCSI adapter.

SCSI terminator The SCSI interface must be correctly terminated to prevent signals echoing on the bus. Many SCSI devices have built-in terminators that engage when they are needed. With some older SCSI devices, you have to add an external SCSI terminator that plugs into the device's SCSI connector.

sector The smallest unit of storage on a disk, usually 512 bytes. Sectors are grouped together into clusters.

seek time Time it takes the actuator arm to move from rest position to active position for the read/write head to access the information. Often used as a performance gauge of an individual drive. The major part of a hard disk's access time is actually seek time.

semiconductors Any material that, depending on some condition, is either a conductor or non-conductor.

serial cables Cables used for serial communications. See *serial communications*.

serial communications   The transmission of information from computer to computer or from computer to a peripheral, one bit at a time. Serial communications can be synchronous and controlled by a clock or asynchronous and coordinated by start and stop bits embedded in the data stream.

serial mouse   A mouse that attaches directly to one of the computer's serial ports.

serial port   A computer input/output port that supports serial communications in which information is processed one bit at a time. RS-232-C is a common serial protocol used by computers when communicating with modems, printers, mice, and other peripherals.

serial printer   A printer that attaches to one of the computer's serial ports.

server   In networking, any computer that makes access to files, printing, communications, or other services available to users of the network. In large networks, a server may run a special network operating system; in smaller installations, a server may run a personal computer operating system.

service   A service is any program that runs in the background on a computer and performs some sort of task for that computer or other machines on the network.

Session layer   The fifth of seven layers of the International Standards Organization's Open Systems Interconnection (ISO/OSI) model for computer-to-computer communications. The Session layer coordinates communications and maintains the session for as long as it is needed, performing security, logging, and administrative functions.

share name   The share name is used to identify a network access point. Share names can be the same as the directory they are sharing or they can be different.

shell   Every operating system needs to have some sort of interface that allows users to navigate the system. The shell is the program that controls how this interface works. For MS-DOS, the Windows Program Manager was its most popular shell. For Windows *9x* and 2000, Explorer (`explorer.exe`) is the standard shell program.

shielded twisted-pair   See *STP (shield twisted-pair)*.

Simple Mail Transport Protocol (SMTP)   SMTP is used to send mail from a client to an e-mail server. SMTP servers do not store mail for users to pick up; they simply send the mail out, and another server (such as a POP3 server) is used to store incoming mail.

Single Inline Memory Module (SIMM)   Individual RAM chips are soldered or surface mounted onto small narrow circuit boards called carrier modules, which can be plugged into sockets on the motherboard. These carrier modules are simple to install and occupy less space than conventional memory modules.

Single Inline Package (SIP)   A type of semiconductor package where the package has a single row of connector pins on one side only.

single-purpose server   A server that is dedicated to one purpose (e.g., a file server or a printer server).

site license   A software license that is valid for all installations at a single site.

slave drive   The secondary drive in a IDE master/slave disk configuration.

small computer system interface   See *SCSI*.

socket services   Part of the software support needed for PCMCIA hardware devices in a portable computer, controlling the interface to the hardware. Socket services is the lowest layer in the software that manages PCMCIA cards. It provides a BIOS-level software interface to the hardware, effectively hiding the specific details from higher levels of software. Socket services also detect when you insert or remove a PCMCIA card and identify the type of card it is.

software   An application program or an operating system that a computer can execute. Software is a broad term that can imply one or many programs, and it can also refer to applications that may actually consist of more than one program.

software driver   Software that acts as the liaison between a piece of hardware and the operating system and allows the use of a component.

solenoid   An electromechanical device that, when activated, produces an instant push or pull force.

source   All computer programs—operating system or application—are nothing but a collection of program code. This is the source code or "source" that defines what a program is and how it works. The open source movement is involved with allowing you to see and even modify this code.

spin speed   An indication of how fast the platters on a fixed disk are spinning.

spindle   The rod that platters are mounted to on in a hard disk drive.

SRAM   See *static RAM (SRAM)*.

ST506 interface   A popular hard-disk interface standard developed by Seagate Technologies, first used in IBM's PC/XT computer and still popular today, with disk capacities smaller than about 40MB. ST506 has a relatively slow data transfer rate of 5 megabits per second.

stack   Another name for the memory map, or the way memory is laid out.

standard peripheral power connector   Type of connector used to power various internal drives. Also called a Molex connector.

star network   A network topology in the form of a star. At the center of the star is a wiring hub or concentrator, and the nodes or workstations are arranged around the central point representing the points of the star.

start bit   In asynchronous transmissions, a start bit is transmitted to indicate the beginning of a new data word.

Start menu   As the main focus of the Windows 9x/NT/2000 user interface, the Start menu allows program shortcuts to be placed for easy and organized access.

static RAM (SRAM)   A type of computer memory that retains its contents as long as power is supplied. It does not need constant refreshment like dynamic RAM chips.

static-charge eliminator strip   The device in EP process printers that drains the static charge from the paper after the toner has been transferred to the paper.

stepper motor   A very precise motor that can move in very small increments. Often used in printers.

stop bit(s)   In asynchronous transmissions, stop bits are transmitted to indicate the end of the current data word. Depending on the convention in use, one or two stop bits are used.

STP (shield twisted-pair)   Cabling that has a braided foil shield around the twisted pairs of wire to decrease electrical interference.

stylus   A pen-like pointing device used in pen-based systems and personal digital assistants.

subnet mask   The subnet mask is a required part of any TCP/IP configuration, and it is used to define which addresses are local and which are on remote networks.

superscalar   See *parallel processing*.

SuperVGA (SVGA)   An enhancement to the Video Graphics Array (VGA) video standard defined by the Video Electronics Standards Association (VESA).

surface mount   See *Quad Small Outline Package (QSOP)*.

surge suppressor   Also known as a surge protector. A regulating device placed between the computer and the AC line connection that protects the computer system from power surges.

SVGA   See *SuperVGA (SVGA)*.

swap file   On a hard disk, a file used to store parts of running programs that have been swapped out of memory temporarily to make room for other running programs. A swap file may be permanent, always occupying the same amount of hard disk space even though the application that created it may not be running, or is temporary, only created as and when needed.

synchronization   The timing of separate elements or events to occur simultaneously.

1. In a multimedia presentation, synchronization ensures that the audio and video components are timed correctly, so they actually make sense.
2. In computer-to-computer communications, the hardware and software must be synchronized so that file transfers can take place.
3. The process of updating files on both a portable computer and a desktop system so that they both have the latest versions is also known as synchronization.

synchronous DRAM   A type of DRAM memory module that uses memory chips synchronized to the speed of the processor.

synchronous transmission   In communications, a transmission method that uses a clock signal to regulate data flow. Synchronous transmissions do not use start and stop bits.

syntax   Syntax is a term used to describe the proper way of forming a text command for entry into the computer. Many commands have a number of different options, each of which requires a particular format.

system attribute   Attribute of DOS that is used to tell the OS that this file is needed by the OS and should not be deleted. Marks a file as part of the operating system and will also protect the file from deletion.

system board   The sturdy sheet or board to which all other components on the computer are attached. These components consist of the CPU, underlying circuitry, expansion slots, video components, and RAM slots, just to name a few. Also known as a logic board, motherboard, or planar board.

system disk   A disk that contains all the files necessary to boot and start the operating system. In most computers, the hard disk is the system disk; indeed, many modern operating systems are too large to run from floppy disk.

SYSTEM.INI   In Microsoft Windows, an initialization file that contains information on your hardware and the internal Windows operating environment.

system resources   On a Windows 3.x or 95/98 machine, the system resources represent those components of the PC that are being used (memory, CPU, etc.).

system software   The programs that make up the operating system, along with the associated utility programs, as distinct from an application program.

tabs   On many windows you will find that, to save space, a single window will have many tabs, each of which can be selected to display particular information.

tape cartridge   A self-contained tape storage module, containing tape much like that in a video cassette. Tape cartridges are primarily used to back up hard disk systems.

tape drive   Removable media drive that uses a tape cartridge that has a long polyester ribbon coated with magnetic oxide and wrapped around two spools with a read/write head in between.

target   Another name for the backup media, it is the destination for the data being backed up. It is usually a tape drive or other backup device.

taskbar   The area of the Windows 9x/NT/2000 interface which includes the Start button and the System Tray, as well as icons for any open programs.

TCP/IP   Acronym for Transmission Control Protocol/Internet Protocol. A set of computer-to-computer communications protocols that encompass media access, packet transport, session communications, file transfer, e-mail, and terminal emulation. TCP/IP is supported by a very large number of hardware and software vendors and is available on many different computers from PCs to mainframes.

temporary swap file   A swap file that is created every time it is needed. A temporary swap file will not consist of a single large area of contiguous hard disk space, but may consist of several discontinuous pieces of space. By its very nature, a temporary swap file does not occupy valuable hard disk space if the application that created it is not running. In a permanent swap file the hard disk space is always reserved and is therefore unavailable to any other application program.

terminal   A monitor and keyboard attached to a computer (usually a mainframe), used for data entry and display. Unlike a personal computer, a terminal does not have its own central processing unit or hard disk.

Terminate and Stay Resident (TSR)   A DOS program that stays loaded in memory, even when it is not actually running, so that you can invoke it very quickly to perform a specific task.

terminator   A device attached to the last peripheral in a series or the last node on a network. A resistor is placed at both ends of a coax Ethernet cable to prevent signals from reflecting and interfering with the transmission.

text mode   A video display mode for a video card that allows it to only display text. When running DOS programs, a video card is in text mode.
   The VL bus is a 32-bit bus, running at either 33 or 40MHz. The maximum throughput is 133 megabytes per second at 33MHz, or 148 megabytes per

second at 40MHz. The most common VL bus adapters are video adapters, hard-disk controllers, and network interface cards.

thermal printer   A nonimpact printer that uses a thermal printhead and specially treated paper to create an image.

thick Ethernet   Connecting coaxial cable used on an Ethernet network. The cable is 1 cm (approximately 0.4") thick and can be used to connect network nodes up to a distance of approximately 3300 feet. Thick Ethernet is primarily used for facility-wide installations. Also known as 10Base5.

thin Ethernet   Connecting coaxial cable used on an Ethernet network. The cable is 5 mm (approximately 0.2") thick, and can be used to connect network nodes up to a distance of approximately 1000 feet. Thin Ethernet is primarily used for office installations. Also known as 10Base2.

thrashing   A slang term for the condition that occurs when Windows must constantly swap data between memory and hard disk. The hard disk spins continuously during this and makes a lot of noise.

token passing   A media access method that gives every NIC equal access to the cable. The token is a special packet of data that is passed from computer to computer. Any computer that wants to transmit has to wait until it has the token, at which point it can add its own data to the token and send it on.

Token Ring network   A local area network with a ring structure that uses token-passing to regulate traffic on the network and avoid collisions. On a Token Ring network, the controlling computer generates a "token" that controls the right to transmit. This token is continuously passed from one node to the next around the network. When a node has information to transmit, it captures the token, sets its status to busy, and adds the message and the destination address. All other nodes continuously read the token to determine if they are the recipient of a message; if they are, they collect the token, extract the message, and return the token to the sender. The sender then removes the message and sets the token status to free, indicating that it can be used by the next node in sequence.

tolerance band   Found on a fixed resistor, this colored band indicates how well the resistor holds to its rated value.

toner   Black carbon substance mixed with polyester resins and iron oxide particles. During the EP printing process, toner is first attracted to areas that have been exposed to the laser in laser printers and is later deposited and melted onto the print medium.

toner cartridge   The replaceable cartridge in a laser printer or photocopier that contains the electrically charged ink to be fused to the paper during printing.

topology A way of laying out a network. Can describe either the logical or physical layout.

touch screen A special monitor that lets the user make choices by touching icons or graphical buttons on the screen.

Tracert Used to trace the path of a packet across a TCP/IP network.

trackball An input device used for pointing, designed as an alternative to the mouse.

tracks The concentric circle unit of hard disk division. A disk platter is divided into these concentric circles.

transfer corona assembly The part of an EP process printer that is responsible for transferring the developed image from the EP drum to the paper.

transfer step The step in the EP print process where the developed toner image on the EP drum is transferred to the print media using the transfer corona.

transistor Abbreviation for transfer resistor. A semiconductor component that acts like a switch, controlling the flow of an electric current. A small voltage applied at one pole controls a larger voltage on the other poles. Transistors are incorporated into modern microprocessors by the million.

Transmission Control Protocol/Internet Protocol See *TCP/IP*.

Transport layer The fourth of seven layers of the International Standards Organization's Open Systems Interconnection (ISO/OSI) model for computer-to-computer communications. The Transport layer defines protocols for message structure and supervises the validity of the transmission by performing some error checking.

TSR See *Terminate and Stay Resident (TSR)*.

twisted-pair cable Cable that comprises two insulated wires twisted together at six twists per inch. In twisted-pair cable, one wire carries the signal and the other is grounded. Telephone wire installed in modern buildings is often twisted-pair wiring.

UART Acronym for Universal Asynchronous Receiver/Transmitter. An electronic module that combines the transmitting and receiving circuitry needed for asynchronous transmission over a serial line. Asynchronous transmissions use start and stop bits encoded in the data stream to coordinate communications rather than the clock pulse found in synchronous transmissions.

Ultra DMA IDE Also known as ATA version 4 (ATA-4), it can transfer data at 33Mbps, so it is also commonly seen in motherboard specifications as Ultra DMA/33, Ultra 66, or UDMA.

uninstall   To remove a program from a computer. This generally involves removing its configuration information from the Registry, its icons from the Start menu, and its program code from the file system.

Universal Serial Bus   See *USB*.

Unix   Pronounced "you-nix." A 32-bit, multiuser, multitasking, portable operating system.

upper memory area   See *reserved memory area*.

upper memory block (UMB)   Free areas of memory that can be used for loading drivers and programs into the upper memory area.

USB   Acronym for Universal Serial Bus. A technology used to connect peripheral devices to a computer. Each USB channel will support 127 devices and has a total transfer rate of up to 12MBps.

USER.EXE   Windows core component that allows a user to interact with Windows. It is the component responsible for interpreting keystrokes and mouse movements and sending the appropriate commands to the other core components.

username   In order to identify themselves on the network, each user must provide two credentials—a username and a password. The username says, "This is who I am," and the password says, "And here's proof!" Each username must be unique on the network and is generally used by only one person.

user profiles   In order to allow each user to customize their Windows experience, user profiles save a particular user's desktop appearance and preferences so that when they log on, they will always have there own desktop, even if they share the machine with others.

utility program   A small program or set of small programs that support the operating system by providing additional services that the operating system does not provide.

UTP   Acronym for unshielded twisted-pair. A type of unshielded network cable that contains multiple conductors in pairs that are twisted around each other.

vaccine   An application program that removes and destroys a computer virus. The people who unleash computer viruses are often very accomplished programmers, and they are constantly creating new and novel ways of causing damage to a system. The antivirus and vaccine programmers do the best they can to catch up, but they must always lag behind to some extent.

vacuum tube   Electronic component that is a glorified switch. A small voltage at one pole switches a larger voltage at the other poles on or off.

variable resistor   A resistor that does not have a fixed value. Typically the value is changed using a knob or slider.

version   Each time that computer software is modified, new features are added and old problems are, hopefully, fixed. To tell these modified programs apart, computer programmers use versions. These are incremented by one digit (for example, from 1.0 to 2.0) for major revisions, or by a tenth of a digit (for example, from 2.0 to 2.1) for minor modifications. Higher version numbers mean newer versions.

VGA   Acronym for Video Graphics Array. A video adapter. VGA supports previous graphics standards, and provides several different graphics resolutions, including 640 pixels horizontally by 480 pixels vertically. A maximum of 256 colors can be displayed simultaneously, chosen from a palette of 262,114 colors. Because the VGA standard requires an analog display, it is capable of resolving a continuous range of gray shades or colors. In contrast, a digital display can only resolve a finite range of shades or colors.

video adapter   An expansion board that plugs into the expansion bus in a DOS computer and provides for text and graphics output to the monitor. The adapter converts the text and graphic signals into several instructions for the display that tell it how to draw the graphic.

Video Graphics Array   See *VGA*.

video RAM (VRAM)   Special-purpose RAM with two data paths for access, rather than just one as in conventional RAM. These two paths let a VRAM board manage two functions at once—refreshing the display and communicating with the processor. VRAM doesn't require the system to complete one function before starting the other, so it allows faster operation for the whole video system.

virtual memory   A memory-management technique that allows information in physical memory to be swapped out to a hard disk. This technique provides application programs with more memory space than is actually available in the computer. True virtual-memory management requires specialized hardware in the processor for the operating system to use; it is not just a question of writing information out to a swap file on the hard disk at the application level.

virus   A program intended to damage your computer system without your knowledge or permission. A virus may attach itself to another program or to the partition table or the boot track on your hard disk. When a certain event occurs, a date passes, or a specific program executes, the virus is triggered into action. Not all viruses are harmful; some are just annoying.

VL bus   Also known as VL local bus. Abbreviation for the VESA local bus, a bus architecture introduced by the Video Electronics Standards Association (VESA), in which up to three adapter slots are built into the motherboard. The VL bus allows for bus mastering.

VLSI (Very Large Scale Integration)   Technology used by chip manufacturers to integrate the functions of several small chips into one chip.

volts   Unit of electrical potential.

VRAM   See *video RAM (VRAM)*.

wait state   A clock cycle during which no instructions are executed because the processor is waiting for data from a device or from memory.

WAN (wide area network)   Network that expands LANs to include networks outside of the local environment and also to distribute resources across distances.

warm boot   Refers to pressing Control+Alt+Delete to reboot the computer. This type of booting doesn't require the computer to perform all of the hardware and memory checks that a cold boot does.

wide area network   See *WAN (wide area network)*.

window   In a graphical user interface, a rectangular portion of the screen that acts as a viewing area for application programs. Windows can be tiled or cascaded and can be individually moved and sized on the screen. Some programs can open multiple document windows inside their application window to display several word processing or spreadsheet data files at the same time.

Windows 95   Windows 95 is a 32-bit, multitasking, multithreaded operating system capable of running DOS, Windows 3.1, and Windows 95 applications; supports Plug and Play (on the appropriate hardware); and adds an enhanced FAT file system in the Virtual FAT which allows long filenames of up to 255 characters while also supporting the DOS 8.3 file-naming conventions.

Windows 98   The home PC operating system released by Microsoft, as the successor to their popular Windows 95 operating system. Basically the same as Windows 95, it offers a few improvements. For example, Windows 98 improves upon the basic "look and feel" of Windows 95 with a "browser-like" interface. It also contains bug-fixes and can support two monitors simultaneously. In addition to new interface features, it includes support for new hardware, including Universal Serial Bus devices.

Windows 2000   The newest Windows operating system that incorporates the "look and feel" of Windows 9x with the power of Windows NT.

Windows Desktop   See *Desktop*.

Windows Installer   A new method Microsoft is using to allow users to customize their application installations more easily. The Windows Installer also makes it easier for users to install approved software on secured workstations and can automatically repair damaged installs.

Windows Internet Name Service (WINS)   WINS provides a database for the storage and retrieval of NetBIOS computer names. Each client must register with the WINS server to be able to be added to and query the database.

Windows NT   A 32-bit multitasking portable operating system developed by Microsoft. Windows NT is designed as a portable operating system, and initial versions run on Intel 80386 (or later) processors and RISC processors, such as the MIPS R4000 and the DEC Alpha. Windows NT contains the graphical user interface from Windows 3.1, and can run Windows 3.1 and DOS applications as well as OS/2 16-bit character-based applications and new 32-bit programs specifically developed for Windows NT. Multitasking under Windows NT is preemptive, and applications can execute multiple threads. Security is built into the operating system at the U.S. Government–approved C2 security level. Windows NT supports the DOS FAT file system, the OS/2 HPFS, installable file systems such as CD-ROM systems, and a native file system called NTFS. Windows NT also supports multiprocessing, OLE, and peer-to-peer networking.

Windows Program Manager   Windows 3.*x* file that contains all of the program icons, group icons, and menus used for organizing, starting, and running programs.

WIN.INI   File that contains Windows environmental settings that control the environment's general function and appearance.

WINIPCFG   In Windows 9*x*, this is the utility that allows you to view your current TCP/IP configuration. It also allows a user to request a new IP configuration from a DHCP server.

wizard   Wizards are pre-programmed utilities that walk the user through a particular task. Each wizard generally includes a number of different pages, each of which allows you to enter information or choose particular options. At the finish of the wizard, the computer will then perform the requested task based on the information it has gathered.

word   In binary communications, multiple bytes associated together are usually called a *word*.

workgroup   A group of individuals who work together and share the same files and databases over a local area network. Special groupware such as Lotus Notes coordinates the workgroup and allows users to edit drawings or documents and update the database as a group.

working directory   Programs that need to save temporary files or configuration data while they are running do so within their working directory. Users can also have a working directory to save their temporary files.

workstation   1. In networking, any personal computer (other than the file server) attached to the network.

2. A high-performance computer optimized for graphics applications such as computer-aided design, computer-aided engineering, or scientific applications.

World Wide Web (WWW)   This is the graphical extension of the Internet that features millions of pages of information accessed though the use of the Hypertext Transfer Protocol (HTTP).

write-protect   To prevent the addition or deletion of files on a disk or tape. Floppy disks have write-protect notches or small write-protect tabs that allow files to be read from the disk, but prevent any modifications or deletions. Certain attributes can make individual files write-protected so they can be read but not altered or erased.

write-protect tab   The small notch or tab in a floppy disk that is used to write-protect it.

writing step   The step in the EP print process where the items being printed are written to the EP drum. In this step, the laser is flashed on and off as it scans across the surface of the drum. The area where the laser shines on is discharged to almost ground (-100 volts).

x86 series   The general name given to the Intel line of IBM-compatible CPUs.

XGA   Acronym for Extended Graphics Array. XGA is only available as a micro channel architecture expansion board; it is not available in ISA or EISA form. XGA supports resolution of 1024 horizontal pixels by 768 vertical pixels with 256 colors, as well as a VGA mode of 640 pixels by 480 pixels with 65,536 colors, and like the 8514/A, XGA is interlaced. XGA is optimized for use with graphical user interfaces, and instead of being very good at drawing lines, it is a bit-block transfer device designed to move blocks of bits like windows or dialog boxes.

zero insertion force (ZIF)   A type of processor socket where you don't have to "snap" the chip into the socket. Rather, you simply set the chip into the ZIF socket and push a bar down to secure it.

zero wait state   Describes a computer that can process information without wait states. A wait state is a clock cycle during which no instructions are executed because the processor is waiting for data from a device or from memory.

ZIF socket   Abbreviation for Zero Insertion Force socket. A specially designed chip socket which makes replacing a chip easier and safer.

Index

Note to the reader: Throughout this index **boldfaced** page numbers indicate primary discussions and definitions of a topic. *Italicized* page numbers indicate illustrations and tables.

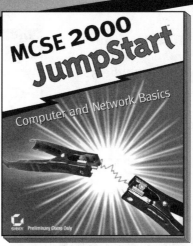

The Best A+ Book/CD Package on the Market!

Get ready for CompTIA's A+ exam with the most comprehensive and challenging sample tests anywhere!

The Sybex EdgeTests feature:

- Chapter-by-chapter exam coverage of all the review questions from both books
- Random tests that simulate the exam format from CompTIA
- Four bonus exams available only on the CD

A+ Complete Study Guide: Core Hardware Service Technician Exam
File   Help

A+ Complete Study Guide: Core Hardware Service Techn

Chapter Tests »	Chapter 1
	Chapter 2
Objective Tests »	Chapter 3
	Chapter 4
Assessment Test »	Chapter 5
	Chapter 6
	Chapter 7
Practice Exam »	Chapter 8
	Chapter 9
Bonus Exam »	Chapter 10
Random Test »	

A+
Core Hardware
Service
Technician
EdgeTests

©2000 Sybex, Inc. Produced by Matt Sheltz and the Edge Group   SYBEX

A+ Complete Study Guide: Core Hardware Service Technician Exam
File   Help
1:28:59   Item 14 of 65   ☐ Mark

To increase system performance, what should happen to ROM at system start-up?

- ○ A. ROM should be copied to the hard disk.
- ○ B. ROM should be copied to RAM.
- ○ C. ROM should be copied to the printer's RAM.
- ○ D. ROM should be copied to the CPU cache.

Previous   Next   Answer

Use the Electronic Flashcards to jog your memory and prep last-minute for the exam!

- Reinforce your understanding of key A+ exam concepts with more than 200 hardcore flashcard-style questions.

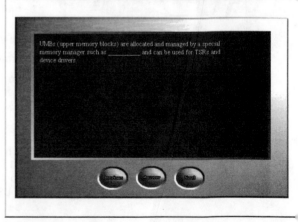

A+ OPERATING SYSTEM TECHNOLOGIES FLASHCARDS

UMBs (upper memory blocks) are allocated and managed by a special memory manager such as _____ and can be used for TSRs and device drivers.

Question   Answer   Next

Electronic Flashcards now available for your Palm device as well!

- Download the Flashcards to your Palm device and go on the road. Now you can study for the A+ exam anywhere, any time.